BRITISH LIGHT AVIATION
A SHIFTING EMPHASIS
A Study in Two Volumes
Volume One

Arthur W.J.G. Ord-Hume

Beagle was to be Britain's last major light aircraft manufacturer. From its Pup light monoplane to the larger Bulldog military trainer, the company produced a variety of machines and in so doing spread its dwindling resources too thinly and in the end went under. One of its greatest products was the Beagle B.206 aimed, boldly, at a market already established by American and European designs. Built at its Shoreham factory and first flown by John Nicholson on August 15th 1961, production versions of the all-metal five seater were powered by two 340 hp Rolls-Royce Continental GTSIO-520C engines. The Series 2, pictured here, saw a production run of just 28 machines for the home market and 19 for export – hardly enough to break even.

Stenlake Publishing Ltd

First Published in the United Kingdom, 2022
Stenlake Publishing Limited
54–58 Mill Square, Catrine, KA5 6RD

01290 551122
www.stenlake.co.uk

© Arthur W. J. G. Ord-Hume, 2022

ISBN 978-1-84033-923-9

During the period covered by this book, a majority of individuals who held sway in high places in both Aviation and Government were of Public School education and background. Two Edwardian schoolmasters, Dr Norwood and a Mr Hope, writing in 1909, made an interesting observation, hopefully satirical, but one that subsequent events have proved may just have a ring of truth…

The public schools generally produce a race of well-bodied, well-mannered, well-meaning boys, keen at games, devoted to their schools, ignorant of life, contemptuous of all outside the pale of their own caste, uninterested in work, neither desiring nor revering knowledge.

Dr Cyril Norwood: The Higher Education of Boys in England, 1909, p.187

Let me make this clear to you. Nothing you will learn [at school or college] will be the slightest possible use to you after life [but] if you work hard and intelligently you should be able to detect when a man is talking rot, and that, in my view, is the main, if not the sole purpose of education.

Harold Macmillan: 'Oxford Remembered', The Times, October 18th 1975

The right of Arthur W. J. G. Ord-Hume as author of this work has been asserted by him
In accordance with the Copyright, Designs and Patents Act, 1993.

All rights reserved. No part of this publication may be reproduced, stored in a retrieval system, or transmitted in any form or by any means, electronic, mechanical, photocopying, recording or otherwise, without the prior permission of Stenlake Publishing Limited.

British Library Cataloguing in Publication Data:
A catalogue record for this book is available from the British Library.

Printed by
Blissetts, Unit 1, Shield Drive,
West Cross Industrial Park, Brentford, TW8 9EX

Contents

Volume One

	Foreword	iv
	Preface	1
	Introduction	9
Chapter 1	Peaceful Skies; Inspiration and Confidence	27
Chapter 2	Light Aviation: an Uphill Struggle	47
Chapter 3	Is Britain really an Air-Minded Nation?	75
Chapter 4	The Post-War Aeroplane Industry	89
Chapter 5	The Home-Made Aeroplane Triumphs!	111
Chapter 6	Engines: the Chicken-and-Egg Situation	121
Chapter 7	Our Aircraft Industry Suffers as Imports Grow	137
Chapter 8	Chronology of Light Aircraft and Engines	149
Chapter 9	The Makers of British Post-War Light Aircraft	165
Chapter 10	British Light Aircraft Engines and Propellers	193

Volume Two

Chapter 11	British Light Aircraft 1946 – 1970 in Detail	207
Chapter 12	Projects and Designs Unfulfilled	423
Appendix 1	Light Aircraft Manufacturing Totals	462
Appendix 2	The Rollason Midget Racer Competition of 1964	470
	Peroration	475
	Acknowledgements	485
	Bibliography	483
	Index	485

Note to Readers:
Throughout this book, reference numbers in italicised square brackets, *i.e. [27],* or
Penrose [49] relate to a source listed in the Bibliography.

Foreword

When my late friend Harald Penrose, Westland's renowned test pilot, produced his monumental series of books under the banner title *British Aviation*, his five-volume history stopped at the onset of the 1939-45 war. This present book, while concentrating on light, civil and private aircraft, takes the story through the quarter-century that followed the war. It is thus offered as a continuation of his work and a salute to his outstanding contribution to aviation history. It also follows on from my own volume, *British Light Aeroplanes: Their Evolution, Development and Perfection 1920-1940* published in 2000.

This book has had a confused gestation not helped by the terrible Covid-19 pandemic which threw everything into turmoil during 2020-21. I have since heard it referred to as the year that the world was switched off. Looking back on those straitened times I see no reason to challenge that assertion. Private flying spent almost eighteen months from the early summer of 2020 well and truly grounded by the lockdown. Air shows were cancelled while the airlines saw business collapse as travel restrictions decimated passenger numbers.

Since the end of the war the British light aircraft has had a disturbed history. In the two decades between the two world conflicts, UK manufacturers were acknowledged as the best makers in the world thanks in no small part to the expansion of aviation that took place in the First World War and the subsequent development, itself hampered by a burgeoning civil market awash with dirt-cheap ex-military aircraft.

What this would do was to foster a fragmented aircraft industry that would be accustomed to extremely small production runs while at the same time maintain the highest-possible standards of performance, instrumentation and performance. Such attention to expensive detail was both essential and expected for an industry which comprised too many manufacturers and was ever be-laden with too small a market. And once we began exporting we gave our skills to countries far better equipped to capitalise on them.

All this sounds a good scenario for a West End play or a TV drama. The only problem is that it's about reality, real people, real situations – and there is no strand of fiction in sight. The nub of the tale is that while in 1946 we had the remains of an enthusiastic and capable light plane industry, by the 1970s it had been snuffed out. Quite thoroughly, in fact. In an unexpected twist of fate, as the light plane industry dwindled it was replaced by a meteoric rise in home-built aircraft.

We will see from the Acknowledgements section that many of the people who participated in this tumultuous and uncertain period of British aviation history are no more, so there is a degree of urgency in getting this tale told in print as soon as possible. And, as it turns out, the choice of publisher is no less essential for it is here that I must relate an unfortunate experience.

The subject covered by this present volume was originally produced as a two-volume work which I was commissioned to prepare for another publisher earlier this century. This was a small and specialist outfit located in a far corner of Europe but with a UK office. For them I laboured long and hard incurring expenditure, spending much time and money to generate the promised work. All went well up to the point of production when suddenly the firm ceased publication. I was offered neither compensation nor explanation. This was some years ago now. The present volume is, if you like, a 'fresh and revised edition' of that unfulfilled work, up-dated with additions and numerous new pictures.

Out of chaos and calamity emerges opportunity and here my survey has been brought up to date as the intervening decades have revealed more history and insight, while the photographic content is similarly revised with images that have come to light as time has progressed.

The smallest two-seat jet? The all wood Somers-Kendall SK.1 was powered by a Turboméca Palas gas turbine and first flew on October 8th, 1955. Planned production was thwarted by various problems, not least of which was difficult engine-starting and the inabillity to produce enough thrust to overcome resistance to taxi over rough grass.

In summary…

Over the course of just twenty-five years, British Light Aviation underwent a sea-change that saw first a coalescence of our remaining companies followed by their rapid collapse. Where once Britain led the world in lightplane design and production, we ultimately failed the test of a post-war revival. The reasons are set out in this work. Despite this litany of failure, we have a thriving lightplane aviation sector today in the main stimulated by amateur-built aircraft. Industrial production may have failed but that is only part of a story that future historians will look back on as charting a fascinating chapter in British light aviation. The picture section that follows picks out some high spots.

A military serial number and a large letter 'P' in a circle show this was the first of the aircraft that we would come to know as the Auster. It is a Taylorcraft E Auster 3 pictured at Rearsby with the cowlings removed. Built for the RAF as a Mk.II in December 1942, it was retained by its makers, Taylorcraft Aeroplanes (England), for evaluation until converted to a Mk.III in April 1944. It was shipped to Australia in April 1944 later becoming VH-SNI with the Queensland Flying Club. This aircraft survives in its original RAF markings. It heralded a series of Austers of many marks and types and would become the mainstay of many a club. An example was Taylorcraft Plus D, G-AHNG, below, of Biggin Hill's Alouette Flying Club.

When Bernard Leak and Richard Christoforides formed the Chrislea firm before the war they had hopes that their Airguard trainer would be accepted for the Royal Air Force which wanted an ab initio training aeroplane. It was rejected and they spent the war years having to make parts for bombers. But you can't keep a good man down and while the conflict progressed, Christoforides and his business partner were designing a novel four-seat light plane. It was to be very different and cheaper than anything else on the market. As it was, its only real difference was in its peculiar control system. Nevertheless, the Ace, portrayed above, turned out to be a handsome beast that was well loved by its devotees. Meanwhile the RAF had enormous numbers of Percival Proctors, four-seaters derived from the pre-war Vega Gull. Many came onto the civil market once the war was over and this one, G-AKIU, a Proctor V, was one of them. The drawback was its big and thirsty Gipsy six-cylinder engine which, with petrol costing about 2/4d a gallon, was expensive to run.

September 1948 and the very first Farnborough Air Show. The jumble of new aircraft brought largest and smallest together. Somewhere in the middle is the Portsmouth Aerocar, the Gipsy-engined Pioneer and, smallest of all, an Auster. Not that airshows were the safest of places to visit. While later rules banned Cobham-style aerobatics over the crowds and turns towards public enclosures, post-war events were unfettered. The Proctor (below) is landing over people's heads!

Frederick George Miles was one of those quiet geniuses among men. He began designing first-rate sporting aircraft before the war and continued into the 1950s. First planned for military use, the Messenger, below, became a popular private aeroplane post-war. Its wing was so good that it was altered to take two engines: so was born the Gemini. While praising 'FG' one ought not to overlook his wife, ever known as 'Blossom'. She, too, was a talented aircraft designer for her husband's company.

Scottish Aviation at Prestwick made its name converting military aircraft to airliners but in 1947 announced its STOL Pioneer for general purposes. The first, above, had a de Havilland Gipsy Queen 32 engine but production examples were Alvis Leonides-powered. Amazing of performance, it finally won military contracts but a number found civilian use.

While designed in Canada, the Chipmunk (above) was produced in Chester and once the RAF had declared them surplus to requirements, they were snapped up by flying clubs and private owners. Slingsby Sailplanes produced the JAP-engined Motor-Tutor (below) for low-cost flight tuition. The authorities vetoed it and so only three were built. A fine idea lost.

The world's oldest jetplane! G-ADNL, above, was a Miles Sparrowhawk built in 1935. In 1952 it was carved up and converted into a single-seater with two small jet engines. Tipsy Aircraft was Fairey Aviation's Belgian subsidiary. They designed the Junior, below, two of which came to Britain. Mikron-powered G-AMVP was one of our earliest ultralights.

In April 1956 Harold Best-Devereux of the PFA flew to France and returned in this Druine Turbulent, F-PHFR, powered by a converted VW engine. The smallest plane many had seen, it created a huge stir and led to the adoption of the design for amateur construction in Britain. Here at Elstree Aerodrome, Auster test-pilot Ranald Porteous poses before taking it aloft.

After the Sparrowjet, F G Miles had one final go at designing a jet plane, this time an all-metal low-cost side-by-side-seated trainer. The result was the M.100 Student constructed at Shoreham and first flown in May 1957. Miles hoped for a military order and planned to make 200 costing some £13,000 apiece which was half the cost of the Jet Provost. An excellent and economic flyer, in the end it was too late and Hunting got the order. The sole Student, G-APLK, marks a long-forgotten design that could just have been a winner.

Cierva's pre-war style of autogiro lost popularity in favour of Bensen's 1950s 'gyrocopters'. Improved from the original, many were UK made including a fine series by Wallis, above. Last British lightplane maker was Beagle which launched its Pup (below), Bulldog and others but at a huge cost to the taxpayer. In the end the company simply imploded. *Triste vale...*

Preface

Throughout the brace of decades that separated the two great wars of the 20th century, British light aeroplanes were considered among the finest anywhere in the whole world. They enjoyed a richly-deserved reputation right around the globe from America to Australia and Scandinavia to Africa.

Aircraft such as the de Havilland Moth and Avro Avian, the diminutive Comper Swift, the competitive Miles Hawks and the sleek Percival Gulls were synonymous with quality, dependability and reliability.

For long distance flights, speed records and durability, the world turned to Great Britain. The results were both proven and justly earned. It was an accolade shared between the British makers of airframes and the makers of British engines.

Attractive though this situation may sound today, it was a dangerous one for there is always somebody somewhere waiting to pick you off at the first chance. And what finer opportunity can there be than a war! This opportunist approach was not so much a conspiracy as an inevitability.

At the outbreak of the 1939-45 war we were riding the crest of a wave that represented our supreme success in this field. British light aeroplanes and their engines had reached a pinnacle of perfection recognised the world over. Britain was great and we designed and built the best. This was an unchallenged fact for British light planes were exported to every nation on the map.

The only problem was that to a large extent we were protected by the Atlantic Ocean from any risk of competition. Very few American light aircraft came awkwardly by sea to our shores. We became a victim of our own success which was in part due to being an island. We were blind to the possibility – even the very thought – that any other nation could touch us in our hallowed light aeroplane market. We did not notice that the Americans, ever astute, self-assured and always self-sufficient, felt that they needed their own light plane industry and so, although rather late starters in the business, they went about creating one. And British handbuilt craftsmanship counted for nothing in the country where mass-production was conceived.

Bolstered by the natural barrier of the Atlantic Ocean, we could not realise that what we had achieved through years of careful development and hard work might now be vulnerable. That it might be matched and even bettered by others in a fraction of that time-span, could not be countenanced. A remote outside possibility of such a challenge would need investment in skills, and even then success

In the bleak days of war when just survival was uppermost in people's minds, deep down inside, many cherished memories of peaceful skies and longed for a return to the private and club scene of the 'thirties. We all reckoned it would be an easy transmission. What we would actually face in the immediate post-war era was a degree of aeronautical austerity the likes of which nobody could ever have visualised.

Throughout our darkest hours we fervently looked forward to the time when there would be a return to the carefree and peaceful skies of our youth and with it the joys of private flying. There was also the recurring dream that everything would pick up just where it all left off. As the years of conflict passed and austerity continued, even the diehard daydreamers began to realise that those rich days of the 'thirties were gone forever. Here we see a group of DH.60 Moths of the Yorkshire Aeroplane Club photographed at Yeadon just before Christmas 1935. G-AAPC in the foreground was to meet its end a few months later: on March 22nd while approaching to land between the hangars and close to a roadside garage in misty conditions it collided with the notorious row of telephone wires that fringed the road alongside the field. It stalled and crashed into a car park.

The pre-war decade was that of thrills, record-breaking and epic flights. Here the racing track at Brooklands in Surrey provides a familiar backdrop for this evocative picture of G-AARB, a DH.60M Moth. This was the aircraft used by 25-year-old Jean Gardner Batten on her amazing 15-day solo flight to Australia. She arrived in Darwin on May 28th 1934 and this picture, taken the week before her departure by a news agency photographer, was issued to the Press the moment word of her arrival 'down-under' was received. A little over a decade later, civilian flying was struggling to find its very existence, let alone achieve any sort of return to those memorable days when the sky was free from red tape. The excitement of long distance aviation did not survive the war and those epic flights of old were forgotten. There would still be commendable solo flights that covered great distances but the instant stardom and glory that they brought a decade earlier was now at most a small paragraph on a back page if it was a slack news day.

Once peace was declared we hoped private flying would instantly restart and a shout of 'Contact!' would once again echo out across our grass aerodromes. Time would suggest that it wasn't that easy. The picture shows Avro Avian G-ABEE about to start off from Hatfield for the Isle of Man Air Race on May 27th 1939. Swinging the prop is pilot Sqdn-Ldr H R A Edwards while his wife commands the throttle. They would fly via Blackpool's Stanley Park to Ronaldsway where they would win the £100 first prize in the Tynwald Race at 106.5 mph. In its report of the event, *Flight* magazine referred to their mount as 'ancient'. In the year 2010, that 'ancient mount' is still flying and the author flew it 50 years ago!

would not be certain. After all, it would need skills and an unbridled quantity of money behind it. Now America in the mid-1930s was a wealthy nation that had the will and the ability to do just that – and they did.

We attached an unrealistic importance to the incidental fact that the idea of flying clubs had originated in Britain and that America didn't have 'clubs' as such, only 'flying schools'. Whether they had clubs or not was, in the end, of no importance whatsoever. Clubs had no definable effect on the demand for light aircraft, nor were clubs a guarantee of aeroplane sales. The club was, like many things, a British thing redolent of brown leather armchairs, port, monocles and cigar-smoke.

While our light aircraft industry was stopped in its tracks when civilian light aviation was prohibited at the end of August 1939, the American light plane business carried on more or less unfettered, at least until America finally decided to join in the war in Europe in December 1941. From then onwards there were few restrictions and then mainly regarding manufacturing materials in the later war years. America thus went on improving its designs and when ultimately war was over, the United States was ready with developed and thoroughly modern designs. They had caught up with us, overtaken us – and galloped off into the distance!

Only five weeks before war was declared we had an inkling of what might lie ahead although very few had the nouse (or the courage) to speak out. We all flew over to France for the Deauville Rally that July and found in the midst of a vast acreage of Royal Aero Club members' aeroplanes and visitors to the Plantagenet Rally several sleek German light aircraft. We also had the chance to peer curiously through the windows of a US-made Beech 'Staggerwing', one of four that were actually already on the British Civil Register

In the fullness of time, and after the shadow of war was passed, we were in for an even nastier shock emanating from much closer to our shores. Within a few years France would embark on the path to light plane contention as would the Germans and even the Italians.

We were left with some pre-war aircraft that had fortuitously survived dereliction or Impressment and the bombing of airfields and storage hangars. We had to rebuild our nation and, above all, a tortured economy. There was no room to encourage something as inconsequential as private flying and light aircraft manufacture. Albion was looking decidedly less than perfidious. For the British light aeroplane, not only had the clock stopped in September 1939 but the mechanism of its very movement was now thoroughly derelict.

Throughout the war years, many aviation and economic pundits had looked at what would (or might) happen when private flying could re-start. Inevitably, reading their words today can be nothing but fusty and amusing; curious glimpses into antiquated concepts and incorrect thinking. The ever-optimistic who are supposed, like the poor, to be 'always with us', believed that we would immediately pick up where we had left off and the spirit of the 1930s would be re-kindled as surely as the Sun rises daily in the East. For others, equally bullish in their beliefs, no ideas or opinions in any direction could shift that unassailable dream to build the ideal aeroplane come what may.

Michael Young's slim book [62] appeared during 1944 – one of the war's bleakest years – and looked at what we might expect of and from aviation after the war. After a long look at how commercial aviation might shape up (and anticipating that the pre-war network of internal air services would not only be sustained but greatly expanded), Young's thinking into what might happen regarding private aircraft when peace returned was really not very encouraging. It certainly proved to be both thought-provoking and, with hindsight, ill-informed:

> The extent of private flying is a very much more uncertain matter. For long distances there will be no great advantage in

Some pictures reek of nostalgia, bringing back recollections of a time that, perhaps, we can't ever remember. This picnic party was photographed near Cheltenham on August 5th 1933. The man unscrews the Thermos flask as the woman on the right shades her eyes from the sun as she listens to the clockwork portable gramophone. The other woman has opened the hamper of food next to the carefully-packed travelling picnic case with its serried ranks of plates and cutlery. Not a bad load for four-year-old Desoutter Mk.I G-AAPT. Two women, a gramophone and a tent! What more could any man want! The aircraft survived until the summer of 1938 when it was scrapped.

travelling by private plane once there is a network of air transport services. Before the war the position was rather different in so far as the commercial services, at least in Britain, were not highly developed, and many air enthusiasts owned planes like the outstanding DH Moth. After the war there will be even more enthusiasts, but the limits to the really large-scale use of private planes will be set by the degree to which the collision risk can be reduced, by the possibility of using planes for short distances and by the cheapness with which they can be manufactured and operated.

So serious is the first limitation held to be that some aviation experts doubt whether there is any future at all for the private flier except in out-of-the-way districts remote from the main air trunk routes. Radio aids would only meet the difficulty if you could be sure that the man in charge of the private plane was every bit as responsible as the man in charge of the airliner.

What! No comprehension of how the car would dominate home transport? And no mention of the railway system which, in those days, was outstandingly good and had trains that regularly visited all the major towns not to mention many villages across the land. This was before the sabre-swinging misguided Dr Beeching severed the rail links to half of Britain and had much of the priceless permanent way uprooted for good.

Not that one can blame Mr Young for predictions that proved wide of the mark: politicians have been performing that trick for years. And remember that, in March 1936, Under Secretary of State for Air Sir Philip Sassoon (1888-1939) declared that the aeroplane would eventually become the most effective of all instruments for promoting and maintaining world peace. Wisely, he died three months before the outbreak of the Second World War. Those who offer forecasts need the salvation of a fast pair of heels or the call of God to escape the wrath of those that listen in good faith to their prognostications.

Back in 1946, as a nation we were to all intent and purpose bankrupt. This was the virtually inevitable outcome of a dedicated and concentrated war effort that had sapped not just our strength but cash reserves for five long years. We were forced first to restrict imported goods and then to ban them completely because we simply could not afford the foreign currency, least of all the US dollar, the currency in which most useful commodities traded. This forced trade barrier kept American light aircraft at bay for so many years to come that by the time they entered our skies it was an unhappy revelation just how far America

Shades of a long-gone age. In the pre-war days, arriving at Lympne Aerodrome often necessitated first making a low pass so that the sheep could be cleared to make space for landing. Shepherds tended several hundred of sheep which were employed to keep the grass down. It is January 16th 1936 and our aircraft circles while sheep dogs, upper centre right, start clearing a strip.

had progressed in the intervening years. We still had a few 1930s aircraft and war surplus machines yet the truth was clear to see: we'd been beaten at our own game.

Money was tight at home and Purchase Tax of one-third on light aircraft pushed them beyond the reach of many aspiring pilots and private owners. Private flying was moving into the realms of the super-wealthy.

In the light of all this one might be excused for thinking that we would have cherished the stock of pre-war British aircraft which we had, those machines which, come what may, had survived the conflict to take to our skies once more. Not a bit of it! They were considered collectively to be of no worth at all to us. We were only too glad to sell them abroad to countries that had fewer restrictions and more money than us. And we desperately needed foreign currency. Yes, they were worth selling, not flying!

The Board of Trade, acutely aware that every penny we could earn by export was important, encouraged overseas sales by offering a variety of financial incentives. We thus sold our light plane heritage in order to pay our way, some would say in order to survive. Each week, the big aircraft brokers such as W S Shackleton (who had once been a brilliant light aircraft designer), and R K Dundas advertised for sale a mouth-watering portfolio of classic pre-war British aircraft in the aviation journals.

With a sick home economy, small wonder these aircraft left our shores like the aeronautical equivalent of rats vacating a sinking ship. Looking back now, these were the years of the 'plane drain'. There was nothing to replace the dwindling stock of aeroplanes. If you sell your family silver, soon there's nothing left of your heritage to sell. And that's what happened to us. Like impoverished stately-home-owners with a leaky roof to fix, we flogged off the family treasures for short-term gain.

Through this, people quickly forgot any surviving compunctions regarding sales abroad. After all, money was scarce and so many of our fine aircraft went out to places like Africa, Australia and New Zealand where high temperatures and low humidity (not to mention the occasional termite infestation) sounded a premature death knell for casein-glued wooden structures. Not long afterwards and after one or two instances of structural failure, the airworthiness authorities in those countries, probably quite rightly, forced them into early retirement. At a time when aircraft preservation and restoration were practices yet to be discovered, many were hastily burned and lost forever.

As for our diminishing core of ageing light aircraft, their utilisation and consequent useful survival was limited by over-zealous operating restrictions at home. These mainly concerned the increasingly tough (and expensive) requirements of our own airworthiness authorities. Words like 'unrealistic' were often used around inspection sites as the tendency to ground aircraft for minor problems grew. This is not to suggest that maintenance standards should have been compromised, but merely to highlight the situation where frequently principles and limitations that were intended to apply to military and commercial aircraft were being unfairly applied to private and club machines. In most cases the demands were impossible to meet either in terms of engineering requirements or financial viability.

Those persons with the ability to 'ground' a plane often interpreted the rules in black and white with no opportunity for 'grey' areas. It indicated they were unwilling to shoulder responsibility and preferred that peace of mind that comes to some by unswervingly following their mandates. But to my knowledge several private owners, exasperated at the demands of inspectors unaccustomed to light aircraft, gave up, sold their aeroplanes and took up some less demanding activity. And for those aircraft where pre-war documentation had been lost or destroyed, they became the displaced and the disenfranchised. 'No paperwork, can't fly' was the rule. This was interpreted as 'no documentation, therefore doesn't exist' The easy solution was, all too often, a box of Bryant & May.

It would be nice for this to be a happy tale but it's hard to be very up-beat about the decades following the war. There were bright moments, there were triumphant times, but they have left no legacy. The good times tended to be short-lived and most are forgotten today. Like our once-great cotton industry, our light aircraft factories are either derelict and empty or have long been converted into something profitable to their owners.

The fact is that the story of our post-war light aircraft industry makes rather dismal reading. But it had a curious and unpredicted offshoot that developed into full blossom after the last of our light plane factories had shut up shop.

Immediately after the war, all amateur-built aircraft were technically banned. Their effective prohibition came about in an interesting way. The category of certificate of airworthiness that amateur aircraft fitted into had been abolished by the Air Ministry (then responsible for civil aircraft) and replaced by a 'permit to fly' system at the time of the 'Flying Flea' craze of 1936. When, shortly afterwards, it was found that the Flying Flea could be unstable under certain conditions, the PtF system was withdrawn in a move that affected all home-made aircraft that were not eligible for a Certificate of Airworthiness or a temporary PtF to act as a 'C of A pending' licence. The outbreak of war left sufficient time for the circumstances to be forgotten by most.

In 1946, the gap caused by the dismantling of the old Air Ministry PtF system was neatly papered over by the newly-formed Ministry of Civil Aviation which inherited the Air Ministry's increasingly onerous task of dealing with civilians and their aeroplanes. If aircraft were not factory-built to qualify for a C of A, then they did not exist and there was no available pigeonhole into which they might be fitted. Aeroplanes that operated comfortably on a PtF up to the outbreak of war were now grounded, to all intents, 'in perpetuity'. The paperwork tree closed in over them leaving them with nowhere to go.

This ludicrous situation was challenged by a half-dozen or so enthusiasts amongst which I was one. Repeated pestering and letter-writing achieved nothing and personal pleas seemed to serve no purpose and neither did the now-popular approach of going and sitting on the front doorstep of the Minister and berating him as he arrived home. Not the least of the problems that beset these immediate post-war campaigners was that the office of Minister kept changing as fresh ones were appointed. Lobbying the Minister was all very well only there was a real chance that he'd be out of office long before he had the chance to do anything constructive. The turnover of politicians was rapid and regular.

Eventually a practice was adopted that, in another situation, might be described as blackmail. A home-built aircraft that was fully inspected by certified engineers, carried correct registration and insurance documents, was to be flown by a licensed pilot before an invited crowd of daily newspaper journalists at a North London airfield. The police were to be notified that the aeroplane had no authorisation to fly from the Ministry and that they would be invited to arrest the pilot on landing. The Ministry, confronted by an inevitable showdown, relented and my Permit to Fly was delivered by motorcycle messenger ten minutes before the 'illegal' flight was scheduled to take place. It made a good newspaper story, but its ramifications were far-reaching. It broke the stalemate and once more made it possible for aircraft to be built by Britain's amateurs.

This crisis legitimised the home-built aeroplane and brought a level of freedom to the amateur aircraft movement that was beyond everybody's wildest dreams. Post-war people still associated home-made aircraft with Mignet's Flying Flea of the mid-1930s. For years after the war we

Those pre-war days may have been remembered as care-free but they were also somewhat disorganised. Here is the scene at Le Touquet on August 17th 1936. The occasion is the aerial fête and the airfield below is well scattered with aeroplanes of all sizes and shape arranged in the sort of jumble associated with a poorly-kept knitting-basket. In the group centre left is a Belgian Tipsy S.2 while far left on the 'runway' is G-ACOX the Boulton & Paul P.71A. Just three weeks later this aircraft, Imperial Airways' *Boadicea*, would be lost in the Channel.

British Light Aviation – A Shifting Emphasis

The 1930s were characterised by Sir Alan Cobham's National Aviation Display days when he took his 'flying circus' of aircraft on a gruelling summertime whistle-stop tour of the British Isles giving displays and joy-rides from fields all over the country. Here it is June 29th 1934 and the venue is Petersfield in Hampshire. A joy-ride passenger points his camera over the side and manages to snap four other aircraft plus his own, capturing on one exposure the excitement of the close-in formation flying that was the stamp of a Cobham event. Two Avro Cadets at distance are close enough but between them and the lens are Handley Page Clive G-ABYX (scrapped at the end of that season) and DH.82a Tiger Moth G-ACEZ. This whole genre of aerial entertainment died with the war and despite 'circuses' such as the Tiger Club formations from 1957 onwards, such images as this would never be recaptured. We had invented 'Health and Safety'…

tried to cover up that episode, considered then to have been an unfortunate one. Now, though, we are older and wiser and realise that Henri Mignet was indeed the inspiration of all that has followed. Henri Mignet encouraged the 'man in the street' to make his own aeroplane. In fact, Mignet made it perfectly possible for the ordinary man to build and fly his own aircraft. With the wisdom of hindsight, we can re-appraise Mignet's enterprise and see that it was he who single-handed demystified aviation for the masses. His problem was the age-old one of being too far ahead of his time.

The background that has made possible the acceptance and the integration of the home-built aeroplane in the difficult years that followed the end of the war makes, I believe, a remarkable story, the details of which are already being forgotten.

One might ponder as to what government help was given to light aviation during this crucial period. While, as we shall see, the governments of other nations in Europe (France in particular) backed their private and amateur flyers to the hilt, Britain was different. Our parliamentarians tut-tutted, made pacifying noises, assured us that they quite understood the problem, and promised faithfully to help – but then forgot. It is that characteristic thick skin of politicians that denies them any sense of shame. For the sake of equality it is probably as well that neither Socialist nor Conservative administrations emerge as more inclined towards private flying: both committed heinous crimes in aviation and each was determinedly detested by those lonely outcasts who wanted to fly their own aircraft.

As Margach wrote [30], 'for fifty years there has existed in Britain a state of ceaseless warfare between Prime Ministers and the media'. It is to our credit that, in aviation, at that time we had a good, strong and trustworthy media that pulled no punches in its criticism of successive political party ineptitude; it is merely unfortunate that the very pachydermatous nature of the perpetrators of these aeronautical sins made them oblivious to criticism.

Published works on post-war aviation mostly blur the demarcation line between British-conceived light aircraft and British-registered light aircraft which can include those from around the world that just happen to fly here with a 'G' registration. Some foreign aircraft have been built here. French aircraft designed by the likes of Roger Druine, Édouard Joly and Jean Délémontez, Yves Gardan and others abound. We also have American, Australian and aircraft from many other nationalities that have been built in Britain and fly here. They are in a different category.

This book concentrates on the quarter-century that followed the end of the Second World War. I will explain why. The year 1946 was the date when private flying was once more permitted after the total ban from wartime skies. And some 25 years later the last of our light aircraft companies was fading away. So 1970 becomes a convenient, if perhaps arbitrary, cut-off point that neatly draws the story to an end following the closure of Britain's last commercial manufacturer of light aeroplanes – Beagle. The period that ended with that year was memorable for a number of other reasons – the collapse of Handley Page, the withdrawal of Britain from the originally-proposed equal-pact European Airbus agreement, the abandonment of countless other military and civil aviation projects that began with TSR.2 and V-1000, and extended into the MRCA fiasco, and the aeronautically ruthless autocracy of the despotic Socialist, Anthony Wedgewood Benn.

Of grimmer significance, however, was the realisation that 1970 was the year in which Britain broke with centuries of insular sanity and sensibility and began the miserable process of 'going metric'. It is typically British that, more than forty years later, we still haven't completed the process. Soon afterwards, even, we allowed ourselves to be joined by Europe in the Common Market. Much later we dug a tunnel to France so foreigners could come and see us. That we subsequently chose to leave the European Community through the so-called 'Brexit' movement after having poured so much into making the partnership work, is just another illustration of the fact that, if pushed, we can be as inconsistent as the next man. There are, however, no moves to fill in the Tunnel – yet.

But 1970 also embraces the start of the great expansion of home-made and amateur-designed light aircraft. It is significant that shortly after this date John W R Taylor, editor of *Jane's All the World's Aircraft* found it necessary to insert a whole new, separate section into this great and respected annual to cater for sport and home-built machines. By the mid-1980s this accounted for no less than one-fifth of the entire volume. For this present book to continue beyond 1970 would thus swamp the real British light aeroplane story with increasing numbers of amateur-built aircraft and, despite my personal pleasure that this would be the case, I have sadly to accept that my story must only concern those final 24 years of our one-time commercial light plane industry.

The next volume in this series will itemise the concluding decades of the twentieth century – 1971 to 2000 – but this will not be needed for half a century yet and I cannot expect to be around to produce it!

Attend a light aircraft 'fly-in' (a term imported from the United States in the 1960s) today and you will find a large number of visiting aircraft. They will be divided into two categories – home-builts and factory-produced. The second category will be redolent with fine machines but most probably none will be British unless they are vintage stock. You might ask if it really matters since they are all aeroplanes and they are 'ours' and we are enjoying flying them.

The fact is that we used to have a champion-status light plane industry but we gave it up. For half a century ordinary people battled to try to keep it ticking over. Good sound and honest men made light aviation their life's work pouring in blood, sweat, toil and tears. They believed fervently in flying both the Union Jack and light aeroplanes. In the end, most of them went to their graves without seeing

It is July 1939 and no fewer than 57 of the 68 entered British aircraft have descended on Deauville in Northern France for the Royal Aero Club's annual rally which this year included the first Plantagenet Rally. The weekend of 22nd-24th was largely spoiled by persistent rain but it was to be the last social gathering of the rapidly-disintegrating peace. Just over five weeks later, all private flying would be stopped and many of these aircraft would never fly again. With the deteriorating situation between Britain and Nazi Germany it was a weekend that people enjoyed to the full despite problems with wet magnetos. Among the aircraft seen here in Deauville's forest clearing are two DH.87A round-winged Hornet Moths, three square-tipped DH.87B examples. Puss and Leopard Moths, a BA Swallow Mk.II (Cirrus engine) and another Pobjoy-powered, BA Eagle, Percival Q6, Avro Avian and, as a harbinger of things to come, third row back at the right is a sleek Whirlwind-powered Beech 17, G-AESJ.

fulfilment. Their efforts have in general long been forgotten which is in itself sad for it means that their energy and devotion to flying and their dedicated struggle that we might fly today – all has been in vain. Those that battled and strove to give us the freedom of the air today have with only a few exceptions passed on, their triumphs and tribulations now taken for granted.

This book aims to chart the history of what really happened after the war and to tell the story of those that engaged in the often thankless task of believing in light aircraft. If for nothing else, I earnestly believe we owe it to those that have breathed their last that we might fly today, and can have no more say in the world they loved so much. Many were my friends and acquaintances and while I am sure that, given the chance, their modesty might prevail, it is their contributions to the aviation world that should be preserved if only for the fact that they might just make a good read. It may not be the ultimate 'human interest' story, but it's nevertheless a good one!

Now historians and authors are fallible and I shall be the first to admit that if you get several people together and get them to recount their experience of an event you are likely to receive several different – possibly *very* different – accounts of the same occurrence. Those that write war memoirs and popular histories frequently fall into the trap of failing to appreciate this basic truth of life. This story, then, is my personal interpretation of the events of history. Wherever possible I have quoted from other writers, contemporary and subsequent, in an effort to corroborate or substantiate my account.

Not completed until after the declaration of war in September 1939, the Marendaz Trainer was an early and quite unmissed victim of the conflict. Designed by an unknown hand hired by the larger-than-life Donald Marcus Kellway Marendaz (the story of whom is told in Ord-Hume [37], the Trainer was proffered as a Civil Air Guard machine. Of course, it was too late since all CAG activities ended, like those of the flying clubs, at the end of August. Powered by a 90 hp Blackburn Cirrus Minor I engine, the sole example, G-AFZX, made its first flight in November of 1939 at the hands of test pilot R A Wyndham. The machine was notable for its highly-stressed undercarriage, the poor geometry of which suggested a minimal fatigue life. Here it is pictured at first roll-out in unfinished state.

To many, history is considered to be a boring subject. This is an unfortunate viewpoint from which to consider those past events that have shaped our lives and made us what we are today. History is the life-blood of not just our heritage but of each and every one of us! It is the explanation behind us, what we are and what we do. It is the story, then, not of mere happenings, but of those events that directly affect us for today. History is the lens through which we will define the focus of the future. I have genuine compassion for those that find history as anything other than an opportunity to understand where we have come from and assist us in where we are going.

Inevitably some of my readers will be bored with mere words so for their benefit I have included a large number of pictures chosen, in the main, for their rarity, pictorial interest and/or relevance to the story.

I have been proud to have played a small part in the light plane scene in the immediate post-war years both as an observer and as an active participant and, at a crucial time, a prolific campaigner. It is all past now but, unlike the reality of life's experience, it doesn't hurt us to look back.

Post-war private flying would bring us sleek all-metal low-wing monoplanes. This target of the light plane world finally happened but even when eventually it came we made a mess of it though poor management where enthusiasm reigned over economics. This combined with a worryingly scant understanding of the world marketplace for this type of aircraft, and an intransigent government that lacked the nouse to put in a nominated management team to save the business from itself. The picture is an evocative night-time scene showing the Beagle factory at Shoreham in 1964.

Introduction

The various production operations are broken down into stages and planned more elaborately in America than in this country. Much time and effort is put into pre-preparation work of scheduling, process planning, machine loading, labour-loading and shop layout, and this is carried out in greater detail in America than is customary in many of our factories. This is considered to be an essential part of obtaining efficient production

Sir Roy Fedden:
Report on a British aircraft industry fact-finding mission to the United States, 1943

If you study history you will find that those that win wars are inevitably trumpeted as victors. Reality, though, suggests such adulation is frequently misplaced. It does not necessarily follow that the conqueror achieves either the economic supremacy or the domestic stability that is popularly associated with winning and being victorious. It seems so often the reverse and time and time again we find that the successful outcome of a conflict generates in the defeated nation conditions conducive to rapid business and domestic revival while the titular conqueror suffers heightened deprivation, not the least economically.

So it was with Britain in 1945. With the war with Nazi Germany in Europe over at last (May 8th 1945) and, on August 14th, that with Japan in the Far East, there was an understandable feeling of national euphoria. After the increasing privations of wartime living which, for those at home, meant meagre food rations, making do with patched-up clothing and linen, coping with uncertain and restricted fuel allocations, battling the authorities for permits in order to try to buy materials to repair the huge numbers of damaged houses, restrictions on public entertainment and travel as well as a host of other activities that had been prevented 'for the duration', suddenly to have the end within grasp was a relief beyond compare.

But this euphoric period was a dreadfully short-lived illusion as living conditions and the economy, unbalanced during the years of war, demonstrated a resolute resistance to any form of rapid recovery. Earlier we had experienced what they called the 'phoney war'; now it was the 'phoney peace'. In fact, in the years that followed the war's end, life became even harder in Britain. Food rationing, introduced in 1939 and endured with resolve throughout the war, continued and, in some cases, allowances were actually further reduced.

It was not until 1954 that the British could finally discard their ration books and buy food without restriction. The shortage of new clothing generated the 'drab' years and, in the perverse way of things, elevated the wearing of old and patched apparel with twice-turned collars and leathered suit-jacket elbows to middling fashionable – even in what remained of London's 'square mile'.

At a less mundane level, there remained huge financial penalties – called disincentives in taxation circles – against acquiring anything, especially luxury goods. The scourge of Purchase Tax, introduced on October 21st 1940, would

In the 1930s, a well-known motor car showroom made a bold attempt to 'normalise' aircraft buying and dispel the myth that they were upper class commodities and very special. London department store Selfridges had displayed famous aircraft starting with the wreckage of Hawker and Grieves' Sopwith Atlantic aircraft after their failed transatlantic flight in May 1919. They then put a Comper Swift in one of the store windows in 1932, and went on to show Lord Sempill's BAC Drone G-ADPJ which had flown from Croydon to Berlin and back on 25 shillings'-worth of petrol in 1936. But displaying aircraft for sale was another thing. Credit for being the first went to this Bond Street automobile showroom that displayed a two seat Cirrus engined Blackburn Bluebird Mk. IV, G-AAIR, in 1929. It carried a price tag of £700 and that included a spare engine on a wooden stand. It is not known if any lunch-time shoppers actually nipped in and bought any but we do know that early in 1930 the Hon Mrs Victor Bruce spotted Bluebird G-ABDS in this self-same window and managed to buy it for £550. The enterprising lady, with just 40 hours in her logbook, then flew it round the world. Leaving Croydon that July she returned the following February and her aircraft became the star attraction in the booking hall of Charing Cross Underground Station – today called Embankment. Three years later in 1932, the Southsea department store Handley's opened an aircraft showroom, complete with Robinson Redwing. Moths were also shown in some stores across the country – Selfridges Aviation Department had 'sold' Amy Johnson her Gipsy Moth G-ABDV and later displayed it with its pilot in one of its windows – but there is little evidence that any aircraft were actually retailed as a result of these ventures. In 1946, Auster Aircraft also placed aeroplanes in stores around the Midlands but not until the 1950s did aircraft appear in a London store again. This happened when motorcycle dealer Raymond Way, having secured a distributorship for the American Piper PA-18 Cub, showed an example in his Kilburn High Road showrooms opposite the railway station. Again it is unlikely that any were ever sold as a result but it certainly got some publicity for the motorbikes! Raymond Way was, at that time, also head of aircraft dealers W S Shackleton of Piccadilly.

remain on 'luxury goods' until its abolition on April 2nd 1973 – to be replaced by Value Added Tax! More on this in a moment, though.

At the end of the First World War, the Armistice was the solution to cease the war rather than subject the Germans to total military defeat. The American army commander, General John J Pershing, would have much preferred this sword-twisting course especially as it was within striking distance: without their supply system the German army could have been driven back into their own territory, but at yet more cost to our gallant but battle-weary servicemen.

Now, at the end of the Second World War, the Americans got what they wanted – the total military defeat of the enemy. Heavy-handedly they revenged Pearl Harbor by sinking the last seven ships of the Japanese navy – now neutralised sitting ducks – in their own harbour at Kure naval base. They could then go home and get on with life again in the embrace of the strong American economy. Their God had truly blessed America! Naturally we, too, wanted the annihilation of the Nazi regime, but the cost of achieving it in both manpower and resources was something we had to live with. Unlike the Americans, we couldn't simply dust down our hands, sail away and forget: we had to live amidst our ruins while reviving and rebuilding. America was a long way off but, at that time, so was Europe and never before had we been quite so isolated in our poverty.

Through a measure of chance and opportunity, we won our war with Nazi Germany and Japan. Unlike the stuff of boys' papers across the years, it wasn't a walk-over for we fought a tyrannical regime staffed with personnel no less resolved than ourselves. And when it came, ours turned out to be closer to being a pyrrhic victory. And actually *how* we won has puzzled analysts ever since, but succeed we did with the help of the Americans and stalwarts from around our Commonwealth.

It is increasingly hard today to recall the enormous task that we were faced with in 1946. Around one-quarter of Britain's wealth had been expended on the war effort and thanks to government-induced poor pre-war policies on the growth of our Services and their equipment (not the least of these being the Royal Air Force) our foreign exchange reserves were all used up by 1941. When the war ended, we were only able to pay for about 40 per cent of our overseas expenditure.

Of greater concern to the rank and file British civilian was that almost one-third

The war years were not healthy for light aircraft. Many were 'impressed' (taken into Service use) where they endured mixed fortunes and, usually, short lives. Others were stored. However, as the war progressed and hangar space became more and more precious, those aircraft deemed worthless were simply turned out into the open for the duration. Cirrus-engined B A Swallow Mk 2 G-AFHU spent five years parked out to face the elements at Hanworth. First registered on June 8th 1938, her working life was short and in the post-war clear-up she was scrapped in December 1946, logbooks and surviving paperwork used to stoke the wintertime boiler in the workshop.

The end of the war revealed the remains of many of the aircraft that had not made it. Here behind the old hangars at White Waltham there lies a pair of Avro 671 Cierva C.30A Autogiros abandoned to rot. G-ACXW had been impressed as BV999 while the other one had been G-ACWF, impressed as DR624 and then allocated G-AHMR in 1946 but not proceeded with. George Cull photographed these in the late 1940s.

This is what five years in the open does to a wooden airframe. Klemm L.25C-1A G-ACXS lies rotting in the grass at Walsall in 1947. First registered on September 15th 1934, this Swallow suffered the same fate as countless other machines up and down the land.

INTRODUCTION

By the time the war ended, comparatively few of the pre-war light aeroplanes survived. While a number had been impressed, not many emerged unscathed after half a decade of pretty rough service. Of those not commandeered for military use, a high proportion had been destroyed. Some had been used as outdoor decoys or obstacles to be left with old cars parked in fields to deter invading German aircraft from landing until the elements reduced them to worthless scrap. Others had been unceremoniously turfed out into the open to clear valuable hangar space. There were several notable heaps of wasted aircraft in the South of England, that at Gatwick Racecourse (later Gatwick Airport) being one of the more infamous. The sheer numbers of aircraft left rotting in the grass at Gatwick may never be known for sure. What is certain is that one man found a derelict Hornet Moth being prepared for a bonfire – and arranged to steal it. That machine, superbly restored, is still flying today – some 60 years on. The pictures here, taken by the late Mike Hooks, show two views of part of the Gatwick Pile. The fuselage of the Spartan Three Seater, G-ABTR, looms over an unidentified wooden DH.60 Moth split open on the grass while behind it is the only Porterfield 35-70 to have been imported into Britain, G-AEOK.

Registered to Surrey Flying Services Ltd on December 11th 1936, this Porterfield was used for tuition until the outbreak of war. With its 70 hp Le Blond radial still in place and the legend 'Porterfield Aircraft Corporation, Kansas City, Mo' on its tail, these were all burned where they rested in 1947.

Less recognisable beneath a tattered and rotting tarpaulin are these two Aeronca G-AEOO and G-AEOP. Brought over from Hanworth in the early part of the war they were stored in the open behind a blister hangar at Denham. There were actually seven wings but only two identifiable fuselages. Absolutely nothing serviceable remained on these rusting hulks.

of our housing had been damaged or destroyed by enemy action. Factories, offices, schools and hospitals had also been hit, so affecting both blue-collar and white-collar workers, the young and the sick and embracing that entire anonymous group known collectively as 'the needy'.

In practically every respect the Second World War had been vastly more costly than the first. While fewer men had been killed than in the 1914-18 conflict (battle deaths were about 264,500[1] against the 750,000 earlier), it had been a war of increasing-costly machinery. This had imposed a far greater strain on our economic and productive resources than had the first. The bottom line was that the National Debt increased by about £14,800 million or almost exactly twice the increase incurred in 1914-18.

Admittedly the comparison is suspect for prices and wages were somewhat higher in 1940 than in 1914 but more significantly, and as had happened in the First World War, annual government expenditures far exceeded the total national income of any pre-war year. British national income in 1938 had been £4,671 million. In each of the seven fiscal years, from the year ending March 31st 1940 to March 31st 1946, the government spent an average of £4,734 million, reaching a peak of slightly over £6,000 million in the year 1944-45.[2]

The strain on capital resources, although massive, would have been worse had the government been less successful in controlling it. Personal civilian expenditure, then, was restricted far more efficiently during this period than during the First World War.

One principal key to this success was the imposition of Purchase Tax first raised by the Finance Act of 1940. As stated earlier, it came into effect in October that year and was to remain in force for 33 years, ultimately to be replaced by Value Added Tax. There were, of course, other taxes that had been brought into force. Among these was Entertainment Tax that imposed a levy on all theatre, concert and cinema seats. But the principal expenditure-limiter was Purchase Tax which was levied on virtually every commodity (the few notable exceptions including books and newspapers) at different rates, the highest band (33⅓ per cent) being for so-called 'luxury goods'

Forerunner of the Proctor, many examples of which spearheaded the revival of the private owner sector in 1946, was the Percival Vega Gull which was first flown as far back as November 1935. Here is the prototype G-AEAB which, for the first part of its life, was mispainted G-AEAD as seen here. This was the confusion between the letters 'b' and 'd' as spoken over a pre-war telephone. This particular aircraft took part in the South Africa Race in September 1936 only to crash by Lake Tanganyika. Ninety Vega Gulls were built in the 1930s, most going for export. By March 1940, some 19 of the British-owned examples had been impressed: only six survived the war. This one didn't make it having crashed in Tanganyika in September 1936. The real G-AEAD was a Flying Flea.

within which light aircraft, cars and radios were to be included after 1946.

Throughout the war years, Britain had been forced to buy from abroad, a trade that was to become increasingly one-way as the war progressed. The inevitable outcome was economic bankruptcy alleviated only in part by sterling credits earned on sales to Britain by foreign nations, chiefly (but not exclusively) within the Commonwealth. These nations agreed to deposit them in London in pounds sterling that earned interest: it was part of an enmeshed policy that would ultimately make our balance of payments maintenance all the more difficult.

The crucial reason for Britain's economic doldrums, however, lay with the Lease-Lend agreement with the United States and Mutual Aid from Canada. Increasingly we depended on these (plus other credits from, in the main, Sterling area countries) as the war progressed until towards the end we were effectively totally dependent on this transatlantic aid. We were, in effect, a nation without funds of our own fighting what was then the most costly war in the history of Mankind.

Lord Keynes (John Maynard Keynes, 1883-1946) was a member of that rare breed – a highly-intelligent and motivated economist. Hired by the new Labour Government's Chancellor of the Exchequer Hugh Dalton as principal Treasury economic adviser, Keynes produced a penetrating and comprehensive analysis of the position of the United Kingdom, highlighting that war-vital foreign aid was 'enabling us to overspend our income at the rate of about £2,100 million a year'. Dalton circulated the damning memorandum to his Cabinet colleagues on August 14th 1945 – the same day that Japan surrendered.

What came next was swift. On August 21st 1945, just a week after the end of the war in the Pacific, President Harry S Truman abruptly ended the lease-lend agreement (as he was required to do by law and in accord with the existing agreement between both Britain and America), and we were precipitated headlong into a massive financial crisis. As Barnett [6] suggests, the end of the war presented an illusion of British power at a new zenith: instead it was a stark indication of American power and wealth and the decline of Britain into a warrior satellite of the United States. Under the spell of victory celebrations, the British public completely failed to grasp this simple truth and acknowledge that Britain was now bust.

We were forced to go cap-in-hand to Washington and beg for a fresh loan. It was poor old Lord Keynes who was the unfortunate emissary chosen to represent

---

1. True figures may never be known but the reliable estimates are 264,433 armed forces dead, 60,595 civilians were killed, and 30,248 in the merchant navy lost their lives. There were thousands of Australians, Indians, New Zealanders, South Africans and others who died as members of the British Empire armed forces. By comparison, Germany lost an estimated 3.25m service dead and 3.6m civilians. Although they did not participate in the war until 1941, the United States armed forces suffered a proportionately higher death rate at 362,561. In terms of total losses, estimates vary widely from 35m to 60m – a vast variation.

2. Gilbert, Bentley B: *Britain since 1918*. Batsford Academic & Educational, London, 1967, 2ed. 1980.

INTRODUCTION

Among the notable pre-war survivors with which we seeded sporting flying in the late 1940s was G-AEXF, the last-remaining of the six Percival Mew Gull racers. Built in 1936 it was raced by Alex Henshaw who flew it to the Cape and back in February 1939. After 13 years in storage it appeared to race through our skies once more.

the Treasury and charged with carrying the begging-bowl to America. Once more we were successful and the loan began in July 1946 being $3,750 million from the United States and $1,250 million from Canada. Attached, however, were the hard conditions that Imperial trade preferences should be ended and that the £ should become freely convertible to the dollar for current transactions as from July 1947. This last requirement would contribute to making 1947, like 1931, a year of crisis.

This, then, was the background to the re-birth of private flying and light aircraft manufacture in 1946. It was the era of Clement Atlee whose period as Prime Minister was endowed with an almost evangelical enthusiasm. His Labour government is remembered for its initial oblivion to all matters of international financial concern thanks to Lord Keynes' loan-negotiation. This 'glad confident morning' of his administration was soon to be overtaken by reality and from 1947 until his welcome resignation in October 1951 Atlee's administration was overshadowed by the struggle to keep Britain afloat economically.

Even so, that Socialist interlude can take credit for seeing through the Bill to nationalise the Bank of England, the coal industry and the railways (through the Inland Transport Act), the enactment of the National Health Service (first mooted in a coalition Government White Paper of February 1944), the Cable and Wireless Act of 1946, and the Electricity Act of 1947.

Amidst all this there was the Civil Aviation Act of 1946. This brought into existence two new corporations under the auspices of the Ministry of Civil Aviation – British European Airways and British South American Airways – which would join British Overseas Airways Corporation, a business that had existed since 1939. On top of that there were no fewer than 69 independent airlines and charter companies, the greater majority of which were one-man operations equipped with just one aircraft, usually a converted surplus wartime bomber. The survival rate of these businesses was poor and within the period covered by this book the number fell back to sixteen.

The year 1947 was remarkable in many ways, not the least being its astonishingly long and bitterly cold winter – the coldest on record since that of 1880-81. Many compared it to the winter of 1927 and the Christmas blizzards which had so memorably trapped trains and travellers. What underscored this post-war winter, however, was that it went down in history as the one that we couldn't cope with and the one that precipitated the end of one of our most respected light aircraft-makers – Miles Aircraft.

It was long and without let-up and people were ill-prepared at every level. On February 7th the Minister of Fuel and Power, Emanuel Shinwell, announced that due to a shortage in the production of coal, electric power would have to be cut off to a large number of industrial establishments and seriously rationed to domestic consumers. To make matters worse, what little coal was available could not be shifted because of the snow and the ice that gripped the national transport system effectively paralysing road and rail links. This was a heavy blow to the government in particular since the official nationalisation of the pits had occurred only a little more than a month before on the first day of the year.

But worse was to come. Nationalisation had unexpectedly resulted in a rise in unemployment. Now the crisis meant that men were being laid off across the nation. The numbers out of work spiralled within two weeks from the almost irreducible minimum of 350,000 to 2.3 million – 15.5 per cent of the nation's work force. The forced closure of factories, which was to last about three weeks, came as a heavy blow to the export drive and that alone cost the nation an estimated £300 million in lost foreign currency.

Of greater long-term concern was Britain's chronic deficit in trade with dollar areas. In a worsening situation, the dollar now became highly restricted. This affected not just the import of American goods but also imposed hardship on those who travelled for business to the United States; very, very few went for pleasure. If the onset of a late spring ended the freeze-up it merely intensified the general economic hardship. By August of 1947 the government was forced to consider draconian measures to stave off national bankruptcy and the immediate outward sign of this was increased domestic austerity. Food rationing, including bread (which had been rationed since July 1946), was tightened and travel outside Sterling areas was first restricted and then, in October, prevented altogether. If today we take for granted the facility of worldwide air travel, communication with the United States, for example, was now back to the postal services and the costly telephone.[3] The currency restrictions affected sea travel as well. Not for a very long time had Britain been so much of an island as she was that year.

---

3. Until the end of 1946 all public telephone services to the Continent were suspended. International services were all based on a three-minute minimum charge and telephoning the United States (all states except the Western ones) cost £3.0.0. Calling those Western States was, for a three-minute connection, £3.15/-. When telephoning the Continent became possible again in 1947, a three-minute call to France cost 6/-, Austria 18/- and Spain 21/-. New rates were introduced for America: 60/- by day and 45/- by night. It was a prodigious cost at a time when the minimal wage for workers was £4.14/- for a 47 hour week and junior to middle management earnings were between £10 and £15 a week. At that time the present author earned, with flying pay, an annual salary of £750.

British Light Aviation – A Shifting Emphasis

B A Swallow 2, G-AELG, a 1936-vintage product of the Hanworth factory of British Aircraft Ltd, returned to fly again in port-war skies until August of 1962 when it was sold to a Mr P A Doyle in Ireland becoming EI-AMU. It was written off in 1963. Here it is pictured at the Royal Aero Club Garden Party in 1952 by Timothy R Wrixon.

Some pre-war light aircraft ought to have had a second chance in 1946 but instead were mere lost designs. The year that war broke out is remembered for a flourishing of the British light aircraft industry. The culmination of two decades of refinement in design and concept had brought a high degree of perfection to the machine. Now the fruits of all that hard work were within the grasp of the private flying world. General Aircraft Ltd had bought the design rights to Chronander and Waddington's Cygnet Minor and spent considerable time and money in perfecting both its design and production. It was a revolution in British light aircraft design being foolproof to fly and both all-metal and blind-riveted in construction. It also had landing flaps and a tricycle undercarriage. David Leonard Hollis Williams, who went on to become Technical Director of Westland Aircraft, flew many a brilliant demonstration in the months leading up to the start of the war. The company, under the control of far-sighted Eric Cecil Gordon England, planned to produce the Cygnet as the people's aero-car and spoke of 500 being built. In the end, just nine Cygnets were made, four survived the war and production was never resumed. G-AGBN with its 150 hp Blackburn Cirrus Major II is today a museum exhibit.

It was this worsening economic crisis that actually generated the means for partial solution. One has to remember that, with Britain so economically weak in world terms, the situation was now having a global effect and there was an economic backlash in America itself. The proportion of American goods traditionally exported to Britain was now under scrutiny as never before. Other than tobacco, there was precious little trade. Our own Board of Trade was required to issue a permit for every import and the instruction was that there had to be a very strong reason for the Treasury to authorise dollars for anything.

Speaking at Harvard University in June 1947, the American Secretary of State, the erudite George C Marshall, proposed a scheme for economic aid for Europe and Britain in particular. This became the so-called Marshall Plan or, to give it its official title, the European Recovery Programme. It should have been our salvation.

However, what had begun as a British problem had by this time grown to such proportions that the economy of the whole western world was fragile. If the Marshall Plan transformed the economic gloom of 1947 into prospects of better times in 1948, the respite was short-lived. The United States now suffered a slight economic depression that reduced the demand for British goods. In normal times this could have probably been shrugged off as a short-term glitch: in reality it was like running in a quagmire and poor trade reports in the spring of 1949 created a sustained attack on the British currency. The 'bad news' cycle generated its own impetus as the world looked elsewhere for trade and investment. For us it meant that the low point of 1931 that had been initiated by the Wall Street Crash two years earlier was exceeded. There were now no reserves to tide over the British economy until we might once more be able to pay our way.

On the domestic front, British Chancellor of the Exchequer Hugh Dalton's ultra-cheap money policy (low Bank Interest Rate) was running out of steam and share prices began to fall – even Dalton's averred 'never-never' stock (repayable in 1975) dropped from 100 in January to 81 in July. Dalton did the only thing he knew how – set a draconian Budget. This was the famous November 12th 'bludgeon-the-people' occasion when he doubled Purchase Tax on everything. Sadly it proved to be the last gesture of a desperate man because he deliberately and very foolishly leaked details of his Budget to the Press before his House of Commons speech. Admitting his stupidity, two days later he resigned. It had no effect on our problems, but merely increased the desperation of the public.

Now came the shock-horror news story – so-called 'tabloid journalism' had yet to be developed so the press merely reflected the emotions that Britain really felt – that the £937m loan which the now-deceased Lord Keynes had negotiated in 1946 was almost exhausted. Spending on the loan had to be cut urgently otherwise we would have no money for those bare essentials – foodstuffs and engineering machinery from the United States.

A wildly-impossible book-balancing act presented the government with only two alternatives – to cut imports or increase exports as the gap between the two accelerated to nine million pounds a week. Hardened city-types knew that increasing exports was no over-night panacea and took a long time to make happen. That only left the import-cutting alternative. Admittedly easier and quicker to deploy (goods-in-transit would cease in a maximum of two months), it would still be a last act of anxiety. Clearly neither was really achievable or palatable, so government took a fresh initiative or, more correctly, dreamed up a new slogan that the suffering public could chant as a mantra of salvation. The 'Work or Want' campaign was started. No way could that stem the outward flow quickly enough. Every day brought the nation nearer to crisis.

With our gold and dollar reserves depleted below what the Treasury considered to be a safe minimum of $2,000 million, the crisis flash-point was reached on July 15th 1948 – the day that saw a total halt on all purchases from dollar areas. The cuts were announced to the British public on August 20th and, for the 'man in the street', the immediate effect was a stop on showing the latest Hollywood films (which, of course, had to be bought with US dollars), the banning of some foodstuffs, and sharp cuts in petrol supplies. Concurrent with this announcement, new priorities were given to exports although it was abundantly clear that the cuts which had been made would not suffice unless there was a rapid increase in exports. On the domestic front, much more coal was the most pressing need.

Along with these fresh austerity measures the Chancellor of the Exchequer, now Sir Stafford Cripps, dramatically devalued the pound, slashing it from $4.03 to $2.80. So great was the effect of this that what little travel there was (almost exclusively business) ceased immediately. Nobody could afford to journey abroad anywhere, least of all to America, unless they were sponsored and their trip paid for in America. Those of us who, as part of work or study, had to buy copies of books or reports from America were placed in the same boat. Universities quickly learned to barter publications in the interests of the exchange of learning. Nobody could afford dollars, *ergo* America was a rich nation and we were a poor one. Eastern Bloc countries had plenty of experience of this sort of cash crisis and would continue to experience it for decades to come; for the British it was a bitter pill to swallow. The dollar would eventually oust that most attractive currency – the Swiss franc – as the currency of European trade and commerce. Businesses began working in dollars and even street prostitutes in some sensitive parts of Europe offered special discounted rates for their services if paid for in hard currency.

At the time these actions were initiated, we had only £190m of that American loan left – roughly about thirteen weeks' existence until we would be totally insolvent.

These hard times, seen by many as symbolising the end of Britain's useful position in the world market, nevertheless marked the turning-point in our fortunes although whether this was entirely due to the revaluation of the pound versus the dollar, or to the expansion of the American market that began with the outbreak of the Korean War on June 25th 1950, remains a moot point. Certainly the resulting lower prices for British goods abroad was a shot in the arm for exports and served to initiate the slow return to stability that followed.

It has been argued that a devaluation of 30 per cent was larger than necessary and that Britain's failure to export was less the result of high British prices than of a sheer inability to produce.[4] Of course much of the advantage that Britain had at this time was to prove short-lived as devaluations in other countries generated what might be termed a 'global parity'. But over the following four years one consequence of an almost 25 per cent inflation in British prices that resulted in the main from Britain's own rearmament programme in 1951 was the blunting of our fundamental problem – the basic imbalance between low productivity and high consumption.

What transpired was that our own economic weakness became less of an encumbrance against a backdrop of the rising standards of living throughout the western world plus the immense and seemingly unstoppable affluence of the United States. We could allow ourselves to be carried along by the tide of whatever it was that abrogated our immediate responsibilities to anybody else. This was made easier because war had diminished our importance as a trading nation to the point where we had ceased to be influential in world terms. Now others had at last shown that they could grow their own economies without Britain's influence or interference.[5] While we were all-too happy to have the responsibilities of Empire-leading relieved at the moment, it was no short-term let-up and the longer we delayed showing our mettle the harder it would be to pick up the pieces ever again. Time would prove we were no longer able to resume the challenge: hindsight would establish we were no longer fit to do so. This was a fundamental turning point in our world status and one from which there was no way back.

Paradoxically, as a nation we retained the mindset of a great empire-builder[6] and world power but as we increasingly became dependent on others, particularly hand-outs from America, things would change. In the half-century that followed,

Post-war light-aircraft flying relied heavily on the resuscitation of whatever pre-war aircraft could be mustered from Service Impressment, storage and abandonment. G-ADPJ was a BAC Drone powered by a 23 hp Douglas Sprite flat twin engine. Built in 1935 it made history in the hands of enterprising enthusiast Lord Sempill (born 1893) who flew from Croydon to Berlin in 11 hours on April 2nd 1936 – all for 25/- worth of petrol. Here he is pictured taking off from Hanworth en-route to Croydon for the proper start. In 1946 in the hands of Albert C Waterhouse, G-ADPJ was restored with a 32 hp Bristol Cherub and eventually flown again in October 1950. It crashed in April 1955 and was approaching completion of rebuild when it was totally destroyed when a gale blew a heavy hangar door on top of it and squashed it very flat. Note the cross-axle undercarriage which meant that take-off in longish grass was impossible.

---

4. Gilbert, *op.cit.*

5. Gilbert, *op.cit.*

6. The British Empire had, contrary to common belief, long ceased to be an asset to Britain and by the late 1930s had become both a political and a military liability. As *Barnett* [6] puts it the empire became 'one of the most outstanding examples of strategic over-extension in history'.

British Light Aviation – A Shifting Emphasis

Another popular pre-war survivor was Comper Swift G-ABUS raced by Anthony L 'Tony' Cole who replaced the standard 75 hp Pobjoy 'R' engine with a 90 hp Pobjoy Niagara III. It is pictured here at Whitchurch Aerodrome, Bristol, on June 11th 1955. The logo on the lower part of the forward fuselage is that of 'The Throttle Benders' Union' of which Cole and a dozen or so other top post-war racers were enthusiastic members.

One distinct type of aircraft which the post-war revival of private aircraft curiously excluded was the autogyro. In spite of a mounting following before the war, the building of the light gyroplane was not resumed. Cierva's greatest years were in the early 1930s and the two seat 175 hp Salmson 9NG-engined C.40, introduced in the summer of 1939, never entered production. Prototype G-AFDP was widely demonstrated by company test pilot Reginald Brie at Hanworth that summer and much was made of its side-by-side seating and its comfortable large windscreen. After the war, autogyros had been overtaken by the first generation of helicopters and not until the invention of American Igor Bensen did the first generation of small and basic home-made rotorplanes once more capture the interests of the civilian market. A formula exploited and expanded by men like Wing-Cmdr Wallis and others produced a fresh candidate for the private autogyro, but these were more enthusiasts' machines as distinct from practical light aircraft. Despite attempts by Beagle to produce machines, autogyros remained but a byway of the amateur aircraft movement. In this picture, taken at Hanworth on June 12th 1939, Cierva test pilot Reginald Brie, nearest the camera, is describing details of the machine to representatives of the military.

Home-built aircraft made up a significant if small sector of the private flying movement in pre-war days. While these were in the main based on interpretations of conventional formula, one design was to stand out as unique. This was the revolutionary vision of two young Nottingham brothers who, inspired by Geoffrey Terence Roland Hill's work with Westland Aircraft, chose to move into virgin territory (as far as amateur design was concerned) and produce their own swept-wing tailless single seat ultra-light. Arguably the most significant development in home-designed and built aircraft in the between-wars years, the Granger Archaeopteryx demonstrated originality and creative thinking of a high order. Four years in the design and construction, this unique aircraft was powered by a 30 hp Bristol Cherub twin-cylinder engine fitted with a Fairey metal propeller. First flown by co-designer R F T Granger on October 19th 1930, it is pictured here at Nottingham Aerodrome with its two creators, 24 year-old Richard John Turney Granger (left) and 30 year-old Richard Francis Turney Granger. Later to be registered G-ABXL, the Archaeopteryx demonstrated a level of original aerodynamic thinking not to be equalled in Britain for another half-century by which time the American designer Bert Rutan had gone a long way to show the world that conventional aircraft were passé.

as the young aspired to leadership and the 'old brigade' died off, and as the British Empire disintegrated around our shoulders starting with the independence of that jewel in our crown, India, we came face to face with our relentless slide in importance and global market share. We gradually became locked into a vicious circle of poor profitability, declining investment and uncontrollable costings. By the end of the century our self-confidence would be quite gone and we would have settled for a national attitude of graceful decline. In 1946, however, any notion that we were a dying star destined for industrial oblivion was quite unthinkable. We were still devoutly British with all that that entailed.

The public, thought government, needed to see a return to status quo: they were not yet ready to face anything vaguely progressive. And those in government shared a morbid fear of apple carts, and the dread of upsetting them produced a generation of so-called leaders who thought in merely hierarchical terms. Any vestige of planning for the future – what Americans were to dub 'linear thinking' – was to put one's job on the line. To be seen to be alert to such matters was neither ideal nor expected, let alone needed. After all, it was peacetime and the urge for looking ahead was, happily, behind us! We could coast along with the undemanding regime of the 'old boys' club' and wait for the British Empire to stabilise by itself. It was a diminishing resource that few recognised.

There were one or two that thought otherwise, but they quickly had any influence taken from them since power and thinking forms a dangerous mix in an administration already dead worried about an immediacy centred on the economy and ready-money in particular.

Britain's poverty affected our light aeroplane business in several ways. Predominately, it isolated us from outside competition. More specifically it forced self-sufficiency. While it preserved British markets by comprehensively preventing American intervention, it denied British aircraft manufacturers any opportunity of intercourse that might allow their availing themselves of the benefits of American technology. We could not, for instance, buy American engines, instruments or equipment.

Just as efficiently, it isolated us from most developments elsewhere outside the American cauldron. It left us bereft of input either through reciprocity with, or influence by, other non-UK designers and aero-engineering procedures. We remained firmly in the realm of the Moth while the rest of the world looked to advanced construction methods and better aerodynamics.

Since the economy was so weak and because it sustained this weakness for such a protracted length of time, it forced us to move forward with whatever limited resources we might muster by way of dated technology and hardware that could be appropriated from the late war effort. Measures that encouraged us to practice total self-sufficiency, while probably good for the soul, meant that we advanced towards the 1950s with pre-war equipment and ideals. Meanwhile other countries such as France and Germany had no dollar trading restrictions and consequently could source material from a global market. We could only look inwards while Germany, in defeat, accepted its new position in Europe and rapidly built a strong economy with brand new factories and equipment supported by a European currency that was second only to the Swiss franc in strength.

This matter of production facilities was to haunt us into the closing decades of the 20th century. At the end of the war virtually all of the significant German factory premises had been destroyed and so Germany had to build modern plants from scratch. We, the victorious ones, had preserved our mainly Victorian buildings and so industry made do in century-old buildings that were long beyond their 'scrap-by' dates. Trying to set up new technical processes in these antediluvian structures was neither cheap nor, in the end, particularly efficient.

Our economic isolation seemed reinforced in April 1951 when the then Chancellor of the Exchequer introduced a swingeing Budget. Purchase Tax on luxury goods was doubled to 66⅔ per cent; petrol prices increased by 4½d to 3s 6½d a gallon and Income Tax went up by 6d to 9/6d in the £. As might be expected the effect on public morale was devastating while home industries, especially the motorcar makers, were well and truly hobbled. Auster Aircraft Ltd was equally manacled when it came to inland (domestic) sales and markets.

When finally the Conservative government of Harold Macmillan, blighted by the aftermath of the Suez crisis of 1956-57, found the courage and resources to restore the illusion (if not the substance) of British prosperity in 1958 (he cut Purchase Tax from that murderous 66⅔ per cent on so-called 'luxury goods' down to 25 per cent), the cosseted post-war days of the British light aeroplane industry were numbered. By eliminating restrictions on hire purchase and gradually reducing Purchase Tax at a time when international commodity prices were falling together with the British Bank Rate, by December he was able to announce a return to unrestricted convertibility for sterling. There were still

The shape of immediate post-war private and club flying was established just prior to the outbreak of the war when Leicester-based Taylorcraft Aeroplanes (England) Ltd embarked on the design and construction of a version of the American-designed Taylorcraft Model B light aircraft. The Army used these for liaison duties and named it the Auster. Fitted with a Cirrus Minor, the rugged little Auster was the forerunner of the Autocrat, Autocar, Aiglet and a host of other models produced at Rearsby. Pictured here in June 1942 is the 'first military example' – actually it is HH985 described as a Taylorcraft Plus C-2 and originally G-AFVB of June 1939. As such it was the fourth of the Army's first batch of seven machines but it was short-lived: on September 25th 1942 it was damaged beyond repair and scrapped.

practical limitations on the availability of money, but it meant that it was now possible to import light aircraft and engines from dollar areas – at a price.

The long-standing argument against American aircraft (and cars, come to that) was that they had 'funny screw-threads' and curious hardware. Engineers and mechanics shook their heads and sucked in through clenched teeth when confronted with US products: tales from pre-war Gatwick where several early American machines were housed and serviced brought forth curious accounts of 'even the locking-wire's a different thickness'. This one-time defensive ploy proved to be as insubstantial as the will-o'-the-wisp and it was no excuse for the real reason we resisted the Yankee planes. We were really afraid that they might be good or even, Heaven forefend, better than things made here.

Opening the flood-gates to such competition was to hit British industry hard. Following an unequal struggle during which the few real advantages of 'buying British' were extolled, industry had to accept that the growing influx of American aircraft, far from being derided by the aviation users – industry's customers – was welcomed. It could now be only a matter of time before one of two things happened: either British makers packed up and surrendered in the face of challenge, or they rallied round and attempted to make something at least as good as the American merchandise on offer.

In the event, the industry chose to pursue both these routes. The smaller makers (there were, in truth, precious few) were unlikely, statistically, to survive, so as the weakest link in an already weak environment they gave up or were driven out. The remainder copied the few surviving major commercial/military aircraft makers and combined into groups, one to be precise. The plan was to combat the type of aircraft British flyers were now being confronted with from across the Atlantic. The outcome was Beagle with the philosophy that if America could do it, so could we and never mind the lack of experience.

A final lesson had still to be learned. And that was the simple economic reality that American mass-production methods could produce very good aircraft at a realistic price. America's home market was huge and their export market to Britain was, in economic terms, very small indeed. That small market was not viable for a mass-produced British aeroplane and certainly the cost benefits of American-

The first of many! G-AGOH was the prototype Auster J-1 Autocrat. Built from a modified Auster 5 fuselage and powered by a 100 hp Blackburn Cirrus Minor 2, it was actually registered to Blackburn Aircraft Ltd and used as an engine-development hack. It differed from all production aircraft in retaining the extended rear window of the original Auster 5.

It was not only light aircraft that enlivened the post-war skies. This Gloster Gladiator Mk.1 was found derelict by Vivian Bellamy at Eastleigh who rebuilt it in 1952. Formerly the RAF's L8032, G-AMRK was a popular sight around the 1950s air shows with the throaty roar of its 840 hp Bristol Mercury VIIIA. One of a batch of 527 built at Hucclecote between 1937 and 1940, it eventually passed back to Gloster Aircraft Ltd and thence to the Shuttleworth Trust.

style assemblage were beyond the wildest hopes of our industry. The leap from insular 1939 technology to that of international 1950 was too great and too costly. Britain's light aircraft industry did the only thing that it could do – it quietly folded up its tent and retreated into obscurity.

One might conclude that this was a wholly bad thing and that it marked the end of British innovation and creativity in light aircraft. On the contrary, it exposed very fertile ground upon which would flourish an area of private aviation that had been, if not exactly moribund, then quiescent for a long while. Out of this economic, financial and political maelstrom, there emerged a whole new era of light aircraft and aircraft makers. From hesitant beginnings in pre-war Britain, home-built aircraft and amateur designs began to proliferate. The reasons behind this extraordinary sea-change in light aviation's direction are all-too clear to see when we view them today with the supreme ocular acuity of near-faultless hindsight, yet even the expansion of this sector very nearly did not come about.

In the fullness of time, Britain has been judged as a loser in a field in which she once led the world. The great names of de Havilland, Auster, Miles, Blackburn, Bristol and countless others are no more, yet today we have one of the largest populations of new small light aircraft to be found outside the United States. That is the most satisfying, curious and reassuring outcome.

Whereas in the decade and a half from 1925 to the outbreak of war the name of de Havilland dominated the light aeroplane scene, this company was significant by its virtual absence from the post-war private arena.[7] But 'DH' was not the only big name to have disappeared from the picture. Its contemporaries such as Avro, Blackburn, Bristol and General Aircraft had moved on, too. Gone also were Desoutter and Comper, Parnall, Heston and others. The major companies all saw the club machine and private owner market as no longer economically viable.

One exception was Miles Aircraft Ltd which went bankrupt while trying to sustain a market position that was now mere memory. And this was despite having a highly-successful four seat aeroplane to offer – the Messenger. But Miles had a rich portfolio of other designs for the private flying sector, none of which got as far as the other side of the drawing-board and almost all of which are forgotten today. A factor contributing to its demise was that awful 1947 winter when restricted production brought income too far below expenditure.

Another exception, but only really by association, was Fairey through its Belgian subsidiary of Tipsy and here the Hayes-based company was careful to keep Avions Fairey (or Tipsy, depending on the colour of the moment) at an arm's length from its core business, by then the building of the curious Naval Gannet and embarking on its costly Gyrodyne projects.

The post-war light plane business began as a two-horse race – the Auster enterprise, built up from an impecunious small-time pre-war importing business run by genuine enthusiasts to market leader thanks to war-production contracts, and Miles Aircraft, a business with two factories and a struggling order-book. Other names came and went such as Elliotts, Chrislea, Portsmouth Aviation and Thruxton as did a clutch of other hopefuls.

One name, however, is almost always overlooked and that is the name Folland.

Folland's private aircraft designs of 1946 and 1947 were so far ahead of their time that their demise must forever be viewed as Britain's biggest light plane lost opportunity. Had Folland succeeded, then a good proportion of Beagle's contribution of fifteen years later would have been redundant to the benefit of the taxpayer.

Folland, like Miles, continually brought out good ideas. Perhaps unlike Miles, many of these concerned metal aircraft designed for volume construction. Henry Folland flourished in his later years but when he retired in 1951 he had been forced to accept that there was no room for Folland light aircraft in the British skies. What a tragedy!

There were others. If the decades are determined by the popularity of wonder-metals and materials, the position of boron fibre today usurped that of titanium which in turn had usurped stainless steel. But in the 1940s the wonder-metal was magnesium. With lightness and strength, what more could you want? Essex Aero laboured to give us the equivalent of the Volkswagen of the Air pressed at low cost out of magnesium. The Sprite sounded fine, but was never completed. And all the things the Beagle Pup offered in 1967 had been offered by the Bianchi Survey designed two decades earlier into an age when materials to build an aeroplane were not just scarce but impossible to obtain.

Designing an aeroplane was one thing, building it and gaining a C of A was another, while as we have seen earlier on in this Introduction the manufacturer was absolutely on his own without any government assistance and, for much of the time, neither incentive nor permits to buy material to build so much as one aeroplane. The uncertain journey from drawing-board to roll-out and first flight was clearly a path plagued with pitfalls. Like Nature's superabundance of sperms and eggs from which success was a hit-and-miss job, a small number did manage to make it. With the probable exception of the Hants & Sussex Herald and one or two others that were ill-cast in one way or another (the Planet Satellite and the Tawney Owl spring to mind), all were practical designs worthy of some success in the marketplace.

So much for the aircraft themselves. What about engines? In the 1920s Britain showed the world how to make an air-cooled inline engine that was light and economic. America almost exclusively used radials while we made a whole raft of fine inline as well as radial motors. We made big and powerful engines that evolved to be our saving grace in time of war. What happened with peace? There was no shortage of good progressive ideas and the rebirth of private flying saw the promise of fine engines such as the Jameson, the Monaco and, best of all, the

Designed by the Belgian E O Tips and first demonstrated at Charles Fairey's new private all-grass aerodrome at Heathrow on May 14th 1937, the Tipsy B was a delightful light all-wood two seater having the distinctly odd arrangement of slightly staggered cockpit seats so that maximum elbow room was obtained without discomfort. A British firm, Tipsy Aircraft Ltd, subsequently built 15 at Hanworth. Somewhat modified from the original, these were called the Tipsy Trainer 1. After the war, Tipsy was reformed at Slough and built three more of which G-AISA was the first to fly in 1947. Operated by the Royal Naval Flying Club at Gosport and powered by the 62 hp Czech-built Walter Mikron engine, this remains one of a handful of the type still flying. When Tipsy closed down in 1952 it saw fit to burn its remaining stock on site – Tipsy B G-AFCM and Trainers G-AFGF (the UK prototype) and G-AFGT.

---

7. De Havilland in Canada had introduced the DHC.1 Chipmunk as a Tiger Moth replacement. Many were to see use for Royal Air Force training in Britain and elsewhere. This delightful aircraft was then produced in England in large numbers as a Service aircraft, but it subsequently proved both difficult and expensive to civilianise when the RAF declared them surplus. Nevertheless, it was to enjoy a small but bright career in the club and private ownership sphere in the 1950s and '60s and earns itself a place in the Chapter devoted to British aircraft designs further on. Although Canadian in origin, its development was entirely within our shores.

Nuffield. All were horizontally-opposed motors of the latest style. Their designers had observed American trends.

The Nuffield seemed to have everything going for it, but the jinx that had forced Wolseley engines from the pre-war market had a last trick up its sleeve. Prior to the war, Lord Nuffield (William Richard Morris) had had a blazing row with the Air Ministry in the shape of Air Minister Lord Swinton as a result of which he interested himself more in making tanks than furthering aviation. This all came about because the Air Ministry had objected to the size of engines that Wolseley Aero Engines was developing. As Sir Miles Thomas [59] wrote:

> Although a constant spate of redesigns for the Scorpio and the Leo and other models (the signs of the Zodiac were chosen as names for Wolseley Engines) were instituted, their size and characteristics did not seem to keep pace with the ever-growing weight and speed requirements of the rapidly developing fighters and bombers that were then being visualised.

A man who was by nature a philanthropist and visionary, Nuffield considered that his efforts were not being properly recognised and the hoped-for big production orders never came. Curiously denied membership of the SBAC and with his fine range of radial engines ignored, he justifiably pulled the plug on all further development. After Swinton had gone, his successor Sir Kingsley Wood took some measures to appease Nuffield but His Lordship remained stoically unmoved: it required considerably more skill and ministerial tact before Nuffield would later agree to building a Spitfire production factory at Castle Bromwich.

Now, in times of peace, William Morris's enthusiasm returned, at least in part, but the obstructions placed before him, mostly by the Air Registration Board and its demands for more and more paperwork, resurrected memories of the sour times of the 'thirties. Why we (officialdom, that is) perpetually bashed Lord Nuffield on the nose with a corporate frying-pan remains a mystery. The 1952 merger of Morris Motors Company with Austin to create the giant British Motor Corporation (later British Leyland) marked the final *finis* to William Morris's brave and respected long-term attempt to be accepted into the elite coterie of aircraft engine manufacturers. It would not be stretching fact too much to summarise the sad tale of his exclusion as merely because, in today's mid-Atlantic parlance, his face didn't fit.

Meanwhile de Havilland still made Gipsy engines and Blackburn still made the Cirrus, light aircraft engines that owed their origins to the First World War and first saw the light of day in the workshops of the Aircraft Disposal Company at Waddon (*see Ord-Hume [39]*). A whole raft of inverted inline motors suitable for light and medium aircraft was available, yet soon all this evaporated. Even the bigger makers, such as Bristol and Napier, were destined not to survive and Britain's world leadership in light engine market would not just be lost but would be denied so much as second or even third place. Instead it died on its feet.

As for those 'thirties hopefuls like the Cross two-stroke and, going back as early as 1934, General Aircraft's clever inverted V four-cylinder air-cooled side-valved motor, well, they turned and fell the way the leaves of even a much-loved tree must fall in autumn. Unloved, unfunded, even the best must fail.

While 'Health and Safety' was still years away from rearing its bandaged head, some of the air displays in the immediate post-war years were a little hairy from the spectators' point of view. In the 'thirties one had been accustomed to Cobham's National Air Day where ultra low-level aerobatics were often conducted directly over the heads of the crowds. The less well-informed thought them brilliant and clever while those in the know were more inclined to use the description 'foolhardy'. Something of those days was rekindled in the summer of 1948 as Chrislea Super Ace G-AKVB is put through its paces perhaps a little too low (and close) for comfort.

In the 1960s, the American National Aeronautics and Space Administration was evaluating Francis Rogallo's 'discovery' of the curious aerodynamics of what NASA chose to call the bi-conic flexible wing and which subsequently gave impetus to the hang-glider movement. The Americans apparently were quite unaware that this same principle had been experimented with in Britain for almost a quarter of a century. Our failing was in not patenting it or cooking up a fancy name for it and then performing a roof-tops-shouting exercise. Here we see one of NASA's experiments with what it described as a 'dynamically scaled, instrumented, radio-controlled, lifting-body parawing model' on May 16th 1968. Our 'floppy-winged unpredictable flying thing' or FUFT for short, was behaving just like this in 1946! Picture by NASA.

Yes, there were bright spots. Rover Gas Turbines was one – but where are they today when their products would be most desired? Budworth was another, in this case a potential never exploited after the talented designer and company founder was killed in an unrelated accident to an American light plane. No, we abandoned the production of light engines as surely as we abandoned light aircraft and, not unexpectedly, for the same reasons. We had so many ideas and opportunities, so many of which never came to anything. If not a litany of failure, it was certainly an age of unfulfilled promise.

Less than two weeks after civil flying had begun again after the war, a rather special anniversary came and went. It was one which, like so many non-personal anniversaries, few people noticed or, maybe, even thought twice about. That January 12th of 1946 saw the Royal Aeronautical Society celebrate its 80th birthday. It was hard to imagine that this august body with its great history and record of learning in the young science of flight was so old as to have been established in the same year that the gas mantle was invented.

There have been equally profound changes, perhaps none less significant than the manner in which aviation and the national press have a changed relationship. At one time every newspaper worth its salt had at least one air correspondent and anything to do with aviation made the headlines. These air correspondents were not mere newspaper-reporters or journalists, nor were they of the 'news-hound' type that predominate in today's world of the 'tabloid' low-brow press. These were senior men of intellect and ability; strategists who had an opinion that was worth reading. They were highly-perceptive, observant journalists of the old order who could interpret news in the correct sense and commentate, meaning that they *understood* things. And they were respected. Their words mattered. What they wrote was noted by industry and government alike, occasionally with trepidation.

During the period covered by this book, the 'air correspondent' still survived as a principal member of the senior editorial staff of real newspapers, and I was privileged to know many of them. Times, though, changed and their survival as a breed became unlikely. Two things happened. Aviation became well established and was no longer the exciting headline material that once it was. And newspapers collectively moved down-market – some to a surprising degree – in order to cater for a readership that was increasingly less interested in technology and achievement. The march of sport and TV 'soap-operas' deprived many readers of the need and the ability to read or form opinions of their own in a world that relegated everything else to a very poor second place after football, pop idols and film stars. Aviation and the thinking man thus declined together.

When one remembers the enormous debt of gratitude aviation owes through the backing and financial sponsorship offered freely by the great newspapers of the past, the *Daily Mail* and the *Daily Express* in particular, not to mention the enthusiasm of the air-minded 'newspaper barons' such as Kemsley and Northcliff, it is a sad reflection on changing times to see where those papers are today. It is no idle statement to suggest that aviation and its development would have been the poorer had it not been for the two newspapers just named. They demonstrated wisdom and foresight – and a good measure of entrepreneurism – recognising the adventure of flying at a time when many around them thought that aviation was a foolish chimera. And so the noble ranks of newspaper air correspondents, unquestionably the elite amidst the traditionally lowly ranks of scribes, were culled. Some of their members, including Michael Donne of the *Financial Times* and Arthur Reed of *The Times*, went on to write valuable and analytical books on the post-war aviation scene. None was tempted to move down-market, though.

Equally, both the trade and technical press have changed. As recorders of events as they happened, these journals once played a crucial role. An important industry demands an informed, intelligent and independent professional trade press. The power of such a mouthpiece should never be overlooked and the role of a magazine is thus extremely influential. Nowhere was this better demonstrated than with the first editors of *The Aeroplane* (Charles Grey Grey) and *Flight* (Stanley Spooner). Both of these men were highly educated, observant and outspoken. Above all they had a super-abiding interest in their subject. When they championed it was seldom without good reason, but when they criticised it was a thunderous roar that could make the other side, whether industry, Royal Air Force, airline, government or anybody else, sit up and think again.

Aeroplane's forthright Grey (1875-1953) was eventually to be partly responsible for his own demise as editor: having published several pieces in praise of the way 1930s Germany had built up the Luftwaffe (in truth a sarcastic and oblique reference to the slow growth of the Royal Air Force and hence a prod at our own Establishment), the magazine's new owner, Roland E Dangerfield (head of Temple Press) did not appreciate the message behind his words and quickly eased him out. Even then, irony in high places didn't always pay off.

'CGG' was succeeded at *The Aeroplane* by Edwin Colston Shepherd (1891-1976) from September 1939 until 1943 when he joined the *Sunday Times* as air correspondent. After an interim period of restricted staff during which the 1939-45 managing editor W/Cmdr Theodore Stanhope Sprigg (1903-1977) was also editor, the office was then filled from December 1945 by Thurstan James (1903-1975) who had been Director of Aircraft Production during the war years. He was replaced in 1965 by John Cormac Seekings (*b.* 1931) who had been economics officer to the International Civil Aviation Organisation (ICAO). He remained in the big chair until the end when, in 1968, owners and publishers Temple Press Ltd were taken over by Iliffe, owners and publishers of *Flight*. Seekings now had the job of closing the door and turning the light out at the delightfully-named Bowling Green Lane offices, for surely one of the most important titles in all aviation history had bitten the dust.

An unhappy amalgamation of the two titles was dual-masted for a short while, but finally *Aeroplane* was allowed to die as a weekly title. Much of its priceless archive was destroyed before some of the remainder could be thoughtfully stolen by those with greater wisdom than the new owners. But almost all the photographic prints were dumped and burned before anybody had the opportunity to liberate them. Of the vast and priceless collection of glass-plate negatives, under ten per cent was saved. It was a sad day for aviation journalism and more so for the honoured one-time staff of *The Aeroplane*.

If *The Times* newspaper had the one-time nickname of 'the thunderer' then in its time *The Aeroplane* was the equivalent. Not that CGG was always right: sometimes he was wrong by a mile, but what he wrote was invariably read with great interest and if he was occasionally adrift, then at least it brought a reappraisal of whatever the situation was in order to justify a complaint or seek a correction.

Flight's Stanley Spooner (1856-1940), who retired in April 1934 when 78 years old, and died in his 85th year, was equally powerful although, being somewhat older than CGG, he was viewed very much as the senior commentator. A founder of the Royal Aeronautical Society and the Royal Aero Club, he lived through and supported the two great industries of the turn of the century – the birth of the motor car and the development of aviation. A gentleman in every respect, in general he was, particularly in his later years, too much of an enthusiast for his new subject to be forthright. This did not prevent him from being critical and some of his editorials of the 1920s are magnificently-penned attacks on the administration and the operation of the Royal Air Force.

If Spooner was an all-round commentator of the finest quality, it did not diminish his ability to apply foresight and judgement. He did, for instance, foresee the tremendous strides that aviation would make. And if sometimes he was editorially aghast at the stink that the younger and hotter-headed CGG could kick up on the early pages of *The Aeroplane*, he learned from such exposure that the pen was indeed mightier than sword. Towards the end of his tenure, he regained the powerful position that the early maturity of his publication had justly earned. The monocled Grey may have been taller and more dignified in appearance, but it was nevertheless the more rotund and shorter Spooner who was really missed from his editorial desk.

His successor was the quiet and rather meek Danish-born Carl Marcus Poulsen, a man with a good, strong engineering background (in 1919 his Patents described him as an 'aeronautical engineer'), but a hatred of exposure who was always a 'we' and never an 'I'. Nevertheless he quickly became, if not exactly a face, then certainly an outspoken voice for aviation. He confronted the challenge of the re-birth of peace in 1945 under the command of G Geoffrey Smith (b. 1885) who was an early authority on gas turbines, with Smith's son Maurice as assistant. No doubt encouraged by Smith, he fearlessly championed private aviation.

Poulsen, for whom no dates or other information survive, was replaced in 1949 by the man who had been his assistant, Maurice Armstrong Smith (b. 1916). Under Smith's leadership, with Horace Frederick King (35-year-old former RAF Sqdn.Ldr) as associate editor, *Flight* regained some of its past prestige. In 1957 he was promoted to managing editor and was replaced, suggesting that the post of helmsman in the modern age was not in any way as permanent as it may once have been.

The magazine was to have some resurgence of its former glory when, in September 1964, John Michael 'Mike' Ramsden (1929-2019), a former student at the de Havilland Technical School, took command. The Ramsden years embraced the closing days of the era covered by this present book. In more recent times, *Flight* has changed both its appearance and its editorial direction, now concentrating on defence matters, space exploration and commercial aviation. After the Covid-19 pandemic, the worldwide retrenchment in commercial and military aviation forced *Flight International*, as it was by then called, to cease weekly publication after 111 years and go monthly.

Most today have long forgotten that short-lived periodical *The Light Plane and Private Owner*. It began bravely in December 1946 but was gone before the decade was out. It was run by Henry M Berney and Arnold V Clifford. They championed the cause of private and amateur aviation before anybody else and they asked the light plane enthusiasts what they wanted. Their cause was influential and their legacy important.

Of the rest of the journals from the post-war era, only one other really proved to be a voice to contend with. This was *Air Pictorial*, a monthly that succeeded the original wartime *Air Training Corps Gazette* which in turn became the *Air Reserve Gazette* (edited by *Aeroplane*'s E Colston Shepherd) from April 1950. The founding editor was Frank Norton Hillier (b. 1894). Hillier was secretary-general of the Air League of the British Empire and proved to be a good observer of aviation matters. Like CGG before him, what Hillier wrote, the aviation world read.

Poor Hillier, sickly in his last years, died in harness in 1958 to be succeeded by his assistant editor Edward Shacklady who quickly branded *Air Pictorial* with his sharp observations. Shacklady's tenure finally came to an untimely end when he and the new Air League secretary general failed to agree on some aspects of editorial policy. Shacklady was succeeded by David Dorrell who successfully continued Shacklady's fearsome approach to the idiocies of government and ministry alike. It is perhaps Dorrell's period of control that marked *Air Pictorial*'s peak of importance as a recorder of events. This coincided with the time when John Seekings' *Aeroplane* at Temple Press approached closure by amalgamation with Iliffe's *Flight*, and *Flight* was less willing to offend the establishment (or, most importantly, upset advertisers) by offering any critical judgement.

Between them, Air Cmdr Gerard John Christopher Paul (1907-2003) as secretary general of the Air League and David Dorrell made *Air Pictorial* some of the hottest reading of the age. The sad thing was that, because the magazine had ascended from being the Air Training Corps house journal and 'spotters' magazine' it was not taken too seriously and not read by too many of the right people.

One other magazine was the glossy and expensive monthly *Aeronautics* owned and edited by Maj Oliver Stewart.[8] Born in 1895, Stewart had served in the RFC and RAF and had been an early test pilot at Orfordness and Martlesham Heath before becoming a respected aeronautical journalist. In 1939 he founded *Aeronautics*. Curiously, this was a revival of an old name, for the first magazine to carry this title ran from 1907 to 1921, initially as a supplement to *Knowledge & Illustrated Scientific News* published by Benn Brothers and edited by Maj B Baden-Powell, but after three issues quickly becoming an independent and respected 6d weekly quality periodical edited by John Henry Ledeboer (1883-1930).

Stewart's magazine, with a post-war cover price of a colossal 2s 6d, was published by C Arthur Pearson Ltd from the famous George Newnes building, Tower House, Southampton Street, Strand, 'for the proprietors, British Aviation Publications Ltd' of the same address. *Aeronautics* became aviation's *Vogue*, *Fortune* or *Country Life* class of publication. It set itself to cater for all aspects of its subject, private, commercial, club, RAF, manufacture and engineering, design and aeronautical theory, gliding, airline operations – and in many ways this omnifarious approach was its downfall. While always a 'good read', it tried to be

---

8. As an aside it is of some minor interest that Oliver Stewart's daughter, Madeau Stewart, joined the BBC as a musicologist and, during the period concerned in this book, she both presented and produced many programmes, including a large number of my own, for what was then known as the BBC Third Programme. At a time when women in senior positions in the BBC were uncommon, it is worth adding that Sir Samuel Instone, a founder of the pioneering Instone Air Lines that later became part of Imperial Airways, also had a musical daughter at the BBC. Anna Instone was an author and musicologist known to millions for her weekly Third Programme classical music record production *Music Magazine* presented in collaboration with her husband, Julian Herbage. Started in 1944 it ran for 29 memorable years and hosted my first-ever radio broadcasts on music with Noël Goodwin.

INTRODUCTION

everything to all men. Stewart wrote good controversial 'leaders' that were ever critical of government stupidity. He was always a great protagonist for all things British.

Valuable though it was, the readership of *Aeronautics* declined in favour of the more specialised press. Gliding enthusiasts, for instance, didn't want to have to have a major supplement on the Handley Page Herald and its airline operating costs, or details of RAF squadron operations in various parts of the world. Economics finally got the better of Oliver Stewart and his prestigious magazine and in March 1962 he produced his last issue.

Since those rich days of aviation press coverage, the attitude towards the technical and professional press seems to have changed. Editors (and their writers) seem less comfortable at taking a stand when they believe something to be adrift. Despite the acceptance of offensive aspects of media, TV programmes and life in general, good aviation journalism after the style of the 'old brigade' as typified by Grey and Spooner, Poulsen, Shacklady, Dorrell and Stewart has suffered as a consequence of the sea-change in magazine presentation where publishers consider advertisers more important than editorial, where readership *numbers* are more important than readership *quality*, and where any risk of 'boat-rocking' is sanitized into blandness by decree from the publisher/business manager. Political correctness means don't upset the advertisers or the readers! Result? News and no strong comment; reporting but no firm opinion, urbanity but never the dogmatic, vanilla rather than vitriol. And above all else, sell more copies than your rival! It is an age when the picture-editor selects his (or her) best for the cover – and then splatters textual tasters of inside contents all over it!

True, aviation journalists have been quick to identify popular and safe causes like Brabazon, London Airport, the TSR.2, V-1000 and Concorde, but with the notable exception of Beagle which involved large sums (relatively speaking) of taxpayers' money, light aeroplanes and their politics are relatively unimportant toys to them these days. Unless it is approaching the supersonic and has defence importance, then it has no news-value. Stories about military helicopters that cannot carry weapons, aircraft carriers that cannot carry aircraft, and fighters that cannot fly with all their attachments – that's much more appealing to columnist and reader alike than the rising costs of operating a small aeroplane! But to be fair Beagle did

He was popularly dubbed 'the mad Major' and Sqdn Cmdr Christopher Draper (1892-1979) used this as the title for his autobiography published in 1962. A First World War 'ace' and recipient of the DSC and the Croix de Guerre, he was a 1930s air show stunt pilot and actor but is remembered today as the man who flew under bridges. It had started back in 1931 when, on September 30th, the then unemployed Draper, determined to draw attention to his abilities. Penniless but a self-publicist, he managed to borrow a Puss Moth from Stag Lane and set off to fly under 14 Thames bridges. He managed Tower Bridge but turbulent air forced him to fly over the next seven before taking the central span of Westminster Bridge. Strategically-placed cameras recorded the 'secret' event and the pictures went worldwide. Meanwhile the Air Ministry found he had no valid licence and the police prosecuted for dangerous flying. In Court his plea of being a penniless actor seeking to promote himself was accepted: he was bound over for a year. Still, though, he nurtured the idea of netting all the bridges. On Tuesday May 5th 1953 he borrowed Auster G-AGYD from Herts & Essex Aero Club at Broxbourne and the job was on. He managed 15 of the 18 he targeted. The *Daily Mirror*, which happened to have a suitably-placed and extremely alert cameraman close by, got this remarkable picture as he flew under Westminster Bridge capturing both shadow and reflection of the Autocrat in the Thames. None on the bridge seemed aware that an aircraft had just flown under their feet. Draper was once more in trouble with four charges of dangerous flying. This time it cost him his licence, ten guineas in costs – and a magistrate's warning. Today it would probably be a capital offence!

generate some first-rate dirt-digging in parts of Fleet Street.

So much for the part the press, both popular and specialised, played in post-war light aircraft. One excuse offered is that everybody was too preoccupied with the broader picture of politics and the economy.

Since 1970 there has been a resurgence in the number of aviation magazines, but few are devoted solely to light aircraft. And those business-breathing publishing myrmidons that work the editorial strings on some magazines display a curiously narrow-foreheaded, bird-brained approach to light planes. These people, given responsibility for shuffling the pennies in a perpetual quest for profit at all cost, devoutly believe a cover picture of a light plane to be a reader turn-off. For this reason, choice must always go to a shot of a grimly-painted military jet screaming upwards – or downwards. The psychology (they say) is that the cover showing a fast fighter jet will act on the sensibilities of prospective buyers like a picture of a big-breasted young female in a black latex-rubber cat-suit when it comes to stimulating those 'must-buy' nerves. This ignores the unpalatable counter-argument – that there are some out there who are fed up to the back teeth with big fighters and loud jets and instead harbour a love of the grass strip and its incumbents. And intelligent ladies with clothes on!

Having dealt with the important players in post-war private flying we find that a recurring theme throughout the whole saga was government. In fact you could not pursue much of the history of post-war aviation without coming up against the administration. The main problem was that men in top jobs (ministers) were, in general, ignoramuses. They knew precious little of the subjects they represented: it was the inevitable consequence of the political game of musical chairs that Parliament has become. It fell to the Wilson administration to create a Ministry of Technology but, as Childs[9] postulates, it wasn't much of a ministry with not much of a minister. Of the eight junior ministers who served between 1964 and 1970, for example, only two had a scientific or technological background. This lack of specialist training was nowhere more noticeable than in aviation where the level of interest, never mind straight knowledge, was pathetic. I used to work in an office with a certain well-known publisher-cum-politician who was forever asking me rather simplistic questions about flying. One day I tried to explain to him Concorde (then in the early design stage) and quickly realised he hadn't a notion what I was talking about. Within a year he'd left his family publishing firm and become Minister of Aviation!

In conclusion it should be recorded that for the duration of the time covered by this present book the restraints on travel and currency were maintained to the detriment of those that flew and not just the burgeoning travel industry. Government currency restrictions were finally eased at the beginning of January 1970 when it was announced that the restrictions on the spending of no more than £50 of currency overseas was ended. It was substituted by a £300 limit. Sir Anthony Milward (1905-1981), a long-

BBC Television came to Denham Aerodrome in Buckinghamshire to make a feature programme on private flying on June 29th 1955. One of the personalities it featured was legless flyer Douglas Bader. For the benefit of the cameras, a fine nostalgic line-up of aircraft was paraded outside the sheds. Framed by the tail and wing of Autocrat G-AHSN, there was Gloster Gladiator G-AMRK, Hawker Tomtit G-AFTA, Avro Club Cadet G-ACHP, Blackburn B.2 G-EBJ, the veteran DH.60 Moth G-EBLV, and finally the Spartan Arrow G-ABWP.

For many pre-war flyers, memories of the super-fast, long distance achievements of Comper Swifts were legendary. Several aircraft did service the war, notably Tony Cole's G-ABUS and Ron Clear's G-ACTF. But so did another – G-ABPE, owned by a young man called Adrian B Golay who had it expensively restored to showroom condition in light blue and silver. – and then destroyed it on an early flight by trying to get through rather than over a hedge. Bits of Golay's Swift hung around for a long while. But it was beyond repair.

---

9. David Childs: *Britain since 1945: A Political History*. Routledge, London, 1997, p.126.

standing opponent of the restriction, said 'It will cause the greatest joy to those who believe that travel is one of the basic freedoms of mankind.'

On February 15th 1971, Britain introduced decimal currency: the following November, we decided to join the Common Market. We were on the run-down to two significant events of the closing years of the 20th century – the birth of the 'Nanny State' and the arrival of 'Political Correctness'. Sharpening our own pencils risked prohibition on the grounds of Health & Safety, while mentioning the colour of somebody's skin risked alienation, even if it only alluded to muddy knees. Much would be laid at the doors of our new off-shore Parliament in Brussels.

Then we decided to leave Europe and paddle our own canoe…

This lengthy *Introduction* goes some way to setting the scene for the story of Britain's post-war light aeroplane revival and the manner in which its ramifications have been covered by the press. Without an understanding of the economic situation and the reasons behind the tardiness of government in participation, the impression would be that as a nation we were congenitally backward. Still, in the light of the bleak years of the late 1940s and 1950s, I hope this at least partially justifies why both private and government money was not forthcoming.

This is not to say that some incredible situations and stupid courses of action were not the root cause of certain events that took place during these years, merely that the events of history as they touched our post-war light plane movement are generally forgotten. And that is to do an even greater disservice to our once-great light plane industry than it actually deserves. As explained earlier, our industry operated with fetters, blinkers and enforced isolation. Small wonder we could never attain the status the British light plane had in the 1930s!

The kernel of this book is Chapter Eleven which analyses British light aircraft by type. Of the 121 aircraft selected for description, just over half are provided with three-view drawings and these predominantly relate to the less-common types. This is because drawings of the more common types are already widely accessible to the enthusiast and historian through Jackson's works and others in the series of company histories published by Putnam. In this present work, for example, there are drawings of many less well-known types such as the Tawney Owl, Hants & Sussex Herald, Planet Satellite, Portsmouth Aerocar and both variations of the Britten-Norman B-N1F. The Chrislea Ace in its original single-tail form and Auster Aircraft's only model with swept-back wings – all these appear in three-view for the first time in a single volume.

Wherever possible, details of design and construction are provided together with, in many cases, wing sections and performance with a choice of power units.

Chapter Twelve looks at the unbuilt projects. The industry may have been small but it produced a prodigious number of these projects from which I have selected just 25 as representing the thought-processes of our designers. Of these almost three-quarters are accompanied by three-view drawings. It is thus suggested that in this area alone this book offers a unique insight to those turbulent years that saw the re-birth of club and private aircraft at the end of the Second World War.

Post-war civil flying coincided with the arrival of a curious atypical nostalgia for the days of war. More and more films were made about the conflict with Nazi Germany and this meant we needed something that looked like a German aircraft to make the movies seem real. A parasite industry sprung up making aircraft that looked the part. It is hard to see but this aircraft is a Percival Proctor grotesquely modified to resemble a Junkers Ju 87 Stuka. Created out of war surplus Proctor airframes for the film *The Battle of Britain*, three were made, only one of which actually flew in the movie. The fate of the aircraft remains a mystery. Throughout the post-war years, film work has called for the building and flying of a variety of singularly odd aircraft.

The Percival Mew Gull G-AEXF was a potent reminder of the pre-war days of worldwide racing. Now in post-war Britain, the same machine was once more star of the skies. Raced by luminaries such as Hugh Scrope, Fred Dunkerley and Nat Somers, this tiny aircraft was comprehensively smashed and re-built several times over. Each owner seemed to have his own idea on cockpit glazing and the very sleek lines created by Edgar Percival's designer, Arthur Bage, were systematically mutilated culminating in the extraordinary bulbous excrescence created for Fred Dunkerley with the aim of improving visibility for racing turns and pictured on page 13. It has since been 'corrected' as seen here.

In 1945, our vastly depleted stock of pre-war light aircraft represented a resource that we neither recognised nor cherished. Percival Vega Gull G-AFBC from 1937 is seen ready in its paint scheme and racing number for the ill-fated and never-to-be staged 1939 Kings' Cup. Soon afterwards it was impressed (X9340) along with many others, yet miraculously it managed to survive to enjoy a post-war career. It met its end at Eastleigh on July 12th 1954.

The majority of aircraft around were thus either pre-war or ex-RAF machines that had been sold off surplus to requirements. Percival Proctor Mk.1 was essentially a pre-war Vega Gull built for military service. The Proctors were familiar occupants of our skies in those days. One made the headlines by force-landing in London's Hyde Park in 1946: he was forbidden to fly out and the aircraft had to be taken apart for removal. Some of the Mk.V Proctors built during the war were assembled by unskilled labour using 'beetle-glue' – one of the early synthetic resins. These had a habit of drying out and separating over time allowing the wood to be peeled apart and the 'sheet' of glue to be taken out. The author was involved with one of the affected aircraft when the wings disintegrated during flight in turbulence, the spars being retained in place by the fuel-tank lugs and the fabric forming a flapping bag containing fragments of unglued wing-ribs. The subsequent landing proved terminal for the aircraft but left its pilot running along the ground still strapped to part of his seat... G-AHDJ was a civilianised RAF machine (P6264) and was written off in an accident on June 18th 1954.

One biplane trainer that rivalled de Havilland's Tiger Moth was the Avro 631 Cadet and 638 Club Cadet. Both were derived from the larger 621 Tutor and variants. The Club Cadet differed from the ordinary Cadet in having unstaggered wings which, like those of the DH.60 Moth, could be folded. Built for clubs and private owners, the Avro 638 was available with a choice of three types of engine – the Gipsy Major I, the Armstrong Siddeley Genet Major I or the more powerful 140 hp Cirrus Hermes IVA. At the end of the war, of seventeen British examples made, only G-ACHP survived with its Gipsy Major Mk.I engine. Cared for by the Vintage Aeroplane Club at Denham it was treasured by those privileged to fly it until on January 1st 1956 a chap took it aloft into a line-squall – and it was wrecked in the adjacent woods.

Before the war, the cause célèbre of the private flying scene was the Flying Flea, the French-designed home-built that became a short-term worldwide talking-point. Several accidents caused the Air Ministry to cease issuing them with Authorisations to Fly. When, soon afterwards, war broke out, peoples' memories appeared to have ground to a halt with this event. The upshot was that for a while after the end of the war, people spoke of Flying Fleas, how they had killed 'hundreds' and how dangerous amateur flying was. And, of course, anyone talking of home-made aircraft meant one of these. It took a surprisingly long while to re-set the common human mind. Here is Don Burgoyne's Scott-powered G-AECN, flown at Knowle near Solihull in 1936. The registration also appeared post-war illegally on the Burgoyne-Stirling Dicer.

CHAPTER ONE
Peaceful Skies:
Inspiration and Confidence

During the two decades that separated the First and Second World Wars Britain experienced years that were indeed rich in terms of aviation achievement and development. Light aircraft flew greater and greater distances, systematically challenged and defeated those early dragons of the pioneers – darkness and bad weather. They reached out to far-off continents and ascended to ever greater heights. Boundaries were pushed, endurance stretched, dogmas overturned. Yesterday was old history while today was always a fresh adventure.

In my earlier books on the history of aircraft up to 1939, *British Light Aeroplanes* [37], and *British Commercial Aircraft* [38], I referred to this as the 'Golden Age' of the light aeroplane. Admittedly the 'twenties began in post-war stagnation and uncertainty followed by periodic economic uncertainties while the 'thirties were blighted by fears of impending war. Despite all this there existed a quiet confidence that came with the certain knowledge that Britain built the best light aeroplanes in the world, that our engines were the most reliable and dependable, and that British products were both the preferred and affordable choice being sought-after worldwide. They had earned respect as the hallmark of quality.

Whether or not this was strictly true is a moot point. History has a cruel way of viewing optimism as jingoism and looking back on this period was no exception. But what is undisputed, certainly at the time, was the confidence that it gave to our industry. A succession of record-breaking long distance flights, many carried out by heroic pilots who themselves were recipients of public acclaim that occasionally bordered on adulation, appeared to prove the point. Designers, both amateur and professional, began to move into that curious area of euphoric auto-imagination and confidence that may only be reached through the hyper-elation inspired by the *joie de vivre* of certainty. In pure aerodynamic research there is no question we were generally alongside, if not decidedly ahead of, the world's best. The roll call of pioneers of progress in aeronautical engineering and theory comprised at least three-quarters British brains. It is merely a quirk of usage that elevated the memory of American Virginius Evans Clark (1886-1948) above that of German-born naturalised Briton Gustav Victor Lachmann (1896-1966), yet the pioneering work on slow and safe flight undertaken by Handley Page at Cricklewood was at least as important as Clark's contemporary amazing and time-proven airfoil sections.

In 1939 we were on the verge of introducing a transatlantic air service and large aircraft were pioneering this last great difficult air route. The quest for the high-speed mailplane brought the remarkable Short-Mayo composite that was as much a technological marvel as it was a wildly misguided solution to a problem that had not been thought through properly. Projects were launched that were clever, ingenious and breathtaking. Hardly a week passed without some acclaimed sensational new development. It was an age of excitement and achievement.

At the private and amateur level, flying clubs thrived, while the choice of light aircraft was ever increasing. There were something like 1,200 private owners and those who flew tended to be members of the reasonably-well-off class. There were notable exceptions and London Transport's subsidised club (based at Broxbourne) proved that even bus drivers and their conductors could learn to fly if they wished. Safe amateur aircraft construction was also within our grasp as lessons were learned from the Flying Flea craze that swept Europe and Britain in 1935 and 1936.

The performance and operational envelope of aviation, although rapidly expanding, was still containable: the separation between light aircraft and the larger and faster transport and military aircraft was not really all that great and the club end of flying might still associate with the professional end.

On the general front, there never seemed shortage of finance for the people who wanted to set up an aircraft manufacturing business or form a flying club. Money was made – but mostly lost – on a large scale in the late 1930s. All this was brought to a sudden end with the outbreak of war.

The fine lines of the Comper Swift single seat racer date right the way back to 1930 yet the little Swift was to distinguish itself for decades to come. The most famous survival of the radial-engined Pobjoy machines was G-ABUS which graced the air show circuits in the two decades that followed the rebirth of private flying in 1946. But there were other survivors – the author's G-ABTC, G-ABPE, G-ABUU and this one, G-ACTF the last built and named *The Scarlet Angel* restored by Airspeed test pilot Ron Clear at Christchurch in 1951.

The RAF's Miles Magister became a popular trainer with many clubs. Although civilianised as the Miles Hawk Trainer, they were always known as 'Maggies'. G-AIUA was a popular Elstree Flying Club machine. Here C Nepean Bishop takes off from there on July 3rd 1949.

The axe had already fallen when war was announced on September 3rd 1939. All private flying in the British Isles was prohibited 'for the duration'. In Ireland the curious situation existed where flying was prohibited in the Six Counties, yet across the border in Eire things carried on as usual. Finally on May 28th 1940 the Eire Minister for Industry and Commerce, Seán MacEntee, fell into line and prohibited private civil flying. This meant closure of the flying school in County Kildare yet allowed the continuance of the civilian Aer Lingus Dublin-to-Liverpool service.

As Britain suffered the consequences of war, light aircraft were either impressed (literally commandeered for military service, mostly as communication and VIP transport) or put into storage in one form or another. Those impressed were invariably two seaters and larger. Single seaters and racers had no value in time of conflict and, with few exceptions, they were ignored and their individual fates of no importance. As the war progressed and valuable covered space became increasingly scarce, those machines hangared on aerodromes were turned out into the open to face the elements. The comparative few that survived best were usually those that had been dismantled and stored away from aerodromes in barns, outhouses or garages.

A war which many optimists, among them notable soldiers and politicians (neither group being renowned then, as today, for prophesy, let alone informed opinion), considered would be over in a matter of 'a few weeks', went on for six long years. In the manner that the Great War of 1914-18 actually marked the effective transition from the Victorian era to the Edwardian age, the protracted privations of the second Great War which extended for a decade and more after it was officially concluded marked the transition from Georgian England into the Second Elizabethan age that began in 1952.

There were those who genuinely believed that the exciting carefree days of pre-war British light aviation would be re-kindled once war was at an end. Man (and woman) would once again have the freedom of the air in small brightly-coloured aeroplanes, and the projected ideal of every major town (including those that believed themselves to be in that category) having its own aerodrome would pick up where it left off. The government would once more pay the clubs to offset their charges and ordinary people could afford to fly again. Of course there would be government subsidy…

These optimists were not only veterans of the Avro 504K that sat in the sun with the shiny little windmill of its Rotherham fuel-pump spinning at the centre-section strut. It included 'thirties King's Cup entrants that had flown Bluebirds and Hawks, B.2s and Couriers. It even included newly demobbed Royal Air Force men, among them the *jeunesse dorée* who still had a love for the romance of flight in their young bones.

People who thought those things were in for a nasty shock.

The pre-war government Subsidy Scheme for Light Aeroplane Clubs was inaugurated as far back as 1925 and had done much to reduce the cost of flying training and practice for the growing band of flying enthusiasts. The idea culminated, in 1937, in the Civil Air

PEACEFUL SKIES: INSPIRATION AND CONFIDENCE

Miles Aircraft is probably best remembered for its Messenger and Gemini four seaters. It all started with the wartime communications aircraft which George Miles built as a replacement for his brother's Whitney Straight of 1936 and his own Monarch of 1938. The outcome was the M.28 series, soon named Mercury by its designer. The first Miles aircraft to have a retractable undercarriage, the Mercury was first flown on July 11th 1941. Six aircraft were built, each slightly different. This is the Mk.IV, U-0243, built in 1944 which later became G-AGVX – before being sold to Australia. Each moved closer to the famed M.38 Messenger with its flaps positioned behind and beneath the wing trailing-edge and its triple fins and rudders.

The ultimate development of the Mercury was the Messenger and this went through several stages of refinement. Seen here, G-ALBR was a Miles Messenger 4A – observe the square window aft of the cockpit. On July 2nd 1949 it crashed into woods at Aldenham House shortly after take-off from Elstree Aerodrome and was damaged beyond economic repair.

G-AILI was a Miles M.38 Messenger 2A built at Woodley in the autumn of 1946. This marque is identifiable by the tear-drop-shaped rear cabin windows and this particular example made history when, in 1947, Miles used it as a flying test-bed for the Czechoslovakian Praga E engine. It subsequently reverted to its original 155 hp Blackburn Cirrus Major 3 engine but on May 23rd 1964 it crashed at Beauvais in France and was destroyed.

Miles' twin-engined M.65 Gemini 1A was another popular machine of its day. Created as a twin-engined version of the Messenger – it had the same wing – it was fitted with a retractable undercarriage. The Elstree club offered twin-engined training on one for seven guineas (£7.7s) an hour in 1952. This example, G-AHKL, first flew in March 1946 and was withdrawn from use at Lympne in February 1966. These aircraft were well built but lightly constructed with the result that whereas, for example, the Percival Proctor was tough, the Miles' designs were less durable.

A special example of the Miles twin was Nat Somers' Gemini G-AKDC described as a Mk.3, which had Gipsy Major 1C engines. Re-engined with Gipsy Major 10s, this won the 1949 King's Cup at 164.25 mph and became the Mk.3C. Possibly the most successful example of its breed, it went on to win the 1953 Siddeley, the 1954 Kemsley and the 1955 Goodyear Trophies. On December 28th 1957 it was sold to Tanganyika.

Guard scheme that brought pilotage almost within the reach of the masses. The measure of success achieved by the government's efforts may be judged from the fact that the number of subsidised clubs rose from five in 1925 to 63 in 1938. Gliding, too, received State recognition and encouragement in subsidy form.

By March 1939 there were 68 flying clubs that between them had (at the last known count in March the previous year) 385 assorted aircraft. That final year of peace was the year of the DH Moth Minor and many clubs had modern aircraft on order, almost all of them being the new low-wing monoplane from Hatfield.

Now, though, things were very different. Just as in the years following the First World War (by this time no longer referred to as The Great War, save by veterans), government had no money and was not at all keen on returning to the pre-war subsidy route. After all, private flying, club or otherwise, was a luxury and Britain was in a state of extreme economic privation. Nor was government going to restart the CAG (Civil Air Guard) scheme despite being urged to by would-be pilots with no money. It should have been apparent that the CAG was quite redundant and its revival would have been both political and economical anathema.

It was thus not surprising that in mid-February 1946, with post-war civil flying less than two months old, the government's eagerly-awaited announcement concerning its intentions regarding flying clubs was received more with sighs of exasperation than gasps of astonishment. By then, those who had still harboured lingering thoughts of reviving subsidies had begun to give up hope. This helped to soften the blow that came like a bang on the nose from a deftly-wielded frying-pan.

'At this juncture', announced Minister for Civil Aviation Lord Winster in response to the recommendations of the [Whitney] Straight Committee, 'there can be no subsidy for private flying.' In spite of the undeniably good 'second-line' work (as *Flight* described it) done during the war by club-trained pilots, the Air Council remained unconvinced of their possible value in any future emergency. The Treasury was clearly unwilling to spend even the comparatively tiny amount that the pre-war level of subsidy was worth. Even worse, the belief was now that in this new era of the government's neo-Nationalised scheme of things, the Minister could see no place for the flying club movement.

Perhaps vaguely aware of the circumstances by which the nation had sequestered flying club (meaning *private*) property at the start of the war and mindful of the unpopularity which greeted the decision to drop any question of subsidy, the government attempted to suggest its more philanthropic side. It announced that it would provide, at nominal price, a total of one hundred light aircraft for the clubs.

This outward display of good-intentioned benevolence was naturally received with howls of righteous indignation. The very thought of having to buy back their own property was totally repugnant. It was interpreted as a downright insult to the flying club movement which had not shunned public-spirited responsibility when, in time of national need in 1939, it had allowed its aircraft to be summarily commandeered. The simple truth that, in 1939, the clubs had no option but to accede to Air Ministry pressure on impressments was neither here nor there. At the outbreak of war clubs and private owners had between them dutifully handed over to the government (in the name of the war effort) some 600 aircraft. These machines had in the main been in tip-top condition with full civilian Certificates of Airworthiness. They were all 'state of the art' light planes.[1]

The MCA's derisory offer of replacement by a few second-hand planes at give-away prices was seen as pretty feeble as was the accompanying statement that no further aircraft could be expected. In the fullness of time it turned out to be even less of a bargain and ultimately would prove more of a liability. There were 60 de Havilland Tiger Moths, 30 Taylorcraft Austers and 10 Miles Magisters that would be sold off at £50 apiece. However, they were generally in such poor condition it was felt that in order to get a full Certificate of Airworthiness (vital for club and flying-school work) each aircraft would probably first require a staggering £400 worth of work to be carried out. The total cost to the clubs, then, would be in the region of £40,000 which was almost as much as might have been needed, in pre-war days, to buy the same number of suitable aircraft in new, or near-new, condition.

By Easter, the deal had turned even more sour when the Royal Air Force suddenly announced it wanted to hang on to 19 of the Austers that, it felt, it would continue to need. Distributing the diminishing number of aircraft around the clubs increasingly reminded one of the parable of the seven fishes and the seven loaves.

So much for the public-spirited gesture that saw club secretaries hand over club property (meaning, literally, the *members'* property) to help defend the Nation! Material sequestered in that way was originally intended as a defence loan: six years later the 'loan' bit had conveniently been forgotten. True there had eventually been a payment by official valuation but this was a fraction of book value and took no account of loss of earnings.

The clubs were now in a real quandary. Aeroplanes were very few and far between and funds were strained to the limit. If they hesitated or declined the offer, they

The 1940s and '50s were renowned for flying displays that were verging a little on the wild side. Fortunately Health & Safety had not yet reared its ugly head so usually things went off OK. Here the cameraman attracts the full attention of a London Aeroplane Club Tiger Moth at Panshanger Aerodrome. The long black shed next to the blister hangar, far right, was the 1960s home of the North London Aero Club. The spacious grass airfield, once known as Holwell Hyde and famously employed during the war first as a DH factory decoy then as home to a RAF Reserve Flying School, and afterwards as home to the London Flying Club, is now obliterated by a mass of close-packed cheap housing. In the 1950s it was used for making several films.

would have to wait that much longer before flying could start again. And there was tremendous pressure from within each club to regain operational status as soon as possible.

Already at that time 52 clubs had announced their intention of reforming at some time in the immediate future. Assuming that every club would want its fair share of the clapped-out Tigers, Austers and Maggies, the Government's offer therefore represented exactly 1.923 aircraft per club. It only requires elementary economics to work out that, even at the highest hourly flying charges, it would not be possible for any club to operate successfully with two or, at the most, three aircraft under such terms.

The irony was that between 1949 and 1950, no fewer than 239 Tiger Moths were broken up under a contract placed by the Ministry of Supply allegedly 'to recover components and spares needed by the RAF'. During the same period, the RAF itself had broken up a further 81 Moths.[2]

For the clubs there seemed no easy answer other than retrenchment. Few of them, save, perhaps, the larger pre-war ones, could afford the sort of initial outlay needed to buy, finance and sustain aircraft. And, as we have already seen in the Introduction, purchase abroad was not an option.

Neither was it feasible to consider a case where all the clubs might pool resources and approach a manufacturer to order new aircraft direct. This was because the manufacturer would not have the physical ability to produce new aircraft since every maker was forced into the schism of 'export first'. By law, a high proportion of any manufacturer's

---

1. During the war, the majority of flying clubs, and virtually all of the small or newly-founded ones, shut down. Some remained as merely social clubs to preserve their identity. Existence was not easy: their aircraft had either been taken over by the government or put into long-term storage while their officials, instructors, ground engineers and many members had been called up for military service. In the summer of 1941 a final settlement was reached between the Air Ministry and the General Council of Light Aeroplane Clubs for payment to be made to the former flying clubs. A sum of £25,000 was paid by the Air Ministry to help the clubs meet their liabilities in addition to a sum amounting to between £60,000 and £80,000 which had already been paid to the sixty-eight clubs that had participated in the pre-war Civil Air Guard Scheme to account for the flying hours that had been interrupted by the outbreak of hostilities. This distribution was not entirely fair since not all clubs belonged to the General Council either for reasons of independence or because they were newly-formed and not yet elected. It also specifically excluded those that did not participate in the CAG either because they had not applied or because they had been rejected. In consequence a number of the smaller and newer clubs which had aircraft not wanted by the government were left badly off. This contrasted with the older and more established light aeroplane clubs which were left solvent.

2. This information was provided to the House of Commons on June 19th 1950 by the Minister of Supply George R Strauss in reply to a question by Air Cmdr Arthur V Harvey (*Cons.*, Macclesfield).

production had to be for foreign currency-earning. Until that quota (variously positioned at about 80 per cent) had been reached, there could be no home sales. Put simply, for every ten aircraft built, eight had to be sold overseas *before* the balance could be sold to domestic users. And with America's position in the world market of light aircraft, our machines stood little chance of a look-in on an export market that was now more favourably inclined towards the United States.

That is not to say that British manufacturers did not try. Far from it. They shifted Heaven and Earth to take demonstration machines around the world. This was far harder than it might sound, since rigid foreign currency restrictions meant that everything that the sales and demonstration party needed on their tour had to be taken out with them. As commercial travellers, these were the new-generation suitcase men and, although the job sounded like a Rolls-Royce of a jolly, it was anything but. Usually the cheapest accommodation was too expensive for the strictly-enforced cash allowance and one either slept in the aircraft (if it was big enough) or unfurled a sleeping bag in the corner of a hangar. The British were truly the world's poor relations at that time.

Curiously it wasn't that there was a shortage of actual aircraft, merely that the right type of machine was just not available. Unlike after the First World War, the greater majority of ex-military aircraft were of little use to the budding private pilot. The Second World War fighters and bombers were vastly different from their First World War counterparts and, with but a few exceptions, civilian use – and most certainly flying club use – was out of the question. The vast stocks of warplanes were simply melted down and turned back into the saucepans from whence the general public (entreated to surrender its hollow-ware during the war years) would wish to believe they came. The American authorities in Europe, faced with the task of destroying thousands of unwanted military aircraft left over from the war, found that the most economical way of rendering them into scrap (to comply with the terms of the Lease-Lend agreement) was to blow them up with 20 lbs of TNT placed around the centre-section spar.[3]

The sheer waste of aircraft and materials was unbelievable. Many new and serviceable machines were taken out and dumped at sea while an unknown number were bulldozed into disused quarries and hastily-dug burial pits. When the American services[4] vacated Hendon Aerodrome (as late as 1952), a huge pit was gouged out alongside the railway embankment and filled with brand new Pratt & Whitney engines, tools and spares – and then grassed over, presumably still there to this day beneath somebody's back garden.

In the meantime, on March 6th Parliament was told, in answer to a question about aircraft scrapping, that the RAF had scuttled 23 of its 59 Sunderland flying boats and the Air Ministry had declared its stocks of Albermarle, Battle, Blenheim, Botha, Defiant, Gladiator, Hampden, Lerwick, London, Lysander, Manchester, Stranraer, Wildebeeste, Whirlwind and Whitley aircraft obsolete. Clearly there would be no repeat of the post First World War activities of an Aircraft Disposal Company-type operation

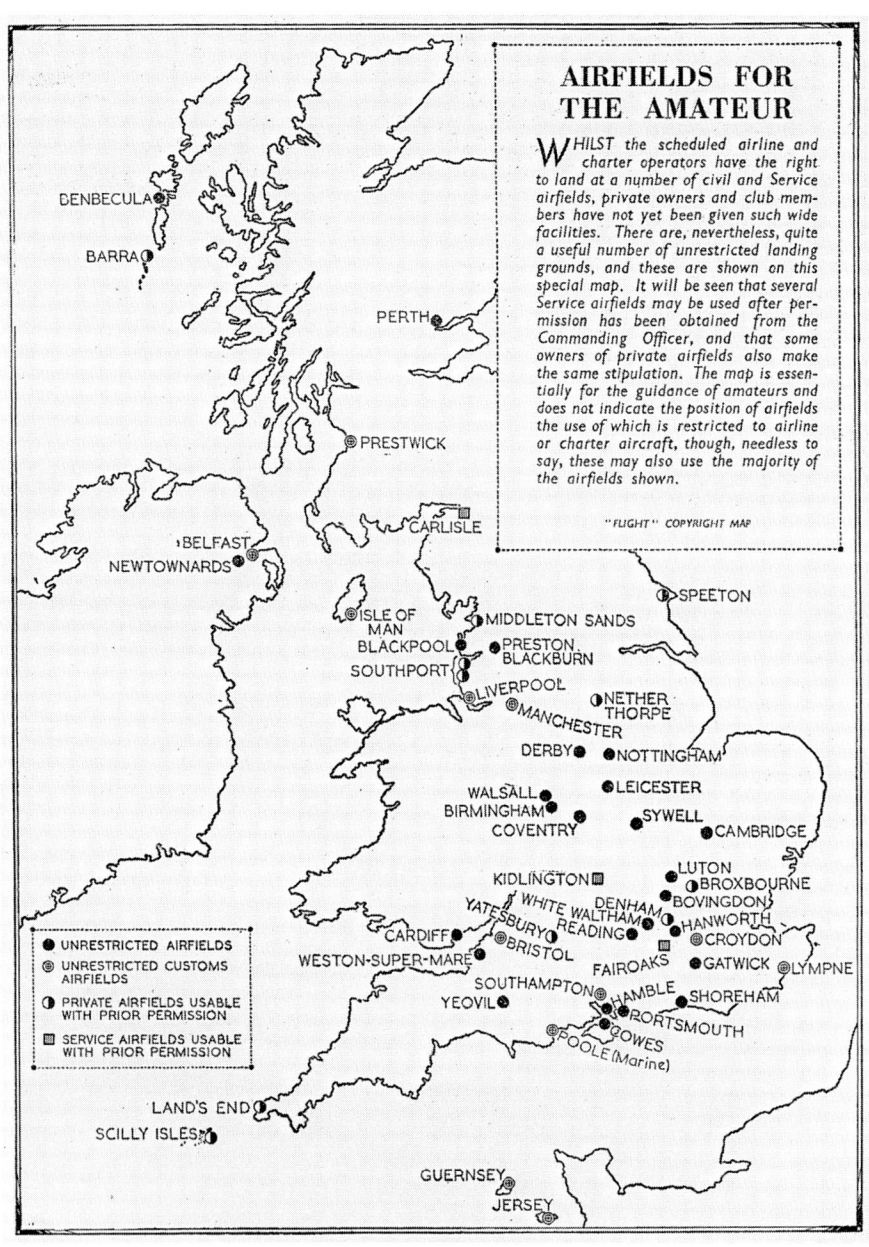

In its issue of November 28th 1946, *Flight* published this special map to show those airfields that were open to amateur (meaning club and private) fliers. The south-east was particularly well served although both Heston and Elstree (Aldenham) were operating at this time, the former as a PPO, the latter unrestricted. Hanworth was also still open. Fuel was not available at all airfields, though, and fliers had to make careful plans to avoid running dry far from base.

---

3. *Flight* April 4th 1946, p.353.

4. This detachment was the curiously-named United States Navy Air Attaché operating the R4D-8 variant of the DC-3.

Last staged there in 1938, Paris's ornate Grand Palais des Champs-Elysées was the setting for the 17th *Salon de l'Aéronautique* in 1946 and, despite the many problems of supply and transport, it turned out to be an impressive event. It had been expected that Britain would represent about a third of the international show with a major presence from America. In the event, this very crowded exhibition was dominated by the French and British while America's aircraft industry could only muster two or three exhibitors. Germany, USSR and Italy were, of course, missing. The show opened on November 15th and ran until December 1st. SBAC president 34-year-old William Reginald Verdon-Smith (a director of Bristol Aeroplane, also Rotol) announced that 'the space taken by the British aircraft industry [shows] an earnest resolve to secure a bigger share of the world's aircraft markets than it has ever obtained before. The fact that [our] share in the window is larger than that or any other foreign country indicates that the wish to gain new markets is backed by an ability to deliver the goods, and that the range of goods is wide and comparable with the likely demand.' Britain's 50 exhibitors were densely packed into the hall along with everybody else. In this snapshot of the crowded exhibition hall can be seen the exhibits of Percival, Miles and Short Brothers with the newly-finished prototype fuselage of Merganser G-AHMH just visible (centre) the Gemini in the distance and the foreground dominated by Armstrong Whitworth's AW.52 Flying Wing, yet to be fitted with an engine and still a glider, in the foreground.

This second snapshot from the 1946 Paris Salon shows some of the austere furnishings that revealed the haste in which France was recovering from the ravages of war. Here we see the M.65 Gemini 1A G-AIHI registered just days before its positioning flight to Paris. In February 1948 it was sold in France as F-BENP. The irony of the Handley Page sign in the background would become apparent 18 months later when Sir Frederick bought up the remains of an unnecessarily bankrupted Miles Aircraft Ltd.

(see The Great War-Plane Sell-Off [39]). While, as we shall see, disposals did take place, they were not on anything like the scale of the previous post-war bonanza.

Not that this prevented vast stocks of aircraft surplus parts entering the market. Aircraft wheels, in particular Spitfire and other fighter types as well as bomber tailwheels, were advertised in *The Exchange & Mart* for a fraction of their original cost. Eagerly bought up by mechanical enthusiasts (war memorabilia collectors had yet to materialise: surplus was no more than salvage then), many were to see an extremely short life used on boat trailers for the beach: the salt water corroded them to powder in a single summer season. And the summer of 1946 saw the disposal to the public of more than 100,000 inflatable rubber survival dinghies. This was later rued by the authorities and new owners were entreated not to let them drift out in the ocean since air-sea rescue people were still on high alert to seek and rescue any ditched airmen.

Lack of suitable aircraft was all very well but there was a more fundamental problem which had emerged. Whereas before the war pilots, aircraft and flying had been the stuff of adventure, excitement and general interest, there was now a sea-change in the public attitude towards aircraft and fliers. A war-weary population had transformed. The man-in-the-street had become bitter and gave the impression of having had enough of flying and flying machines. A discernible undercurrent objected to the resurrection of private flying and would disavow having an airfield on its doorstep. Such protestations began with those people who had been traumatised by destruction from the skies but, in later years, their numbers were gradually replaced by a new and younger generation which, while probably not remembering the war, still objected to private flying 'on principle'.

This disturbing reversal of the popular image of private flying served to cancel out all the expansion and achievements of the days since the Wright Brothers and threatened to put aviation back into the Dark Ages when, it is recorded, wealthy landowners campaigned to sue balloonists not merely for landing on their property but for trespassing in the airspace above it!

The anti-light aviation lobby began almost imperceptibly in 1946 and has been gathering momentum ever since. The effects have manifested themselves in two ways. First were those who simply objected to light aeroplanes. Second were those who decided to object because they had chosen to live near aerodromes. In the majority of instances it is this latter category that to this day comprise the most determined and troublesome bunch. These are in so many instances people who have opted through property-purchase to live close to an airfield, and then campaigned to have it closed. In recent years many airfields have been subjected to this process.

One that comes to mind is Denham where campaigns to shut down this thriving and ancient airfield are most vociferous – from newcomers who have moved into new houses built in the area within very recent times. Short-sighted and narrow-minded minority groups like this will never fit comfortably into a community accustomed to living near an aerodrome and they merely demonstrate only their own selfishness by attempting the impossible. Usually they fall into the category of 'young and upwardly mobile' and most did not see the light of day until the war was well and truly over. And often they are the same people happy to rob

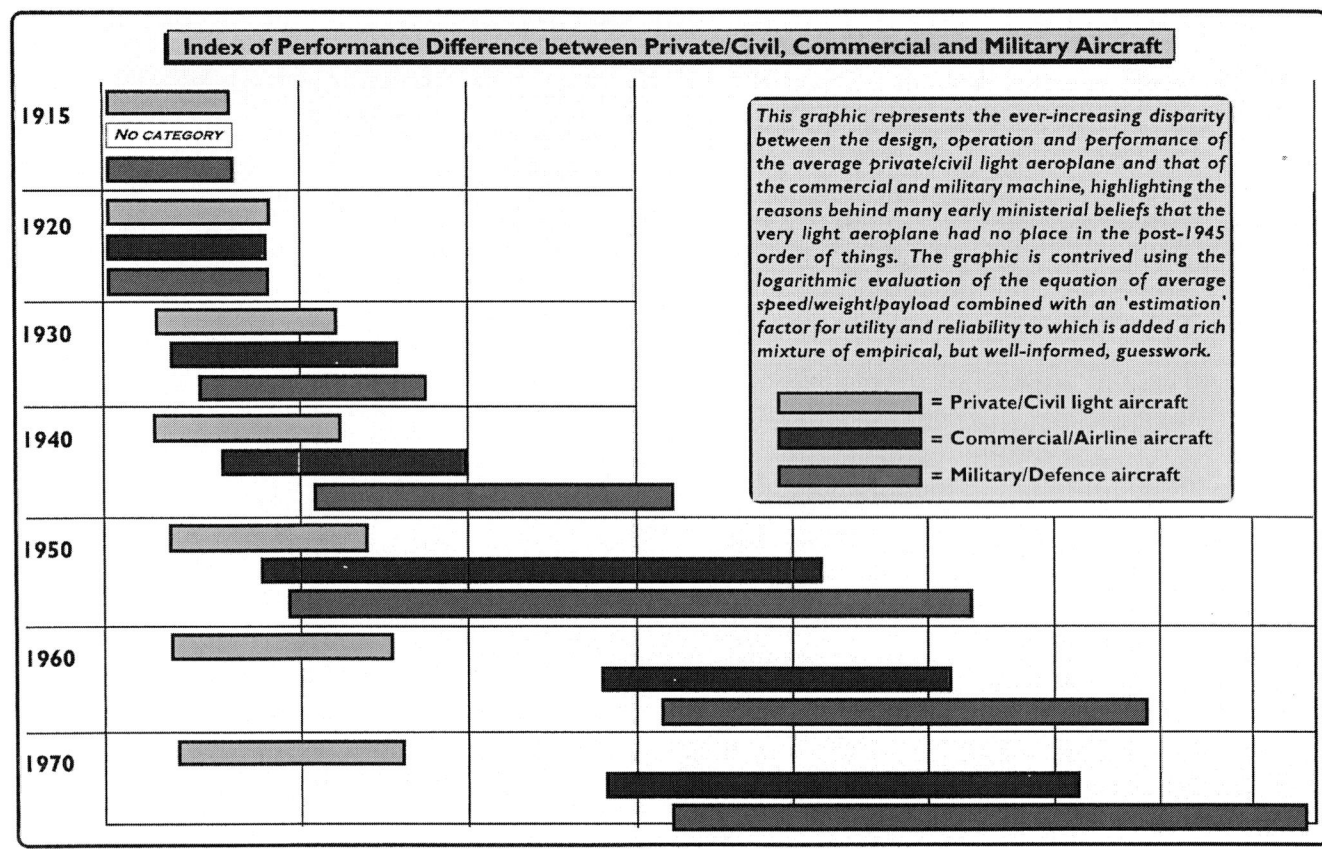

This chart shows the relative position of three classes of aircraft at seven significant stages in their development. These classes are (top) private, civil light aircraft, (centre) commercial/airline aircraft, and (bottom) military/defence service aircraft against an arbitrary performance index. This shows how far the majority of private and civil aircraft had become separated from Service/military aircraft.

In 1946 if you owned an old cart or a trailer you might well get inveigled into helping somebody collect his aeroplane from a government sale. Here in exchange for five crisp white five-pound notes a team of would-be aviators load up AX791, a 1938 Tiger Moth G-AFGJ, from a West Country disposals site.

Buying an aircraft at these government sales was a gamble. The author once bought four Tiger Moths for £100. Two were almost immediately flyable and were removed by air, the third needed a couple of days' work on it and the fourth was slightly damaged so it was broken up for spares. Today that fourth machine could have been lovingly restored in a mere month or so! And an airworthy DH.82a sells for quite a few thousand!

natural resources in order to maintain their invariably new golf club and drive a multi-wheel'd environmentally-unfriendly truck!

But Denham's noisy minority of VILERs (Vociferous Indignant Local Egotistical Residents) are not the only ones living in the Dark Ages. Town councillors, not normally associated with respecting the wishes of those that elected them once they have got into office, have almost to a man taken to objecting to flying fields – even their own town aerodromes. When Portsmouth Town Council, for instance, voted to abandon its fine and convenient aerodrome thereby uprooting one of the most successful local flying clubs in the area (not to mention several important aviation engineering concerns), it proved just how supremely unimaginative a public authority could be. But across the country those who have tried to establish landing strips have almost always received nothing but hostility and antagonism from local authorities.

It remains a curious heterodoxy in human nature that the noisiest machines in the modern skies – helicopters – attract little public outrage, yet the sound of a small light aircraft going about its own business relatively quietly generates an outburst of almost Peléan intensity.

If the 20th century went out on a sour note, the pattern for its five-decade second half was established as early as 1946. It was in that year that the hopeful private aircraft owners and pilots began to see that the so-called freedom of the air, an attitude established in the 1930s, had become subjective. The owners of some aircraft could more or less do as they pleased – there were as yet no 'airways', few restricted flying areas and no call to carry radio. However, the owners of some other aircraft, which had been classified in pre-war times as 'ultra-light', were now 'frozen out' of the flying scene. A letter from a Mr R Allen published in *Flight* on June 13th 1946 under the heading 'Ultra-Light Aircraft Grounded by Official Muddling' explained all:

> I wonder if any of your readers are in the same unfortunate position that I am at this moment.
>
> Before the war I used to fly a Tipsy single seater, G-AFVH. This machine, like all other ultra-light aircraft in the country, was flown on a 'Permit to Fly' and the C of A regulations were waived.
>
> Now I want to get the machine flying again, but on writing to the ARB [Air Registration Board] for a permit I was told that no permits would be issued except for experimental aircraft, and that I must get a C of A. As soon as I tried to get a C of A I came up against a brick wall.
>
> No C of A can be issued for an ultra-light aircraft because the engines used by these machines are non-approved engines. No approved engine can be fitted, as there are none available of the required power. Also, in my case, the airframe is of Belgian origin, and on applying to the Belgian authorities for a copy of the original Belgian C of A, I was informed that all documents had been destroyed during the Occupation and therefore they could not produce a copy.
>
> I am therefore in the delightful position of being allowed to fly the machine as soon as I can get a C of A, but under no circumstances may I have a C of A: and this situation is unaffected by however many replacements, overhauls, renewals, etc, that I may do on the machine.
>
> Could anything be purer 'Gilbert and Sullivan'?
>
> I have been writing now for months to the Ministry of Civil Aviation about this business and I still cannot get any sense out of them. I have been up to London to see them, and I have written to Lord Winster [Minister of Civil Aviation] asking for an interview, but 'the matter is still under review'. It has apparently been under review since at least January 1st of this year!
>
> It is quite clear, to me at any rate, that this decision not to issue permits to fly has been taken by somebody who 'hasn't a clue' as to its effect. If it has been taken deliberately, the whole matter becomes much uglier, as it means that the Government is out to kill the ultra-light aircraft movement despite the fact that these little machines were amazingly good and surprisingly cheap to fly.

Pictured on May 3rd 1947 are members of London Transport Sports Association Flying Club seen in this publicity photo shot at its Fairoaks, Surrey, base. The unsuitable flying kit is only matched by the elderly six-wheeled single-decker 1920s omnibus in which the lucky drivers and conductors have been transported from their depôt. Only the Tiger Moths look ageless.

One pre-war design that was showing every sign of being an outstandingly successful private aeroplane was Errol Shapley's Kittiwake gull-winged monoplane. Built above his works in the centre of Torquay, G-AFRP emerged after the war to complete its flying trials. A new company and finance had been secured to fund production once airworthiness was assured. Shaping up nicely and with glowing recommendations from a number of pilots who had flown the machine experimentally, Shapley's Pobjoy-powered pride and joy was entrusted to a Ministry recommended test pilot who was to undertake altitude handling trials. At some 18,000 feet over the Devonshire moors the aircraft entered an inverted spin, the sort of manoeuvre which a skilled pilot usually has a pretty good idea how to get out of, certainly with that amount of height to play with. Instead of using his controls, the pilot panicked and took to his parachute. The Kittiwake, when finally it came down, was consequently destroyed. Shapley rightly blamed the erstwhile test pilot and was so bitterly upset – he was, after all, a 'one-man band' – that he emigrated.

PEACEFUL SKIES: INSPIRATION AND CONFIDENCE

New aeroplanes in those early post-war years made reassuringly frequent stories in the newspapers and trade press, but only rarely did they prove more than a brief light in the sky of hope. One amazing contender for the private and executive light twin market was Portsmouth Aviation's Aerocar first flown by Francis Luxmoore on June 18th 1947. All who saw it and flew it recognised its peer position and it was one of the star attractions at that September's Society of British Aircraft Companies (SBAC) Show staged at Handley Page's Radlett Aerodrome.

Access to the Aerocar's instruments and controls was unparalleled. Clamshell access panels opened to reach flight controls, the rear of the instrument panel and all services. Because the designer was worried about the risks of a wheels-up landing, the fuselage pod actually had rear skids so that, with the nosewheel projecting a little even when retracted, a safe 'wheels-up' landing could be considered in the event of some system failure. The order book for the Aerocar reached the 'impressive' level.

Mr Allen's letter concerned a Belgian-built Tipsy S.2, OO-ASB, fitted with a 32 hp Sarolea Epervier flat-twin engine imported in June of 1939 and re-registered in Britain. This was the first intimation to the light aviation world that the suspected 'them and us' demarcation feared in post-war flying actually existed. As time would tell, it existed not just with one class of aircraft, but with aircraft manufacturers as well. In the short term, Allen's predicament encouraged support from other correspondents but, in the event, G-AFVH was finally returned to Belgium for preservation under the registration OO-TIP.

Behind the scenes, though, what today would be described as a 'hidden agenda' was being played out. As ever, there were two sides to it, one being a simple statement of facts, and the other the intransigence of the authorities. First was that in the five or so years since private flying had been stopped, aviation had advanced tremendously. Military aircraft were bigger, faster and more advanced and they had ruled the skies. To cater for the new generation of civil aircraft, airworthiness and operational requirements had been upgraded by leaps and bounds. This left the pre-war light plane superseded in virtually all aspects, overtaken by the expansion of aviation and now left standing like a loin-skin-wearing mediaeval native transported to the middle of Piccadilly Circus in the rush-hour.

The inflexibility of the authorities was not helped by the proliferation, in the Civil Service, of retired (or redundant) officers from His Majesty's services. The fact was that all (or virtually all) of those who were now responsible for civil and private aviation had been pressed down from military duties. Not for the first time would a misguided dependence on Service discipline and procedures be applied to civilian matters with consequences that were less than beneficial. If at one time there had been equality amongst airmen, Joe Public in his tweed sports jacket and plus-fours now rated a very long way down the ladder that led to the perceived administrative Heaven of non-military flying.

Without any shadow of doubt, the Ministry policy was to rid the nation of all aircraft that did not have, or could not qualify for, a full Certificate of Airworthiness. The reason why an aircraft such as Mr Allen's Tipsy or any 'permit to fly' type light aircraft could not ever hope to obtain a full C of A was that it was built under conditions that did not meet the administrative standards now demanded by the Air Registration Board. These included the maintenance of bonded stores for all materials, the complicated managerial procedures of Release Notes for all materials, the employment of approved inspectors to monitor the movement of approved materials and their conversion into aircraft parts, and a whole ancillary pantomime of paper-chasing, rubber stamps and inspections.

Not that this was in itself wrong, but it was the necessary (and vastly expensive) background to a proper aircraft manufacturer, procedures quite unsuited and unattainable by the small company; certainly the amateur light aircraft-builder.

By insisting on the full C of A for all private and club-operated aircraft, the Ministry autocracy demonstrated an inflexibility that would hamper private flying for some years. For hire-and-reward flying club machines, of course, a C of A was essential as much as anything else for the well-being of the club members and the sanity of the insurance companies.

What emerged as a vast unknown quantity was the resilience and devotion of the aircraft enthusiasts in this country. Those who wanted to fly, be it privately or as a member of a flying club, were actually a very powerful lobby and one that would become increasingly vociferous. The other unknown was what the Ministry of Civil Aviation and Lord Winster in particular felt in private about light aircraft and private flying. In truth, Winster was extremely worried about private flying, a concern that would dog several subsequent ministers until they had the courage to bite the bullet and engage in a dialogue with the bodies concerned.

But in January and February of 1946 there was a lack of co-ordination of the private flyers' efforts. Winster admitted later that he was uncertain what to do about light aviation and how far it could or [even] should be encouraged. The Royal Aero Club was one of the strongest lobbyists of government and in the years that followed it welcomed joining forces with the newly-created Ultra Light Aircraft Association and the BGA (British Gliding Association). As one body, it then represented a formidable number of individuals and their needs. Government

Portsmouth Aviation's SBAC Show stand revealed a scale model of the Aerocar fitted with floats for this was just one of the numerous variants planned by the company. The fundamental problem, though, remained capital and the mechanics of manufacture. The state of the nation's finances prevented any thought of government aid or finance of any sort. The Aerocar's makers gallantly battled for a year and then gave in. G-AGTG was broken up and a brilliant design tossed to the ravens. If we were desperate for the Yankee dollar (we were) then this was a golden goose with nothing to rival it elsewhere in the world at the time – and that included Hamburgerland.

had only one need and that was to do with election and it knew that the path to election was not to be seen to be offending too many sectors of the public. It was an interesting situation over which the RAeC/ULAA/BGA combine held ever-increasing sway. But this is an occurrence well ahead of the story, for we are still exploring those bleak years that marked the close of the 1940s.

It is generally considered that arrival on the scene of the Ultra Light Aircraft Association, formed at Easter in 1946, was the first move to consolidate post-war amateur aviation. A splendid thought though this may appear, it is not exactly true, for the ULAA was neither the first champion of the raw amateur end of private flying, nor was it the first group to represent the interests of its members. That kudos goes to the Harrogate Aircraft Club, a long-standing group of enthusiasts based in Yorkshire and co-ordinated by Erik Addyman who had been a significant figure in Yorkshire aviation circles pre-war.[5]

So it was that the first group of amateurs who got together to fight officialdom (actually they did not succeed in the end) was Addyman's HAC. His club, already active again by the start of 1946, tried hard but while failing to overturn ministerial intransigence, managed to get some flying done even if it was not all 'official'. Yorkshire, conveniently distant from the hawk-eyed gaze of moustached military-trained zealots of Westminster, went as far as it could along its own way.

Most important, however, was the fact that the Harrogate Aircraft Club (which had boldly changed its name in January 1935 to The Aircraft Club) made sufficient of a nuisance of itself to inspire others and at the same time give the Ministry a taste of what was to come. From its headquarters, White House, Starbeck, Harrogate (Addyman's home address), club members bombarded the aviation press with 'letters to the editor' under various, but generally transparent, noms-de-plume. A case for the amateur end of aviation was gradually being played out under the spotlight of influential correspondence pages. Soon other observers were sucked into the argument

---

5. Born in 1889, Erik Thomas Waterhouse Addyman was the son of a Norwegian-born solicitor. During the First World War he worked at the School of Mines in Portsmouth developing the depth charge. Then with the Arrol Johnson motor works in Dumfries he designed an aircraft engine and perfected a carburettor before returning to his family home at Belmont House, Starbeck, Harrogate in the 1920s where he worked as a railway engineer. An early advocate of diesel locomotion, Addyman designed and built racing cars, one being the Addyman Vortex. With the start of the British gliding movement in the 1930s he designed and built several gliders: in one of these he suffered a serious accident at Ingleby Greenhow breaking both legs and losing his right arm but this did not stop him from continuing with gliding and flying. A staunchly independent man, he died in 1963 aged 74.

Occupying a factory in the unlikely setting of North London's Mornington Crescent, Chrislea Aircraft Ltd had built the Airguard Trainer in 1939 before switching to war-effort production from 1939 to 1945. During much of that time founder Richard Christoforides honed ideas for a civil four seat light plane. Design work began during the war as, unofficially, did construction. In fact, first announcements were made before the war ended! Called the Chrislea Ace, it was small, perky-looking, and housed four people in a wrap-around glazed cabin. Designed by ex-Miles Aircraft engineer Ralph Marshall, the Ace made its first flight at Heston on August 19th 1946. Unfortunately, turbulence from the relatively enormous cabin upset airflow over the very small tail and test pilot Rex Stedman found he could not turn, a normally simple procedure additionally hampered in this case by a highly unconventional control system devoid of rudder-bar. Having completed possibly the longest circuit on record for a light aircraft, Stedman managed to edge the Ace round and head back over Southern England to Heston. Here, after the Ace's unconventional first flight, designer Ralph Marshall (left) and company founder Richard Christorophides (right) discuss the problems of the aircraft with test pilot Rex Stedman.

The answer lay in a larger tail, in fact, in a twin fin-and-rudder tailplane that was to become standard with all subsequent Ace models. And a large central trim-tab! Foot-operated rudder controls were also eventually installed, largely through widespread criticism from the many pilots who flew the aircraft on its extensive in demonstration tours and nervously pounded the carpet seeking rudder pedals when all they had to do was to turn and push a wheel. Or was it push and turn?

The Chrislea Ace settled down to become a successful design and its tricycle undercarriage was, for a time, a unique feature for a post-war British production light aircraft. Easy to fly and comfortable, the Ace was also quieter than the comparable Auster. The massive dihedral of the prototype's wings was reduced to aid rudder response.

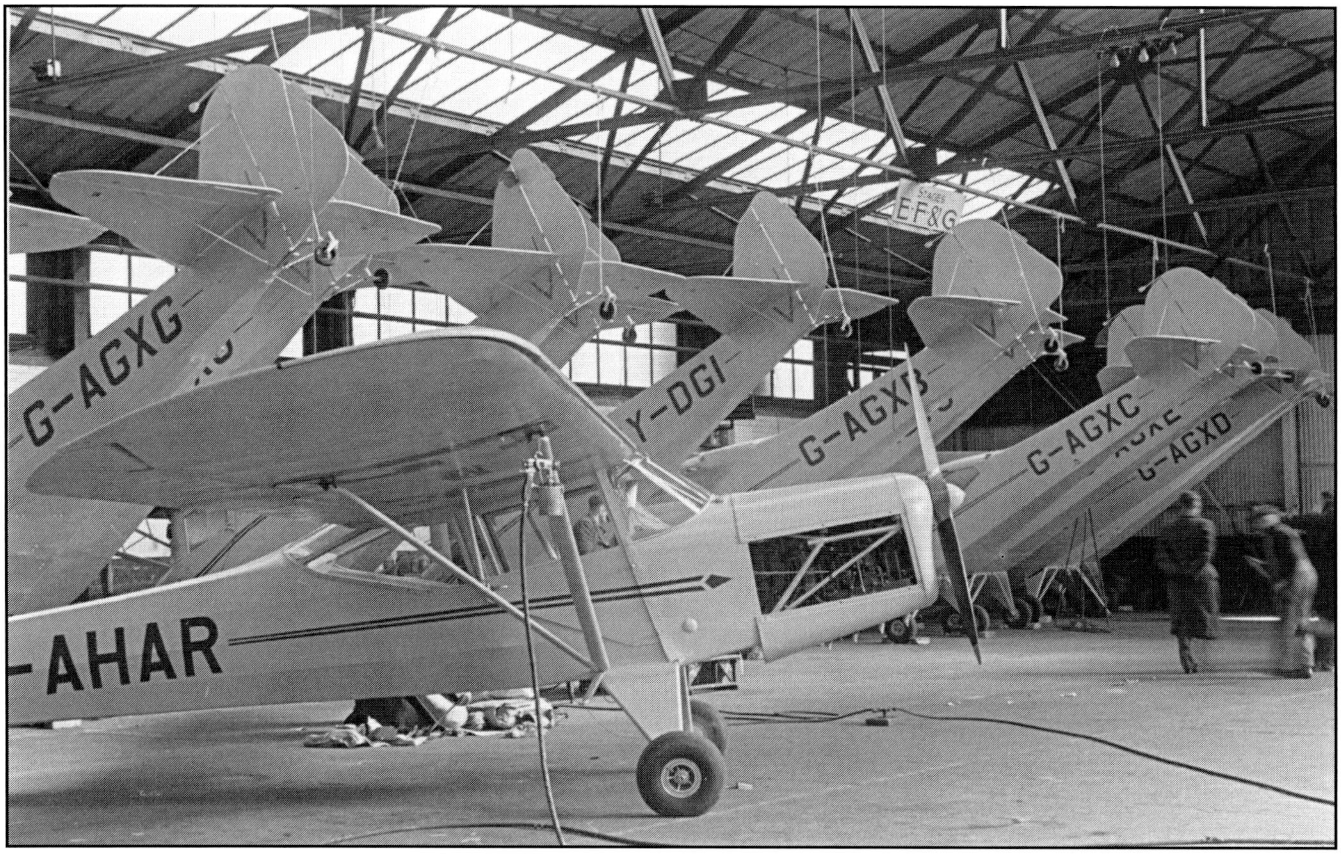

Above: Auster Autocrats in full production became victims of the Auster factory's chronic and on going shortage of space. Here finished fuselages are tied by their tails to the roof beams awaiting the installation of engines and wings. Already at this early stage the company had begun to make inroads to an export market – in the centre is OY-DGI destined for Denmark. *Picture by Mike Hooks.*

Above: As time progressed there were gradual changes and improvements to the basic J-1 Autocrat. G-AGTP was fitted with a silencer to reduce the cabin noise level, the rear cabin glazing was improved and there were other refinements. This one is fitted with the long-range fuel tank under the fuselage and also a glider tow-hook. First registered on October 2nd 1955 it survived until May 31st 1978 when it crashed at Enstone. *Picture by Richard Riding.*

The standard first-production Autocrats were very popular not just with private owners but with flying clubs. This one, G-AGXJ, bears the cowling logo of London Aero & Motor Services which operated the United Services Flying Club at Elstree. First registered on February 1st 1946 it was sold to France on March 1st 1953 becoming F-BGRX. The USFC became the Elstree Flying Club. *Picture by Richard Riding.*

and The Aircraft Club's seed had germinated!

At a meeting staged in Harrogate, members put forward a number of bold proposals for the future of amateur flying. Wisely national rather than parochial they ranged from the provision of a 400-yard square landing field to the haze-free west of every centre of population, to urging designers to go back to the 1923 and 1924 Lympne trials and then develop new types of aircraft with modern improvements. They were sound and well-evaluated proposals that others would later attribute to their own endeavours.

Addyman's club had, in 1935, 43 members with Maj The Rt Hon J W Hills, MP (*Con; Ripon*), as president and John Slingsby, brother of the famed sailplane-designer, as one of its vice-presidents.

The part played by Erik Addyman in the revival of the post-war private flying movement is cruelly forgotten today, yet it was his early burst of enthusiasm that fired others into action. My personal belief is that it was his very amateur status that sparked others, who perhaps thought they were better qualified (*i.e.* senior ex-RAF personnel rather than mere civilians) and considered themselves to be more learned and qualified, to take those steps which eventually led to the Ultra Light Aircraft Association. Addyman played no part in the formation of the ULAA: as an adopted Yorkshireman he did not see any point in aligning with a bunch of Southern toffs when he knew exactly what was wanted. But Addyman was getting on in years and gradually The Aircraft Club faded and its founder eventually died in 1963. The national characteristic of an inbred dislike of forceful individuals made Addyman unpopular with authority, yet he was in his own way a pioneer. For all this he is to be remembered.

When private flying was once more allowed on January 1st 1946, petrol was rationed to the extent that full and free use of aeroplanes and the air was still effectively curtailed. Restricted to four hours' worth of petrol per month, the return to pre-war standards of flight freedom was, for the private owner, a long way off yet. Flying clubs were allowed sufficient fuel for 50 hours for each machine per month. For the club with four aircraft and, say, 250 flying members half of whom were under instruction, then it is clear that so little flying would be possible for each member that those who were students might never have the chance to go solo, let alone qualify for their licences.

In pre-war years there had been a certain club atmosphere that permeated the whole flying movement. It has been said that the golf club is the place where social barriers are broken down and camaraderie fostered. This erroneous image of golf clubs is only projected by those who have never been a member of a private golf club, often institutions that thrive on the class structure and occasionally foster it with an almost religious fervour. The flying club, on the other hand, really did see all classes and ranks of members genuinely socialising and mutually sharing the experience of flying. And perhaps nowhere was this atmosphere more prevalent that at the leading clubs in the land such as Yorkshire Aeroplane, Hanworth, Brooklands, Surrey, and Herts & Essex. Friendships formed in the flying club tended to rival the kinship of Freemasonry for durability.

The halcyon days of the late 1930s had created a nationwide light-aircraft fraternity that had a deep and sincere love of flying. Not all members passed automatically into the RAF when war was declared, and not many survived the bleak years that followed. But what it had created was a rich nostalgia: a veritable craving for the return to the grand days of Yorkshire, Brooklands and Hanworth and a hundred other small fields and clubs across the land. The longer the war lasted, the deeper this craving became for many and even in times of the greatest stress, men would still go glassy-eyed at the thought of a Heaven where brightly-coloured Moths serenely cavorted. And just as everybody longed for a return to those great days, most knew deep down inside that they were now beyond reach and had gone forever.

Perhaps because of the way in which private flying restarted after the war, that special pre-war ambience had departed. True the small clubs and later the Popular Flying Association (precursors of today's Light Aircraft Association) groups saw a measure of return to the pleasurable days of old, but there was a difference. While flying in 1946 was restricted merely by fuel rationing, as the years progressed, flying became less care-free as more and more artificial restrictions and responsibilities were heaped upon the amateur flyer. True, aircraft were becoming faster and more complicated and there was, thankfully, less scope for ignorance, inexperience or slipshod behaviour, but the fact remains that post-war flying was separated from pre-war flying by a gulf that was measured in many ways other than mere years.

During the summer months of 1946, there were sales of surplus aircraft and engines held at RAF stations up and down the country. While these attracted

The Auster company bought back a large number of the original military Taylorcraft Auster V machines and rebuilt them for civilian use. G-ALFA, formerly RT607, demonstrates the salient characteristics of the type namely the snub-nose of the Lycoming flat-four engine cowling and, most noticeable, the extensive cabin glazing. Issued with its C of A on October 20th 1948.

While so many aircraft to emerge from Rearsby were 'made over' at least once in their lives, when it came to the J-1 Autocrat, this was a wholly-new concept with its own special jigs. Gone was the curious port-side under-tail trim paddle to be replaced by a proper elevator-mounted trim-tab. Later, of course, even Autocrats were upgraded and rebuilt, mostly as Alphas. Here is an early Autocrat, G-AIZU. The flaps are set to first-notch for take-off. Observe the static mass balance to the top of the small, straight-hinged rudder. Later modifications involved a slightly larger tail, the rudder carrying an aerodynamic mass balance to its top. *Picture by Richard Riding.*

An early-build Autocrat, G-AGYK shows off its metal propeller and general lines. The stub exhausts did nothing to calm the staccato sound of the Cirrus engine at full throttle but a silencer was available and many club machines featured this refinement as an aid to protecting the instructor's voice.

An early development of the Autocrat was the J-1B Aiglet which, in the case of G-AJUW pictured here on the apron at Elstree, was converted to a J-1N Alpha. Notice the long-range 'slipper' fuel tank and the enlarged, balanced rudder.

considerable interest, because of the remote locations of most of the airfields concerned, as well as the lack of detailed information regarding both the condition of the aircraft and even conditions of sale, many potential buyers, although tempted, did not take an active part in the sales nor did they submit a tender. Also one has to remember that both car petrol and aeroplane fuel was rationed at the time. Travel was limited to public transport meaning the then-extensive railway network as yet unsullied by the criminal antics of axe-wielding ex-grammar-school boy, Dr Richard Beeching.

These government sales were also bound by some curious if not downright archaic conditions. All sales were by 'offer' or tender and it had to be stated clearly on the proposal form for what purpose the aircraft was required and what uses it would be put to. To put down 'flying' somehow seemed unlikely to be sufficient! Perhaps the real message was to prevent anybody from forming a private fighter squadron.

Prices, naturally, varied and an occasion might arise where £650 would secure, say, a Hornet Moth at one sale while at a later one £900 would be required for the same type of machine. At airfields around the country, but predominantly at RAF Kemble, the variety of aircraft available was interesting. Magisters, Dominies, Whitney Straights, Ansons and Queen Bees were more commonly available. The Queen Bee was always described as 'only suitable for spares' since it wasn't considered to be a real aeroplane. The fact that it was built of perfectly good Tiger and wooden-fuselage '60' Moth components seemed neither here nor there and many went for under £10 apiece. A large number of these ended up in a blister hangar at Redhill where, after several years of poor storage (and thoughtful pilfering by those with 'real' Tiger Moths to maintain), they were turned out and burned.

Buyers could be sure, however, that most of the aircraft were airworthy and had been flown in for the sale within the previous six or eight weeks and then been inhibited and stored in hangars. Inevitably, some were unairworthy and these machines had been brought in by road. These were readily identifiable and usually had to depart the way they came.

The conditions of sale all stated that: 'Aircraft and aero-engines will be sold as lying with no guarantee as to condition,

Without doubt and despite a good influx of Tiger Moths and Miles Magisters, by far the most common of the club and private owner light aircraft seen around the club-scene post-war was the Auster J-1 Autocrat, this one, G-AGYN, being pictured at White Waltham in June 1952. Note the Cirrus engine's wooden propeller. The engine cowling bears the logo of The London Aeroplane Club of Panshanger.

serviceability or airworthiness. During the period allowed for inspection the Service logbooks of all aircraft are available for examination and checking delivery; after sale, a civilian logbook is raised and the Service one despatched to Records'.

Like all sales of this sort, *caveat emptor* was the ruling factor. While there was usually fuel available for those who could fly their purchases away (presumably after de-inhibition and a reasonably good inspection), a crane was also available for loading non-flying aircraft on to lorries and waggons. The cost of a C of A for these machines was the major uncertainty and provided the encouragement for attempting to 'buy low'. Prices quoted ranged from £75 to as much as £600.

There was a downside. The Director of Disposals (Air) at Thames House, Millbank, was more comfortable dealing with companies rather than with individuals. Furthermore, decent-sized batches of bids could be expected from companies and these were less time-consuming and offensive to process than having to deal with the common man and his sweaty hand clutching a grubby bunch of once-white five-pound notes. The reality was that individual bidders were discouraged. That some flying club secretaries armed with club cheque-books, were recently-discharged Holders of the King's Commission did not exempt them from this blanket condemnation. The much-vaunted public sales were thus anything but public.

This is an aspect recalled by Albert Hawes of Hants & Sussex Aviation Ltd at Portsmouth who describes Tiger Moths purchased from the MOD Disposal Branch at £50 each and 'would not pay that sort of money unless the aircraft was in a fully serviceable and flying condition'.[6] Surplus de Havilland Dominie aircraft (twin-engined Dragon Rapides) were bought for between £350 and £500.

On one occasion Hawes recalled buying more than 100 Tiger Moth machines on a job lot at £5 each adding that 'this particular batch had been dismantled and were partly cannibalised, lying at the RAF Maintenance Unit at Llandow'. He adds that he and his brother had to transport them all by road to Portsmouth on a lightweight trailer. 'We worked from dawn to dusk and finally became completely exhausted and had to abandon some 30 or so airframes which we burned on site.' Later, back at Portsmouth, Hawes relates:

> With several hundred Tiger Moth wings stacked on the airfield we were selling these 'as is – where is' at one pound ten shillings each or £4.00 for a set of four. Customers sorted out what they wanted and carted these away on trailers. Our standard re-furbished Tiger Moth (when ordered in pairs), including an Export Certificate of Airworthiness was sold for exactly £400 each! Most were supplied in pairs because they were invariably shipped abroad, mainly by W S Shackleton Ltd, and this was achieved economically by packing two aircraft in a large shipping container.

Completing something out of the tattered surviving remains of the pre-war days' flying scene was uphill work. Many small club aerodromes and their buildings, unused or unmaintained for the duration, required enormous amounts of work in order to make them serviceable. Since building materials were still either rationed or in short supply, restoration was often dependent more on cunning than skill and very little was accomplished without 'scrounging', be it materials or

---

6. *Hants & Sussex Aviation Ltd* by Albert E Hawes, OBE. Privately printed and published Portsmouth, 1985. See p.36.

tools. A national cement shortage was just another obstacle to progress. The resourcefulness demonstrated by these early post-war enthusiasts brought a whole new interpretation to the wartime exhortation of 'make-do and mend'.

If 1946 was the year of struggle for private aviation and flying clubs, they survived the first year of the peace in the acute awareness that they were the pariahs in the world of real aviation, meaning that part of the flying scene populated by airliners and military aircraft. Private flyers were second-class citizens whose needs were shunned by the Ministry and who could best serve their nation by giving up and emigrating. Pre-war days when all aviation existed merely as different facets of one medium were gone, for as we have shown time and time again, war and expansion had widened the gap between civil and military flying. Besides legislation and restriction, the operating conditions of military and commercial flying were so different from those of private flying that the gulf separating the small aeroplane from Service and airline operations was now irreconcilable.

Suddenly, however, some inkling of this feeling must have got through to the House of Lords for when, on November 26th, their Lordships debated the first year of nationalised British aviation, the new minister responsible for civil aviation – Lord Nathan – unexpectedly spoke up for the formation of a new private flying committee. His Lordship publicly stated for the first time that a committee was being formed to advise him on the whole question of private flying. This was the celebrated Straight Committee whose findings would emerge the following year[7].

Surprisingly enough, remembering the way in which the value of club-trained pilots to the RAF had been repeatedly denied in high places, Nathan opened his heterodox statement by saying that 'the private flying clubs were responsible for providing some of the finest pilots serving with the RAF in the last war,' adding that he was anxious to encourage both private flying and gliding. Chairman of the new committee, he said, would be Whitney Straight who was also chairman of the Royal Aero Club.

Was he guilt-ridden – or genuinely mindful of the nation's debt (however small) to private flyers? Those that knew his Lordship considered that he was unlikely ever to be susceptible to guilt and probably didn't know what it meant, so perhaps he might just be genuine? What a radical thought! Truth was more likely that it was a dam' good dinner, rather a lot of brandy and a pledge given while partially sedated.

But for the present at least things were looking up. As time would tell, though, for a good while to come every moment of good cheer in the world of the private flyer would be followed by plenty of gloomy moments.

All sorts of flying clubs and training schools appeared up and down the country. Sqdn-Ldr G C Wright of Liverpool (second right) based his flying school at Hooton in Cheshire. This happy snapshot shows Autocrat G-AIGP, first registered October 21st 1946, with rather more than a full load and taken no doubt to mark a successful joy ride early in January 1947.

---

7. Whitney Willard Straight was one of the most significant influences on private and civil aviation in general from the mid-1930s up to the mid-1970s. Born in New York to American parents on November 6th 1912 he was the elder of two sons and a daughter. After his father had been killed in the First World War, his mother married again, this time to an Englishman, and the family moved to England. The young Whitney eventually went up to Cambridge where he took an interest in motor-racing (in which he was greatly successful at Brooklands) and also, from 1934, in light aircraft. In 1935 he married and became a British subject. A skilled and competent pilot, his rise to power was meteoric and recognising both the advantages and opportunities attainable through sheer size he founded the Whitney Straight Corporation. This acquired and operated a chain of airlines, aerodromes and flying clubs. Seeking a design for a fast touring light aircraft and inspired by Charles Lindbergh's confidence in Miles Aircraft, he commissioned the design of a Hawk variant that was named after him as the Miles Whitney Straight. His achievements and aspirations were cut short by the outbreak of war in 1939 by which time he had already recognised the threat and joined the Royal Air Force. His distinguished Service record earned him numerous awards and he was made CBE in 1944 ultimately leaving the RAF with the rank of Air Commodore. Joining first British European Airways as deputy chairman, in 1947 he was appointed managing director of British Overseas Airways Corporation and in 1955 became executive vice-chairman of Rolls-Royce Ltd. Throughout this time he remained active in the Royal Aero Club of which he was long-serving vice-president. He lived at 'The Aviary', Windmill Lane, Southall, Middlesex, where he died on April 5th 1979.

The average club and private flying aerodrome hangar in the 1950s had a good mix of aircraft types within. Here from around 1950, we see some of what lived in the main hangar at Thruxton.

Percival Prentice G-APIU saw service at Biggin Hill with the Surrey and Kent Flying Club between 1958 and 1964 and was scrapped in 1967.

Among the smallest single seat aircraft ever to have been built and flown in Britain was the Ward Gnome powered by a 14 hp Douglas motorcycle engine made in 1925.

British Light Aviation – A Shifting Emphasis

The post-war years may have been rich in the restraints of austerity, yet the National Air Races brought back some normality into the aviation scene quite quickly. Here is a moment of excitement from the 1946 event showing Proctor 1 G-AHMV *Windmill Girl* taking the higher option over Gemini G-AKGE at an airfield turning point.

Below left: It is July 12th 1958 and John Heaton's Thruxton Jackaroo G-AOIR, displaying a rather time-expired paint job, rounds a pylon at the King's Cup race staged at Baginton, Coventry's airport.

Below right: Same place on July 11th the following year when another Jackaroo, this time G-ANZT flown by Beverly Snook, takes a pylon above Turbulent G-APNZ flown by Margo McKellar.

CHAPTER TWO
Light Aviation: an Uphill Struggle

From the very beginning of civil flying in 1919 up to the outbreak of the Second World War, the responsibility for licensing and certification of civil aircraft, both private and commercial, lay with the Air Ministry. The Air Ministry dealt with everything that flew, whether civil or military, private or commercial. However, as military machines became larger, faster and heavier, the disparity between the private civil sector and the Services revealed an ever-increasing gap.

The point was reached where the arrangement was virtually unworkable. From the Air Ministry's point of view, club and other private aircraft were hindering what they saw as more important matters while, for the private flyer, having to deal with the Air Ministry became ever more like an audience with the Deity.

It was a recognition of the virtually impossible task imposed upon the Air Ministry with its obligation to looking after military aircraft and the industry's better-organised manufacturing facility alongside the different needs of civil and private aviation that led the Gorell Committee (which had been appointed by the Secretary of State for Air to report on the control of private flying) to recommend as early as 1933 that an independent board be established to control the airworthiness of civil aircraft.

Initially this recommendation had been implemented by creating a small committee working in association with the executive appointed by the Air Ministry. Under the authority of the Air Navigation Act of 1936, powers were invested in the Board to take over the major portion of the Air Ministry's work in connection with the control of airworthiness of civil aircraft. Clearly the Board, hitherto operating on an *ad hoc* basis, now needed to be established as an independent entity outside the skirts of the Air Ministry and its Kingsway grim brown and green-painted offices. It should become a proper business.

The eventual outcome of this was the establishment of the Air Registration Board (ARB) which was actually a pre-war institution. Registered on February 26th 1937 as a company limited by guarantee and without share capital, Air Registration Board Ltd was created to assume responsibility for all airworthiness matters affecting civilian aircraft, the Air Ministry retaining the formality of issuing Certificates of Airworthiness on the ARB's recommendation. Responsible directly to the Minister, the ARB was in some respect an aeronautical version of the Lloyd's Register of Shipping. It had eighteen members, two of whom were appointed by the Minister, a dozen who represented constructors, operators and insurers of aircraft, and four members who were co-opted.

Its management board comprised leading figures from virtually every aspect of the civil aviation industry. Under the chairmanship of Frederick Handley Page, it mustered a panel of expertise and astuteness that was unique in the annals of British aviation.

Some of the names are familiar even today: Whitney Willard Straight (for whom Miles made and named one of his Hawk touring variants), George Harris Handasyde (who had been one half of the greatly-respected Martinsyde aircraft company in Woking and was then involved in many other aviation activities), Alfred Gilmer Lamplugh (key figure in aviation insurance, aero clubs and airworthiness committees), Henry Nigel St Valery Norman (aeronautical consultant, partner with Alan Muntz in Airwork, developer of Heston Airport, &c) and, eventually, Lord Brabazon of Tara (who, as John Theodore Cuthbert Moore-Brabazon, was the first Englishman to gain a pilot's licence) as chairman.

The General Aircraft Company was based at the London Air Park, Hanworth, and in the mid-1930s it absorbed the British Aircraft Company, makers of the Swallow and Eagle. The story of how it came to buy the rights to the Owlet and the Cygnet all-metal light aircraft has been related in an earlier book (37). The first production Cygnet Mk.II, G-AFVR, gained its C of A on July 5th 1939, less than two months before the outbreak of the Second World War. Its makers continued to advertise the Cygnet well into 1941, no doubt in the hope that the war would be over 'very soon'. Of the eight examples built, the majority were completed during the early years of the conflict, the last in the summer of 1941. The firm's Christmas cards were always up-beat and that for 1940 is seen here, a full-colour artist's rendition of an imaginary scene in what appears to be far-off Cape Town. Inside, the text reads: 'That there soon may be a happy issue from the present troubles and problems is the sincere Christmas and New Year wish of the Directors and Staff of &c'. There was no doubt that GAL was poised to restart manufacture again as soon as hostilities ceased. As time would tell, it was not to be so and the business changed so much during the latter days of the war that it would never again build a light aircraft. The Cygnet was forgotten. As for G-AFVR, it was impressed as HL539, survived the war, was returned to the Civil Register and ended its flying career on August 26th 1969 in a fatal crash at Wœrth, Alsace, Northern France.

Headquartered in new offices in Brettenham House off the Strand, the mandate of the newly-established Board was to take over and properly organise the airworthiness aspects of all civil machines from airliners down to the smallest ultra-light. Its duties covered details of design, construction, and inspection. It also ensured that only 'approved' materials were used in construction, repair and maintenance. The actual processes of manufacturing, materials, and the certification of component parts remained the job of the AID or Aircraft Inspection Department (itself founded in 1925), and final airworthiness certification, meaning the issue of the authority of fly, remained with the Air Ministry.

Ultimately the ARB would take on the enormous responsibilities of certifying civil aircraft for their annual Certificates of Airworthiness, in particular the airworthiness of those commercial aircraft used for airline operations and for which the demands were far more exacting than those for military machines.

In post-war Britain, the position of the ARB was ratified with some up-datings to its terms of office. These were to allow for the developments in aviation during the war years and for the fact that commercial aircraft were now rather different from those around when first the body was formed.

One specific aspect of the ARB's 'tidied-up' mandate was, perhaps unwittingly, to prove an obstacle – initially considered to be insurmountable – to any possible hope of return to the pre-war Permit to Fly system, let alone permit amateur aircraft construction. This was the statement that, save in exceptional circumstances, no civil aircraft would be allowed to fly unless it had a valid Certificate of Airworthiness. It was also stipulated that any aircraft, if it had been manufactured in this country, must have been designed and built in accordance with the British Civil Airworthiness Requirements by constructors approved by the Air Registration Board.

This criterion, clearly aimed at commercial aircraft and despite being non-conducive to popular flying, was assumed by all in authority to embrace all types of aircraft. Nobody from the Minister downwards (including the ARB) interpreted it in any other way. Its restraints were to be felt throughout private flying for many years to come.

An immediate effect was to permanently ground (meaning potentially destroy) all aircraft of pre-war origin, whether airworthy or otherwise, that

Even as late as the closing years of the 1940s there remained a strong feeling of frustration within some people as to why private flying was taking so long to return to the 1930s level. The truth was that as a nation we were bankrupt, there was no money to make aircraft any more and the machines upon which so many real hopes were pinned in 1939 had been rendered not merely obsolescent by the wartime flying interregnum, but quite obsolete. Things had moved on and the great light plane builders of the 'thirties had ratcheted up their sights to military and commercial targets – far and away beyond the club and private owner. The example of GAL's Cygnet is a good case in point. Displayed at air shows around Europe in 1939 – here G-AFVR is seen at the Brussels Exhibition – it was ready and waiting to go into production. Jigs and tools were in place. And after five years of war effort, they were not. It was as simple as that.

We still had a number of good pre-war machines such as this Miles Mk.2W Hawk Trainer, G-ADWT. One of the few M2 Series to survive, this was pleasingly fast and took part in the re-started National Air Races. It is pictured here at Whitchurch Aerodrome, Bristol, on June 11th 1955. Soon, though, aircraft like this would be seen as commodities with which to earn valuable hard currency. In 1964, we sold it to the Canadians as CF-NXT.

The re-starting of events such as the King's Cup Race brought a degree of sanity into an increasingly moribund aviation sector. Here at the 1949 event we see Hawker Hart G-ABMR piloted by Hawker test pilot George Bullen above the low-flying Miles Gemini, G-AKKB, of Fred Dunkerley. Both these aircraft are still airworthy at time of writing.

LIGHT AVIATION: AN UPHILL STRUGGLE

The first 'new design' based on original thinking rather than the civilian development of a military light plane was Richard C Christoforides' compact little Ace cabin four seater. This had rather a head start in 1946 in that construction actually began well before the end of the war at the Chrislea factory in London's Mornington Crescent. Here it is seen at Heston Aerodrome (the famous gas-holder can be seen beneath the starboard wing) for a publicity photo. Designed for the 90 hp American flat-four Franklin engine, Christophorides quickly changed this in favour of the up-coming 100 hp Monaco but as this faltered he installed a 125 hp Lycoming as seen here.

Company test pilot Rex Stedman stands in front of the prototype Chrislea Ace prior to the first flight, The small single fin and rudder assembly proved to be the aircraft's weak link and Stedman found that after take-off, the large glazed cabin created so much slipstream disturbance behind the aircraft that the rudder was ineffective. After a long outward flight in more or less a straight line, Stedman managed to get G-AHLG to turn by using just aileron drag. It was a long circuit, especially with the unconventional controls.

Close-up of the prototype Chrislea Ace showing the highly original control system. It was also unconventional in that there was no foot-operated rudder bar, all three axis movements being obtained by pushing, pulling, turning and bending the control wheel in various directions. A major fault was that there was no 'self-centring' feature so that you did not know where the level/straight flight position might be. The author was one of the many club pilots invited to try out the Ace. One was thankful that Rex Stedman was sitting on the right-hand cushion! Note also the sideways-hinged top engine cowling.

could not produce a valid set of documents. After five and more years of war, even aircraft that had been carefully stored did not always still have their original logbooks, old C of A, Certificate of Registration and so on preserved intact with them. This period, the true 'dark age' of private flying, cast shadows of Cromwellian proportions on the movement and created the unshakeable belief that it was the correct paperwork that made an aircraft fly – nothing else really mattered so long as the right documents were presented. I wrote in 1955: 'Only when the weight of paperwork matches the bulk of the aircraft at maximum authorised take-off weight will the Ministry so much as consider allowing you to fly!'

It was clear that in the six years since last private flying had been possible, aviation had advanced enormously and along with it the ruling legislation. The whole process had moved up a gear, creating a widening gap at the bottom in which restricted space private flying floundered. Beneath that was the place where once home-built aircraft had been allowed. Now a sea of official demands such as approved workshops, bonded materials stores, material release notes, inspectors and their certificates, white coats, rubber stamps and filing systems full of paperwork obliterated the enthusiast's old work-bench at the bottom of the aviation tree. He had been driven off and, in the minds of many still mindful of the saga of the Flying Flea, good riddance!

At this point I would like to summarise the events that concerned civil aviation over the next 30 years to avoid continually having to return to the subject. During the Second World War, planning for the re-starting of civil aviation was put on the back burner but was not abandoned altogether. One of the decisions taken was that the Air Ministry should no longer have to become involved with civilian matters and so, in October 1944, the Ministry of Civil Aviation was established under Viscount Swinton as the first minister. It was more an offshoot of the wartime Ministry of Aircraft Production than the Air Ministry.[1]

Swinton was succeeded on August 5th 1945 by Lord Winster and the following April Air Vice-Marshal Sir Conrad Collier was appointed to head a new technical division of the MCA. Meanwhile Ministers came and went with alarming

---

1. The Ministry of Aircraft Production was formed in May 1940 under the auspices of Lord Beaverbrook. It was dissolved on April 1st 1946 and its functions transferred to the Ministry of Supply. Beaverbrook was probably better known as newspaper baron William Maxwell Aitken (1879-1964).

alacrity: Lord Nathan (1946-1948), Lord Pakenham (1948-1951), and Lord Ogmore (for a few months in 1951). That October saw the appointment of yet another new Minister – the Hon John Scott Maclay. His tenure was equally short-lived and he resigned due to illness the following May to be replaced by the Rt Hon Alan T Lennox-Boyd. Both of these gentlemen also doubled their duties with those of Minister of Transport.

All went well until February 1953 when Prime Minister Winston Churchill announced that he proposed later that year to amalgamate the Ministry of Transport and the Ministry of Civil Aviation to create the twin-headed monster, the Ministry of Transport & Civil Aviation (MTCA). Lennox-Boyd was replaced in July 1954 by John Archibald Boyd-Carpenter who held office until he was replaced by Harold Watkinson in December 1955. The game of musical chairs, Westminster style, fostered wry grins throughout the aviation world while, in irreverent circles, the MTCA was referred to as the Ministry for Buses and Planes.

This augured badly for any attempt at minister-lobbying for as soon as some progress seemed to be made with one chappie, his rapid departure and replacement inevitably meant returning to the beginning again. Private flying only just survived in this era of the two-step – one forward and one (or two) back again.

But government had not yet finished with the business of changing the names of ministries and by the end of 1959 it was again plain and simple Ministry of Aviation and the man running with the title of Minister of Aviation was Duncan Sandys. By the start of 1966 we had our thirteenth Minister – Fred Mulley. The fluidity of our political thinking on matters aeronautical soon dispensed altogether with any ministry carrying in its title so much as a hint of things aeronautical and, in a brisk wind of change, by 1968 it had become the Department of Trade & Industry and the Minister himself had the impressive handle of 'Minister for Aerospace'. This quickly became the Ministry of Technology with an overall Minister in the form of the Rt Hon Anthony Wedgewood Benn, later to re-market himself as plain de-porcelainised Tony Benn. Analogies about level playing-fields and moving goal-posts could not mask the reality that nobody really knew what was going on while overall the feeling was that nobody really cared.

Across the years there had appeared an almost wilful approach to the appointment of Ministers of Civil Aviation. Despite holding high office, their actual influence was minimal. The only one who tried hard and showed some promise was Lord Nathan, but even he was unable to move the Whitehall mountain. By the end of 1948, the brief period since the war's end had seen two ministers come and go and behind them leave absolutely nothing of consequence. Then came Lord Pakenham.

While accepted as a non-flying man, for great administrators do not necessarily have to be great exponents of the practices they preach, it would not have been a bad idea had Pakenham at least been air-minded. This he was most certainly not and his administration proved as anodyne as most that had gone before. His level of complete ignorance on his subject was such that it earned him droll plaudits for consistency. Pakenham's appointment underscored the words of ancient Vitruvius who proclaimed that 'neither talent without instruction, nor instruction without talent, can produce the perfect craftsman'. Yet this, remember, was the crucial time in which private flying was trying to re-establish itself. We needed talent and leadership, not a parade of hereditary peers.

And still we had no new engines.

Meanwhile Australia and New Zealand had their Civil Aviation Authority (CAA) and America had its Federal Aviation Administration (FAA). It could not, surely, be long before Britain followed with a similar-acronymed title. But it was. In fact we had to wait a whole quarter-century before we got rid of government ministries and their morass of paperwork, pedantry and procrastination. It wasn't until Saturday April 1st of 1972 that the formation of the Civil Aviation Authority was announced. Ignoring the significance of the date and demonstrating commendable lack of originality, this new body proclaimed that – just in case we hadn't yet sussed it out – it would be known as the CAA for short. Some feared that the new body was merely a fresh ministry in disguise and that we were leaping from the frying-pan straight into the fire. 'It's only Coats An' 'Ats!' proclaimed cynics with a sigh who remembered the old London department store called C & A that first inspired the 'clean' version of this ancient quip. The birth of the CAA, though, took place outside the period covered by this study and hence an evaluation is irrelevant here.

Just about the first thing to emerge when private flying was officially resumed after the war was a new series of Notices to Airmen, those small sheets of paper, some single, others stapled into sections of four, eight or, rarely, more pages, produced at what seemed to be ever-increasing frequency by the

Air shows in the decades following the end of the war were rich in old pre-war designs. This DH.87b Hornet Moth designed in 1934 was one of two brought over from Canada and impressed during the war years, this one as P6785. Originally CF-BFN, when it emerged in peaceful skies once more, it was restored and registered on February 6th 1946 as G-AHBL. It is seen here on an open day at Hatfield on a cold June 26th 1946. Built in 1936, it still flies today.

Ministry of Civil Aviation with the intention of making sure that private flyers knew what they could and could not do. Usually two or three would drop through the licensed pilot's letterbox every week, notifying of restricted and prohibited flying areas, firing ranges, other changes to maps, and suchlike. Even before the January 1st 1946 lifting of restrictions, these Notices began to flutter through the letter-boxes of all licensed pilots. In the closing days of December 1945, some 25 of these ubiquitous pieces of paper were issued. All were posted out in individual wrappers at great expense: most were deemed irrelevant to particular users and were consigned to the dust bin ('garbage' had still to be invented together with its can).

Poulsen in *Flight*, a shrewd man who understood that the true purpose of a memo was not to inform the third party so much as to protect the sender, was moved to write (on January 3rd 1946):

> Necessary though it is to formulate rules and regulations to cover the movements of individual aircraft, we cannot help feeling that the new series of directions designed to this end are primarily the result of a desire to 'pass the buck' rather than to clear the air.

By November 1948, 381 of these Notices had been mailed to every licensed pilot in the land – roughly 1.59 for each working day. The majority dealt with revisions to the times of working of various control and radio services. There was a growing feeling that these were something to do with keeping civil servants busy at the expense of the taxpayer. Few seemed relevant to the actual business of private flying.

At the same time, the ARB announced the issue of eleven additional sub-sections to British Civil Airworthiness Requirements. The full set of BCA Requirements and amendments could be bought for two guineas (£2. 2s. 0d) or half that price if you were a licensed ground engineer.

In general, the conditions were very similar to those applying before the war. However, there were only 25 airfields that had been officially allocated for the use of civil aircraft. Twenty-one radio stations were also to be available, listed as having Standard Beam Approach facilities.

Little of this was of concern to the flying club member and the private flyer to whom a 'standard beam approach' was a merely a welcome hand-rail or bannister after one too many in the saloon bar.

The end of the war in Europe was celebrated on May 8th 1945, and the

Air-racing, a tremendous pre-war attraction, never regained its immense public appeal after the war. This was partly because people were more accustomed to aircraft plus the fact that machines were faster and covered greater distances. In short, for those who attended an air race, the time between visible thrills (the start, lapping and the finish) was too long. Organisers countered by holding races in conjunction with air displays but the fact remained that while racing remained ever popular with its participants, the excitement of it as a spectator sport had dwindled. For the 1949 King's Cup one of the entrants was Miles Hawk Trainer G-AIUA, formerly Magister T9769. It was entered by R H Young and flown by the legendary Cyril Albert Nepean Bishop, seen here standing with his mount. A formidable figure in civil and light aviation in the 1930s and 1940s, 'Bish' became the first CFI of the famous Tiger Club founded at Croydon in the 1950s by Norman Jones of Rollason fame. He was also a prime mover in the Seaplane Club at Lee on Solent. His death at the beginning of 1968 at the age of just 67 robbed us of a great man who had been a passionate devotee of practical light flying since 1939.

world marked the end of the war against Japan on August 15th. In anticipation of the word of command, just before Christmas the first two Auster three seaters came off Taylorcraft's peacetime production line at Rearsby and were handed over to their respective purchasers – a brace of businessmen, one each from Birmingham and Nottingham. The Nottingham chap was a Mr T W Shipside of Tollerton who, with his wife and 17-year-old son Kenneth, claimed to be the first English family to use their light aircraft like a 'family car'. In March 1946, *Flight* published a photograph showing the family pulling G-AGTO out of its home-made hangar on a private landing strip next to their home.

This splendid news concealed the hidden problems of operating a light aeroplane. Taylorcraft's chief test pilot was Geoffrey Edwards and at the end of 1945 he made a sales trip to Denmark in a civilian Auster III series J/1. The flight from Rearsby took in Manston, The Hague, Oldenburg, Lubeck and Copenhagen. The 1,600 mile trip used 84 gallons of fuel which, flying at 100 mph, gave a fuel consumption of 19 miles to the gallon. The Cirrus engine, which had more than 250 hours in its logbook at the start of the flight, used no oil. Flying at a constant payload of 600 lb, the entire trip (apart from personal expenses) cost rather less than £10. The average price of petrol then was a little over 2s per gallon.

Although business owners of light aircraft were promised 'special consideration' from the fuel-rationing authorities, the sobering fact was that this particular pleasant little jolly would, for the private owner, be quite out of the question since it would have involved the use of nearly *four months* of fuel entitlement. At this time, a family saloon car (the latest was the Austin A40) cost £325 plus £91.0s.6d Purchase Tax, road tax was £1, a pint of beer 1s.5d and a top newspaper 2d while a six-bedroomed house in Wimbledon could be bought freehold for £7,250.

The first civil flying fuel allocation announced on January 1st 1946 was 60 hours for charter and taxi aircraft, 50 for flying clubs and, for the poor private pilot and private owner, just four hours a month.

The government relented – slightly – by August 1946. Charter and club-flying benefited to the equivalent of 75 and 60 hours' flying per month respectively while the private owner could now obtain fuel for six hours of flying per month. While this represented by far the biggest percentage increase in the allowances, and was thus better than before, it remained nowhere near what keen flyers wanted. Car owners, incidentally, were still heavily restricted and the flyer was probably actually better off when it came to miles that could be travelled.

Taylorcraft Aeroplanes Ltd had changed its name to Auster Aircraft Ltd on March 7th 1946 yet it was not the first light aircraft manufacturer to offer a post-war civil aircraft. That distinction fell to Chrislea Aircraft. When war broke out, General Aircraft Ltd at Hanworth had just begun production of the Cygnet and for a long time after hostilities had begun the company continued to advertise the aircraft almost as if the war was a mere temporary inconvenience. Chrislea followed a somewhat similar approach, actually beginning work on its four seat Ace unofficially (and, technically, illegally) during the war. VE Day (May 8th 1945) was a full six months away when Chrislea first began to advertise its private aeroplane in the trade press. The only possible clue to the fact that this was merely a demonstration of hope was the legend '£475 approx ex-works'.

The first private flying school or club to re-open on January 1st 1946 was Cambridge which also happened to be one of only six places in the British Isles where 73 and 83 octane fuel could be obtained. Marshalls Flying School made a tentative start using one Tiger Moth for training and a Falcon Major for other purposes. The rate for tuition was £5.10s/- per hour. By early spring, the Wiltshire School of Flying & Club, founded in 1931, had restarted at their High Post base. Two of the former pre-war organisers were back in charge – Sqdn-Ldrs James Edward Doran-Webb and M F Ogilvie-Forbes. The club used Taylorcraft Austers for which they charged £3 per hour either solo or dual: by 1948 they had eight Austers of various models, five Magisters and a Proctor. Marshall's continued to expand and by October had begun a training scheme for the first 'B' Licence technical course.

Brooklands, held by many to be the cradle of private flying, had its fate sealed on January 7th when a general meeting of the company that owned it, Brooklands (Weybridge) Ltd, agreed to the sale of the whole site to Vickers-Armstrong Ltd. This meant that there could be no return to motor-racing and, as it turned out, nor was there to be a return to civil – meaning private – flying, at least not on a regular basis.

April 1st saw the re-starting of two important flying clubs. The first was the RAF Flying Club based at Panshanger, membership being open to past and present members of the three Services as well as the RAFVR, AAF and Dominion Air Forces. Annual subscription was £5 and an associate membership was available for £2.10/-. The minimum flying qualifications in all cases was 250 hours as first pilot, so this was not a novices' training outfit, rather a club for officers and gentleman. The other opening was that of a real training club – Luton which formed the first of a proposed group of Hunting Flying Clubs Ltd. Well-placed for London, Luton had been developed during the war and now had a hard runway as well as the normal grass strips.

Other flying clubs followed during that summer – Wolverhampton, Portsmouth, Weston, County Flying Club, Leicestershire, Yorkshire, Strathtay, Border, Wiltshire, Derby, Airwork, and Oxford were among those that were kick-started back into life. By June there were 18 clubs in active operation with more being formed. Despite the Ministry's refusal to offer any form of subsidy, the club scene had returned and the average flying charges were between £3 to £4 per hour.

A novel form of club was formed at the former Aldenham Aerodrome near Elstree that spring. This was the United Services Flying Club open to all ex-Service personnel regardless of rank or Service. The CFI was a former Naval commander, John Temple-West (nick-named 'Twist'), who had been in charge of a flight of Barracudas. Now chief pilot to Elstree-based London Aero & Motor Services

Owned by the Marquess of Londonderry, Newtownards, Northern Ireland, this Miles M.38 Messenger 2A, G-AJFH, was first registered on May 8th 1947. Here it is pictured at Elstree Aerodrome in the summer of 1949. This model is recognised by its 'tear-drop'-shaped rear cockpit windows. The hangar visible behind the open cabin doors is that used by the Watford-based Monaco Engine Company, then engaged in running its new flat-four aircraft motor on an outside test-bed facility.

So successful was the Miles Messenger seen in the previous picture that the wing was used, with very little modification, in the twin-engined Miles Gemini. The last step in the development which began with the Miles Falcon and progressed through Mercury to Messenger, the Gemini first flew at Woodley on October 26th 1945. This particular example, G-AILK, was later sold to Australia as VH-BJZ and its ferry flight at the hands of Grp-Capt Alan Francis 'Bush' Bandidt (1912-1969) on February 7th 1947, marked the first solo long distance flight after the war ended.

(owners of the club, in fact) he doubled as an instructor on Auster Autocrats and a Percival Proctor. Assistant secretary of the club, and also doubling as aerodrome manager, was former Royal Tank Regiment officer 'Jock' Renton.

With its mixture of newly-civilianised and largely wild personalities, the USFC was something of a happy-go-lucky club which, inevitably, could not be sustained indefinitely. Frequent infringements of rules regarding low-flying, reckless aviating and suchlike were just one reason behind the transformation of the old into the new as Elstree Flying Club – but it was to be a long time before the last of the lunatic fringe of frustrated former wartime flyers sobered up.

In this regard, Elstree was little different from a few other clubs across the land. Post-war private flying was, for many, a release of tension in a manner that only those that had been through the war years could understand.

Teaching people to fly was the mainstay of these establishments and was the manner in which they earned most of their money. There was, accordingly, some sense of shock when, in August 1948, the Hampshire Aeroplane Club announced it would teach you to fly for just £30 provided the cash was paid in advance. For this, the pupil got full membership of the club for a year and took lessons, each of around 30 minutes a go, until after five hours in total the CFI made an assessment of the pupil's ability. Those that failed would have £15 refunded to them. Since the average pupil was said to take between 10 and 15 hours to qualify and the maximum number of hours to be given under the scheme was 15, it was a bold move. Any pupil who had not qualified at the end of that time had to continue at normal club rates. The scheme worked on the principle that people would not necessarily fly seven days a week, that English weather would prolong the process, that there would be very good pupils and drop-outs – and meanwhile the full capital could be invested. It would not work if overheads and tax on fuel rose, nor if the pupil completed his course in double-quick time.

There was, of course, a catch: 'teaching to fly' was not quite the same as 'qualifying for a pilots' licence'!

But back to 1946 and pilots from times past knew that things were getting at least partially back to normal when, on January 7th, Airmet restarted. Airmet was the dedicated wireless station for flyers and broadcast weather 'actuals' and forecasts. The Air Ministry Meteorological Station at Borough Hill had begun its transmissions in the 1930s but it was now under the control of the Air Ministry Continuous Forecasting Station at Dunstable. This invaluable service operated seven days a week on 245 KC/S (1,224 metres) from 07.00 hrs to 18.00 hrs GMT during the winter, and 06.00 hrs to 21.00 hrs GMT in the summer.

The restoring of the Deauville Rally on France's northern coast put back onto the Royal Aero Club's calendar once of the most popular of inter-war events. The first post-war Rally took place on the weekend of July 13th-15th 1946 and was attended by a number of British pilots, mostly in their own machines, some in club aircraft, but all with light hearts. Old lags found the atmosphere and certainly the airfield greatly changed while others accepted it as the first opportunity they had had to fly a light plane across the Channel since before the war. And without fear of being shot at! The beaches of Northern France bore still the dreadful scars of the too-recent conflict and the old and friendly town had yet to recover its full dignity having been horribly damaged. It was, though, France and it was a first move towards normality. And the French, as ever, were great hosts despite their austerity and food shortages which made even ours pale into insignificance. Tea and coffee were hugely expensive and almost impossible to find but when it was available, they willingly shared it. France and Britain were very close.

A month later, Britain's first post-war air races were staged at Lympne on the South Coast. Heats and the finals for the Siddeley Trophy and the Folkestone Trophy plus the High Speed Handicap were flown on August 31st and September 1st by an assortment of aircraft predominantly pre-war in origin but including Percival Proctors (wartime military-specification pre-war Vega Gull developments), a Vickers Viking airliner and a de Havilland Dove not to mention a Hornet (the Mosquito variant, as distinct from the Moth type) and a Vampire jet. The winner was, to the delight of everybody except the handicappers, a lumbering Vickers-Supermarine Walrus biplane amphibian! No King's Cup Race, though. The last (the 17th) had taken place at Hatfield on July 21st 1938 and the event would not restart until 1949 when, on July 30th, it was run at Elmdon.

At the end of August 1939 there had been 69 licensed aerodromes across the country plus approximately 50 others that were for private use. It was recalled that at the annual meeting of the Aerodrome Owners' Association in February of 1940, president Lord Londonderry had urged members to look after their airfields and keep them ready for a return to peacetime use. He referred also to something that Lord Mottistone had said some years previous when he urged that there should be a network of aerodromes across the country never more than 25 miles apart. The war years sired many, many new

George Miles designed the M.57 Aerovan in 1944 for the short-haul transport of bulky loads. Powered by two Cirrus Major Mk.3 engines each of 155 hp, the all-wood Aerovan could carry a ton of freight, eight passengers or a family-sized car. In the hands of Tommy Rose it made its first flight at Woodley on January 26th 1945 under the markings U-0248. Subsequently bearing the civil registration G-AGOZ it flew at all the early post-war air shows demonstrating its short take-off and landing capabilities and that October it flew to Switzerland with 5,000 ball-point pens, Miles having secured the licence-manufacture of the Biro pen from its inventor, the Hungarian newspaper editor Lásló Bíró. Later models of the Aerovan had a slightly longer fuselage, circular windows and plain, unbalanced outer rudders.

airfields and many, particularly in East Anglia, were far, far closer together than that arbitrary 25 miles.

A significant development occurred on October 30th 1946 with the formation of a business called British Gliding Association Ltd. A company limited by guarantee and thus with no share capital, it was formed with 100 members each of whom carried liability up to the value of £1. Its directors were glider pilots Dudley George Oliver Hiscox and John William Sutton Pringle, the noted zoologist. The BGA as it became known would become a powerful and early force for the interests of private flying.

Besides the private pilots who formed the kernel of the membership of the Royal Aero Club (and could afford its membership fees), there was a small but increasingly vociferous body of impecunious enthusiasts possessed of little spare money but abundant enthusiasm. Some were ex-RAF men, a few were aged zealots from the 1930s, a few were students with grand ideas, others were frustrated designers and engineers that believed in the freedom of the air and the duplicity of the family garage.

A handful of like-minded people met in a flat in south-west London early in 1946. Most had been in communication with each other by telephone, correspondence or face-to-face meeting. Two gets-together were held to discuss mutual interests and to define what would be needed to bring back the sort of amateur aviation that existed in the 1930s. The upshot was the distribution to a circle of other enthusiasts an invitation to attend an informal meeting in London that April. The outcome was the creation of the Ultra Light Aircraft Association, a body that was to have a far-reaching impact on private flying.

The ULAA began to grow rapidly, attracting many that felt, prematurely as it turned out, that here was a body that would make amateur flying at low cost a reality. Five years later, when it changed its name to the Popular Flying Association, it was well on the way to becoming an organisation far and away larger and more powerful than the Royal Aero Club. To begin with, though, it was like many neophytes, rich in enthusiasm and somewhat sparse on achievement.

Indeed the ULAA ran a dire risk of steeple-chasing before it could crawl and that November secretary Maurice Imray wrote to *Flight* castigating the misplaced enthusiasm of other correspondents. He lamented what he described as a 'curious fact' that nobody wanted to talk organisation. 'It appears they would rather talk on design... than try to get down to the admittedly hard and unspectacular business of founding an organisation. It is only through an organised association that the amateur designers', constructors' and pilots' efforts can be co-ordinated and brought to full fruition... A well-organised and efficient movement will be in a far better position to approach the Ministry of Civil Aviation on such matters as C of A and "permits to fly" etc, than any single individual, however enthusiastic he or she may be'.

Imray was, of course, right, especially since the ULAA was sizing up to the paper-ridden, organisationally-rich world of government ministerial ministries. The path to our success indeed lay through many hours of mundane business management by a few of us that had the time and the energy to devote to the good of the whole. Rather than the exciting stuff of building aeroplanes this usually meant digging deep into our own pockets to pay for printing stationery, envelopes and postage! My own actual subscription was not paid as such for a year, but I owned the office duplicator!

When it staged its first Annual General Meeting at the Royal Aero Club Aviation Centre established at Lord Londonderry's palatial London home in Park Lane, more than 50 members attended out of the total strength of 200. The formal meeting disclosed several gems of information that members eagerly received. First was that a 'considerable' stock (39 to be exact) of

The majority of pre-war small and low-powered aircraft remained in limbo during 1939-45 and were deemed unsuitable for Impressment. Some, like the Peterborough-built Aeronca 100 G-AEVT, were squirrelled away 'for the duration'. This one was found with the legends 'Clitheroe and District Air Training Corps' painted on its sides. Acquired by Paul Simpson it was restored in the rural seclusion of a Pinner Hill back garden. The original wings were beyond repair and were replaced by those of G-AEVE, built as an Aeronca 300. This latter aircraft had been 'loaned' to the Peterborough Flying Club and, on the outbreak of war, appears to have been 'commandeered' by somebody with the power (and nerve) at RAF Warton in Lancashire. Painted in camouflage and provided with roundels, it carried no RAF markings. It thus continued to fly at intervals during the war as a private runabout but in 1947 was dismantled and stored against a hedge where, in September 1949, its wings were liberated and, although badly deteriorated after two years leading-edge down in the grass, restored to incorporate in the Pinner Hill '100'.

Completion of a long-term restoration in 1949 finds owner Paul Simpson standing with justifiable pride next to G-AEVT at Elstree awaiting its first flight for more than a decade. Unfortunately this machine was damaged beyond repair in an accident at Loughborough College Aerodrome on July 11th 1950, when it was caught in a line squall immediately after take-off.

pre-war Aeronca JAP engines had been found and, thanks to the generosity of Lord Kemsley, a loan had been secured so that these motors could be acquired for sale to members at between £50 and £70 apiece. Second was the news that Ernest Oscar Tips, who ran Fairey's Belgian operation and was also renowned for the Tipsy aircraft, had a new single seater design on the board and that he hoped to offer plans for amateur constructors.

The event ended on an upbeat note as members voted unanimously on two resolutions, first that a telegram be sent to Lord Kemsley thanking him for his support, and a second wire, this addressed to the Minister of Civil Aviation (Lord Nathan), requesting an early re-introduction of Permits to Fly.

It was an anomalous situation that a small number of pre-war ultra-lights existed but there was no mechanisms in place whereby they might be flown. With this regime, there was obviously very little hope for any new generation of home-builder. Whether he built to a pre-war design or one of Mr Tips' promised single seaters, he would never be allowed to fly his handiwork no matter how many times it was inspected by licensed engineers and signed out as airworthy.

In short, the owner of an ultra-light, or the person who wanted to build his own aeroplane, remained excluded from post-war aviation through exactly the same loophole that prevented pre-war-built Permit to Fly aircraft from ever taking to the skies again.

The ULAA lobbied intensively on behalf of those few that owned existing ultra-light machines that had operated on a pre-war Permit to Fly. More feculent than fecund, the Ministry of Civil Aviation's attitude to this upstart group of weirdos appeared to be that if ignored they would go away. And time would establish that negotiations with the Ministry were only consistent in their total lack of progress.

In the belief that 'the usual channels' of communication were regularly flushed, members of the ULAA Committee resorted to less conventional tactics ranging from reasoning to pleading and finally to subterfuge. In August 1947 Lord Nathan's department was virtually forced to relent, having no doubt recognising that the continual presence of the ULAA and its persistent pleas combined to interfere with the Ministry's other, more important activities.

Permits to Fly were now authorised for all existing ultra-light aircraft which had already flown successfully. The

Although slow-selling when new (the Hanworth distributors Aircraft Exchange & Mart Ltd held a large stock of unsold aircraft which is why the Peterborough factory was forced into bankruptcy before the war), a good number of Aeronca 100 machines survived the war. One was G-AEXD seen here at Blackbushe in October 1969. Recently this took to the air again after a 40-year rebuild. British-made Aeroncas are distinguished by three immediately visible features – wooden fabric-covered ailerons, the rudder static mass balance and the J A Prestwich-built engine characterised by the cast rocker-box covers having an inverted 'U'-shaped bottom edge cut-out to access the lower spark-plug.

Auction sales of ex-RAF aircraft continued for some years after the end of the Second World War. It was not always possible to inspect the aircraft you wanted to bid on before the sale and even when you could look over it, these inspections had to be brief and superficial. Sometimes one had to bid 'sight unseen' which is why some prices were quite ridiculously low. Elstree Flying Club, newly formed from the United Services Flying Club, paid £25 each for half a dozen Miles M.14A Hawk Trainers. Only one was actually good enough to be converted to civil standards. Here we see G-ALNX (L8211) and G-ALNY (L8075) arriving at Elstree on September 6th 1950. They were in poor condition and the first was broken up for spares/scrap in October 1952. The second lasted until Bonfire Night – November 5th – 1953. It was not the first time that a flying club celebration would comprise dancing and chanting around an aeronautically-inspired cremation.

reintroduced document was based on the pre-war formula whereby the owner of an ultra-light aircraft need not submit to aircraft to the ordinary routine associated with the obtaining of a Certificate of Airworthiness, but to a simpler form of inspection. The intention behind its relenting, said the Ministry, was to reduce cost by cutting out AID inspection routine.

Restriction on operation was as before: no aerobatics were permitted in a Permit aircraft, nor was it allowed to be flown in visibility of less than three miles or over thickly-populated areas. In short, the pilot could risk his own neck but not those of other people.

The return to the old Permit system was not without strings. The enthusiast could not yet shout 'Hurrah' from the rooftops. It all hung on the interpretation of 'pre-war' and 'restoring'. 'Pre-war' flying had to be corroborated by the original paperwork including the old Permit and logbooks – not always as easy a task as it sounds since the trials and tribulations of war had contributed to paperwork losses. And 'restoration' was specified as being no more than twenty per cent of the airframe and engine. Building a new wing, for example, immediately took one beyond the definition of 'restoration' and officially prohibited any approval or certification of any kind. What today would be a full restoration was then quite out of the question. 'Restoration' meant cleaning, fresh air in the tyres and re-setting the plug-gaps on a pre-war motor.

The form of legislative wording not so much encouraged falsification of fact but more it forced the owner of an old aircraft into all manner of lies and deceit if he was ever to fly it again. Confronted by this sort of dilemma, morals invariably went by the board.

Getting Permits back on the agenda had been one of the ULAA's primary aims. The committee breathed a sigh of relief – and moved on to confront its next challenge – what about those members that wanted to build a new aircraft from scratch or fly a pre-war-built example with a different engine? It was, for example, pointless to build a 1930s design and then try to fly it with a 1930s converted motorcycle engine simply because it had been tried before. We had been told that there was a good supply of Aeronca engines which were airworthy and reliable so it would make sense to build an aeroplane and fit one of these to it. Or wouldn't it? As would emerge over the long years that followed, taking a pre-war approved design of airframe and fitting a pre-war approved brand of engine to it only worked if that combination had been certified in pre-war times.

An example of the sheer bloody-mindedness of the Ministry of Civil Aviation and, to some extent, the Air Registration Board, concerned the famous BAC Drone, G-ADPJ, belonging to Mr A C Waterhouse of Desford. Waterhouse's Drone became something of a *cause célèbre* in 1950. If the owner was driven to unwise language and tactics, then it was understandable. The gist of his gripe with Authority was contained in his famous letter to *The Aeroplane* of June 16th that year and published under the title 'Adding Unairworthiness'. Here is an extract:

> We people who are interested in the sport of flying ultra-light aircraft are completely ensnared in the web of officialdom.
>
> I have rebuilt a BAC Drone and spent 2,000 man-hours making it serviceable – all to no avail. During reconstruction an independent person inspected the work, but unfortunately I improved the design by fitting a better engine than the original converted motorcycle engine that was fitted.
>
> I fitted a Bristol Cherub Mk. III, an engine of repute, noted for its smoothness and reliability, also an Air Ministry type tested engine. Unfortunately this has jeopardized my chances of getting a Permit to Fly.
>
> Negotiations have been going on with MCA since November, 1948, and it is now June, 1950, and I am still officially earth-bound.

> MCA's explanation for turning down the permit is that the fuselage has been rebuilt and fitted with a different type of engine – which change they consider to be fundamental, in spite of saying this they have just granted a permit to the Airways Club Heath Parasol, which has been completely rebuilt and fitted with a JAP engine – an engine with which no Heath Parasol has ever been known to be fitted. Surely this is inconsistent of them?
>
> It appears that the Ministry's left hand does not know what its right hand is doing. ARB must think that people who fly ultra-lights of ancient design are suicidal maniacs and must be kept on the ground at all costs.
>
> The ULAA have ARB approved design and inspection teams... I would suggest that MCA should ask them for their technical recommendation on such aircraft as mine, instead of the ARB, who are obviously not interested and know very little about them. The men forming these teams must have been selected because of their ability and knowledge of ultra-light types.
>
> Why not let the ULAA look after the small aeroplane in the same way as the BGA is looking after the gliders, and once again let us fly.
>
> The past record of the ultra-light aircraft was one of safety and will be again if the Ministry will, give us a bit of air space in which to prove it.[2]

In a case that concerned the author, an aircraft certified in 1938 with a heavy and unreliable converted motorcycle engine that had caused the machine to crash in 1939 would have to be re-installed if the aircraft was to be allowed to fly with a Permit to Fly. By fitting a brand new reliable Aeronca engine a non-approved combination would be created meaning that no Permit to Fly could ever be issued! The battle was long, hard and, inevitably, involved measures not wholly reputable until the authorities relented and put the responsibilities for certification where they belonged – with the newly-named Popular Flying Association.

The private and club scene in 1946 faced an unenviable challenge. The existing supply of pre-war light aircraft could not in all reason be expected to remain as front-line machines for all time and nor could one rely on the dubious economics of restoring (meaning getting Certificates of Airworthiness) for the few ex-Service light aircraft that the Ministry might grudgingly part with. A plan for the future was needed.

Peter Masefield, one of a strong band of young men who had become light plane devotees before the war, took it upon

What is airworthiness? The uninitiated think that it is a state of aeronautical engineering whereby a machine is safe to fly. The reality is somewhat different since it concerns paperwork. Take the case of Bücker Bü.181 Bestmann, a virtually new machine liberated by the occupying forces at the end of the war and brought to Britain as 'spoils of war'. Quickly surplus to requirements, it was bought by an enthusiast, allocated a Civil registration and given a Permit to Fly to enable it to be flown from Farnborough's stock of captured German aircraft to Denham. It arrived there in due course and was picketed in the open behind the blister hangar to await clearance of its paperwork. The vital documentation failed to materialise and poor old 'KAX sat out in the open for almost three years, unloved and unable to fly because it did not have the correct piece of paper! From being an almost new and fully-airworthy machine to becoming a beyond (then) economic repair wreck did not take long and this lovely all-wood aircraft was broken up in 1950.

---

2. Waterhouse did eventually get his Drone flying with official approval – by which time he had already completed many hours of careful but safe unofficial test-flying. His aeroplane, finally officially airworthy, enjoyed but a short life: in a gale a heavy hangar door blew in and squashed it flat like a fly under a boot. Gallant Bert Waterhouse ultimately rebuilt his beloved aircraft. It is still an airworthy aircraft.

himself to find out what post-war private flying was likely to require as a mount. Minister of Civil Aviation Lord Nathan listened to the argument put forward by the tall and rather lanky bespectacled young man and finally agreed to support an investigation into the needs of private flying.

So came into being that autumn one of the more unusual of the committees ever to dissect matters aeronautical in Britain – the Informal Light Aeroplane Committee of which Masefield would be chairman under the rich handle of Director-General of Long-Term Projects & Planning.

Masefield gathered together an executive of leading figures in the club and private flying scene including the Royal Aero Club's Secretary-General, the dapper Colonel 'Mossie' Preston and his opposite number in the Association of British Aero Clubs with input from Whitney Straight and a few others. He promised Lord Nathan a report within three months (things were quicker then than later – or was it merely optimism?) and set about arranging an air display of British light aeroplanes.

It is an unwritten law of being British that only a lunatic would think of organising an air show in the wintertime. January, for example, is not renowned as a month popular with organisers of church fêtes and other outdoor events that involve walking around in fields of long grass. But it was January 18th that Masefield's ILAC selected for its presentation at Fairey's new aerodrome, White Waltham near Maidenhead.

The event must go down in history for being extraordinary in so many aspects, not the least of which was the unseasonably perfect sunny weather. The other remarkable feature was the number of aircraft that Masefield had been able to muster, three of them absolutely new. From close-by Heston emerged the prototype Chrislea Ace, newly flying with its twin tail. Down the road from Heston was Hanworth, home of General Aircraft Company and this firm had brought along one of its Cygnet II cabin monoplanes produced just as the war began. This example, G-AGAX, represented a breed of private machines for which the company held high expectations in 1939, but it never enjoyed the hoped-for post-war revival.

Auster Aircraft turned out not just one but two new aircraft, the Arrow and the J.4, as well as an Autocrat, while Miles Aircraft Ltd down the road at Woodley had no fewer than twelve of its machines in attendance including the unusual M.64 experimental low-wing tricycle-wheeled two seater. This attracted a great deal of attention on account of its large and spacious enclosed cockpit. Airspeed showed its new small airliner, the Consul (which was a hastily-civilianised military Oxford) and, from America, importers Helliwell of Walsall, Birmingham, showed a sleek streamlined tin monoplane called a Globe Swift. A tailwheel job, it featured the 'grinning-face' type of American car radiator grille,

Besides the Cygnet, other pre-war types included a 1938 single seat Tipsy with 18 hp engine alongside Fairey's latest Belgian-built Tipsy Belfair. A veteran from the outbreak of the war was the Austrian Hirtenberg HS.9A, G-AGAK (formerly with the pre-war German registration D-EDJH).

The display was a tremendous success especially when Lord Nathan turned out to give his blessing to the day. He took a great interest in everything and proved that of all the Ministers with civil aviation responsibilities he was the best. It wasn't entirely his fault that he was powerless to do much. He said he looked forward to Masefield's recommendations, but in truth there wasn't much Masefield could suggest at that time. The more powerful Straight Committee would report within a year, so perhaps by that time private flying would have sorted out its likely future needs.

It wasn't that easy, for many clubs had enough to do just with keeping going, never mind answering questions as to what they thought they might want.

Thurstan James wrote in his editorial in *The Aeroplane* for January 24th 1947:

> One does not have to investigate very far to realise that selection of the right design of aeroplane depends on the answers to a number of questions. Who are the people that want to fly themselves as pilots? Are they the young men and women of university age? Are they the thousands of men who flew as pilots during the War? Are they the middle-aged and comfortable placed as regards income? And [at] the other end of the scale, what about the ATC cadets who have been given what our French neighbours calls [sic] their baptism of air in gliders swiftly tobogganing down from the comparatively meagre height attained in a winch-launch?

It was the old problem of asking a dozen people what they wanted – and receiving a dozen different answers, each as direct and as viable as the others. Private aviation didn't really know what it wanted. In truth, it couldn't much care – so long as whatever it was flew well and was both cheap and available.

In fairness to Lord Nathan (*b.* 1889 as Harry Louis Nathan) and to his department, they played an important part in getting commercial aircraft operating again after the war. In that direction they proved thoughtful and helpful, co-operative and practical and without their concerted efforts, commercial flying would have suffered an even more uphill struggle in the post-war decades. The trouble was that Lord Nathan and his team believed that they existed to foster *commercial* aviation and to this extent a load of ordinary amateurs

Here is a historic Autogiro. Originally G-ACUI, this Avro 671 Rota or Cierva C.30A, was impressed as HM581 and spent some of its war years undertaking valuable radar calibration work. It was civilianised on June 11th 1946 being restored with parts from G-ACUU. Re-registered as G-AHTZ, this saw service with the Essex Club before being sold to Rota Towels Ltd. A rare sight in the post-war years, the Autogiro always attracted interest wherever it went. It met its end at Elmden on March 4th 1958, crashing and catching fire right in front of the then Lord Mayor of Birmingham at an air show.

playing around with small planes simply wasn't really their scene. Furthermore, in high places aviation was either military or commercial. Private flying, like masturbation and Morris dancing, was not something you discussed in polite circles while terms like 'Ultra-light' tended to be lumped together in the minds of Whitehall minions with 'models' which meant children's toys and therefore not real aeroplanes. A sad but true conclusion.

A grand scheme emerged during 1948 and it concerned a new light aeroplane built by Slingsby Sailplanes. This was the conversion of a Tutor two seat glider into a single seat light aeroplane by fitting an Aeronca-JAP engine on the front. The Motor-Tutor was amazingly easy to fly and people with a little gliding experience could easily handle it. Several people proclaimed that here was the chance to gain a power flying licence very cheaply and that it ought to be possible to train a pilot effectively by solo flying.

It wasn't a wholly ridiculous notion for if you took a competent glider pilot, putting him into a Motor-Tutor was merely an extension of handling something that he already knew. The Ministry was surprisingly warm to the idea and so long as training was under strict supervision handled by approved groups within the Ultra Light Aircraft Association, it would probably be authorised.

The Kemsley Flying Trust, discussed in a moment, was amenable to financing the scheme and negotiations began between the ULAA and Slingsby to build six Motor-Tutors for delivery by the spring of 1949. The economics were interesting. The cost of operating a Motor-Tutor was estimated to be £1 per hour. To be eligible for participation in the scheme, the ULAA 'approved group' would have to pay out nearly £100. Of that sum, £50 per annum would be repaid to the Kemsley Trust and nearly £50 would be paid in insurance. To achieve the necessary profit, the group would have to fly a minimum of only 150 hours a year.

In the event, the sums were never put to the test: problems at a number of levels, not the least of which was finding the half-dozen suitable ULAA groups, eventually led to the cancellation of the Motor-Tutor scheme and Slingsby never entered the hoped-for production phase of this attractive light aircraft.

While private flying (and amateur flying in particular) was still rather struggling in Britain, we looked with envy across the Channel for, despite the German occupation (of Northern France), the end of the war had brought an immediate return to private and club flying in France. As early as the autumn of 1945, light (meaning private) aircraft production was in full swing. It is said that some light-aircraft designers had already produced 'post-war' designs during the war and so were well-placed to come out into the open the instant the occupation ceased. Holland and Belgium were also getting organised quickly.

In was, however, in France that the most rapid advances were being made. Four classes of aircraft were being built: single seaters of 45-45 hp, single seaters of 75-90 hp; two or three seaters with 140 hp engines, and the luxury four seater with 220 hp engine. In the main wooden construction was favoured by the French. The cost of motors for aircraft in France was, though, quite prohibitive standing at around Frs. 2,000 per horsepower or twice what was desirable.

Not that flying itself in France was cheap. In 1946 the French complained that their flying cost them something like twice what we had to pay in Britain. At the then exchange rates, a single seater aircraft cost around £600 to £700 while a four seat cabin aircraft could be anything over £4,000. Flying in club machines was also a costly business then working out at Frs.1,300 to Frs.1,500 per hour.

The Vice-President of the Flying Club Federation of France, a splendid enthusiast named Joannes, was aiming to get this reduced to around Frs.400 to 600 per hour. At that time the rate of exchange of the old franc was around 440 to the £.

Gallic enterprise had thus generated for the enthusiast the rapid return to the freedom of the skies, but had not yet the economy to make it cheap and universally available.

Back here a major row broke out in the autumn of 1946. It had been brewing for all of the summer months and it concerned the high charges for both landing and hangarage at State-owned airfields. It was apparent that when the Minister for Civil Aviation had thought about charges he was thinking only of charter and executive travel and had forgotten (or chosen to forget) the impecunious amateur and average club member. *Flight's* editor, Carl Poulsen, ranted in his October 3rd editorial:

> The landing fees… are grossly extortionate in proportion to the facilities offered – which are often almost non-existent. To find oneself forced to pay 17s 6d (to quote an average figure) for a refuelling or other temporary stop, and then to discover that one has to fetch one's own chocks and start one's own engine is nothing if not irritating. Yet the case of the private owner who is forced by circumstances to keep his aircraft at a State airfield is likely to be even more financially disturbing, since he cannot take his machine out for a few practice circuits without being faced with a quite unreasonable bill. We have heard of one owner who bought an aircraft before completing his training and is now faced with the prospect of paying 17s 6d for every one of the score of landings still likely to be necessary. Meanwhile, his aircraft languishes in a hangar at the cost of 8s a night.

In the heady days of the 1940s, a popular theme of many an air show was the presence of very old and early aircraft. The types owned by the Science Museum and the Nash Collection included Blériot Monoplanes, a Deperdussin, Sopwith Pup and others. Incredibly not only were these machines continually dragged out and put together as static exhibits, they actually flew as well unless there was a gale blowing. A regular and popular exhibit was the little Hawker Cygnet G-EBMB which, with its translucent fabric-covering, revealed its ribs and spars to the satisfaction of the curious in the crowds that watched. Thanks to the supreme skill of their pilots, none ever sustained serious damage by this regular usage.

Poulsen feared that the authorities were reckoning that if a man could afford his own aeroplane then he could afford the high charges. He was perfectly correct and the campaign to lower State-owned airfield charges was to go on for a while to come. Tempers grew frayed and there were countless letters in the aviation press. Fortunately some of these were read and understood by the ministerial collar-feelers who agreed to rethink the procedure. One complaint was from J Cecil Rice (ARAeS) who was horrified to be charged 17s 6d for landing his Miles Whitney Straight G-AEVA at Tollerton on a courtesy visit to see how they were faring since the war. He wrote:[3]

> That airfield was founded by the foresight, and for the use of, the citizens of Nottingham. With present Government control and entirely uneconomic scale of charges, the use of the airfield, which should be a national asset, is denied to private flying. This follows mention by the BBC that the Ministry of Civil Aviation expects business men to use aircraft more. What sane business man would tolerate a fee of 17s 6d for landing at a place like Tollerton? At Derby, run by the Corporation, the fee is 5s.
>
> I have just returned from a three weeks' tour of many Continental airfields, and nowhere did I find such extortion. At Brussels the fee was 1s 2d (with 1s 2d for hangarage if desired). From Deauville to Prague I have noted fees of a few shillings only. Why should our present Government obstruct and penalize private flying while other countries foster it? In Czechoslovakia I found posters urging every man to fly; 'The Air is our Sea', 'Everybody should join his aero-club'. The population there totals little more than London (14,000,000), yet they have 200 live aeroclubs of which 85 per cent run gliding schools… Instead of helping the youth of Britain to fly, the present Government is doing everything to prevent it.

The powers-that-be decided that if size was difficult to determine (perhaps, because aircraft were always referred to as feminine in gender, defining size was thought indelicate), then weight must be the governing criterion. And so the official solution was to base the landing fee on how heavy an aircraft was. Initially it was decided that aircraft under 6,000 lbs would pay the same fee on either grass-only or runway aerodromes. For aircraft not exceeding a weight of 2,000 lbs the charge was 5s, not exceeding 4,000 lbs was 12s 6d and for those up to 6,000 lbs £1.5s 0d. It was also stated that landing fees would not apply to club machines flown either solo or dual when operating at their own base.

Meanwhile, Miles Aircraft was quick to identify a good public-relations opportunity and within a month had let it be known that their airfield at Reading could be used free of all charge by all private owners, adding that 'duty crews will always be available and every effort made to facilitate the entry, exit and servicing of aircraft. This, to encourage that most discouraged kind of aviation – private flying.'

This still left the independent private owner in a tricky position although in the end it was partially resolved (if not adequately solved) by individual arrangements and verbal promises. In one case, known to the author, landing fees were replaced by an occasional (and untaxable) half bottle of whisky. In the end, though, by the 1960s landing fees had crept back in to the pilot's overheads and charges of between 2s 6d and 5s per landing became the norm at many airfields. Generally these were the ones that pilots learned to avoid. The new tariffs came into operation on October 20th but with a warning that these were 'temporary and may be modified when a permanent system is introduced'.

The first twelve months of peace had brought a deal of disillusionment to the light aircraft movement. Times had been tough before but now, with petrol rationing, they were tougher. A cartoon in a popular aviation magazine showed an irate farmer remonstrating with a light plane pilot who had force-landed in his meadow. 'I'll be back in six weeks and fly it away when I've got my next petrol allowance!' the flyer is telling the landowner.

This situation continued until 1950 when the first relaxation of the rationing allowed the light plane pilot to exchange all his coupons in one go if he wanted, so enabling him to make a long flight. The six-month allowance for my own aircraft was 36 gallons and the price of petrol at that time was 2s 10d a gallon. If you wanted to take advantage of this benefit and exchange your coupons in one fell swoop, you had to do it at one place at one time for one delivery of fuel directly into your aircraft's tank. Whoever thought this one up must have had a wicked sense of humour for most aircraft fuel tanks held a maximum of ten gallons. The concession was thus quite unworkable for the average light plane owner. Very soon afterwards, though, two events occurred

On May 8th 1949, the Royal Aeronautical Society staged its annual Garden Party at White Waltham near Maidenhead and, as usual, the display was enlivened by the presence of a clutch of the real 'old-timers'. Here the Blériot Monoplane is being viewed by Sir Francis McLean (1904-1998) who had served as the chief engineer to the Psychological Warfare Division of the Supreme Headquarters Allied Expeditionary Force (PWD SHAEF). A brilliant man, it was he who pioneered colour TV in Britain and recommended our broadcaster to adopt the German PAL colour system. He was knighted in 1967. This evocative image was captured by the renowned aviation photographer Charles E Brown.

---

3. *Flight*, October 17th 1946, p.431.

that created fresh turmoil. First was in April 1950 when Chancellor Sir Stafford Cripps put another 9d tax on a gallon of petrol, both for motoring and flying. And the second was shortly afterwards when, on May 29th, the whole coupon thing came to an end and petrol was off ration.

That was also the year when a significant change in the licensing of pilots took place. Until then, in order to be able to fly the pilot had to hold either the celebrated 'A' Licence or, if he wanted to fly for hire and reward (*i.e.* commercially) the 'B' Licence. The requirements for these were disarmingly simple and there were many that felt the training and testing – certainly for the 'A' Licence – left much to be desired.

Now it was proposed to replace the whole system with a better scheme that was demanding of more adequate (and, by this time, relevant) training. To start flying you had to have a Student Pilot's Licence for which you had to pass a medical examination carried out by your own doctor using a Ministry form. The basic training was 40 hours of which a given proportion had to be undertaken solo. At certain flying schools that operated an 'approved' training programme whereby the student completed his whole flying training within a short and concentrated period of time, this could be reduced to a total of 30 hours. At the end, this qualified for the issue of a Private Pilot's Licence. For hire-and-reward flying, the old 'B' Licence was similarly replaced by the Commercial Pilot's Licence.

Back in 1947, the year had begun with a real buzz of excitement. Lord Nathan's Ministry of Civil Aviation set up its Special Advisory Committee on Private Flying on January 22nd under the chairmanship of Whitney Straight. Whitney Willard Straight (1912–1979) was the man who, before the war, had been a driver besides playing an increasing part in flying club and aerodrome administration. He now held the sober rank of Air Commodore.

A naturalised British subject, American-born Straight was just 35 years old but was a good man for the job. He worked hard on his task and finally issued a lengthy report on October 31st. In summary, it was very good. Just what the clubs and private flyers wanted. Sensible, sober and responsible. The report found that the claims of the light plane movement were not mere selfish ones of self-survival and argued that our light plane industry 'cannot figure in the export drive unless it has the support and

When Auster Aircraft Ltd developed the Autocar four seater from its Autocrat three seater, it created a fuselage that was wider and deeper aft of the wing trailing-edge. This bulk tended to cause what is best described as variable air-flow and turbulence over the tail depending on the airspeed. The result was that at certain speeds and aircraft attitudes the standard-size of fin and rudder was less effective.

encouragement of an air-minded nation behind it'. It recalled that in the past many of our larger manufacturers had been saved by entering the light plane field when heavy aircraft production had been curtailed and that this situation, he added darkly, would arise again.

Straight's report recommended that power flying clubs should receive a subsidy that would rise to a maximum of £900,000 at the end of the first three years. £84,000 was to be set aside for the initiation and development of suitable aircraft and a further £1,170,000 was to be available for interest-free loans for their bulk production over two years.

Dealing specifically with ultra-light aircraft, Straight considered that these machines should be sponsored and developed and that home construction, under supervision, ought to be encouraged.

On flying training, the report recommended an establishment of 200 full-time and 300 part-time flying instructors and a body of 400 maintenance engineers as 'an absolute minimum'. There should be a general limitation of control zones with reference to light plane flying and a general reduction of landing and housing charges as well as a reduction in petrol tax.

The report went on at great length and in great detail on suitable aircraft designs and specifications that should receive government sponsorship and financial backing, the importance of gliding, and a whole range of similar subsidies for gliding clubs and gliding tuition.

This rich package suddenly converted a mere Government White Paper to the paperback of the moment and, as well, 'a damned good one-and-threepence-worth'. Naturally the private and club flyers were all elated and so when nothing happened

immediately (contrary to what everybody had naively hoped), representatives of the Association of British Aeroplane Clubs (of which, coincidentally, Whitney Straight was also chairman) invited the Minister Lord Nathan to a lunch to find out when he was going to do the expected.

It was an unfortunate juxtaposition of people, policies, hopes and promises that met the Minister on Friday, February 13th 1948. Vice-chairman was Freddie Miles of Miles Aircraft Ltd. He was as hopeful as the rest as they eagerly pressed the Minister for news as to when he was going to implement the recommendations of the Straight Committee's great and wonderful report.

Lord Nathan acknowledged his obligation by responding very simply that there were no funds available with which to take any action whatsoever and consequently the Association could not expect any support from the government – except, he coyly assured everybody, of the moral variety.

To use the idiom of the 21st century, everybody was gutted. Their hopes had been elevated to the highest-possible level by the Committee's proposals, but now the Minister couldn't (or wouldn't) help. And soon, of course, Nathan himself would time-expire and a new minister (Lord Pakenham) would take over who naturally knew nothing about all that had gone before. It was a losing game.

So what could you buy for your money in that first spring of peacetime? Aircraft brokers W S Shackleton of 175 Piccadilly advertised the following machines as available ex-stock: A BA Swallow Mk.II fitted with a Pobjoy Cataract III engine, described as 'the best Swallow in the country' with the statement that it had just been completely overhauled at a cost of £250, was available with renewed C of A for £595 with the additional advice that the engine had been completely overhauled by the makers in 1939 at a cost exceeding £200 and there had been only 10 hours running since. For just £100 more than the Swallow you could have a Gipsy Major-engined Miles Sparrowhawk with 12 months' C of A 'property of a well-known test pilot'. The same sum would buy a De Havilland Hornet Moth with a Gipsy Major engine (only 48 hours total) fitted with a starter. 'This was the best Hornet offered in the recent [ex-Impressment] disposals and was specially selected', added the vendor.

Shackleton also had a Taylorcraft 'A', American built with less than 30 airframe and engine hours since new. Powered by a Continental A-40-5 engine and with full dual controls, brakes, wheel spats and tailwheel, this came with eight months' C of A for £595. At the other end of the scale was a whole airliner! Priced at £4,000, the 11 passenger DH.86B Express was offered ex-Perth, Western Australia, with 12 months' C of A and an 'enormous inventory of airframe spares, also 2 spare overhauled engines: this aeroplane is in perfect condition'.

The small ads were equally interesting. Available at undisclosed prices were a DH.85 Leopard Moth described by its Box Number seller as having flown only 430 hours total (Gipsy Major) since new. '... delivery at once; make offer'. A Cirrus-engined 1936 Simmonds Spartan with dual control was described as 'good condition; view by appointment'. For the speed freaks, A B Golay of 7, Maychurch Close, Stanmore offered a Comper Swift with 75 hp Pobjoy engine and a 600 mile range complete with 12-month C of A for £445. A sad 'fact-of-life' tale no doubt lay behind the advertisement from Mr Lindesay of 19 Thorncombe Road, East Dulwich. 'Spartan 2 seater (dual control) with Cirrus Mk.III engine, overhauled for C of A before war, but since damaged (chiefly fabric) through exposure during storage; £75.'

There were also pre-war engines offered for sale – Carden-Fords, Scott Flying Squirrels, the occasional Bristol Cherub and Blackburne Tomtit. These were probably ex-Flying Fleas but it would be hard to find anything to fit them to that would be capable of *legal* flight in 1946. Pobjoy motors, Blackburn Cirrus, DH Gipsys – these were fairly plentiful but if you bought an engine as a spare for your existing C of A aircraft, unless it had a complete logbook the chances of getting it flying again were equally limited. Once more, it was paper that made aircraft fly. Of course, you could get a logbookless engine overhauled by one of the professional aircraft establishments that were authorised to do such work and who could issue a new logbook for a freshly zero-houred motor – but the cost would be prohibitive.

What were the operating costs of the average private owner aircraft? Naturally it varied from place to place and from aircraft to aircraft, but it was in an attempt to reduce the operating costs of light aircraft that the Royal Aero Club launched a novel initiative. As early as 1948 the club introduced its own system of maintenance schedules for aircraft and engines. The largest item faced by the private owner was the cost of the annual Certificate of Airworthiness. Usually this was based on the premise that the aircraft had received no maintenance throughout the previous year. The Royal Aero Club considered that a programme of scheduled maintenance during the year could work out cheaper. The upshot was a system of monthly checks with an additional engine inspection after every ten hours, a six-monthly inspection with an overriding maximum of 120 hours, a twelve-monthly inspection to coincide with the renewal of the C of A, and a three-yearly complete overhaul as formerly associated with the C of A with an overriding maximum of 500 hours.

This sensible programme meant that the ARB surveyor could take into consideration the fact that regular inspections would have detected small problems as they occurred and therefore the cost of the overhaul was lower. In simple terms, rather than take the aircraft to pieces every year, scheduled maintenance would only require the machine to be stripped once every three years.

The schedules were intended solely for privately-owned aircraft and not for club aircraft or those operated for hire and reward. They also applied only to single-engined aircraft not exceeding 3,500 lb maximum weight and 220 bhp. A special dispensation was agreed whereby this scheme could also embrace the twin-engined Miles Gemini.

In 1950, the club produced some representative figures to illustrate how costs had panned out. The owner of a particular Auster Autocrat had compiled the following: ten monthly inspections at 15s each = £7 10s; one six-monthly inspection at £2 10s; one twelve-monthly inspection = £10 making a grand total of £20. Work found necessary as the result of the inspections totalled 18s. This compared favourably with the normal cost of an annual C of A renewal inspection which, for the Autocrat, was in the order of £50 plus necessary work. On top of this was the £5 renewal fee to the ARB.

Other aircraft for which annual maintenance fees had been compiled were a Miles Gemini (£32 plus £11 ARB fees); Miles Whitney Straight (£43 plus £8); Auster Arrow (£34 14s 6d plus £5); Auster Autocrat (£42 13s plus £5).

In close co-operation with the ARB, the RAeC was able to create a basic figure showing the number of hours which, under normal conditions, were required for an aircraft inspection. For monthly inspection, an Auster required three hours and a Miles Messenger four hours. A Percival Proctor required five hours and a Miles Gemini also five. The six-monthly inspection needed six, eight, fourteen and ten hours respectively.

Auster's solution was to increase the area of both fin and rudder, taking the opportunity of incorporation an aerodynamic balance to the rudder. These two pictures, the previous G-AJYK and this one, G-AJYM, reveal the solution. The enlarged fin and rudder became the standard design for a number of Auster variants starting with the Autocrat's first improvement as the Alpha.

This move to establish private aircraft operating costs went some way to curbing a disturbing element that crept into private aviation in the immediate post-war years – the great variation in the amount charged by firms and engineers for routine maintenance.

These were peculiar times when there was a relative wealth of choice yet so little opportunity. With very few prohibited areas or control zones to worry about, the private flyer could virtually go anywhere he liked so long as he kept his eyes open. Instrument ratings were luxuries that only commercial flyers might be able to afford: the ordinary pilot with his single-engined licence flew VFR. The man who formed the Ultra Light Aircraft Association, electrical engineer Ronald W Clegg, issued a prophetic warning at Christmas 1947 when, writing in that short-lived but excellent magazine *The Light Plane & Private Owner*, he suggested that 'the time is rapidly approaching when the use of any aircraft not fitted with two-way radio will be severely restricted, if not completely prohibited, in certain specified Control Areas and Control Zones.'

One of the sets that he subsequently reviewed was the GEC lightweight single-channel VHF airborne Transmitter/Receiver, 'probably the smallest on the market today'. It measured four inches wide, eight inches high, nine-and-a-half inches deep and weighed eight and a half pounds. The range was 25 miles at 1,000 feet and the cost was £90 – based on average second-hand prices, that worked out about 17 per cent of the cost of an aeroplane! And that was before one considered a battery to power it!

Generally speaking, then, radio and light aircraft didn't mix. For the really small aircraft, there was simply no room for the radio and its necessary power source. Neither was there enough margin for the weight of the radio and its very heavy battery. Add to that the need for engine ignition screening and suppression, licensed installation and maintenance and so on, and you begin to see that radio was a difficult subject that was expensive in more ways than merely buying the box of tricks. A radio installation could cost the aircraft owner between 20 and 25 per cent of the value of his machine while adding only four to six per cent to its sale value.

As far as amateur flying was concerned, the Ultra Light Aircraft Association offered status to the many enthusiasts that made up its steadily-growing numbers. One of its foundation 'wings' was the Experimental Group, a grand name for 30 members with some largely unflyable aircraft based in a leaking and draughty blister hangar at Elstree. With the occasional use of a Magister and an Auster Autocrat for training, members paid 10s monthly subscription and 37s 6d per hour for flying.

The difficulty with the ULAA was that it was a totally amateur spare-time organisation that had been expanding faster than its status could cope with. Too late did the executive appreciate what was happening. On March 15th 1952 the Association's Annual General Meeting was dominated by news of impending doom and gloom not from the usual sources, but this time from within. The treasurer had been unable to maintain the books with sufficient diligence with the result that the finances were in a terrible mess and the ULAA could not continue. ULAA President and Chairman Peter Masefield had already approached Colonel Preston of the Royal Aero Club for management help.

Two years earlier, on November 6th 1950, the association's executive had had the wisdom to foresee a possible time when the amateur status of the ULAA might render its existence uncertain. There was also the simple fact that in its dealings with other authorities, in particular the Ministry, it was sometimes necessary to have more potential 'clout'. On that day the executive formed a new £100-capital company called Ulair Ltd for the purpose of accepting the funds of the ULAA and generally to control the business of the ULAA. Founding directors were Ronald W Clegg, Edward L Mole. Maurice O Imray, Louis E E Martin, John E Fricker, Gabriella R M Patterson, Norman H Lester, Hubert Lewellyn Pitt, Alfred R O Weyl, Rosemary W Lindsay Neale, and others.

Now in the summer of 1952 the ULAA could not meet its debts. Ulair Ltd, one fortunate step away from the Association's problems, instigated urgent talks with the Royal Aero Club. An Extraordinary General Meeting was called at Londonderry House on November 3rd starting at 6.30 pm. Mrs Lindsay-Neale, the secretary, found herself unable to continue in office due to the pressure of the task, Maurice Imray had already resigned as had several others of the executive. The treasurer did not attend the meeting, but had also long-since vacated his job. ULAA was a hollow shell.

An era came to an end when, at precisely 7.05 that evening the Ultra Light Aircraft Association was officially wound up and chairman Peter Masefield left his seat. Colonel Rupert Preston now took the chair as interim head of the meeting and proposed the formation of a new body to be called the Popular Flying Association. The Royal Aero Club would not only administer all finances but would generously absorb the old ULAA's £186 debt. The proposition was accepted, the Popular Flying Association was born and Maurice Imray was elected honorary secretary with Peter Masefield back as president.

In the curious manner by which oft-repeated errors, by virtue of being so oft-repeated, attain an almost unassailable and unchallenged historical credence, it is popularly believed that the PFA arose by changing the name of the ULAA and that

Our skies tended to be given over to pre-war types, especially when it came to racing. The Percival Mew G-AEXF was a regular participant in 1950s events – despite being comprehensively crashed several times. However, the age of appreciation and restoration was just beginning and this particular machine was one of the earliest to undergo rebirth. In this restoration it was a hark-back to Arthur Bage's original minimalistic shape for Percival where the front of the tyre was exposed. Visibility from the cockpit was always very dubious in the original. Here the seat has been raised – and a vast bubble cockpit erected to give excellent visibility rather at the expense of the aircraft's original streamlined profile. An even later rebuild took it back to its original tight streamlines profile. See also pages 13 and 25.

the PFA was founded in 1946. This is untrue. To be strictly accurate, the PFA was created after the ULAA had been officially wound up (admittedly only by a few minutes!) and therefore was not founded until 1952.

Early on in its existence, the newly-formed PFA succeeded, through the financial provision of two members, in buying the title to the pre-war *Popular Flying* magazine from owners George Newnes Ltd – a move which saw the revival of a famous and distinctive title that became PFA property in perpetuity – truly a jewel in its crown!

Two years later the new Popular Flying Association achieved its first great triumph. As the direct result of a deputation led by myself and Imray, the Ministry of Transport and Civil Aviation agreed to allow Permits to Fly to be issued to newly-constructed amateur-built aircraft so long as they were built to designs approved by the PFA and had been constructed under the PFA's supervision. This marked a memorable relaxation in the requirements for airworthiness certification and placed a rich burden of responsibility on the shoulders of the PFA. The aircraft inspectorate comprised Douglas E Bianchi of White Waltham and myself.

There were, of course, conditions. The aircraft must not weigh in excess of 1,200 lb, nor must it have a stalling speed in excess of 45 mph and the engine power was not to exceed 75 hp. The aircraft was to be used solely for private purposes, must only be flown within the UK and then not over populous areas, must not be used for aerobatics and must only be flown by day and under Visual Flight Rules (VFR). In all cases third-party insurance was necessary. It was a great step forward as now ordinary people could build new aeroplanes such as the Luton Minor (the first post-war British design to be approved), the Turbulent (the second) and the Turbi – the first two seat home-built design.

Lord Kemsley (he was the newspaper baron James Gomer Berry born in 1883) had always been a great supporter and patron of aviation and in 1947 he created the Kemsley Flying Trust with the aim of providing funds to further interests in light aviation. There was an interest-free loan system to cover flying training while there were similar schemes to enable groups to buy aircraft and engines. For the impecunious and invariably struggling aircraft co-ownership groups and clubs, this was an absolute godsend. The whole running and administration of the trust was managed by Basil Alfred Gregory Meads, MBE, who was its secretary. The Trust became one of the principal benefactors of the Ultra Light Aircraft Association in its early days. It was, though, wound up with the death of Lord Kemsley in 1968.

In a commendable and benevolent move to continue where Kemsley left off, a consortium led by the Society of British Aircraft Constructors (SBAC) set up a £100,000 Private Flying Loan Fund in 1961 to assist flying clubs and approved groups to obtain financial aid through low interest loans for the purchase of aircraft. Shell-Mex and BP put up £25,000 and the balance came from the SBAC. That this marked a continuation of the good work begun by the former Kemsley Flying Trust was assured by the appointment of Basil Meads as secretary of the new fund.

Sadly, this proved a short-lived venture: by the summer of 1967 the SBAC announced that it had decided to scrap the system stating that 'the principal [sic] circumstances prevailing when it was created no longer apply since other more orthodox means of financing the purchase of aircraft have subsequently become available.' This was a body blow to the flying and co-ownership groups within the PFA for those 'more orthodox means' unquestionably meant money at high interest rates. The loss of the SBAC arrangement once more put aircraft ownership out of the reach of many who wished to own their own aircraft.

The fund added in its defence that 'the scale of support now required by the UK Gliding and Flying Movement is beyond its available budget and should be tackled on a national level, particularly if the current shortage of qualified airline pilots is to be relieved'.

Successive post-war governments had consistently demonstrated a signal lack of interest in the private flying movement which meant that the UK held a dismal place internationally in the world of private and club flying. Nevertheless the SBAC Fund had tided over the movement for six years, lending £177,745 which had assisted in the purchase of more than 150 aircraft.

In 1958, John Blake, then editor of the house magazine of the Royal Aero Club, compiled an interesting analysis of the aircraft in the class below 10,500 lbs all-up weight. Of the 1,200 aircraft in this category, only 129 were ten years old or less and of this number 98 were Austers.

Curious anomalies existed in the rich world of the materials from which aircraft were constructed. Steel and aluminium, for example, were readily available so long as you had a permit to allow you to purchase more than, say, a sample piece maybe two feet in length. Aircraft timber, on the other hand, was free of restrictions, but simply very hard to obtain since the restrictions of wartime production demand had not entirely been lifted, nor had sufficient time yet elapsed to allow the free flow of material on to the consumer market.

An acute shortage of natural rubber during the war (it was all channelled into the war effort) meant that aircraft tyres had for some years been made of synthetic rubber. The real stuff had been retained for inner tubes, however. One of the curiosities of the synthetic rubber used for outer covers was that it did not naturally deteriorate as quickly, but it wore out more rapidly in use than genuine rubber. Owners of aircraft learned that tyres on aircraft left standing in the open or in oil were usually all right, yet after a few landings the tread would have been noticeably scuffed down. The return to real rubber types (in fact to a semi-synthetic added compound) did not come in quantity until the start of 1947.

The perils of having too much of a good thing, *i.e.* surviving Tiger Moths, was demonstrated in the grounds of a nightclub near the old Hamsey Green aerodrome on Guy Fawkes night in 1956. Nine ex-RAF DH.82a Tigers were burned in a fireworks display. They were G-AMIN, G-AMIO, G-AMIS, G-AMIT, G-AMIW, G-AMIY, G-AMJA, G-AMJB and G-AMJC. Seldom can a bonfire of such value have been lit in the furtherance of the brief entertainment of a group of moronic, drunken bystanders.[4]

It was in 1956 that the British home-built aircraft movement received both a kick-start and an irresistible opportunity. It was at the beginning of April that the

---

4. Tiger Moth vandalism continued well into recent times. When, in the summer of 1969, the enormous numbers of examples used in Belgium's State School of Civil Aviation were declared redundant, they were packed into a hangar at Grimbergen near Brussels. In order to save space, the front spar bolts were withdrawn from top and bottom wings which were then folded back. As most people know, the Tiger Moth was developed from the DH.60 Moth which did have folding wings. The Tiger Moth, on the other hand, while built using DH.60 Moth components and retaining the hinge fittings, did not have folding wings, the stagger preventing this being done because the hinge pins were no longer in line. Forcing back the wings on the Belgian examples thus succeeded in tearing the wing-root fittings out of the wing spars.

As post-war air-racing became more popular, rare types from the 'thirties emerged. One was the Leeds-built Arrow Active single seat biplane. Only two were built, each slightly different, and Alex Henshaw had owned and raced one – until it caught fire in mid-air and he had to bale out. Survivor G-ABVE successfully raced in the second half of the 20th century rekindling some of the thrill of super-fast biplanes of an already well-past age.

French-designed Druine Turbulent F-PHFR was flown to England from France by Harold Best-Devereux. Best-Devereux, later to be PFA President, was an enthusiastic private pilot, a staunch advocate of amateur construction and, importantly, an ARB inspector. This curious mix brought him into conflict with his superiors at times, but in the end was to prove immensely influential for the burgeoning Popular Flying Association on whose executive committee both he and I sat at its Londonderry House, Park Lane, headquarters.

Best-Devereux set off from his Elstree base with the tiny French single seat monoplane and then proceeded to tour England. Between April 8th and May 8th he took it to many parts of the country. The fact that a full set of engineering drawings was available immediately and at a reasonable cost and the knowledge that the aircraft would qualify for the issue of a British Permit to Fly quickly encouraged builders to take up the challenge and start home-construction.

The PFA Annual General Meeting on May 9th 1956 discussed one principal notion, namely that the PFA should apply for proper affiliation to the Royal Aero Club. Although its creation had been supervised by the RAeC after the collapse of the old ULAA, the PFA had quickly gained independence and, despite its debt of formation, had officially distanced itself from the club. The PFA was to retain that independence for a while longer.

At that time PFA had 60 affiliated flying groups and was still expanding rapidly as members came to understand the co-ownership group scheme that PFA was proposing over the previous four years. The PFA also wanted to foster amateur construction which at that moment in time was being practiced by a mere handful of its members with the Luton Minor and now the Druine Turbulent.

Now that currency restrictions were a thing of the past we began to see more and more American light aircraft in the British skies. They were objects of great interest but generally considered, by the rank and file flyers, as being costly to maintain on the simple grounds that they were not just foreign but American and that meant that any spares (including expertise) had to cross the Atlantic.

Another objection, more realistic as far as servicing was concerned, was that they were built with American-type nuts and bolts that used the so-called 'unified' screw-thread and therefore normal AGS parts were not able to be used as replacements. Even spanners were different in size besides being described in the American handbooks as 'wrenches'. In those days we took pains to preserve our language as well as our screw and nut threads: we fought shy of adopting anything else American. Enough damage, many thought, had been caused by the widespread practice, rife-rampant from their servicemen here during the war, of chewing gum not to mention the unseemly temptations presented to our young womenfolk and arising from Yankee sweet-talk sustained by curiously-shaped condoms and promises of silk stockings...

The arguments were robust enough at first, but the agents that handled American machines in Britain quickly established strong holdings of American hardware to the extent that even the staunchest Georgian-era pilot or engineer could not really sustain a credible argument against 'going American'.

Not only did we have to get used to club-type aeroplanes that were made of tin but we were also exposed to the pat expressions of Americanese and sales jargon. The first Cessna 150 that was privately-owned in Britain was G-ARAB (registered on April 29th 1960) which, we found, was fitted with a 'Land-O-Matic' undercarriage.

From April 28th to 30th 1961, W S Shackleton staged a weekend of what was by then commonly termed General Aviation aircraft. Held at Baginton, Coventry, it marked the debut of the new Beagle Auster Airedale G-ARKE which was offered in standard form without radio for £4,750. It was fitted with a 180 hp Lycoming. Accompanying the Airedale was the Terrier G-ARLH which was a direct development of the Air OP Auster Mk.6 fitted with a 145 hp Gipsy Major Mk.10. A three seater, it was offered for touring, dual instruction or glider towing at £1,995.

Concurrently with this, the American-built Piper Colt was on offer through Vigors Aviation at Kidlington. A two seater with a 108 hp Lycoming engine, this offered 22.23 miles per gallon cruising at 115 mph. Available on what was called 'the 3-year easy-payment plan' (hire purchase to you and me) this cost £2,795 or £599 down and (if four people were grouped to own it) £18.6s.6d a month.

Shackleton's sales weekend revealed some interesting list prices and serves as a good market barometer. The largest aircraft were the British Avro 748 and the American Grumman Gulfstream. The former was described as a 'de luxe executive aircraft' and carried a price-tag of 'approximately £245,000'. The latter was priced at £420,000 which, in those days, was a great deal of money: the average middle-management salary was still little more than £1,500 per annum and £5,000 would buy a nice three-bedroomed house.

The sector comprising aircraft from £38,500 (DH Dove, Srs 8) downwards included 18 aircraft types of which only one other was British – the Lancashire Prospector at £9,360. Cheapest was the Cessna Skylane at £8,169. Two German twins were included, these being the Dornier Do.27 (£12,815) and Do.28 (£21,785), and also a pair of Czech twins from Omnipol, the Aero 145 (£11,850) and the Morava L-200A (£18,600).

Aircraft priced under £6,000 numbered thirteen and extended from the Cessna 175A at £5,648 down to the Piper Colt and the Piper Tri-Pacer 160 Super Custom, both at £2,795.

In this category, which specifically excluded the new Auster-Beagles which were in effect only just launched onto the market, of the thirteen machines all but three were American. The exceptions were the Jodel Ambassador (£2,800) and the Jodel Musketeer (£4,500), both available from Rollason, and the Czechoslovakian Meta-Sokol, imported by Peter Clifford.

There were cheaper machines for the less well-off, the cheapest being Rollason's standard Turbulent which, complete with 30 hp engine, sliding canopy and wheel spats was priced at just a fraction over £1,000. This little single seater cruised at rather better than 40 statute miles to a gallon. A version fitted with a 40 hp engine and radio (still considered an executive-aircraft novelty and therefore a great curiosity in a single seater) was also available to special order.

Also from the Beagle stable (but the drawing-board of the Miles' family) was the Student jet trainer. This did not have a price tag, though.

This was a time when new American aircraft were being seen (and offered for sale) in Britain only a brief while after their introduction in America. The Americans knew that the British market was only very small but they ensured that they took advantage of every possible selling opportunity. Early in the summer of 1961, then, the Cessna 210 was offered to the UK. Distributed by agents based at Panshanger, the list price, duty paid and ready to fly, was £10,300. It was estimated that with hangarage at £99 per annum, the C of A renewal annual cost of £150 and insurance at 6½ per cent of the initial cost (£669 a year), if one amortised the aircraft's cost over twelve years, the total fixed operating costs for the year worked out at £1,776.

Taking the cost of fuel per hour of flying at £2.12s.6d and maintenance costs per hour of flying at £1.15s.0d, the direct cost per flying hour was £4.7s.0d. If one flew the aircraft 150 hours in the year, the cost in pence per seat-mile (based on the assumption that three seats were occupied for half the time, and four for the remainder) was 6½d. Pushing the annual hours flown to 800 brought this seat-mile cost down to 2¾d.

This, however, was for the 'bare' aircraft. Fitted out to customer's individual requirements could add considerably to the fly-away cost. The demonstration aircraft, for example, was provided with Lear ADC, Narco Mk.5 radio and full instrumentation boosting the total price to £12,723 – an increase of £2,423 or 23.5 per cent above basic list.

Ordinary flying people winced at such huge prices and wondered who could ever afford this category of aircraft. The point was that those people did exist. They were the earliest of the post-war business executive flyers and company aircraft operators. This was the category that British manufacturers had long tried to encourage from the early days. The pre-war Heston Phoenix and de Havilland Dragonfly were aimed at business users. Now the 'off-the-peg' American-built machines fitted the bill very well and it was this fact that highlighted not so much Britain's lost opportunity so much as how far behind America we had fallen through the hiatus of war. America's light aircraft industry had continued virtually uninterrupted for most of the war years and had progressed greatly while our industry had of necessity stagnated. Beagle's brave attempt to counteract this will be looked at in a later chapter.

The delightful Hawker 41 Tomtit dated from April 1939 and saw service as K1786. Restored as all-blue and white G-AFTA, this nifty and aerobatic biplane entertained the air show crowds for a decade or more. Finally withdrawn from use in April 1967, it was restored to its Service markings for preservation.

In the world of flying training, big business was starting to move into the flying club scene as it was realised that there was scope for something between the implied happy-go-lucky social atmosphere of the flying club and the sober pressures of the professional air training establishments. There began to emerge a new breed of flight school – the so-called 'aviation centre'.

It began with the foundation in 1966 of the British Light Aviation Centre, itself an amalgamation of the Royal Aero Club Aviation Centre and the Association of British Aero Clubs and Centres. This was not a flying school: the centres that followed were and they promoted a sober and scholastic approach to learning to fly.

Quite early on it seemed likely that the amateur end of the light plane business was going to form a significant part of the post-war aviation revival. Its early days were, though, fraught with problems.

We have already seen that the British Ultra-Light category permit to fly ruling current up to 1961, stated that aircraft were eligible for inclusion in the scheme provided that [a] the all-up weight did not exceed 1,200 lbs, [b] the stalling speed, flaps up, was not in excess of 45 mph, and [c] the design and construction were of a standard acceptable to the Popular Flying Association

The operational limitations were that [d] the aircraft might not be flown over any congested area of a city, town or settlement or over any assembly of persons in the open air; [e] the aircraft may be used for private purposes only; [f] it may not be used for aerobatic flying; [g] it may not be flown unless it is in a state of adequate repair and in sound working order. Furthermore there were to be no alterations, replacements or repairs, which substantially affected the constructional features of the aircraft without reference to the PFA.

Other conditions stipulated that the aircraft must possess a third party insurance policy for not less than £10,000 in respect of loss or damage caused on any one occasion. The aircraft was not to be flown in any state whereby that insurance coverage would be invalidated and the aircraft only to be flown by day and in accordance with either *(1)* visual flight rules, or *(2)* a special VFR clearance issued by the appropriate Air Traffic Control. The aircraft was only to be flown within the United Kingdom although special dispensation for flights abroad could be arranged provided that the owner had an invitation from a club in the country he wished to visit.

Named after the man who did so much to regularise the somewhat disparate pre-war operation of flying clubs and private aerodromes, the Miles M.11A Whitney Straight G-AEWA was first registered on March 9th 1937 and continued to fly during the war, impressed as DJ714. At the resumption of private flying in 1946, it returned to peaceful skies until March 3rd, 1961, when, while attempting to take-off from a field at Neufchâtel in France, it crashed and was destroyed.

There was a sting in the tail, so to speak, for one of the reasons for operating on a Permit to Fly was to bring cheaper flying to the enthusiasts. It was said that pilots who flew ultra-light aircraft had to be fully-qualified pilots, meaning that they should hold a Private Pilot's Licence. This in effect negated much of the purpose of cheap flying and the PFA wanted dispensation to allow ultra-lights to be flown by student pilots (meaning those pilots who held the Student Pilot's Licence) under the supervision of their instructors.

A case could arise where a person who was learning to fly owned or had built a 'permit' aircraft and wanted to use it for the completion of their hours for a PPL. This came to be allowed although there was, crucially, nothing in writing from the Ministry about this. The discretion of the individual instructor was accepted.

The relationship between what became the PFA and the Ministry was very much a treading-on-egg-shells relationship for the PFA knew that any incident concerning an aircraft operating on a Permit to Fly could jeopardise its relationship with the Ministry and, in particular, call into question the Ministry's dispensation to allow the PFA the right to recommend aircraft for certification under the Permit scheme. The Permit campaign had received a very early knock when, on April 27th 1947, a youthful enthusiast for no-frills private flying had taken to the air in his BAC Drone G-AEJS (750cc Douglas flat-twin) and then come down again rather firmly at Gerrards Cross.

In as long as it takes to hit the ground very hard, this young man managed to break almost every one of the rules of flying, shatter the slender leeway ULAA/PFA had made and in so doing almost destroy the amateur aircraft movement and its achievements to date. It turned out that not only had the pilot no licence of any sort, but also the aircraft had no permit (although he had applied for one which had been delayed because there was no engineer's report) and he had been refused third party insurance because of the lack of the other necessary papers.

The absolute saving grace was that the perpetrator was found not to be a member of the Popular Flying Association either. Curiously there was a positive spin-off. It highlighted the anomalous procedure required by the Civil Aviation Ministry regarding the reissue of Permits to Fly for aircraft that had flown before the war. Had the Ministry come to a proper decision, then the accident might never have happened because the pilot's application for a permit would have led automatically to an engineer's inspection of his aircraft. Intense lobbying actually succeeded in transferring sufficient responsibility for the incident back to the shoulders of the Minister to save the ULAA/PFA's bacon.

It was, though, a close call and this one affair, coming so early on in the unsteady days of the amateur aircraft movement, nearly killed off the permit system before it had got going. Memories, however, are long and the ULAA and its succeeding PFA had struggled long and hard to tread a very safe line.

All this hard-earned progress almost came to an end again on December 6th 1960 when a Rollason-built Druine Turbulent which was operating on the Permit to Fly scheme was involved in a fatal accident near Biggin Hill, Kent. It was said that the pilot was attempting aerobatics – prohibited in a Permit machine. On June 20th 1961, after the necessary inquest, the Ministry of Aviation wrote to the PFA. The tone of the letter, over the signature of the Under Secretary, Aviation Safety and General, R Goodison, was sympathetic but the content meant that the PFA had for the moment at least lost some of its responsibility.

But there was worse! The Ministry letter continued:

> Consideration has been given to pilot qualifications. It is, I think, agreed that it has always been the intention that the pilot of an aircraft flying under a Permit to Fly as opposed to a C of A should be competent to cope with the lower standard of airworthiness such aircraft may well have. I have in mind particularly possible lower standards of controllability. Therefore we feel that those who fly these aircraft should not be student pilots but should at least hold a private pilot's licence. At present this is not one of the conditions under which Permits to Fly are issued for ultra-light aircraft, but it is intended to make it so in the future.

This was something of a bombshell and resulted in protracted negotiations between the Ministry and the other bodies concerned, namely the Royal Aero Club, the PFA and the Air Registration Board. It was highlighted by the Minister that there existed no legal grounds for continuing 'the present legislation unless new legislation to cover this point was introduced' and the Ministry felt unable 'at the present time' to consider recommending such action.

Tracing back the history of the postwar private and amateur flying movement in this country reveals that progress was in the form of a saw tooth: each advance would be followed by a setback; every dark moment would be succeeded by a moment of delight – and then another restriction. The directions these movements took could – and did – concern every aspect of owning and operating a light aircraft, let alone building one. There was the matter of airworthiness rules, aircraft licensing, pilot licensing, air restrictions, ground restrictions, insurance, legislation, design, testing, engines, maintenance, certification, the cost and rationing of petrol and then the limitation and withdrawal of certain types of fuel – the list was as long as your arm.

A curious aspect of both the Ministry of Aviation/Civil Aviation/Transport & Civil Aviation (or whatever was the official flavour of the moment) and also the Air Registration Board was that the private and amateur flying movement actually had very strong supporters within these organisations. While

The growing interest of film companies in pseudo-historic aviation movies created a demand for 'replica' aircraft of the period. Slingsby Sailplanes would later build examples of First World War SE.5a fighters for Hollywood. Probably the most memorable of these efforts was *Those Magnificent Men and their Flying Machines* for which a large number of 'replicas' was needed. One of these was the so-called Eardley-Billing Biplane built at Stapleford Tawney by Harold Best-Devereux and the present author in 1965. In the film it was flown by the supposed German pilots Colonel Manfred von Holstein and Captain Rumpelstoss, while a variant was seen as a Japanese contestant. Here are the two constructors pictured having finished building the aircraft and each having flown a length of the airfield at a ground speed of 25 mph as measured by a pace car – only just in 3rd gear!

outwardly all appeared obstructionist and although many of the manifestations of official benevolence were anything but that, there was a growing core of people who, if not exactly moving Heaven and earth, then shifted papers in the right direction in very high places. The outcome was often very interesting to observe. Meetings with the Ministry were always very friendly but invariably negative, yet within a short space of time afterwards some communication would reveal that, whatever the message was, it had actually slipped through and was being considered.

It was during one of these meetings that the PFA tried to explain to both the Ministry and the Air Registration Board that the existing Permit to Fly scheme was based on a specification pitched just short of the average two seater in terms of weight and horsepower. Since building or operating a safe two seater within existing limits was tempting fate, this class of aircraft was being effectively discriminated against, since the maximum limits only allowed for single seaters. It was pointed out that the sport of popular flying was unlikely to flourish so long as there was no chance of ever getting a modern two seat design to qualify. In many ways, it was the ghost of the 1926 Lympne Light Aeroplane Competitions returning to haunt afresh, reminding us that two seaters need just a bit more power and weight in their specifications. It was also, maybe unintentionally, a warning that sooner or later somebody would create a too-flimsy, underpowered two seater with consequences to be imagined.

This was, as it turned out, the most important submission that PFA had ever made (up to that time) to the authorities. The submission was double-edged. First, a review upwards of the limits would allow the small C of A aircraft (Taylorcraft, Aeronca and suchlike) to be operated on the Permit system. Second it would inspire designers to tackle the hitherto unthinkable – a new two seater design for the home-builder with a reasonable-sized engine.

At the end of 1961, the Ministry and the ARB gave the PFA its best-ever Christmas present – agreement that the limits for the Permit to Fly would henceforth be increased to a weight maximum of 1,750 lbs and engines up to 115 horsepower. The stalling speed could rise to 60 mph using approved engines or 50 mph for non-approved engines instead of the old and unrealistic limit of 45 mph IAS with flaps down.

The Ministry added that the changes 'are designed primarily at encouraging the design and construction of two seat ultra-light aeroplanes. It is also hoped that they will result in aircraft of improved performance and utility with more reliable power plants.' We were indeed staring 1926 in the face!

The news coincided with the announcement of a number of new projects from Rollason and the Beagle company. It seemed that 1962 was going to prove fortuitous for the popular flying movement.

All this while there was another force at work. In an economic situation that was not so much volatile as moribund if not stultified, costs were inexorably rising. This was front-ended by higher fees for pilot training. The Popular Flying Association's devotion to the group-ownership approach had expanded impressively – at the start of 1962 there were about 80 – and was now proving its worth for a Tiger Moth operated under the group scheme could still be flown profitably for between £2 10s and £3 per hour. Even more modern aircraft that were group owned could be flown for around £5 per hour.

A contributory factor to these low operating costs was the petrol duty rebate introduced in the late 1950s. Expressly excluding all privately-owned aircraft, this scheme allowed all flying clubs and affiliated (meaning legitimate) groups to claim back 1s 9d per gallon of duty on their fuel bills. The actual amount given to each club was based on the estimated fuel consumption of the particular aircraft at cruising revs calculated as the product of the flying hours multiplied by the fixed allowance for the aircraft type. The sum was paid every six months and an arbitrary ceiling of £80,000 per club/per annum was agreed.

At the end of 1961 the Ministry of Aviation, in response to fears from the Treasury that club and group flying was on the increase, decided to reduce this rebate allowance to 1s 3d per gallon and to adjust this rate further if necessary by means of quarterly returns. There was no negotiation with clubs or other organisations, just a simple bald statement of intent that offered no room for negotiation, let alone arbitration, by the parties concerned.

What the minions at Whitehall had overlooked was that statistically aircraft do not (perhaps 'cannot' is a better word) fly so much in the winter as in the summer. Extra hours of daylight, better weather – all are regulating factors that flying clubs budget for. The basing of an assessment on the wrong quarter's utilisation for any new applicant could prove a financial nightmare.

It will be seen that this announcement was timed to follow that of the relaxation of Permit aircraft requirements so what was given generously with one hand to one sector of the popular flying movement was balanced by a blow at the general aviation side.

Staunch campaigner for aviation was, of course, the Air League of the British Empire, by this time generally referred to as just the Air League. On October 26th 1959 it celebrated its 50th birthday with a special luncheon held at the Mansion House at the invitation of the Lord Mayor, Sir Harold Gillett. Patron of the Air League the late Prince Philip, Duke of Edinburgh, delivered a sparkling address, some of which is worth recalling.

> At the moment it seems to be fashionable to say that the British aircraft industry is in a muddle simply because there are not enough orders for the aircraft in production or projected to make a profit. If the lack of orders is due to the fact that British aircraft are not wanted because they are no good, then the industry is in a proper muddle. But I do not believe this to be the case. There are many reasons for this state of affairs, and one of the most potent is that the American aircraft industry is providing increasingly rugged competition, not just to the British industry, but to the aircraft industries of all countries outside the United States, particularly in Europe. This problem can only be tackled by governments, operators and industries together.

Of course, it wasn't! Even so, the Duke's address ended with an upbeat reference to amateur aviation and a hint that the Secretary-General had been seen doing some ultra-light flying...

> [among the matters in which the Air League takes special interest] is the question of private flying in the British Isles. I know that the Secretary-General considers this a very turbulent matter, even though he isn't nipping about it in a particularly tipsy manner as yet. I realise that there are many difficulties in the way of amateur flying, but the cost and complication of suitable aircraft is not one of them.

Londonderry House in Park Lane became Britain's established Aviation Centre administered by the Royal Aero Club. Gifted by Lord Londonderry (born as Charles Stewart Henry Vane-Tempest-Stewart, Seventh Marquess of Londonderry, on May 13th 1878) who was one of the greatest aviation benefactors, this fine house with its fantastic marble hall, statues and broad, double-headed staircase had been requisitioned during the war and used as offices and a mess for some obscure military establishment. Now with the vandalism that this had generated repaired, this building became home to virtually every facet of private aviation. By Christmas 1946 the aviation organisations housed there included the Associate Members of the Royal Aero Club, the Guild of Air Pilots and Air Navigators, the Aerodrome Owners' Association, the British Air Charter Association, the British Gliding Association and the Association of British Aero Clubs. It also housed the Royal Aero Club's extensive library superbly run by John Blake.[6]

In due course, and through the influence of Colonel Rupert Lionel 'Mossie' Preston who was Secretary-General of the Royal Aero Club, the Ultra Light Aircraft Association was invited to

One of the attractions at the Royal Aeronautical Society's Garden Party staged at White Waltham on May 14th, 1950, was an astonishing little 'one-off' single-seater from France called the Hurel-Dubois HD.10. It was a flying test-bed for the ultra-high aspect-ratio wing designed by the Hurel Dubois partnership at Villacoublay. The wing span of 39 feet 4 inches was matched by a chord of only 15¾-inches. It caught the attention of George Miles who was sufficiently interested to embark on the planning of a whole range of new designs using the HD narrow-chord wide-span wings. But first he had to try out a wing...

---

5. For those curious to see the old face of Park Lane, a picture of the façade of Londonderry House can be found in *The Aeroplane* for January 10th 1947 (p.31).

LIGHT AVIATION: AN UPHILL STRUGGLE

Miles Aerovan G-AJOF was rebuilt and fitted with a Hurel-Dubois formula wing. Normally spanning 50 feet, the new variant had a span of 75 feet 4 inches. Registered G-AHDM (a special allocation to include the initials of the prime-movers), the new Aerovan proved faster, had a greater rate of climb and a higher ceiling.

The one-off Aerovan with its Hurel-Dubois-formula wing was first flown on March 30th 1957, by which time Miles was in no position to initiate any production. Instead he gave the project to Short Brothers in Belfast. The outcome was the Skyvan, Miles inspired but with a compromise mid-way span/chord wing to ease ground handling ability. Incidentally, the original G-AHDM had been a civilianised Halifax.

Designed by the free-thinking Charles Bower, Reid & Sigrist's two seat Desford Trainer with its two 130 Gipsy Major engines was to have been the development prototype for a four-to five seat private owner's light aircraft. Had this been proceeded with it would have been a commendable rival to the Miles Gemini. The firm's core business, however, was instrument-making and its first foray into making a complete aircraft had come with the whimsically-named Snargasher of 1939. During the war the business built trainer aircraft and operated flight-training schools for the RAF. Here we see the sole example of the Desford, one of the first civil aircraft to be registered in 1946 as G-AGOS.

join this elite group of tenants and so moved its chattels (a filing cabinet, a typewriter and my hand-turned Roneo duplicator) into a room there during 1947. It was a tremendously rich and privileged environment for those of us that devoted all our spare cash to flying.

Sometime after the death of his Lordship (February 11th 1949), early in 1962 it was announced that the building was to be sold and the site redeveloped. This heralded the end of the last great one-time private house in Park Lane and led to the dispersal of all those who together made up the Aviation Centre. This wonderful building where so many formative meetings were held in the burgeoning days of the ULAA and PFA was now demolished and nothing of its fine interior was salvaged. In its place was erected a dreadful modern American-style hotel, the banal architecture of which was in such sharp contrast to the edifice it replaced. That it retains Lord Londonderry's name in its title is but a hollow tribute verging on the insult.

In 1963 came some startling news from across the Channel where the counterpart of the PFA, the Réseau du Sport de l'Air (RSA) had negotiated with the French regulatory body for drastic modifications to the requirements for the French equivalent of the Permit to Fly for amateur-built aircraft. This amateur home-built aircraft organisation had been working away for some while in a move to upgrade the home-built category.

Now came the announcement of its successful campaign: to those in Britain it made mouth-watering reading. In short, the French airworthiness authorities had opened the whole regime and set a precedent then unique in Europe and only bettered in America. Two and three seaters were now admitted into the Permit scheme and they could have engines up to 136 hp in place of the 100 hp previously agreed or alternatively the engine capacity could be seven litres instead of just five.

But there was more. An interesting example of Gallic forward thinking was that a new category had been established with the French authorities for amateur built jet aircraft. Their thrust must be less than 150 kilograms for single seaters and less than 300 kilograms for two and three seaters. The French permit to fly remained as before valid for two years but should the aircraft exceed 200 hours of flight, then the permit had to be renewed.

And there was yet more! 'Acrobatic flight' was now permitted in suitable aircraft subject to documentary authority being included on the permit to fly. The owners of permit-to-fly aircraft in France now had to display a placard visible to passengers that the aircraft was not operating with a normal category C of A and that the use of the aircraft for profit was forbidden.

The Air Registration Board in London watched these cross-Channel developments with interest for at last they were beginning to realise two things. First that home-built aircraft would not go away and, second, that they would play an increasing part in the British private aviation sector. Already, as we have seen, the ARB had within its hallowed walls a sizeable faction of people who were sympathetic to the amateur aircraft owner and builder – even designer. These people looked increasingly to the French for, if not leadership (which might be thought unpatriotic), then example (which was acceptable so long as it was promoted as originally an all-British idea). And if there were those that were yet unforgiving on the surrender of Aquitaine, we could always learn from our buddies across the Atlantic.

Something happened back in 1961 which was to have a far-reaching effect on the future of all flying, especially private and club aviation. This was the first indication that having and using radio would become virtually mandatory if you wanted to traverse the skies safely and legally. It all began at the start of April with one of those innocent-looking 'Notices to Airmen' which, in the abbreviaspeak of the day was already known as a 'Notam'. Notam 51, written in a style that even for a ministerial department was verbose in the extreme, baldly announced that the skies were no longer free but had been carved up for 'public use'. Sequestering the airspace around London created a *fait accompli* for flyers: the London Control Zone had been born!

Except for entrance funnels and the circuits of Fairoaks, Denham and White Waltham, the whole of the Zone which covered more than 250 square miles of the most valuable and important part of England from the ground up to 11,000 feet (the magazine *Flight* helpfully calculated this as being equal to 2.5 billion cubic yards of air) had been appropriated by the Ministry for the benefit of the scheduled airlines. The magazine mentioned took a curiously anti-establishment stance on this and for once failed to realise that the move was in many ways both inevitable and in the interests of safety for all concerned.

The immediate effect was to eliminate all light aircraft from within the Greater London area. Whereas once it was allowed to pass Heathrow under 3,000 feet if you were more than five miles from its boundary and to fly right over the top of it so long as you were above 3,000 feet, now you were kept well away. And no more would small aeroplanes (*any* aeroplanes, come to that) be able to use such occasional private airstrips such as Staines, Middlesex, and Hatch End (Pinner). The long-term effect was to demand that all aircraft that wished to enter the Control Zone or cross an airway had to have radio.

The Experimental Aircraft Association's Fly-In in the summer of 1963 was a memorable event. This American organisation, the equivalent of the ULAA/PFA and largely the effort of one man's dream – that of Paul Poberezny – boasted 16,422 members and estimated that at least 2,000 home-builts were flying in the States with at least 4,000 under construction. Besides introducing the concept of virtual total freedom in amateur aircraft construction and, more importantly, design, the EAA also introduced a new term to this side of the Atlantic – 'Fly-In' meaning rally, gathering, get-together.

Those that could afford to travel from Britain to America for the event – and who could find that essential American hospitality in order that the £50 travel allowance (there were still currency restrictions on travel) would last – watched in awe as literally hundreds of home-built aircraft took part in the week-long meeting. A number of the aircraft, we were intrigued to find, had some sort of radio, but not all. The event took place at a busy commercially-used airport – Rockford, Illinois – and this meant that scheduled commercial movements by airliners were almost continuous. The air traffic control chaps sorted that one out by using light signals, one circuit direction being allocated for the amateurs and a different one for the professionals. The upshot was that many thousands of movements took place without interference or, thankfully, incident of any kind. Some of the British observers in attendance wondered quietly why such an eminently workable, intelligent solution might not be used at home in Britain. Deep down we were becoming resigned to the inevitability of radio in our aircraft. And envious of the Americans as well as the French…

It was several years later (1966) that Poberezny, the EAA President, lectured

Reid & Sigrist's Desford Trainer was also used for trials in a programme to evaluate the possibilities of using a pilot lying down instead of sitting in a cockpit. Here is the Desford but now in military markings as VZ728 with a rebuilt, extended nose for prone-position pilot experiments. After the prone-position pilot concept was ousted – it was decided that the disadvantages outweighed the benefits – all trials stopped, and the aircraft's makers returned to their core business never again to make a complete aircraft. This great enterprise was lost.

the Royal Aeronautical Society in London and showed a colour film of the 1965 Fly-In. Members sat open-mouthed as they watched the flying, landing and parking of the 2,800 aircraft that attended, not all of them equipped with radio, and saw the 4,000 family members that camped around the airfield, some under their aircraft. Poberezny spoke of the 5,500 movements per day of the event. Amateur aircraft 'fly-ins' in Britain at that time tended to major on hopes for good weather and the aeroplane starting first time! One such rally, recalled by the author, managed one visiting aircraft – and that had force-landed miles away in fog and volunteers had to go with a car and rescue the pilot in time for dinner!

The year 1964 began with restrictions of all kinds in place and the British private flyer still facing obstruction at almost every turn. This reduced the number of light aircraft on the register and as regards the numbers of aircraft privately owned put Britain into tenth position in the world following Brazil, Argentina, Mexico and West Germany among others. The 1962 register showed that America had 81,700 general aviation aircraft on the active list, France 4,000 and the UK just 1,000. The Royal Aero Club had some trenchant comments to offer on this situation.

Record-breaking flyer T W 'Tom' Hayhow from Fairoaks was busy establishing new point-to-point records from London to European capital cities. Many of these had first been set in the 'twenties and 'thirties and never challenged since. By the end of 1952 Hayhow had achieved a unique series of 28 new records. His mount was this Auster J-5F Aiglet Trainer, G-AMOS, powered by a Gipsy Major 1G. Named 'Liege Lady', he kept the aircraft at Denham. Early on April 10th he set off on a fresh challenge – London to Belgrade. The next day came news that he had disappeared over the Alps. It was not until May 10th that skiers found his aircraft upside down in the snow, but not badly damaged, in a hollow between the peaks of Gressor and Kleiner Breitstein, some 20 miles south of Salzburg. A lengthy search located Hayhow's body some 600 yards away. Scarcely injured, he had been trying to find a way out of the mountains in deep snow but had been overcome by the cold and died of exposure. It was subsequently established that he had probably got as far as Klagenfurt before becoming weathered in and turned to retrace his tracks. In the end he simply ran out of fuel. As is usual in such instances, once searched, the unsalvable 15-month old aircraft was burned on site and its wreck location suitably recorded.

> The theory usually put forward for our current failure is that the cost of flying aeroplanes today is too high. In our view this is a partial truth only. The cost of Club flying has not increased relatively as much as other sports, including gliding. What is true is that the cost is too high for what we can offer. Thousands of people would be glad to learn to fly if, once they have done so, they can go forward to extract both use and pleasure from being a pilot. A major reason why we cannot do so is because successive governments since the war have failed to provide the basic infrastructure of a flying movement – aerodromes and the associated facilities. Nor have they provided a helpful and sensible attitude towards the minimum number of necessary controls and restrictions. All this is in marked contrast with the action of other leading nations.

The Wilson government of 1964 revealed the hard and short-sighted aspect of the Labour Party. The Defence Minister, Duncan Sandys (1908-1987), told the House that the Royal Air Force would no longer need manned aircraft and with them things like expensive pilot training. *Air Pictorial's* David Dorrell was clearly disgusted with a government that, in its first hundred days, had decided that Britain would not play any further part in what was then called Concord, that it would scrap the revolutionary TSR-2 and, above all, to buy American for commercial and military aircraft.

> Mr Wilson and his colleagues are well on the way to achieving what Hitler and seventy million Germans could not manage in five years: the destruction of British air power.

Strong stuff but one only had to remember that the previous administration had been urging everybody to 'export or die'. The 'brain-drain' was in full swing at that time. Designers, engineers – even draughtsmen and lowly aerodynamicists – were lured from their hovels in British industry by offers of unimaginable riches, high standards of living, subsidised housing and above all the Yankee dollar and vast cars with squishy suspension. They left our shores in droves, few ever returning. Not only had we given America our best and most commercial ideas but also our best brains. By the time we had wised up to what was happening, comments about 'will the last one to leave Britain please turn the light out' were no longer funny.

By 1965 there were only a few older pilots around that could recall the good old carefree days of Hanworth and beyond and still remained vocal. A whole generation had grown up in time of restriction and to these every change for the good or bad, every quirk of the Chancellor's Budget was merely an inevitable and unavoidable event. To them, they were not just accustomed to hard times: they knew nothing different. They positively expected life to be an inordinate struggle where inequality was to be accepted and the pleasures in life were all taxable, curtailable or simply a threat to health and morality.

So it came as no great surprise when one of the few government-sponsored encouragements to flying was summarily suspended. The Ministry of Aviation's Junior Wings scheme had given a small subsidy to clubs to encourage youngsters to take up flying. The reason given for the abolition of the scheme was that of cost. It saved the Chancellor possibly a couple of thousand pounds.

The Air League of the British Empire quickly stepped in to supplant the Ministry's ex-scheme with a replacement Junior Members scheme that enabled flying to be undertaken for around 5s per hour. The body that pioneered this was the Norfolk and Norwich Aero Club at Swanton Morley with the backing of the Norfolk Education Committee which undertook to contribute £50 per head towards the cost of those of its school pupils chosen as Junior Members of the said club. The residue of cash was to be covered by the Air League and local business sponsors.

The deal began with fifteen junior members selected by their school headmasters and headmistresses. By Easter, a third of these had already flown solo with the rest about to. The object of the arrangement was to encourage other clubs to follow this lead. The Air League, founded as early as 1909 to further the interests of the aviation-minded young and to provide flying and engineering scholarships and bursaries as well as careers advice, had come to the forefront in 1935. In that year it sponsored Henri Mignet and his *Pou-du-Ciel* and published the English translation of his famous book. It still exists today, although it has dropped the 'British Empire' portion of its title.

While one scheme seemed set for some success (time would tell that it was an enterprise that quietly fizzled out), a more serious setback for flying clubs was the end of the petrol tax rebate for club flying. In 1965 clubs were faced with increasing their hourly charges in order to stay solvent. This highlighted what many had already suspected, namely that clubs were becoming more and more dependent on their rebates in order to subsidise increasingly unrealistic charges.

Besides pure civilian or sporting flying training, the Air Ministry had a training scheme of its own. Set up in July 1950, the Air Ministry Flying Scholarship Scheme sought air-minded youths and trained them for private pilot's licences at government expense. This, however, was initially restricted to members of the Air Training Corps and the RAF sections of the Combined Cadet Force. In response to pressure from people who were outside these categories, by 1961 the Air Ministry had agreed to extend the scheme to include a hundred scholarships a year to boys genuinely interested in joining the RAF and who were attending schools where there was neither ATC nor CCF representation. Note that girls were denied any such opportunity – and that despite the vital part played in the war by the young girl fliers of the Air Transport Auxiliary (ATA).

The cost of this was estimated at £17,000 a year, each scholarship being worth £170 – approximately the cost of gaining a PPL. At the time it was hailed as the most important development in the British air cadet movement since the formation of the Air Training Corps in February 1941. Over 30 flying clubs received Air Ministry contracts for flying instruction using the club's own aircraft

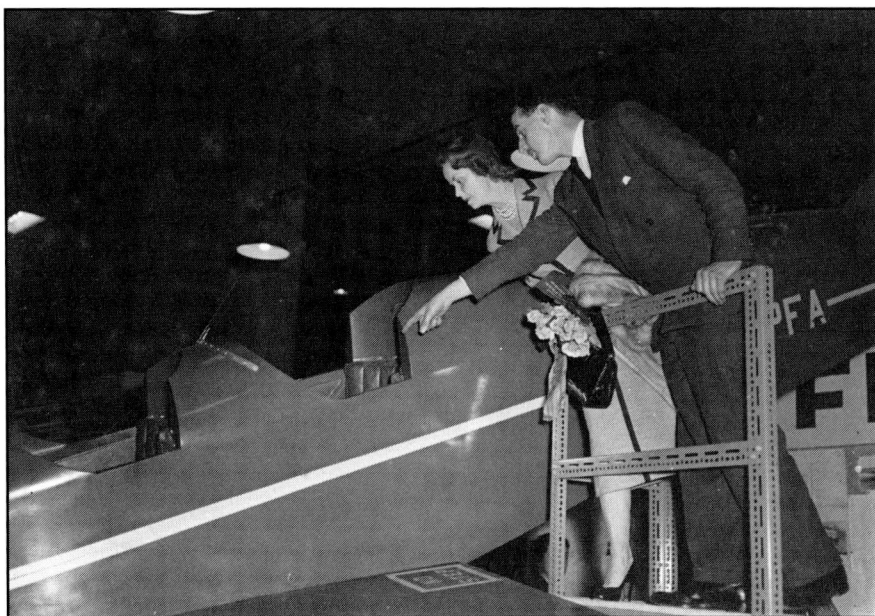

Amateur-built aircraft were never far away, except from the minds of Whitehall. Remembered as the 'Do-It-Yourself' exhibition, the September 1957 event at Earl's Court Exhibition Centre in London was properly entitled the 5th Annual Hobbies and Handicrafts Exhibition. The organiser approached me to see if the Popular Flying Association would like a free stand in a prestigious position on which to show a home-made aeroplane. We said 'yes' and I duly flew G-APFA, the PFA's sponsored Turbi from Bembridge to Elstree where it was dismantled and transported to West London. A full-sized aircraft on display pleased the organisers, drew the crowds and gave us valuable publicity. The Dexion people who made slotted steel angle, offered to build us a free stand to support the aircraft at a rakish angle in return for having their name on show. Everyone benefitted. This Press photograph shows me pointing out some detail to the Duchess of Sutherland, Lady Diana Percy (1917-1978) who opened the show.

and instructors and each course was to include at least 30 hours flying to last about two months and include two consecutive weeks of continuous training. By 1963, 4,637 had been selected and of these almost 4,000 had secured their licences and about half of them had joined the Royal Air Force.

On a broader front, this was the year that the Labour Government wielded its cruellest axe over the British aircraft industry. Five years later, on December 2nd 1970, the Conservative Government proved that it, too, could batter the industry into submission. In the commercial field, the decision not to support the BAC Three-Eleven, an airliner upon which the conglomerate had pinned its future, was a terrible shock that even caught strike-prone unions off guard. With little else in the civil aircraft pipeline, the British Aircraft Corporation was forced to lay off 1,350 workers.

As if this were not enough, Hawker Siddeley was also in trouble and was forced to dispose of more than 2,000 workers. The early months of 1971 showed no let-up in the industry's troubles and the collapse of Rolls-Royce resulted in a knock-on effect with that company's suppliers: some 14,000 people lost their jobs.

In a prophetic insight, David Dorrell, then editor of *Air Pictorial*, warned in his May 1971 editorial column that our aircraft industry was in danger of shrinking fast and might soon be overtaken by the French.

> In December last year the number of people employed by the British aircraft industry was about 228,000. Exports were still running at a fairly high level. The industry had, in fact, done well since the Labour Government's drastic aircraft cancellations of 1965, total aerospace exports for the four years 1966-69 amounting to over £1,000 million, with a record £304.7 million in 1969 itself. The figure for 1970 is down (£277.9 million), but even so is equivalent to an export earning of more that £1,000 a year for each person employed in the industry (which at the same time produces aircraft for the home market as well). There are few other industries that can match this.

What happened militarily and commercially hit equally hard at the private flyer for without a primary aircraft industry, the operation of a secondary or small private-sector industry would become that much more difficult to sustain. Small engines, for instance, were traditionally created on the backs of bigger ones, demonstrating that without a healthy demand for large motors there was no incentive to develop small ones as a spin-off of the technology.

As the 1970s progressed, the first of many major changes, not all of which might be thought for the good of amateur flying, emerged. Among these was the replacement of the ultra-light category Permit to Fly with the Special Category C of A. Then came the announcement in the autumn of 1971 that the Department of Trade & Industry had increased the cost of this 'special category' C of A for PFA members from £3 to £9 per 1,000 lbs of all-up weight. This meant that an aircraft weighing a fraction over the 1,000 lbs mark would be priced at £18. Equally important for Permit aircraft owners was the fact that hitherto expiry of the Permit to Fly (now replaced by the Special Category C of A) had allowed a month's grace to enable any test-flying to be completed in connection with Permit renewal.

The new C of A denied that, meaning that once expired the machine was grounded. For the owner-operator this necessitated planning for C of A renewal maybe four months ahead of the expiry date in order to complete maintenance checks, engine overhauls and the paperwork application before expiry. For some owners, especially those based on isolated private strips, this meant that the new C of A, while titularly valid for a year, allowed barely eight months of use. If this was described as tightening up Ministerial loose ends it was more like the knotting together of boot-lace ends for the poor private owner

The PFA was actually in a far stronger position than it ever knew. The Department of Trade and Industry didn't know what it was doing, the Ministry of Technology couldn't understand why light aircraft were different from Boeing airliners, and the Minister himself was proven to be a fully-paid-up aviation ignoramus. The man with the official title of 'controller of aircraft' had been an admin wallah in the RAF during his latter days and, despite being a Service flying instructor in the inter-war years, was known not to be a believer of the civilian use of aircraft, certainly not small ones.

Most of the old-timers in the PFA had by now departed. This was a shame for had the PFA actually stood up and fought back it would have stood a good chance of re-shaping the Ministry's arbitrary if not maverick behaviour. The arbitrary classification of ultra-light or Permit machines was merely that and a forceful discussion might have had a more advantageous short-term outcome. Unfortunately at that particular period, the PFA executive comprised a fine group of highly-qualified jolly nice blokes unlikely to be numbered amongst the rabble-rousers that were really needed. In defence of the PFA's lack of initiative it might be emphasised that the PFA thought that it had a lot to lose if it fell foul of the administration and that it thought it preferable to play safe, grateful for any crumbs that might fall from the table of General Aviation and commercial flying. Things did change, but not until much later and through other means.

The advance of the 1970s also brought an end to some of the convenience of flying your own aeroplane as more and more airfields around the country were closed. By this time, however, the movement towards establishing new landing strips on farmland was beginning to take off. The numerical transition from a preponderance of factory-built to one centred on home-built aircraft was well advanced and with it a systematic shift from organised airfields with landing fees, expensive hangars and babblespeak, to small fields, friendly farmers and sheds made from hay-bales and corrugated iron.

Elsewhere, the cost of learning to fly was on the increase. Whereas in the 1950s the average hourly rate had seldom exceeded three guineas, in the 1960s this had risen to more than £5 per hour. In 1972 a costing was undertaken by the then PFA president, Air Cmdr Gerard John Christopher Paul. Working on the assumption that the student pilot would attend a club that was approved for the 35-hour shorter course (the normal hours' flying for the licence was 40), he found that the total charge for flying had risen to £327 made up from eleven hours of solo flight at £9 per hour and 24 hours of dual instruction at £9.50 per hour. On top of this the cost of medicals, licenses and examinations, books, maps and navigational instruments came to an additional £28 making the cost of obtaining a PPL £355. Thereafter the possessor of this PPL could continue to fly at £9 per hour and thus it would cost a minimum of £45 per year (five hours' minimum flying experience) to keep his licence current.

Comparison with a club running an 'unapproved' 40-hour course and charging flying at £8 per hour average came to a very similar figure – £320 for the minimum 40 hours training, making a total of £348.

At this time the average PFA group was still able to charge about £3 per hour less than average club rates for both dual and solo flying. This, though, was not the cheapest option and nor were the calculations for the PPL the lowest. That accolade fell to the British Gliding Association which, after years of assessing the ethics of using powered gliders, had accepted the powered glider as the cheapest and most efficient means of giving flying instruction with dual control prior to a small amount of further dual and then the first solo on a pure glider.

This qualified the pilot for the issue of what was called a Motor Glider PPL (MGPPL) the requirements for which were set out as either *[i]* BGA Bronze C Certificate: eight hours' flying in a Self Launched Motor Glider (SLMG) at least four hours dual in SLMG (at least one hour of which must have been completed after going solo), a minimum of three hours P.1 including at least ten take-offs

Home-built aircraft remained a sore point with the authorities and it took much effort to get the concept of amateur-construction accepted. Among the first designs to be approved here were the French Jodel D.9 Bébé. This example was built by Ken Fripp at Lasham. Registered G-AXKJ, it first flew in 1969 powered by a 1,500cc VW conversion. This picture was taken on July 22nd that year.

and landings; three engine stops and restarts in flight; and a solo triangular cross-country flight of at least 100km in a glider or 159km in an SLMG. or [ii] FAI Silver C badge: three hours P.1 on SLMG (within six months prior to application) and three engine stops and restarts in flight.

Meanwhile diehard glidists and sailplaners viewed gliders with engines in the way a concert pianist views a Pianola…

Air Cmdr Paul postulated that 'there is no reason at all why the PFA should not use the same kind of aircraft for our own purposes, and by doing so be able to provide dual and solo powered flying at something like £3 per hour with a consequent dramatic cut in the cost of learning to fly.' Paul's goal was for total flying time for the PPL (assuming a non-approved or 40-hour course) to cost no more than £120. Added to that the 'irreducible minimum' by way of paperwork and inevitables, and the cost would drop to £148 – well under half the cost of gaining a PPL at an approved-course 30-hour school.

While the popular press had latched on to the convenience aspect of private flying and promoted many flights of journalistic fancy, the popular goal of the roadable aircraft or flying motor car was one that quite failed to materialise. The first example seen in Britain after the war was the Fulton Airphibian demonstrated at the *Daily Express* Air Display at Gatwick Airport in 1946. Designed by Robert Edison Fulton (1909-2004) and built for him by Continental Inc, it seemed to have a lot going for it.

With a tour sponsored by the national newspaper and employed on missions like flying and driving blood to a central London hospital, the flying car was something of a nine-day wonder. In the end, and certainly as far as Britain was concerned, the idea was either too fanciful or maybe simply too far ahead of its time and, just like the amphibious motor car that was produced in the 1960s (it drove across the Solent from Portsmouth to the Isle of Wight), reduced to mere novelty or curiosity.

The roadable aircraft (meaning capable of being folded up and towed along behind a car) thus became another moribund class in Britain. Things seemed about to change when the German designer Heini Dittmar, a pre-war international gliding champion, introduced the Dittmar HD.153 Motor-Möve two seat side-by-side seating high-wing single-engined roadable monoplane in the spring of 1956. This was actually a development of the HD-53 Segal-Möve sailplane and, at about £1,200 in Germany, it looked set for a good future, but in the end it did not sell very well even in its home country.

Concerning PFA groups and their flying charges, the target of cheap flying did not go down well with everybody and PFA groups were not always welcome alongside conventional flying clubs. Aerodrome owners sometimes viewed these enterprises in the same way some saw the pre-war Civil Air Guard, namely as destabilising elements meaning possible causes of political instability. This was particularly so when operating alongside any regular flying club that might also be situated on the same aerodrome and, more than likely, owned by the aerodrome operator.

Clearly it was difficult to have two clubs sharing the same basic facilities, with one charging £5 per hour to fly a Tiger Moth while the other was costing its members just £3. Probably the first instance of this problem arose around 1949-50 at Elstree where the regular flying club and then aerodrome owner were positively hostile to a ULAA group that was operating an Auster Autocrat for 35s per hour against £2 17s 6d by the regular club.

The resolution of problems of this sort took much delicate negotiation. Fortunately there were precedents outside the PFA. The Handley Page Flying Club had arrangements with, among others, Elstree Flying Club to hire its aircraft at a special rate and then charge its members a flat rate of between 22s 6d and 25s per hour, the difference being the subsidy paid by the company. In time, of course, increasing regular flying club membership meant that demand on aircraft usage rose within the club and a 'contract' price could no longer be arranged for Handley Page. Gallantly the HP flying group was allowed to continue, still paying the same subsidised rate for hire while Handley Page effectively increased its subsidy to make up the difference.

Ultra-light aircraft had to share the airfield environment with other and larger light aeroplanes. Sometimes even this was a cause for concern and not just because of the old argument about landing fees. One bane of the ULA-owner was hangarage charges: Elstree's then owner charged the present author the same rate for housing an ultra-light as he charged for an Auster – £10 per month. On top of this he wanted a flat-rate landing fee of £25 per year and insisted that all maintenance on the aircraft was to be carried out by the resident club's own engineers. At that particular time, this was exactly the same conditions and costs presented to owners of Miles Magisters, Taylorcrafts and Tiger Moths. Under this form of pricing strategy all the benefits of owning and operating a tiny aeroplane were negated. In the example cited here, the aeroplane in question was not to be long in residence.

Keeping a light aircraft was an expensive undertaking and there were some aerodrome operators that took advantage of the opportunity to make money through over-charging. Fortunately they were few and the majority of airfield owners, especially those that were themselves private-aircraft owners, were friendly and helpful.

Most private fliers were of the impression that a good proportion of the world of officialdom was against them. This apparent paranoia was not without some small justification.

British builders made Druine Turbulents. Redhill's Tiger Club flew these Rollason-built examples – G-APYZ with canopy, and G-APTZ (behind) with original open cockpit. Both flew on a Restricted Certificate of Airworthiness.

CHAPTER THREE
Is Britain Really an Air-Minded Nation?

Statistically the number of licensed pilots per head of the British population was pathetically low. The annual figures published by the Fédération Aéronautique Internationale (of which Lord Brabazon was one of the five *Présidents d'Honneur*) published some disturbing conclusions which caused the editor of the Air League's journal, Air Commodore G J C Paul to ask that leading question – 'is Britain air-minded?' His concern arose from figures for 1958 that showed that the United States had 444,500 licensed pilots. Next in line came France with 10,000 and third England with 6,442. Fourth was Germany with 4,721 followed in fifth place by Italy with 3,800. Australia possessed 3,710 flyers.

If these numbers painted a picture that was not too bad, then they were less encouraging when expressed in terms of licensed pilots per million of population. Now the picture suddenly looked very different. Leading with 2,880 pilots per million was still the United States. Next at 445 pilots per million was Switzerland followed in third place by Australia with 381. France, with 228, was in fourth place with Sweden in fifth with 175 pilots. In sixth place with 163 licensed pilots per million of population was Chile. Finally, in seventh position with just 125 pilots per million inhabitants, was the United Kingdom.

Paul summed it up neatly.

> It would be... dangerous to seek to draw too many conclusions from these figures... In 1957 the US Government provided free flying training for no less than 13,000 'veterans'. That Canada (whose pilot population is not published) subsidised each student pilot to the tune of $100 and a similar sum for each student to the club which trained him; that Australia provided £180,000 towards the cost of replacement aircraft for flying clubs; and that in France the Government provided 40 per cent of the cost of new aircraft; in Sweden, there is no tax on club aircraft fuel.

What is clear, however, is that in a population when contains 2,880 private licensed pilots per million, there is likely to be a far better understanding of the functions and national importance of aviation, than in a population where the figure is only 125 per million. It is liable to be reflected in the everyday attitude of people towards flying; whether they accept it as a normal means of transport, or still regard it as something unusual and rather daring, in short whether or not the people are 'air-minded'.

If... the figures shown can be used as a measure of 'air-mindedness', Britain shows up badly. Moreover, the FAI report indicates that we are getting worse, because our total of private licensed pilots was actually 11.4 per cent less in 1958 than it had been in 1957.

One conclusion therefore stands out. It is time Britain woke up to everyday flying and became air-minded.

What Paul overlooked was that very old saying about leading a horse to water

Airmindedness is one of those loose terms which we all think we understand what it means yet, in the final analysis, it is as imprecise and as fleeting as the hint of a rose on a summer's breeze. In practical terms it all boiled down to two distinct parts – first, was the government (meaning the Ministry) actually interested in keeping light aviation alive. Second, was the general public still enthused, as once they certainly had been, by the sight of an aeroplane? This picture, taken in the summer of 1958, shows a Rollason-built Druine Turbulent at an air show. It is tightly surrounded by people who have obviously been drawn to it. However, only a father and his young son appear actually to be looking at it! Perhaps coincidental, but the world of light aviation could be excused for seeing this evocative photograph as something of a mirror on the real world. This is the one that HRH The Duke of Edinburgh flew in 1952 – G-APNZ.

being rather easier than getting it to drink. He did not so much as countenance the sad thought that perhaps people in Britain couldn't afford to fly, or simply didn't *want* to fly!

The 1957 figures could not have come as a shock. During the debate on civil aviation in the House of Commons as early as March 19th 1951, one MP (George Ward; *Cons.* Worcester) told Members that club pilots and private owners were being slowly squeezed out of the air. The pattern was there for all to see, he proclaimed.

In the first nine months of 1939 the Royal Aero Club issued 3,287 private pilot's licences; in 1946 the number issued was 1,688; in 1947 it was 1,763 and in 1948 1,784. Up to that year (1948) the number had been gradually increasing since the end of the war. In the closing nine months of 1949, however, only 470 were issued and in the first half of 1950 the number stood at just 128.

George Ward concluded that the first really big drop took place in 1949 and coincided with the coming into force of the Air Navigation Order of 1949. This order, it was asserted, made the lives of private flyers almost impossible by producing a mass of rules, regulations and restrictions. Another plea was made to help the clubs. But nothing changed then, in 1958, or later.

We had begun post-war flying with more aircraft than we had a decade later because many of the pre-war survivors were sold off abroad in the quest for 'hard currency'. In 1938 there were 626 private aircraft registered in Britain, a number that had actually declined to 542 by 1939. A decade later this figure had fallen to 306 and by 1950 we had just 257 or less than half the pre-war figure. There were those in influential positions that felt that the job of legislating private flying practically out of existence was being pursued with success.

Data like these, while shocking and depressing, are fundamentally vital. They serve as bread-and-butter reading for financial institutions and government departments should they ever have to consider loans to aircraft makers or subsidies to aid flying. They are valuable weapons in the battle for lethargy. They are also deterrents against the inspiration to try to produce a new light aeroplane. And they also made excellent reading for overseas (meaning American) companies who might view Britain and its aircraft market as either undeveloped or undevelopable. We also know that they're pretty useless since they can be made to prove anything…

The Chrislea Aircraft Company had begun operations before the war in a small shared workshop off Mornington Crescent, Camden Town in North London. There, with four employees, the business stayed through the early days of the war making small parts for, among others, the Fairey Swordfish. In 1941 the firm took over part of The Acme Furniture Company at 77 Fortess Road, Kentish Town, where it stayed for the remainder of the war. With staff numbers increased and working a sixty-hour six-day week, parts for Beaufighters become the mainstay operation. Early in 1944, a young lad called Monty Brown was pulled from production work and given the job of building a mock-up of a private aircraft. This was the Ace. By the end of that year and well before peace was declared, Chrislea saw fit to place its first advertisement for a civil aircraft which it priced optimistically at £475 complete with an American Franklin engine. With the end of the war, Chrislea Aircraft moved out to one of the Airwork hangars at Heston Airport and Ace production began in earnest. A completely new workforce was employed: Monty Brown was the only one to stay with the firm. By the end of the year the sales price of the Ace was being promoted as £1,750.

Aircraft and qualified people to fly them are one thing: suitable places to operate the aircraft are another. Across the country, far from preserving our aerodromes, they were being closed down. Merely within the Home Counties, many flying fields were shut between 1939 and 1960. In that year and in the London catchment area alone, some 16 aerodromes available to private flyers were closed and abandoned. These were:

Abridge; Broxbourne; Canterbury (Bekesbourne); Croydon; Eastbourne (Wilmington); Fairlop; Gravesend; Hanworth; Heathrow (Great West Aerodrome, also known as Harmondsworth, Fairey's private aerodrome); Hendon; Heston; Horton Kirby; Maidstone; Penshurst; Romford (Maylands); Warlingham (Hamsey Green).

To this one could also add a handful of others that were only slightly beyond the London reaches such as Langley, Hatfield and Leavesden soon to be followed by Radlett and so on. This list excludes the Royal airfield at Smith's Lawn, Windsor, and perhaps already de rigueur by 1939. The spread of Control Zones in the 1950s and the redefinition of military low-flying zones further restricted opportunities for private flying.

The untimely closure of Broxbourne in the early 1950s (it was more profitable to mine the field for its underlying gravel which, incidentally, made it so well-drained and such a splendid all-year-round airfield) was now to be the fate of Panshanger in particular following a vociferous campaign from the nearby settlement of Welwyn Garden City where a band of blue-collar rabble-rousing residents (probably best dubbed Denhamites after that infamous anti-flying fringe in neighbouring Buckinghamshire) objected to the freedom of flying. In the end, Panshanger was allowed a stay of execution after a long battle, in particular because it, too, was on valuable deposits of gravel. It didn't survive, being built over by 2016.

Fairlop, thought ideally sited east of London, was to have been the new London International Aerodrome to replace Croydon in 1939, but development work was overtaken by war and, in the end, it would have been too small with no easy room for expansion. But it was a nice flying field for light aircraft. Some private flying did return there after the war but it was never really re-opened and today is quite forgotten.

Peter Masefield (1914-2006) was a powerful figure in post-war aviation. Today he's best recalled as the man who took over as chairman of British Airports Authority in 1960 and turned its £17m loss into a profit of almost £6m by the time he left in 1971. While government wanted Foulness to be London's third airport, Masefield backed Stansted and won. Back in 1945 he was the first British Embassy civil air attaché to Washington and endeared himself to light plane users by flying his own Percival Proctor around America. From there he joined the Ministry of Civil Aviation and quickly showed himself to be partial to light flying. Now chief executive of British European Airways (BEA), he encouraged the airline's participation in the 1953 London-Christchurch (NZ) air race and entered the third prototype Viscount airliner which Vickers was invited to loan for the event. As BEA team manager, Masefield took an interest in every aspect of the attempt which involved carrying huge amounts of fuel to increase the airliner's range. He also piloted the Viscount for some portions of the race. Operating during the event at weights well in excess of its designed maximum, the BEA Viscount came in second in its section which was won by a KLM Douglas DC6A. This was the last of the great air races. After seven years with the airline, Masefield became managing director of Bristol Aircraft in 1955 and pushed through the development of Britain's first (and last) long-range turboprop liner, the Britannia. He was elected president of the Popular Flying Association and operated his own souped-up Chipmunk. By 1960 he accepted the job of managing director (later chairman) of Beagle Aircraft and persuaded the Pressed Steel company to finance the venture, organised the takeover of Miles Aircraft Ltd and Auster Aircraft Ltd, and set up a comprehensive design and production system. By the time he was invited to take on the chairmanship of the BAA in 1965 for his innovative six-year stewardship, Beagle's prospects looked bright enough. The success of Beagle is recounted elsewhere. Masefield was knighted in 1972 and went on to be, among many other things, president of the Brooklands Museum. While much of Beagle's problems were not of his direct making it is recalled that on a rare occasion when he actually attended a PFA meeting he afterwards said to the present author that the secret of success in business was to know when to keep your head down and when to move on... Staffordshire-born Peter Gordon Masefield was a rarity in the world of post-war aviation. His recommendations on the Third London Airport, for example, were at variance with many of his peers yet he had the wisdom to push when others would have backed off. Starting as a junior draughtsman with Fairey Aviation before joining the editorial staff of The Aeroplane in 1937, he was firmly on the management escalator. Latterly he became president of the Royal Aeronautical Society and was knighted in 1972.

But the real loss was Portsmouth Airport. The utter unmitigated stupidity of once-alert Portsmouth Town Council in closing that fine grass field (which even had its own, albeit underutilised, railway station) is almost unrivalled in aviation vandalism. The decision, in 1972, took out the last landing place before the Isle of Wight and dispossessed a good flying club and a friendly staff, not to mention the flying side of Hants & Sussex Aviation Ltd, an accommodating and thriving aircraft building and maintenance business that had just become approved to handle advanced engine overhauls. As for Airspeed Ltd, its famed home on the airfield's south side had been home to Oxford, Consul and Ambassador aircraft. Now it would be obliterated.

What many assumed to be the systematic gradual withdrawal of services for the private pilot was no recent event. It had really begun on March 15th 1950. That was the day that Airmet was unexpectedly and unceremoniously taken off the air. Just four years after restarting its service, the Copenhagen Conference on Radio Broadcasting had allocated the Airmet frequency of 1,224-metre wavelength to a needy high-power radio station. That no alternative frequency was allocated and that the usurper was actually Danish created an uproar in private flying circles that rumbled on for several years. Despite protests to the Postmaster-General (Labour's Wilfred Paling), the MCA and all else and sundry, Airmet was silenced forever. Pilots in that era of non-radio flying were deprived of a key met-forecasting/actual aid. While not necessary now, its closure then created a twenty-year void in vital information-sourcing.

And the same week as Airmet went off the air, Leicestershire's most popular aerodrome was closed – Ratcliffe. Its founder and owner, Sir Lindsay Everard (b. March 13th 1891, Kt.cr 1939) was a great sponsor of private flying in the pre-war years but he had died in March 1949. The home of the Leicestershire Flying Club, Ratcliffe had begun as Sir Lindsay's own private 'strip' – a real 'pocket-handkershief' field which he had systematically enlarged. Associated with the activities of Winifred Spooner (who herself died in 1933 of 'flu) and during the war used as a ferry pool for the Air Transport Auxiliary, Ratcliffe's closure so soon after the re-birth of light aviation was felt by almost every pilot in the land.[1]

It was this on-going dire state of affairs that was the dominant influence in the Air League's Report on General Aviation published in November 1960. Among the predictable comments and recommendations, it urged *(1)* freer use of RAF airfields such as at weekends; *(2)* greater use of disused airfields; *(3)* provision of three or four common radio frequencies for General Aviation. It went on to urge the government to encourage private industry to enter the field of light aircraft manufacture. And so on, concluding in summary with recommendations for *(a)* a lively light aircraft industry; *(b)* a purposeful and active flying and gliding club movement; *(c)* an adequate ground organisation, including airfields and radio facilities to encourage General Aviation; and *(d)* an enlightened attitude towards the framing and publication of essential regulations regarding the organisation of air traffic.

Curiously, and by a remarkably fortunate coincidence of timing, just as this report was being published, Sir Peter Masefield let it be known that he was interested in forming a new aircraft company to produce light aircraft.

It was all good stuff, especially as carrots had been dangled in high places for some long while. Masefield had been managing director of Bristol Aircraft (1955-1960) and the respected international aviation periodical *Interavia* had published a short news item in the autumn of 1959 saying that Bristol Aircraft were working on designs for a series of light liaison and sports aircraft built largely from plastics. Now came the bombshell that Masefield, fresh from Bristol, might be about to start up in a new, modern venture.

---

1. Radio communication was at this time almost unheard of in private flying, in the main because it was deemed unnecessary, but in truth because the necessary equipment was of restricted range, extremely large, very heavy and cripplingly expensive. For those that did use radio, the Ministry of Civil Aviation decided that it was time to have a new phonetic alphabet. The days of 'Able, Baker, Charlie, Dog...' were relegated to history on November 1st 1951 when everybody was expected to change over to 'Alpha, Bravo, Charlie, Delta, Echo, &c' Many a controller had exasperating fun trying to cope with 'George Able Fox Mike Dog' attempting to make the best of a poorly-remembered Information Circular No 133/51...

What happened next was to result in the formation of British Executive and General Aviation Limited, an outfit better known as Beagle. This will be described in detail later on but for the moment let it mark an event that coloured the start of the decade known popularly as the 'swinging sixties'.

For now let's summarise the areas of aeronautical development that characterised that quarter-century following the end of the Second World War.

Since the days of the Aerial Derby in the 1920s air-racing had been a popular event in the private flying calendar. Like the one-time Hendon Air Pageants and Alan Cobham's National Air Days, racing brought thrill and excitement to the public. With the outward similarities to the great national horse-racing events (there were bookies, paddocks, cups, trophies and prizes that were expressed in guineas) there was immediate scope to restart the occasions.

What would emerge as the final events had been scheduled for the day before the outbreak of war. September 2nd 1939 was to have been the race for the King's Cup and that for the Wakefield Challenge Cup held at Birmingham. The worsening international situation and the imminence of war led to their cancellation. The last race to be held that year had been the Folkestone Aero Trophy Race at Lympne. Eleven starters were lined up for the flag: the event was won by a Chilton DW.1A at 126 mph with two Tiger Moths in second and third place at 113 mph and 110 mph

Memories are short and most forget that the mid-1940s gave every indication of heralding a genuine light plane renaissance. A small but significant handful of new light aeroplanes promised a return to the busy skies of old. Time would tell that most evolved as non-starters and only Miles and Auster are remembered today, possibly Chrislea too, but that's all. But there was also the Newbury EoN, curiously spelled that way because it actually stood for 'Elliotts of Newbury'. This all-wood four seater was cheap, sensible, easy to fly and of wooden construction that was ideal for maintenance and repair. It was, in short, an excellent aeroplane. Elliotts was a long-established firm of quality shopfitters and furniture-makers in pre-war days. Now with a war-funded aircraft manufacturing capability, it also built fine sailplanes (the EoN Olympia) but deprived of work by the declaration of peace, the business needed backing, guarantees and, above all, some encouragement from high places. Outcome? Nothing – and when the aircraft pictured here in 1948 unfortunately crashed due to pilot stupidity it was seen as an excuse to forget it.

respectively. The best speed in this handicap event was Edgar Percival who clocked an astonishing 230.5 mph in his Mew Gull G-AFAA.

As related in Chapter Two, the first post-war event was again held at Lympne and was once more the Folkestone Aero Trophy Race. A score of machines entered for the September 1st start. That day also saw the start of a new event – the Lympne High Speed Handicap – which was flown over three laps by four RAF fighters and was won by a Hawker Fury at 342 mph. The problem with this event was that,

unlike the excitement of low-level pylon-turning races of old, it turned out to be too fast and too high and thus made for a poor spectator sport: it was only staged one more time and then allowed to fade.

These events were important to the private pilot because in theory anybody could take part and, in an age before computers took the last vestiges of chance out of handicapping, almost anybody could win whether in a machine that was fast or slow. It was always a matter of regret that the national newspapers, keen supporters of the event pre-war, now devoted less and less space to the event and then only to note the winner of the Royal trophy or, as unfortunately occurred on occasion, the fatal crash of a contestant.

In 1949, the Royal Aero Club decided to combine all the racing events into one major occasion known as the National Air Races. Key event as always was the King's Cup Race. It is worth recording here that, following the passing of King George VI in 1952, Queen Elizabeth II agreed that the trophy should retain its historic title. In addition to this major contest there was a full supporting programme of other events including the Grosvenor Cup, Osram Cup and Kemsley Trophy with an array of ancillary awards including the SBAC Trophy, Air Racing Champion, British Lockheed Aerobatic Trophy, John Percival Challenge Cup, Norton Griffiths Trophy, and the Air League Cup.

During the late 1940s and early 1950s, a small group of pilots whose names regularly appeared in the top places in race winners' lists formed themselves into a

Still, though, Britain could muster a busy apron when one wanted to. Here is the scene at Shoreham Aerodrome in Sussex one summer's day. The line-up includes Dragon Rapide, Chrislea Ace, Miles Messenger and Gemini, Auster Autocrat, Puss Moth, Tiger Moth, Dart Kitten and Chipmunk. Pre-war designs clearly proliferate and this would be the sustained pattern for many years to come.

group that gained both respect and public notice at the time. This was 'The Throttle-Benders' Union' and comprised Sqdn Ldr J Rush, J N 'Nat' Somers, Ronald R Paine, Cyril Geoffrey Alington, Anthony L 'Tony' Cole and Fred Dunkerley. Predominantly Percival and Miles-mounted, the stars of the band were undoubtedly Somers, Paine, Dunkerley and 28-year-old Tony Cole flying what was, for a while, the only airworthy example of the 1930s Comper Swift (G-ABUS): he was, much later, joined by Airspeed test pilot Ron Clear in his own Swift (G-ACTF).

Making an aircraft go fast still represented a challenge – maybe the last great frontier open to the private pilot – in the 1960s. A recurring topic wherever flying men gathered, it was as a result of endless discussions and postulations over clubhouse pints that Norman Jones, founder of the Tiger Club and owner of Rollasons Aircraft & Engines Ltd at Croydon, decided to sponsor a competition to design a midget racer.

Norman Jones was a tremendous enthusiast and philanthropist who ran his aircraft servicing business as an opportunity to fly. He had a production line of Turbulents and Condors and was a true patron of light aviation. He also handled the Ardem-converted Volkswagen flat-four aircraft engines. His real occupation was looking after the family stationery business based in Ware, Hertfordshire, and he frequently commuted by Turbulent from Croydon to Panshanger where a company car would meet him for the rest of his journey to his factory where Butterfly-brand envelopes were churned out.

Rollasons' announcement came at the start of 1964. 'This competition', said the literature, 'is to encourage the production of new practical designs in the British ultra-light aeroplane group. The accent is on the sporting side, as these little aeroplanes can really come into their own by providing pilots with a cheap and efficient racer in the National and International Air Races. Further, a good design can also provide a cheap means of aerial transport for the private owner.'

What a wonderfully straightforward piece of encouragement! It was almost unnecessary to offer a prize after that incentive, but Norman Jones did. The first prize would be 100 guineas (£105), the second prize was 75 guineas (£78.15s.0d) while the third place would earn 50 guineas (£52.10s.0d).

Air shows and races were still richly dominated by old aircraft. Not that anybody objected since there was a certain frisson to be gained from seeing an open-cockpit racer sweep through the skies to the accompaniment of a distinctive engine sound. All that could be found in the 1930 Comper Swift. While the first Swifts to fly after the war were B-G-ABUS and, briefly, G-ABPE, it was Airspeed's Ron Clear who piloted G-ACTF. The red and white Pobjoy-powered midget continues as a show-stopper right to the present day!

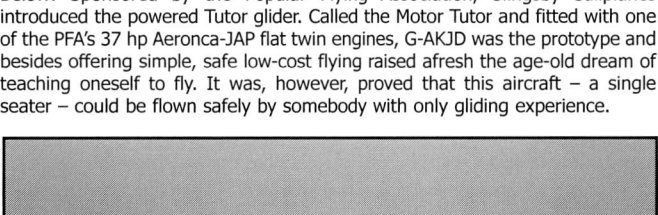

Below: Sponsored by the Popular Flying Association, Slingsby Sailplanes introduced the powered Tutor glider. Called the Motor Tutor and fitted with one of the PFA's 37 hp Aeronca-JAP flat twin engines, G-AKJD was the prototype and besides offering simple, safe low-cost flying raised afresh the age-old dream of teaching oneself to fly. It was, however, proved that this aircraft – a single seater – could be flown safely by somebody with only gliding experience.

The availability of RAF-surplus Chipmunks offered a lifeline to flying clubs up and down the country that needed something other than Tiger Moths and Autocrats. Fully aerobatic with an enclosed cockpit, de Havilland's tandem two seater was an ideal training aircraft. The only problem was that getting a civil conversion meaning a Certificate of Airworthiness was both difficult and expensive. Amidst many arguments centring on how could it be so costly to convert a highly successful military aircraft into a ditto civil one, it was quite a while (and a lot of money) before the event actually happened. An early conversion was Elstree Flying Club's G-AOSY pictured here. One of the difficulties was that engine starting was by Coffman cartridge, the revolver chamber accepting six cartridges. Having explosive cartridges on board and replacing them was a long-term stumbling-block eventually overcome by a change to electrical starting. The old fashioned hand-swinging was increasingly less popular with the younger generation of flyers!

There was also the 'new brigade' – those engineers endowed with the fervour to make something different rather than merely to re-make designs that were already out-moded. The product of one of these avant-garde businesses was the extraordinary Planet Satellite, G-ALOI. A brave, if ultimately misguided attempt at being very different, the all-magnesium centre-engined pusher was the product of impressive lack of experience, considerable faith, extensive hope – and vast quantities of other people's cash. Those with a knowledge of schoolboy aerodynamics saw it at the Farnborough Show in 1948 (where it was a static exhibit) and asked how it was intended to fly. No satisfactory answer was offered but the pudding was proved the following year after which it was scrapped. It was a tragedy that so much effort should have been put into a project so clearly deemed to fail. In the end, the Satellite's only connection to successful flight was that it was built, under contract, in the factory of Redwing at Croydon, a firm forever associated with Mr Robinson's very practical side-by-side two seat biplane of the 1930s.

Conditions were that all competitors had to be British subjects and that the engine had to be the Rollason Ardem 4CO2 Mk.4 flat-four 1,500cc (45 hp) or the Mk.5 of 55 hp. Prospective contestants had a month in which to submit entries, and until September 1st to submit full construction drawings for Rollasons undertook to build the winning design.

Of course, Rollasons' scheme was not entirely altruistic for they got the publicity for the contest and the winner – and the winning design. Plus, presumably, all of the others of which there was an encouragingly large heap. By the close of the contest 159 entries had been received comprising 63 'professional' entries submitted by aircraft companies including the British Aircraft Corporation and Hawker-Siddeley and which would probably be acceptable for Permits to Fly without further investigation. Seventeen of these professional designs were the work of groups comprising designers, aerodynamicists, stressmen and so forth. The organisers commented that 'some remarkable aeroplanes are being born' adding that there were some 'exciting wing shapes and sections' amongst which were at least two delta-winged proposals.

'Non-professional' entries submitted from other trades and professions totalled 65, some of which were biplanes and one being a pterodactyl. A third section comprised 31 entries from students, apprentices and even schoolchildren, the detail of which was described as demonstrating 'an amazing knowledge' of aeronautics and encouraging Norman Jones to propose a special prize for the best design from an entrant aged 18 years or under.

In the end, the three prize-winners turned out to be for rather conventional-looking aircraft. Clearly Rollasons had chickened-out of going for radical designs although besides the final ten that were short-listed, details of the other 156 suggestions have never been revealed. By completion date the 159 entries had sorted themselves down to just over 40 sets of constructional drawings. First prize went to the five-strong Luton Group for a neat low-winger with a projected top speed of 142 mph. Rollasons said that it would be ideally suited to amateur construction in the average garage and kit costs were likely to be about £300-£350 plus engine and propeller.

Second prize went to the Titch, a fine design by the enthusiastic John Taylor working entirely on his own. Both these designs were of all-wood construction. The third prize, however, went to an all-metal design called the Mitchell-Prizeman Scamp. This was priced at £1,350 based on a production of 40 examples, with a kit price of £850 inclusive of instruments, engine and propeller.

The full list of the ten design finalists and details of the winning aircraft together with brief assessment notes on each can be found in Appendix Two.

Ultimately all three prize-winning designs were built and they are described in Chapter Eleven. The competition was a resounding success as a stimulus to amateur aircraft building, it was good for Norman Jones' business, but, apart from stimulating an interest in air-racing, in the final analysis it had little impact on the aircraft scene as a whole. Once again it demonstrated that, as in the days of the 1920s Lympne contests, competitions generally only produce short-term results and occasionally even those are hard to define.

The arrival of the gas turbine first in military aircraft and then in commercial transports was not ignored by the private flying fraternity even though the logistics of small jet engines seemed as insurmountable as the advantages appeared exciting. News from France of the marvellous little SIPA Minijet and the outstandingly small and light Turboméca Palas jet engine spurred British light aircraft designers to forsake the propeller and think pure-jet. The first of these was the famous Miles Sparrowhawk G-ADNL of 1935 vintage.

When in 1950 racing pilot Fred Dunkerley sought a King's Cup winner, he decided to convert an existing Miles machine to a twin-jet racer. With the benefit of hindsight one will conclude that without doubt the best procedure would have been to build a wholly new aircraft instead of which the venerable M.5 Sparrowhawk – the last survivor of a mere five-strong production – was mutilated at Redhill in order to install two Palas engines in its wing-roots.

Of course the fact was that Dunkerley only had a certain sum of money available to finance the project and F G Miles was already existing hand-to-mouth never far from the financial problems that regularly dogged his later years. The project extended across Miles' move from Redhill to Shoreham where it made its first flight on December 14th 1953. After much tribulation, the re-named G-ADNL Sparrowjet did win the King's Cup Race at an astonishing 228 mph. Britain's first – and the world's *oldest* – jet-powered aeroplane met an ignominious end in a hangar blaze in 1964.

By that time there had been a succession of tiny attempts at the light jet, the most unusual of which being the installation of a 70 hp Rover Gas Turbine in Currie Wot G-APWT to create a high-performance turboprop biplane.

In the sphere of the pure jet, though, one machine stands out head and shoulders above the others and that was the word of another racing pilot and a racing designer. Hugh Kendall's design for pilot J Nathaniel Somers was an outstanding machine that was simple, sleek and fast. Powered by a single

In the dark days of the early 1950s we were greatly inspired by our friends across the Channel. The enthusiasm of the French home-builders and their association – Réseau du Sport de L'Air – was boundless. To these men we owe an enormous debt of gratitude because not only did they bring us inspiration but the fact that their aircraft designs were approved by the French airworthiness authorities was instrumental in having them accepted here for our ARB was statutorily obligated to accept what its French counterpart accepted. Even more so, our British rules and regulations governing the building and operating of home-built aircraft were based directly on those legally used in France. That debt to France is, unfortunately, largely forgotten today. This picture shows one of the first French home-builts to be seen in Britain, a Jodel D.9 and, in the background, Britain's second Heath Parasol, G-AJCK.

Is Britain Really an Air-Minded Nation?

The 5th Annual Hobbies and Handicrafts Exhibition at Earl's Court in September 1957 saw the PFA's Druine Turbi centre-stage on an exhibition stand. The show drew many thousands of visitors but although the aeroplane attracted considerable interest, the PFA gained fewer than half a dozen new members and only one set of plans was sold – to an American visitor. In this staged promotional photograph I am showing the drawings to Jill Exell, the Royal Aero Club's secretary-typist at Londonderry House who did a great deal of work for both the PFA and me.

The Popular Flying Association was allocated a prominent stand space on which we showed the Turbi, displayed at a rakish angle on its Dexion-contributed display stand, a set of plans for building the Turbi and a pair of engines on display stands, the Rollason Ardem or RTW engine for Turbulents seen here left of centre. White cotton rope, pillars and strip of red nylon carpet were borrowed from The Davis Theatre, Croydon, owned by our executive committee member, Ted Davis.

This occasion was really the first opportunity the Popular Flying Association had to promote itself. My efforts to get the Turbi on show made certain the PFA was featured in all the London evening and national daily newspapers. This really was the start of half a century of promotion by the end of which the PFA name was known and respected around the aviation world. In the centre here can be seen a spare Coventry-Victor Flying Neptune engine on display stand.

Turboméca Palas, the two seat all-wood SK-1 resembled an amalgam of jet fighter and sailplane. This fine enterprise was dogged by teething problems that conspired to restrict its flying, an activity eventually curtailed by an unexpected in-flight turbine failure.

True light jet flight ran its course in the decades that ended with 1970 and the increasing availability of other internal-combustion engines, not just bona fide aircraft units but adapted units such as the Rotax and Volkswagen, tended to diminish the lure of the turbine.

Had the remarkable little Budworth gas turbine completed its development in the late 1960s the situation might have been very different: David Budworth's death in an unrelated light aircraft accident robbed light aviation of a long-forgotten rich opportunity that has not re-occurred.

Motorless flight is the subject of another book in this series [43]. Details of the progress of gliding is therefore out of place here other that to record the fact that gliding flourished in the post-war environment. It offered a real alternative to power flying and in general provided a low-cost substitute that, unless one wanted to purchase one's own machine, was reasonably within the reach of most.

Simple gliding machines based on kites owe their origins to experiments in Britain during the war years. While hang-glider protagonists eagerly and persistently attribute their origins to Francis Rogallo's 'invention' of the bi-conic flexible wing (experimented with by NASA in the late 1960s), this principle was seen first in Britain in 1945 and

Aerial advertising, pioneered by Major John Clifford 'Jack' Savage (1891-1945) with his modified SE.5A, was a volatile subject in Britain. Sky-writing, banner-towing, night-time flights with illuminated signs and sky-shouting were never officially popular and in 1939 a ban was proposed that would take effect on October 1st 1941. Of course, war overtook events and by 1946 most people had forgotten the controversy – but not for long. Aerial advertising was revived but soon there were questions in Parliament and in 1950 it was very nearly banned. But we were on borrowed time and several incidents involving distractions through illuminated signs flown on Miles Aerovans at night and, in particular, sky-shouting, brought matters to a head. On March 29th 1960 a ban prohibiting all forms of aerial advertising came into force. It was warmly welcomed by our Minister of Aviation Duncan Sandys who was just six months into office. As travel became affordable, younger people commented that on the Continent and especially in America aircraft towed banners around the skies and why didn't we have such charming diversions here! Eventually, commonsense and pressure from the United Kingdom General Aviation Manufacturers' & Traders' Association (GAMTA) prevailed: the ban was lifted in 1963. Here we see Ranald Porteous in Autocrat G-AJIZ equipped with Goodyear castoring undercarriage and underwing loudspeakers for sky-shouting, admittedly the least attractive form of air-advertising.

recurred at frequent intervals up to the time of American Rogallo's 'brainwave'.

Kite wings not only made possible cheap and simple gliders but they developed into the so-called microlight aeroplane which bridged that awkward gap between power-flying and gliding.

However, the inclusion of references to gliding here are not without due cause for, just as before the war, there were legitimate cross-over machines that were part-glider and part powered aircraft and consequently offered some of the benefits of each world. In general, they were like the pre-war BAC Drone and built around existing gliders.

The popular Slingsby Cadet and Tutor machines were fitted up with small engines, usually of the motorcycle variety, to bring low-powered flight to the fortunate few. With the easing of regulations in the mid-1960s this sort of modification was no longer akin to a capital offence. Twin-engined gliders were built, but the most successful of the powered glider conversions was Slingsby's own Motor Tutor, a real light aeroplane with proper undercarriage in place of the normal skid, and a 37 hp twin-cylinder JAP engine. This appeared as early as 1948 and there were plans to put it into production – an event that did not come to pass.

Slingsby went on to produce its Capstan powered sailplane fitted with a pylon-mounted Nelson flat-four engine in true BAC Drone style. There were plans to put this into production but a week after I had visited its makers to fly it the great fire of November 17th 1968 which virtually destroyed Slingsby Sailplanes Ltd put paid to the project.

Motor gliders were never really to catch on in Britain despite the fact that Slingsby built one and a small number of standard Slingsby gliders were converted by their owners. In Germany, however,

Aware that the Fox Moth was a four-seater and used the same engine as a two-seat Tiger Moth, Sqdn Ldr James Edward Doran-Webb of Thruxton Aviation & Engineering Co Ltd had the idea of turning the Tiger, large numbers of which were still to be picked up for a very reasonable price, into a four-seater. Built almost entirely out of standard DH.82a parts but with a revised centre section, the cabin four-seater was called the Thruxton Jackaroo. The designer brought his first machine to Bembridge and invited the Author to fly it with the advice that 'it flies just like a Tiger'. He omitted to say that, like the Percival Prentice, it had to be consciously pulled off the ground thanks to an invisible compensating device that made it always fly as if it were at maximum weight plus overload. Here two are seen on the ground. In recent years, many surviving examples have been re-converted back to Tiger Moths.

there were several prominent types such as the elegant Fischer RW-3, the Pützer Motorraab/Moraa (D-EBAC) and the Me 06 Motor-Segler. Britain imported the Scheibe Motorspatz and Motorfalke, this latter machine being licence-built at Kirkbymoorside for a while, but their popularity was surprisingly restricted.

By a similar token, the 'conventional' autogiro as perfected in pre-war years with the Cierva series of machines proved to be a played-out formula by the end of the war. There seems no direct explanation for this since the alternative rotary-wing machine – the helicopter – was a far more complicated, noisy and expensive device, much of this excess cost being due to the need for a comparatively large engine for a relatively small payload.

Not until the rise in popularity of the small and, initially, single seat autogiro begun in America with the 'gyrocopter' of Russian-born Igor Basil Bensen and perfected in Britain by Wing Cmdr Kenneth Wallis and others did the interest in autogyro-type aircraft re-kindle.

On the other hand, perhaps the most striking development of this period was the growth of the helicopter market, in particular amongst private owners. As the availability of small helicopters increased thanks to the gradual replacement of small and expensive models with piston engines and tiny payloads to more practical small turbine-powered examples, so the private owner market expanded.

In 1945, the Helicopter Association of Great Britain was formed under the presidency of James George Weir (of Weir in Glasgow, also Cierva Autogiro fame) and with Cierva's manager and test pilot Henry Alan Marsh as chairman. Its purpose was to promote the interests of those keen on rotary-winged aircraft.

The HAGB staged its first helicopter garden party at Hanworth Park in September 1950 and planned to repeat it annually. However the second did not materialise until 1956 and that was through the generosity of Charles Hughesdon and his wife, actress Florence Desmond, who threw open their garden and grounds at Dunsborough Park, Ripley, Surrey. It was held at this location every year afterwards.[2]

In January of 1960 the Helicopter Association was merged with the Royal Aeronautical Society and became the Rotorcraft Section of the Society. Set up in the same year was the Helicopter Society of Great Britain the responsibilities of which were aligned towards the manufacture and development of rotary-winged machines.

At the same time, the Royal Aero Club established its Rotary Wing Section and, thanks to the continued hospitality of the landowner, who was deputy chairman of aviation insurance brokers Stewart, Smith & Co Ltd, it remained at Dunsborough Park. The Garden Party staged on June 13th 1970 drew more than 20 machines. Other than British-built (or assembled) Westland Widgeon, Wessex and Whirlwind machines, the bulk of aircraft in attendance comprised foreign-designed and built helicopters such as the Agusta-Bell 206A Jet-Ranger, Brantley 305, Bell 47G, Sioux and Alouette II. It was an all-helicopter affair and no autogyros attended.

At the amateur end of the market, Bensen's popular little autogyros were widely built in America and quickly gained a foothold in Britain where they initially posed something of a headache for the authorities for whom rotary-winged aircraft were by then as much of a legislative anomaly as home-builts had been a decade earlier. Ultimately the followers had their own collective association in the shape of the British Gyroplane Association. This had begun in 1959 as the British Gyrocopter Association under the presidency of Donald Campbell of Campbell Aircraft who, with his wife Nan, subsequently lost his life in a commercial aircraft accident. Because 'gyrocopter' was also the trade-name used by the American Bensen machines and since many alternative designs were now emerging, the name was changed.

The realisation that integration of all aspects of the home-built aircraft movement was beneficial led to the decision, taken at the British Gyroplane Association's annual general meeting held on March 8th 1969, that the group with its 100-strong membership should merge with the PFA.

In the interests of avoiding potential acrimony and accusations of oversight by air-cushion vehicle protagonists, it is best to mention this novel form of transportation in this section. Saunders-Roe's prototype SR-N1 was built at Cowes and made its first crossing of the Channel in June 1959.

Christopher Cockerell's hovercraft was a fine workable device that quickly fell foul of the Establishment for it was ruled that since it was a flying machine you had to possess a pilot's licence to fly it and a commercial licence in order to carry passengers in it. Even after its cruising altitude was so dramatically increased by the invention of the flexible rubber skirt[3] everybody possessed of average intellect knew that the hovercraft was anything but a proper flying machine.

Curious anomalies arose as airline pilots confronted training courses to learn the ways of the water in order that these surface-skimmers could be demonstrated. Experienced water captains thought it rather silly. This stupidity went on for five long years before, at the beginning of 1968, the long-standing debate as to whether or not an air cushion vehicle such as a hovercraft should be classified as an aircraft was settled by the Council of the International Civil Aviation Organisation (ICAO).

To the relief of everybody, as much as anybody else those that believed, quite rightly, that the authorities were steadily falling off their trolleys, that august body debated and finally concluded that the answer was 'no'. It is understood that the author's published description of the hovercraft as being a flying machine in which altitude was measured using a dipstick[4] was reputedly widely quoted, if only partially appreciated.

As a result, the ICAO's council, in deciding that they were not aircraft, stopped short of saying exactly what they were. Possibly frightened by stories of 'the Bermuda Triangle', ghosts and crop-circles, they decided to recognise the hovercraft, but not to define it. It did, though, amend its International Standards and Recommended Practices to exclude such vehicles.

As the 20th century moved on, there seemed only one more hurdle to surmount – that of man-powered flight. A curious step backwards and an irrelevance was how many considered the subject in an age when Man had flown at supersonic speeds, walked on the Moon, and had set his sights on the distant stars. But there was no denying that despite all the advances that had taken place in

---

2. The Helicopter Association produced its own journal up to the end of 1959. It was published by Wm Dawson Ltd of 16 West Street, Farnham, Surrey. This organisation also held reprints of important papers read at Association meetings.

3. The flexible skirt for the hovercraft to enable it to 'fly' at a greater height and clear obstructions was invented by the author in 1961 and subsequently patented by his then business partner, Cecil Hugh Latimer-Needham. The invention was an attempt to defeat what the author referred to as the hovercraft's 'playpen' problem. See *Hoveringcraft & Hydrofoil*, London, July 1962, pp.12-13.

4. *Op.cit.*

Originally known as the Bearn GY-20 Minicab, this French design was acquired by A W J G Ord-Hume in the early 1960s and redesigned to comply with British design and airworthiness requirements and re-launched as the Ord-Hume GY-201 Minicab. The first example to be built in Britain was G-AWEP constructed by F S 'Stan' Jackson of Preston, Lancashire. It was test-flown by Roland Beamont on June 21st 1969.

If the Flying Flea started the renaissance in home-built aircraft in the 1930s, then it has proved a credo that will not easily go away. Henri Mignet's post-war HM-290 was a popular and practical machine. Further improved as the HM-293 and powered by a Volkswagen conversion, G-AXPG was an example built at Purleigh in Britain by W H 'Bill' Cole and unveiled at the PFA Sywell Rally on July 17th 1971. Curiously the Flea formula, still popular in France and with a strong following in America, has never quite caught on again here in Britain.

The diminutive Chilton Monoplane was one of the great success stories of the immediate pre-war racing scene. All four that were completed survived the war. This, the third example built, first flew in October 1938 powered by a heavy water-cooled Carden-Ford motor. Finished in light sky-blue and silver, this cruised at 100 mph and hit a maximum of 112 mph in 1939 thanks entirely to the extremely neat nose cowl. Pictured here at the Folkestone Trophy Air Race on July 30th 1938, F Dawson Paul finished fifth at an average speed of 102 mph. The name painted on the top of the cowling is *Flammenwerfer*, associated more with speed than pyrotechnics. This machine was raced in the 1950s by Hugh Kendall who fitted a bubble canopy from an Olympia sailplane and with a new 55 hp Continental motor hit 129 mph to win the Daily Express Race at Shoreham on September 22nd 1951.

While the pre-war style of Cierva autogiro was not to see a long-term renaissance in the post-war skies (the two remaining examples were not destined to survive for long), a new breed of ultra-light autogiro came from America in the shape of the Bensen Gyroplane. The concept was embraced by Britain's Wing Cmdr Wallis who built this modified Model B-7MC, G-APUD, and flew it at Biggin Hill where this picture was taken in 1960 of its builder in his characteristic 'look, no hands!' posture. It was the first of a whole raft of Wallis Gyroplanes that ended up achieving fame in a James Bond film.

A pre-war design that deserved a post-war come-back was the delightful Currie Wot biplane ever associated with the old Cinque Ports Aviation at Lympne in the 'thirties, Thanks to the encouragement of men like John O Isaacs, John H B Urmston and Viv Bellamy at the Hampshire Aero Club, Eastleigh, the original designer John Currie was persuaded to redesign his single seater for modern needs. Popular with those builders who like building a lot of wings, the Wot was easy to build and a dream to fly. This one, G-AYMO, was built in Sussex by E H Gould and fitted with a Walter Mikron III engine.

Fitted with a French-made four-cylinder inverted inline 45 hp Train 4T engine, G-AFSV was another Chilton Monoplane that graced the skies in recent times. In the Goodyear Trophy Race at Wolverhampton on May 17th 152 John R Batt of Aviation Traders Ltd managed to average 122.5 mph. In 1956 it was fitted with a 62 hp Walter Mikron II engine and a streamlined low-profile cabin-top. The inspiration of the Chiltons encouraged the 1960s interest in midget racing aircraft and the Rollason Contest (see Appendix Two in the second volume).

aeronautics, aerodynamics and structural design since the early days of aviation, the concept of a man becoming airborne through nothing more than his own muscle power still held a curious fascination for certain people.

Of course, many had tried throughout aviation's history from Leonardo da Vinci to bicycling wing-flapping birdmen – and all had failed. That alone was enough to cast down the gauntlet of challenge. The first prize money to be put up for a successful man-powered flight was offered during the First World War. The Peugeot prize of £400 was for the first person to make a flight of ten metres carried out with no other motive power than that furnished by the pilot. It was in abeyance during war but by 1919 interest in it had revived, and there was a lot of strenuous practising. In August 1919 a message from Paris announced that at Longchamps the well-known French cyclist, André Poulain, had made a hop of twelve metres at a height of one metre, his speed being 9km per hour.

There had also been much work in Germany and Italy towards the goal of successful man-powered flight during the 1920s and 1930s and, in 1929, Alexander Martin Lippisch (1894-1976) was involved in trials with a flapping-wing glider.[5]

Early in 1936, an Italian succeeded in flying a bicycle-type sailplane with twin propellers for a distance of 300 feet. Soon afterwards, a catapult launch enabled the same pilot to sustain flight for several hundred metres culminating with a launch to nine metres height and a pedalled flight of one kilometre. That was at Cinisello Airport, Milan, and it took place on March 18th 1937.

Of course, aid such as that offered by a catapult was unacceptable to the purists who, rightly, stated that the true man-powered flight must be made from a standing start and without external assistance. Preferably the use of stored-up energy (falling weights, springs and suchlike) mustn't come into it either.

One of Britain's leading protagonists in the quest for aviation's Loch Ness Monster was Canadian-born Beverley Strahan Shenstone. Born in Toronto on June 10th 1906, Shenstone was based in Germany between 1929 and '31, working with Junkers on the single-engined Ju52, and then at Rhön-Rossitten Gesellschaft. Here he was introduced to the German soaring movement, eventually qualifying for his sailplane pilot's certificate at the Wasserkupf. Years later found him as chief engineer to British European Airways at Northolt Airport and, later, Heathrow.[6]

Engineer Shenstone saw an opportunity and so, in February of 1955, he wrote an article in the *Sunday Times* suggesting a revival of interest in man-powered flight. This started rolling a ball that gathered in both size and velocity, finally maturing into the Man-Powered Aircraft Committee formed in January 1957. Centred on RAF Cranfield, the MAPAC began with a seven-strong team that quickly doubled in numbers as more people became interested. By October of 1959 it had merged into the Man-Powered Aircraft Group Committee of the Royal Aeronautical Society. Suddenly man-powered flight was up alongside space-travel as the ultimate goal of aeronautical mankind!

The little Druine Turbulent was put into production at Croydon by Rollasons and here G-APIZ is seen being started. Because of its diminutive size it was often the subject of clubhouse jokes, one of the more reputable ones said to concern the pilot of a Turbulent who arrived at the petrol bowser and ordered seven pints of petrol. The mechanic, without flinching, responded: 'Certainly, Sir! And shall I cough into the tyres?'

The Tiger Club at Redhill operated a flight of Turbulents that gave demonstrations at air shows around the country. Team leader Norman Jones of Rollasons had his own special example. Fitted with neat spats, long chromium-plated exhausts and a spacious cabin with sliding canopy, G-ARMZ was a very luxurious member of the breed.

---

5. This was the *Schwinguin* flown with the aid of a bungee launch during the spring of 1929. An account of the event appears in the Journal of the Royal Aeronautical Society, Vol 64, July 1964, pp.395-398.

6. Born in 1906, Beverley Shenstone was a significant figure in post-war British aviation. As a member of R J Mitchell's team, he worked on the design of the Supermarine Spitfire, going to the Air Ministry in 1938, thence to the Ministry of Aircraft Production. After a stint as general manager of A V Roe Canada Ltd (during which time he was also president of the Soaring Association of Canada), he returned to Britain to become BEA's chief engineer. He was also a leading figure in the European gliding world, editor of OSTIV, author of numerous technical works and president of the Royal Aeronautical Society for a year. He died in Cyprus on November 9th 1979.

It was at this time that the attention of one Henry Kremer was aroused. A Swiss-educated industrialist, Kremer was born in Eastern Europe. Resident in London, he was chairman and managing director of Microcell Ltd as well as being involved with other businesses. Of an inventive mind, he held a number of patents including those for the plywood process used in the construction of the de Havilland Mosquito fighter-bomber. Now he suggested that man-powered flight was perfectly possible – but it would be an expensive quest and therefore need the incentive of a large cash prize to make it worthwhile attempting.

As good as his word, in November 1959 Henry Kremer put up two prizes. The first, £50,000, was for completion of a figure-of-eight course. The second was £100,000 for the first man-powered aircraft to cross the Channel from England to France. The rest became history. It was to be eighteen long years before the first hurdle was achieved by *Gossamer Condor* on August 23rd 1977, and another two years before the star prize was awarded.

This quest saw the development of a number of contenders and some of these employed new, ground-breaking technologies. The man-powered aircraft project grew from a perhaps fanciful dream into practical reality when, on April 25th 1979 Bryan Allen flew the British-made *Gossamer Albatross* for one hour nine minutes and three seconds over the Harper Dry Lake in California – the longest human-powered flight ever made at that moment in time. Then, on June 12th, the same athletic pilot set off across the Channel in the same machine. The 22.25 statute miles took two hours and 49 minutes and the challenge had been conquered.

The tremendous achievement of pedalling a man-powered aircraft across the Channel to France, with the machine at times merely inches about the water surface, rivals solo round-the-world sailing and rowing the Atlantic in terms of personal stamina and accomplishment. To the designers and constructors of the aircraft, though, goes an equal if different accolade for supremely understanding their materials.

The success of this one man-powered aircraft should not be allowed to obliterate the achievements of other contenders who, while missing out on the actual prize, still succeeding in designing, developing and flying man-powered aeroplanes.

Hot-air balloons, relics of the earliest days of Man's aerial ascents, were revived in the 1950s to form one of the most popular forms of sight-seeing and passenger-flying. The ballooning craze became by far the most expanding sector of private aviation in the latter half of the 20th century, admittedly because it began from what was essentially nothing and succeeded in putting on steady growth every year forward.

At the same time, after Lord Ventry's solo attempts to revive the airship, much derided at the time (the late 1940s), airship design and development has proceeded steadily and by 1970 several British designs were in hand while interest was kept alive by regular tours by the American Goodyear blimp.

The post-war years saw the coalescing of aircraft companies at an accelerating rate. Early in 1960 Westland Aircraft acquired Fairey Aviation. Besides losing one of the oldest of British aircraft manufacturers, the merger also meant that Westland was now the sole producer of rotorcraft in the country. Fairey's expanding helicopter division was now part of the Yeovil-based conglomerate. Not until the rotorcraft division of Beagle (making the little Wallis single seaters) would Britain have another, if rather short-lived, rotorcraft maker.

Back in January 1958, the Royal Aero Club House Dinner, hitherto a somewhat anodyne affair, had as guest speaker racing pilot Fred Dunkerley who emulated

Ord-Hume GY-201 Minicab G-AVRW built by R D Hart coming in to land at Halfpenny Green. This machine received its Authorisation to Fly on April 20th 1968.

The Duet G-AYTT was built by A S Knowles as a side-by-side two seater based on the Luton Minor. Attributed to Phoenix Aircraft Ltd, it remained a private venture project since the company had by this time ceased to trade. Power was provided by a Continental C.90 flat four engine. While preserving none of the aesthetics of the Luton design it did demonstrate that the idea of an open-cockpit all-wood machine remains practical as a proposition.

Edward Shacklady and Chris Paul and asked what was wrong with our light aircraft industry and why was it dying on its feet. This drew a response from Edgar Percival who, in a reply published in *The Aeroplane* the following week, told us what we already knew, namely that it was all a case of finance. Highlighting how successful the American industry was and taking up where Dunkerley had left off, he said:

> … the US manufacturer has an added advantage in that practically every manufacturer of light aircraft has received at some time a sizeable order from either the US Air Force, the Army, or the Navy. These orders sometimes amount to as many as 150 aircraft or more at a time, and it is needless to point out what beneficial effect this has upon amortization of tooling and development costs.

He added that:

> … the building of small aircraft should receive some form of Government recognition or support, until the business becomes mainly self-supporting. It is supported in a most practical manner in other countries… In France, the Army bought 425 Max Holste Broussards, and the German Government has placed an order for over 400 Dornier Do 27s. Both of these aircraft are in the small 'executive' class and have proved to be of great value to their owners. In the national interest, the SBAC [Society of British Aircraft Constructors] will have to play its part and take a wider view than they have in the past.

Unmistakably a 'Rearsby Rooster', yet this was approaching the last to carry the name once associated with 'the All-Steel Aeroplane' of Taylorcraft days. A Beagle Terrier II, G-ASAN had started its life as VX928, an Army Auster AOP 6/T.7 but emerged from Rearsby after rebuild on June 26th 1962 as a Beagle/Auster A.61 Terrier II. It is seen here during its days with the Spalding Gliding Club operating from Crowland airfield in Lincolnshire. Note the tow-hook affixed betwixt fuselage and tailwheel.

So would things pan out as Percival proposed? Well, in the years to come, the RAF did order some light aircraft from Beagle, but then the government decided it was all going wrong and closed the firm down. And did the SBAC help? No.

The 1960s began with a feeling that the doldrums of the British aviation industry were once and for all behind us. In light aircraft we had Beagle appearing to be consolidating into a major production centre and continuing where Auster had left off with its amalgamation into the Pressed Steel conglomerate. As far as commercial and military aircraft were concerned, 1963 had seen the decision to produce 100 of the new TSR.2 fighters for the Ministry of Defence and Pan Am and Trans World Airlines had taken an option on half a dozen of the world-beating Concorde supersonic airlines – a lead quickly followed in the summer of 1964 by Air India which put its name down for a brace.

That year also saw the SBAC change its name, substituting 'aerospace' for 'aircraft' so as to elevate its image while keeping its cherished initials unaltered. It marked the recognition of a yet-wider gulf between light/private/amateur aviation and the activities of the companies and the airlines, defence and military flying.

Along with this was a boost from the film industry with the creation of a number of cinematographic block-busters. These included *The Blue Max* and *Those Magnificent Men and their Flying Machines*, movies that called for the recreation of types of old aircraft. Firms up and down the country gained lucrative, if one-off, contracts to built flying replicas of a variety of aircraft from Bristol Boxkite and Antoinette to Fokkers and SE.5A fighters.

While these films gained immense popularity with the general public, they also brought home to many who had not really thought about it before just how difficult they were to fly. For a small number of lucky pilots, flying these film replicas underscored that fact. It was a rich era.

Were we an air-minded nation? The balance of evidence suggests a reasonable degree of probability but this stops short of rank enthusiasm by the masses. Sure, more people fly, but the statistics with which we began uncovered a stark truth that could hardly be ignored.

The Beagle company marked a last-ditch attempt to get our industry revived. Throughout the ten troubled years of its existence it was to endure the trials and tribulations of an intransigent government yet was far from innocent of the means of its own downfall. Words like profligate and squander became associated with the Shoreham enterprise and yet, throughout all this, it did produce some potentially outstanding light aircraft. Birth of the company was announced on Friday, October 7th 1960. By the time the Ministry of Technology forced the government to put the business into the hands of the Receiver on December 2nd 1969 it had managed to produce some good machines such as the Pup. Here is a Series 1 Beagle 121 Pup coming in to land at Shoreham.

The simplicity of the home-built aircraft's cockpit displays all that is really needed in order to fly properly and safely. Here is the instrument-panel of a Druine Turbulent. Centre top is the turn and slip indicator, below left the airspeed indicator calibrated in knots (nautical miles in one hour), altimeter calibrated in feet, the two ignition switches, one for each of the dual-ignition magnetos, engine revolutions-per-minute indicator and, above it, the smaller oil pressure gauge calibrated in pounds per square inch. The knob below the instrument panel, right, is the carburettor heat control to prevent icing. Out of sight, left side, is the throttle lever. Central in the cockpit with the white hand-grip is the control column and just visible is the right one of the two rudder pedals. The fuel tank filler cap is visible just beyond the windscreen. This has a wire rod that indicates the quantity of fuel in the tank: a float raises the rod for a full tank, and allows it to drop to reveal the diminishing content as the tank empties.

Building wing-ribs for a Rollason/Druine Condor showing the simplicity of the equipment needed. Using Aero-Research synthetic glue provided by Ciba (ARL) and contained in the small canister, the two youthful workers have the special rib-building jig in front of them. A small hand-saw, a sharp knife, a wood file, tack hammer and industrial staple-gun completes the tool list for this, one of the more satisfying jobs in the construction of a light aeroplane.

CHAPTER FOUR
The Post-War Light Aeroplane Industry

Throughout the decade immediately preceding the outbreak of the war, Britain had an increasing number of light aircraft manufacturers. As a result, there were numerous projects that were on the cusp of development. Most were very small yet it went to show how many nascent constructors we had within our shores. These were enthusiastic designers and entrepreneurs like Arpin, Chronander, Helmy, Shapley and others who were prevented from shifting their dreams into reality by two things – shortage of capital and the outbreak of war. While both of these causes pertained, only one was beyond their control.

From this one might have expected that peace would have unleashed a rash of new companies spawned by a welter of pent-up aeronautical passion: dreams that had been suppressed for the duration, a vivacious outpouring of light aeroplane enterprise that would be rather more than just mere rekindling of that which had gone on before.

What actually happened was rather different. Yes, there were those that set off at a canter the moment the stable doors were unlocked, but for most it was a trot, let alone a gallop. There was the basic problem that whatever one wanted to do had to fit within the framework of the austerity that tarnished the UK's post-war economy. It has already been explained that materials of all sorts were in short supply, foreign goods were either impossible to buy or phenomenally complicated to import through bureaucratic red-tape, and the freedom to travel was drastically restricted. Government economies and restraints gave little encouragement to those with ideas of starting up fresh enterprises. Taxation and legislation weighed heavily on the small business. And the sale of finished goods other than for export was highly taxed.

Then there was the non-availability of engines. Motors announced as under development never materialised while those in established production such as Blackburn Cirrus and de Havilland were already 'on quota' to existing manufacturers. Any new business had to export a significant part of its production in order to be allowed to operate. This was another 'Catch 22' scenario for it posed a circular argument. With foreign travel heavily controlled through currency restrictions, competing in overseas markets or opening up opportunities abroad was extremely difficult if not impossible. No travel meant no market research and no market research left you with hands secured firmly behind the back!

Starting an aircraft business, then, was a mountain to climb. Those who attempted it were brave and in the majority of cases already had some experience, perhaps of wartime contract work, that might help in securing permits and other vital paperwork around which business had to operate.

So what did we have by way of an aviation industry? As regards aircraft manufacturers of all kinds, we had about 26 although the process of company amalgamation that accelerated after the 1950s had begun as early as 1935. Forgetting group allegiances, the names that survived into 1945 were:

1. Airspeed
2. Armstrong Whitworth
3. Auster (Taylorcraft Aeroplanes Ltd)
4. Avro
5. Blackburn
6. Boulton Paul
7. Bristol Aeroplane
8. Cierva Autogiro
9. Cunliffe-Owen
10. De Havilland
11. English Electric
12. Fairey
13. Folland
14. General Aircraft (GAL)
15. Gloster
16. Handley Page
17. Hawker
18. Heston
19. Martin-Baker
20. Miles Aircraft (Phillips & Powis)
21. Percival
22. Portsmouth Aviation
23. Saunders-Roe (Saro)
24. Short Brothers
25. Supermarine
26. Vickers
27. Westland

Of these, Armstrong Whitworth, Avro, Gloster and Hawker together with ancillary industries had grouped back in 1935 to create Hawker Siddeley. Supermarine had been taken over by Vickers-Armstrong in October 1938,

Developed from the Envoy and first flown in 1937, around 8,750 twin-engined Airspeed Oxford trainers were built for use by the RAF. By 1945 there were large numbers surplus to requirements. At Portsmouth Airport, while Hants & Sussex Aviation was engaged in chopping up several hundred decommissioned Oxfords at one end of the airfield, the Airspeed factory on the other was busy converting Oxfords into civilian Consul 6-8 seaters as light feeder liners and transports. Some of these became luxury private owner aircraft for the up-coming company executive. The prototype AS.65 Consul was G-AGVY, ex-V3679. Besides Consul conversions, a small number of Airspeed Oxfords took on civilian guise. G-ALTR (formerly PH368) was a standard AS.40 Oxford converted for use by Air Service Training Ltd. It survived until being damaged beyond repair following an engine fire at Christchurch on New Year's Day 1962. While not in the flying club league, these machines joined with the DH Dragon Rapide to form the backbone of the fledgling twin-engined civil market.

while in 1940 Airspeed had become part of de Havilland. In 1944 Percival became part of the Hunting Group.

By January of 1951, Cierva ceased to be an independent organisation and became part of Saunders-Roe (Saro), while Cunliffe-Owen, after an ill-founded attempt to produce an airliner nobody wanted (it was a Dakota replacement that was, essentially, just another Dakota only smaller and more expensive), ceased in 1947.

Company coalescence into groups was thus nothing new and by 1950 most of the major players in industry were 'team members'. Government advocated the integration of the smaller firms into just one or possibly two large conglomerates on the grounds of perceived efficiency. Amongst the larger manufacturers of large aircraft, it was Handley Page that was seen as the 'go-it-alone' maverick: in light aviation it was Edgar Percival. After Hunting took an even greater interest in his former company in 1954 and renamed it Hunting Percival Aircraft, Edgar Percival left to start up his own eponymously-named independent business, surviving until 1960 when he sold it to the firm that became Lancashire Aircraft. It was in that year that Hunting itself became part of the British Aircraft Corporation.

In light aviation, however, the 'real' amalgamations did not occur until the formation of Beagle in October 1960. And this marked what was effectively the final act in the saga of British post-war light aircraft manufacturing. Beagle, top of the pyramid and carrying all that had gone before, was, as we would soon see, in a particularly vulnerable position.

In this chapter I want to summarise the areas of development and achievement in the period of two-and-a-half decades following the end of the war. We shall find a story enriched by some successes and a few failures, along the way assessing the changes that characterised this curious era of post-war aviation. And finally we shall look to the achievements of the industry that did exist. I want to take a look at the events surrounding those that I consider to have been significant and major makers while at the same time attempting to show those events that combined to the ultimate demise of the British light aircraft industry. Some of these companies and their projects I have already mentioned in outline.

As post-war turbulence was in progress, another factor operated in the background that served to retard our development. It is a characteristic of the

The first real new civilian aircraft from Auster Aircraft was the Autocrat and this example, G-AJAJ, took to the skies on February 4th 1947. Like so many Auster variants, this machine was subsequently updated becoming a J/1N Alpha. This example was pictured at Lea Airport, Sandown, Isle of Wight.

The two seat Auster J-2 Arrow was the smallest of the Auster family and was powered by a 75 hp Continental C-75-12 horizontally-opposed four cylinder engine. This example, G-AJAM (first flown February 8th 1947), took part in a novel and unofficial race with a Triumph TR2 car to see who would use less fuel on the journey from Land's End to John o'Groats. Harold Best-Devereux flew the aircraft with a Royal Automobile Club official as passenger. Unfortunately due largely to bad weather the car won – but by a surprisingly small margin.

British that we exhibit an unenviable record of treating our inventors and best brains with what is to all intents and purposes a national disdain. Those who have demonstrated the temerity to come up with something new have never been popular with 'the establishment'.

Although there has long been a stoic if rather patronising trumpeting of British achievement and national leadership, this is a characteristic that has always been merely skin-deep. It was a contributory factor to the so-called 'brain drain' of the 1950s and 1960s when British talent was openly touted for by foreign companies, notably those in America.

The poaching of those clever enough to build industrial empires, usually at design level, was a principal activity of the post-war decades. Overseas recruitment experts set up offices in London hotels and, having perused the financial, trade and specialist press, knew to whom to direct their attentions. Others were enticed by glowing advertisements that were not slow in appealing, perhaps, to wives with mention of luxurious homes and Californian weather.

People with the desired experience and qualifications would then be invited to attend an interview and were well lubricated and dined while being painted an extremely rosy picture of life in a country free from the restrictions and the austerity that still plagued Great Britain. This then culminated with the suggestion that a very good position was available with a parent company in the United States. Mind-boggling salary packages were suggested that invariably included inducements such as removal expenses, housing aid, health and school schemes and, of course, a big brand new car. For the £1,500-a-year senior designer with a British firm, offers tied to salaries equating to £6,000 or more were hard to ignore.

Those who were approached with offers of such fine jobs and positions overseas had to make their own decision in terms of the balance between loyalty and personal living standards, likely future prospects for their British careers, and the potential for bettering themselves abroad. On balance most accepted that staying put would be the poorer choice. One may not criticise the many that succumbed to temptation and chose to seek their fortunes in fresh fields. In any case, very few people could afford (or obtain) a new car in Britain at that time. The present writer was on the receiving end of such an approach but only a fervent wish not to live in America proved the ultimate resistance to a fairy-tale wage offer.

To be fair, there really was little to justify staying put, particularly if you were 'an ideas man'. As an indication of the manner in which we rewarded invention in this country, take the case of William J O'Brien, inventor of the Decca Navigator. He was an American but chose to come to England before the war in order to perfect his radio navigation system. It was to play a significant part in the D-Day invasion. In 1946 he was awarded the prestigious prize offered by the Council of the Royal Society for the invention considered to be the best advancement in the service or practice of navigation. His award? A cheque for £50 which at that time was equal to maybe three or four weeks' salary. Shades of the chronometer-maker Harrison and his 18th century battle for recognition from the Board of Longitude!

Another example of this curious ambivalence to inventors is to be found in Christopher Cockerell's hovercraft. First the authorities to whom he showed his invention failed to see any future in it at all and lacked the imagination to foresee a use for it either militarily or in civilian service. The inventor's perseverance finally triumphed and, in a normal society, Cockerell should have been on course for success and with it, recognition and wealth.

In true British fashion, Cockerell was sidetracked very early on and ultimately rewarded in the manner for which the British Government is world-renowned – nothing. A true patriot, the inventor refused job offers from overseas (particularly America) and is remembered today for his acerbic comments on Britain's failure to capitalise on new ideas. This he blamed on an education system which 'produces engineers who are quite unsuitable for positions of influence, and managers who can do no better than stagger through our highly-technological age.' He later added: 'What our political parties should be spelling out is not different ways of dividing up the national cake, but how to make it bigger so we can all benefit. Our approach to inventors is a serious detriment to the country. People think there aren't more inventions to invent, but there are!'

Cockerell (1910-1999) was a brilliant and accomplished inventor responsible, among other devices, for the Marconi two-needle aerial direction-finder used during the war. Appointed CBE in 1966, he was knighted in 1969. That he is remembered is important: equally that he wasn't rewarded must also not be forgotten.

This is merely one well-known case. The predicting hydrofoil and predictor ski for high speed watercraft in rough seas was another British invention that the inventor, Christopher Hook, could not interest anyone in. With his own limited resources he built the prototype HN-4 Hydrofin powered by a Pobjoy engine and a four-bladed propeller from a Monospar.[1] He paid out of his own pocket for tank tests by the Royal Aircraft Establishment at Farnborough where engineers were deeply impressed by the results and made encouraging noises. Nobody offered him a cup of coffee, let alone a development contract, so he went to America – and made if not exactly a fortune then certainly a very good living.

The oft-repeated tale of Sir Frank Whittle and his jet engine is too well known to reiterate here: it merely reinforces the points already made.

With that sort of track-record, did we want a light plane industry? Indeed, did we deserve one – or would it have been better to pack up our tents and buy American from Day One? This was no idle thought for statistically we were a pretty staid, ground-borne nation. Air Cmdr Chris Paul's rhetoric question 'is Britain air-minded?' would repeatedly return to haunt us!

The event that characterised these lean years was the anomaly of a one-time world leader in light planes which no longer had a significant industry. This unpalatable truth was clear for all to see but if one needed confirmation one only had to look to see what was happening the other side of the Atlantic. In the single month of August 1946, the American light aircraft industry built at least 4,094

The Beagle factory at Shoreham in Sussex took rather a long time to produce its first aircraft but finally the great day did come. Here is the roll-out of the very first Beagle 121 Pup Srs 1 on April 8th 1967. A two seater powered by a 100 hp Rolls-Royce Continental flat four engine, it made its first flight later that same day in the hands of company test pilot John W Charles 'Pee-Wee' Judge (1922-1970).

---

1. The second working Hook Hydrofin was built at Cowes on the Isle of Wight and tested extensively in the Solent under a wide variety of water conditions. The manufacture and detail design of the predictors – small hinged servo-foils arranged in front or, and connected to, the main hydrofoils so as continually to fine-tune their angle of attack to suit the water state – was carried out for Christopher Hook by the late Ron Benton who was subsequently a leading member of the Britten-Norman company and later to distinguish himself as one of the team members associated with Richard Noble in attaining the World Ground Speed Record in the Thrust 2 racing car. For a good summary of the Hydrofin development, together with a three-view drawing and photographs, see *Flight*, November 11th 1948, pp.561-563.

light aeroplanes. These emanated from: Aeronca (798); Piper (also 798); Ercoupe (600); Cessna (547); Taylorcraft (518); Luscombe 280; Stinson (245); Globe (172); Commonwealth (92); Funk (24); Republic (20) and finally an undeclared number from Culver. And fresh records were broken that September as the US industry topped 4,552 new aircraft of which Aeronca and Piper both contributed more than 1,000. The full-year total output of the US industry was a staggering 34,395 aircraft.

On the 9th of December that self-same year Britain had 185 private aircraft, 65 club machines and 80 light aircraft used for business purposes. Taxi and charter operators ran a further 64 machines making a grand total of 394 machines – less than half the production of Aeronca in one single month!

The American Civil Aeronautics Authority published figures at the end of that year of 1946 confirming that monthly output was 5,000 machines and there were more than 14,000 private owners with the numbers rapidly rising. Henry Berney writing in *The Light Plane* in February 1947 suggested that if a light aircraft could be built for about £1,000 – I think he meant *sold* for that sum – then he thought 145,000 people would be in a position to buy a plane. Now I cannot make his sums add up but, whether they did or not, he certainly made a strong case for setting up a thriving light aircraft industry.

On the positive side, shortly after the time private flying restarted, we had a number of projects on the go with contributions from Auster, Chrislea, Elliotts, Percival, Scottish Aviation, Portsmouth Aviation, Miles Aircraft, Cierva and Planet. Cierva gave us the smallest two seater helicopter, Elliotts the nosewheeled closed-cabin EoN (the unfamiliar spelling standing for 'Elliotts of Newbury'), Portsmouth Aviation the clever Aerocar, and Planet the bizarre all-magnesium Satellite pusher. Outside the coterie of established makers and entrepreneurs, there was Essex Aero with its futuristic Sprite.

To summarise, then, during this period there were only three significantly important exercises into the realm of originality that came to fruition. These were the Portsmouth Aerocar (1947), the Planet Satellite (1948) and the Somers-Kendall SK-I (1955). All three demonstrated a high degree of original thinking that was largely absent elsewhere, yet all three were, ultimately, branded as failures for one reason or another. The SK-I was sailplane-derivative and offered jet propulsion at a time when the demand for privately-owned jet-powered racing aircraft was non-existent. The Satellite was in every respect 'a bridge too far' being conceptually and structurally outside the envelope of contemporary knowledge. In addition revolutionary lines and appearance proved no substitute for adequate aerodynamics while the choice of magnesium for construction was curious and even during construction rapid corrosion (to which the special alloy used was alleged to be impervious) should have served as a warning of suspect airframe durability.

The most successful of these three designs was the Portsmouth Aerocar which was theoretically so far advanced that it was to sow the seeds of its own demise. Like the wonderful aircraft built immediately after the First World War by Grahame-White, the Aerocar was aimed bravely at a market that did not yet exist. While exhortations that no fresh market ever existed without there being a candidate to kick-start its promotion, market research could have established that, like Grahame-White's Aero Limousine of 1918-19, one may cast seed as much as one likes yet if the ground be barren, all the promotional energy in the world may not be rewarded by so much as a spark of life!

Curiously the Aerocar flew in the face of conventional sales expectations, for it found a potential market and was on the brink of success. It accrued an impressively-full order book when outside circumstances forced its scrapping. Its failure was neither aerodynamic nor structural; more infrastructural.

In this respect the Aerocar was virtually the exception that proves the rule, for its very success confounded the marketing pundits. It earned an alleged several hundreds of orders but the makers could not raise production finance and government intransigence delayed vital decisions affecting its funds until it was too late to save. Which only serves to show that there are few winners amongst experimenters, whether they are good or merely indifferent. Failure survives when the reasons behind failure are quickly forgotten. Expressed in governmental terms, if uncertain, wait long enough – and it will go away.

In terms of hierarchy, at the end of the war we had three established light aircraft makers who had built light aircraft for military use throughout the war year. These were Auster (Taylorcraft Aeroplanes), Miles Aircraft (Phillips & Powis) and Percival Aircraft, this latter no longer involved with the man Edgar Percival. To this can be added the names of the three other companies that had spent the war years performing important sub-contract work to the aircraft industry yet remained outside the circle (should one, perhaps, say club?) of big-name makers. These were Chrislea Aircraft, Elliotts of Newbury, and Portsmouth Aviation. One other company of significance started from scratch in the immediate post-war years; this was afore-mentioned Planet. The final British light aeroplane company was Beagle built afresh from the foundations of Auster and Miles (and

Identifiable by its extended cabin fenestration, the Beagle B.206S Srs.2 was the production model of the marque. G-ATTL first flew on April 25th 1966 and the following year, on October 20th 1967, was sold to Argentina where it became LV-DMR.

THE POST-WAR LIGHT AEROPLANE INDUSTRY

Left: Chrislea CH.3 Super Ace G-AKVG was first flown on May 9th 1950 but within six months it was sold to Switzerland as HB-EAA. Here it is seen about to touch down in its new markings. Sales of the Ace on the home market were hampered first by the cost of operating a machine with a 125 hp Gipsy Major 10 engine but fundamentally by designer's choice of a wholly-new control system that dispensed with rudder pedals and controlled three-axis movement by a hand-wheel. By the time the designer had been convinced of this 'own goal' situation and reverted to more conventional controls, the market was rich in cheaper Austers and the Ace's reputation was irreparably tarnished. The Super Ace was, however, an excellent flyer.

Above: What would be Chrislea's final effort was the CH.4 Skyjeep which featured a hinged rear decking to allow a stretcher to be carried on top of the rear fuselage. Offered as a single seat freighter or for stretcher case and attendant, the first example, seen here unregistered and later marked G-AKVR, first flew at Exeter on November 21st 1949 in the hands of Donald Lowry, who took over from Rex Stedman as Chrislea's test pilot in 1949. Lowry also assumed the role of sales and publicity manager for the company in its closing days.

Above: De Havilland's DH.82a Tiger Moth remains an ancient design but in the immediate post-war years a number of exciting variations on the theme appeared. While unquestionably Tigers, these were each radical departures from the 1931 prototype. Here is G-AIVW, one of a number of lightweight racing single seater variants built up by Rollason Aircraft and Engines Ltd at Croydon. This cleaned-up model bears the logo of 'The Throttle-Benders' Union' above the oil tank. There are neither slots nor anti-spin strakes fitted.

Right: G-AIVW underwent a further extensive modification and operated for many years as the sole floatplane on the British register. Back as a two seater and fitted with floats as well as replacement strakes, it was unofficially styled the DH.82c Sea Tiger and is seen here on Oulton Broad in August 1971.

Below: The ordinary two seat Tiger Moth allowed room for quite extensive modifications and here is G-ANSA, a much-souped-up model. Formerly N6944, this was granted a C of A on May 13th 1955 having been fitted with a closed cockpit canopy, large lower wind-root fairings, extended exhaust pipes and tightly-profiled wheel spats. It is pictured at Whitchurch, Bristol, on June 11th 1955. Sadly it did not enjoy a long like, crashing in the River Mersey off Speke on March 30th 1958.

Above: There were two special lightweight single seater Tigers built by Rollason for the Tiger Club. The first was G-APDZ named *The Bishop* after the club's veteran instructor-pilot, Cyril Albert Nepean Bishop. This dispensed with both top wing centre-section fuel tank and slots, and was provided with a low-mounted additional tank so that extended inverted flight was possible. After this machine there was a second example, G-ANZZ and this was named *The Archbishop*. These two Tiger variants were stars of the Tiger Club's aerobatic performances in the 1960s. Here we see *The Archbishop* pictured at RAF Station Leuchars in Fife (one-time home to the author's 43 Sqdn) on September 18th 1965.

embodying, in part, Wallis and his autogyros) yet ultimately proving as insubstantial as the others.

Amongst these firms there was no shortage of original thinking with Portsmouth Aviation presenting a wholly-new twin-engined touring design (the Aerocar) on the one hand, and Planet a singularly futuristic all-magnesium four seat pusher (the Satellite) on the other. In the case of the Aerocar, I have already shown that it was both successful and did everything that was expected of it. It also gathered in a large number of potential buyers. By contrast, the Satellite was a move into the unknown and a combination of mistaken aerodynamics and over-optimism ensured that it never flew properly.

Certain of these companies were destined to become intertwined, others to be divided or re-formed. Here they will be considered in a random order since there is no reliable 'common denominator' by which a representative protocol may be established.

1. Miles Aircraft Ltd.

Here was a typically fortunate, successful and happy company operated along ideal lines. It was an environment that fostered design and innovation as demonstrated by the huge number of successful aircraft and innovative design projects that it generated from 1942 onwards.

As a company it was almost too successful and when it came to moving from light aircraft to ambitious and expensive designs like the Merchantman and Marathon for which a greater volume of expenditure would have to be undertaken, a stage was reached where a relatively small event could produce a disproportionately large reaction.

After Miles had acquired a controlling interest in Phillips & Powis from Rolls-Royce in 1941, the firm was propelled into a cash cascade that was containable so long as the money continued to flow in. But the new designs called for more money and, as 1946 came to an end, the business sought re-financing through London & Yorkshire Trust. The goal was to raise £400,000 by the issue of £350,000 cumulative preference and £50,000 ordinary shares.

Almost immediately Britain was afflicted by the worst winter for many years. A national fuel crisis (it was impossible to move coal either by road or rail) combined with roads that were impassable due to thick and unusually prolonged ice led to power shortages, transport and service cuts, and finally to enforced factory closures as heating and electricity had to be rationed. It could not have come at a worse time for the company.

While the Miles share offer was supported by accounts that were made up before the hiatus, by the time the City analysts began looking into the company's finances, things had changed drastically. Difficulties with repayments on existing bank borrowings fuelled concern over the firm's finances and the bank instituted an independent enquiry. It was completed in September 1947 and showed that in the previous six months of trading the company had incurred a loss of more than £300,000. The bank pulled the plug on the cash flow and the creditors marshalled themselves. On November 19th the bank appointed a Receiver.

The matter of the share floatation now arose. Frederick G Miles and Sir William M Mount were the senior directors. William Malcolm Mount (1904-1999) was High Sheriff of Berkshire and grandfather to David Cameron, later to be Prime Minister and leader of the Conservative Party. As 1949 drew to a close it became clear that the problems of Miles Aircraft were, as far as the Inland Revenue and the Board of Trade were concerned, tantamount to fraud if not deceit. At Bow Street Magistrates' Court on February 28th 1950, both men were committed to the April Sessions of the Central Criminal Court for trial. Each faced 24 charges concerning a prospectus issued to prospective shareholders in 1947.

The crux of the case was that immediately after the share prospectus was issued, nine Miles Aerovans, which had cost £6,938 each to produce, were sold for an average of £3,360 apiece while four others, costing £8,519 each, had been sold at £5,000 each. The company's former accountant, Thomas Chandler, suggested that more time had been spent on assembly than had been foreseen and a trading deficit of over £192,000 had been estimated. This sum had been exceeded yet, maintained the Crown, neither Miles nor Sir William had thought to interpret the findings in consideration of what were viewed as the 'clearly false statements' made to investors.

It was an awful, embarrassing and messy business that hung over the heads of the two men for, in all, almost a year. Their crime was not one of commission, merely hopes and expectations that a flaccid market and an apocalyptic winter had not helped. As F G Miles and his honoured business faced ruin, one-time

Besides British manufacture, the Tiger Moth was produced in other parts of the world, predominantly Australia and Canada. For North American use, the bitter cold of winter dictated that a closed cockpit was an essential modification, hence producing the DH.82c or Canadian Tiger Moth. Merely for comparison, here is a picture of Dr Gregg's example on his strip at Guelph, Ontario, displaying the then-new-style Canadian registration C-FBSP (one-time 3847). The Canadian-built Tigers differed from UK models in three major ways of which the large-area sliding cockpit canopy is the most obvious. Besides that, the interplane struts were of streamlined-section steel tube instead of wood, and the cowling bore a large carburettor heater and air-filter.

trade friends behaved like those familiar but nevertheless nasty little rodents that scurry from a sinking ship. Nobody came to his aid and the final petition to wind up the company was brought about by one creditor who, owed far less than most, had pressed for liquidation. Miles had to sell his own house to pay dividends that were due.

Now knowing just who his friends were, poor Miles put on a brave face and founded a shoe-string revival business under his own name and based in half a rented hangar at Redhill.

In the end his real friends were the jurors of the Central Criminal Court who failed to see how Miles and Sir William could have crystal-balled what was going to happen. It was pointed out that had the weather not forced a protracted works shut-down the cash-flow might have been sustained. In a historic move, they stopped the trial on June 2nd – the 17th day of the Old Bailey hearing – leaving the judge with no other course but to quash the charges and free the defendants.

Although he was left with £20,000 costs to pay, F G Miles was immensely relieved at the outcome: it could hardly be called a verdict. But the damage to his health by the strain of it all took a long while to heal and he never came to terms with the ill that had been done to him.

Stripped of his company and assets, Miles was not yet beaten and in the years at Redhill and later Shoreham his new company proved itself as innovative as ever. But when the chance came to unite with the grand opportunities offered by Beagle, one feels he was more than ready to chip in his proud and proven pennyworth and retire in 1961. 'F G' died in a nursing home on August 15th 1976 aged 73, yet *unnecessarily* older. Biographers say he was struck by financial disaster, the implication being that he could have avoided it. As that honourable jury said, that was anything but the truth.

2. Percival Aircraft

Edgar Wikner Percival's company was founded in the 1930s and its pre-war activities have already been recorded in an earlier work [42]. During the war, important military contracts had allowed the business to expand. Much of this work entailed development and production of the military version of the pre-war Vega Gull renamed the Proctor. This machine also played an important part in the civil flying movement in the post-war years, a number of Proctor Mks.III, IV and V being civilianised. The firm also designed and produced the Prentice as a military trainer which made its first flight on March 31st 1946.

Although he was retained by consultancy contract, Percival himself had resigned from the company in 1940 and his former firm lost its independence in September 1944 when it was acquired by the shipping and oil company Hunting & Son Ltd of Newcastle-upon-Tyne.

Under the Hunting Group's leadership, Percival never went back to the light plane business so although, strictly speaking, a machine such as the Proctor Mks.III, IV and V were 'new' machines for the civil market, no wholly-new designs materialised. On July 18th 1944 a new business was registered as the E W Percival Aeronautical Co at 72 Chesterfield House, Curzon Street, London W1 with the purpose of retaining the Percival name in British aviation. When, in 1957, Hunting decided that there was no longer any point in perpetuating the name 'Percival' and simplified its title to Hunting Aircraft Ltd, that decision was justified.

The Hunting Group of companies encouraged the conversion of many Proctors for civilian use. Of these, the Mk.I was probably the best because it was close in many respects to the original Vega Gull. As the design was developed it became larger and heavier with the Model V and VI being the heaviest. The marque with the best performance was probably the Mk.III.

As for the Prentice, designed as a Royal Air Force trainer, this proved eminently unsuited to any major civilian role. Freddie Laker's Aviation Traders bought every Prentice they could lay their hands on – 252 of them – at a bulk price said to be in the order of £100,000 or around £396 16s each. They tried for some while to sell them for various duties yet in the end they were almost all scrapped. It turned out to be a small but profitable move for Laker.

Meanwhile as Edgar Percival Ltd, Percival designed the EP.9 and set up a small business at Stapleford Tawney to build them. Percival, always the entrepreneur businessman and enthusiast (not to mention a good self-publicist), had a winner with this machine. As a light freighter and agricultural aircraft it was very good. The first one sold quickly, Percival built more – and they sold, too. But just when a decent production line was laid down, sales slowed alarmingly. As operating capital haemorrhaged, Edgar Percival sold out to Samlesbury Engineering Ltd which became Lancashire Aircraft Company Ltd.

The post-war contribution of Percival was, therefore, more by reputation than through direct influence. The Proctors kept the name flying while the EP.9 (until it became the Lancashire Aircraft Prospector) earned some respect. The rich contributions of the 1930s, though, were never to be repeated and the name played no significant part in the post-war revival.

Edgar Wikner Percival left his company Percival Aircraft Ltd during the war but returned to the aviation world in 1954 with the formation of Edgar Percival Ltd. With premises at Stapleford Tawney in Essex he designed and built the EP.9 as a light freighter and agricultural aircraft. G-AOZO was an early example and first flew as G-43-8 on March 6th 1957. After the business was sold to Samlesbury Engineering Ltd, renamed Lancashire Aircraft Co Ltd, early in 1960 the type was given the name Prospector. This example, pictured here, completed an extensive European sales demonstration tour culminating at Vienna in March 1960. Ultimately owned by Eagle Parachuting Centre Ltd, it met a fiery end at Lympne on July 2nd 1980 when it stalled and caught fire on take-off killing all six on board. One example, G-APWX, became a joy-riding hack carrying five passengers plus pilot.

Fairey Aviation had initiated a close connection with E O Tips and his Tipsy Aircraft Co at Gosselies in Belgium since the late 1930s. Tipsy aircraft had subsequently been produced in Slough. Now Tips came up with a brilliant if rather heavy two seat trainer called the Tipsy M of 1947 and registered OO-POM. Powered by a 145 hp Gipsy Major 10, it was brought to Britain where it flew initially under the markings G-6-1 and then G-AKSX.

A close-up of the engine, undercarriage and flap arrangement of the Tipsy OO-POM. This prototype was dismantled and used to make drawings and jigs for the first British-made Fairey Primer which was built at Hamble in 1948. Two British examples were built but despite comprehensive evaluation by interested parties, no RAF interest materialised and, consequently, civil interest could not be generated by itself.

Other than the rather accentuated fuselage aft of the cockpit, this side view of the Belgian prototype shows the pleasing lines of what would become the Fairey Primer. Evaluated at Boscombe Down, the aircraft had to be dismantled to create new drawings, the originals having been lost.

3. Auster Aircraft Ltd

The rise and almost inevitable fall of this company was due to one basic cause: the business was run by nice people who were primarily gentlemen enthusiasts rather than hard-nosed businessmen. This was apparent from its unrealistic costings, low price structures and willingness to embark on far too many unprofitable projects. It culminated with the huge losses on the Agricola coming on top of the unrealistic and very costly dream of the Atlantic.

Auster's proximity to financial ruin actually began with its pre-war beginnings, was staved off by wartime contracts, and concluded by being absorbed into the delusional regime of Beagle which encouraged the uneconomic production of, first, the Terrier, then the Husky and finally the supremely unrealistic Airedale.

The British Taylorcraft company and its formation in the last summer before the outbreak of war has already been told in an earlier book [37]. While the Army had an urgent need for light aircraft in the communications role, many impressed pre-war private aircraft were available. It was actually the increasing unsuitability of these that pushed the military to explore the opportunities of a new product. Taylorcraft met that need with its aircraft not just because it was a simple aircraft but because it was good. It also had a British engine produced by Blackburn.

The Army called its new type 'Auster' and, once the war was at an end, the Leicester-based British Taylorcraft firm realised two goals, first that its product had reached a stage of development whereby it was no longer best described as of American origin, and second the time was ripe for an all-British company to assume control.

Since the Army had come up with the name, it was logical to cash in on it, so the new firm became Auster Aircraft. There was also some merit in promoting its American form of construction and those who still used it. Accordingly, the new Auster company adopted the dual slogan 'the All-Steel Aeroplane' and 'the eyes of the Army'.

Auster was to be our most consistently reliable light aircraft maker from the immediate post-war months through to the Beagle involvement. Until August 1963, Rearsby had the distinction of being the only place in England where light aircraft had been in continuous production since the Second World War.

Never outstandingly profitable and with few designs actually earning large production runs, Auster became the popular face of club and private flying. The truth was that it was a rather bland face and for fifteen years the company produced little that was innovative: everything was derivative; merely an ever-gradual improvement on the 1940 Taylorcraft D.

During this period, the basic design was steadily moved forward with bigger engines, better upholstery, a proper elevator trim-tab instead of an external wobble-plate, exhaust silencer, better instrumentation, two seats to three and then four, long-range fuel tank, glider tow-hook, aerobatic version, crop-duster and sprayer, stretcher-carrier, bigger wheels, floats, water skis, and so on and so on. In effect, it was repapering the lounge with little effort to remodel the basic structure of the house.

There were three notable exceptions. First was the ghastly four-wheeled freighter of 1951. Second was the only low-wing Auster, the Agricola of 1955. And finally the 1957 pseudo-American Atlantic. Significantly, only the Agricola managed production and that totalled a mere eight examples. But Auster had already tried to escape from the Taylorcraft mould as early as April 1948 with its curious Queen-powered A2/45. This, though, was for a military market that, probably wisely, rejected the offering.

Having failed with what critics described as 'the Rearsby Cessna', Austers reverted to mainstream and the mundane enjoying a good business in upgrading aircraft. For the observer today this has made individual Auster aircraft histories a tangled maze of confusion. Post-war Autocrats were rebuilt as bigger-engined four seaters with larger tails and different rudders. Other models were revised and revamped so that the task of keeping tabs on model numbers, let alone production totals, often borders on the fruitless.

Significantly it was not until the 1960s that Auster really began to escape from the Taylorcraft incubus when, now under the auspices of Beagle, it cast the past to the four winds and gave us first the Husky then the Terrier and finally the real Yankee look with the Airedale.

During 1959-60, the British Army declared its Auster Mks.6, 7 and 10 surplus to requirements and these were repurchased by Austers and some converted to Tugmasters. After the Beagle acquisition of Auster Aircraft Ltd on October 7th 1960, these became the Beagle Terrier.

In August 1963, the Rearsby production lines were given over to the manufacture of the Beagle 206 and production of the Airedale and the conversion of Terrier 2 aircraft ceased. Conversions of Auster 6 to Terrier I and Tugmaster ended in September 1964: the last new Auster-type aircraft to be built was a Beagle Husky, G-ASNC, which gained its C of A on April 23rd 1964.

Production of the Auster at Rearsby had lasted just over 25 years and in this time a grand total of 3,573 aircraft were turned out.

Auster was probably played out as an individual company by the 1960s. Had Beagle not embraced it there is the probability that it would not have gone on as an individual entity for much longer because by then American and European-sourced light aircraft had already made huge inroads to Auster's core market of flying clubs and private owners. In the very short term, Beagle saved the day and, in the end, severed the final links with 'the steel aeroplane' that had been the eyes of our Army.

However, the Beagle days at Rearsby got off to a bad start with the costly Airedale of which 567 would have had to have been built in order to recoup development costs. In the end just 43 were built. The loss was significant.

4. Chrislea Aircraft Ltd

The Chrislea firm had been founded before the war by Richard Christoforides and Bernard V Leak. Leak soon left the business and worked for Folland during the war but he was already a very sick man, dying aged just 40 in October 1947 by which time Christoforides had reformed his business and opened a factory at Heston. Here he was producing a very attractive little four seat aircraft called the Ace. Not thought quite so attractive was its unconventional control system which, like Mignet's Flying Flea, had no foot-operated rudder controls.

While even then control wheels as a substitute for a 'stick' were not exactly new, control wheels that worked in three dimensions were radical and, most probably, would be thought so today. Christoforides, who did not fly himself, worked out a scheme that was directly related to Blériot's monoplane used for his cross-Channel flight. Louis Blériot's *cloche* allowed his wheel on a vertical stalk to move in all directions: the Chrislea system used a version of the *cloche* mounted horizontally in the control panel with the wheel sticking out on a stalk.

Like Blériot's system, the difficulty of centralising the control wheel without easy reference points proved to be the real Achilles heel of the whole thing.

Following publication of a description of the system in *The Aeroplane* on December 6th 1946, the firm's publicity manager, W Clifford, was moved to respond in its defence, ending with the comment that '… our system reacts to perfectly natural actions'. Curiously this was the one criterion it simply did not meet although those people that made the effort to master the system seemed happy enough. The general feeling, however, was that if an aircraft had a radical control system that was quite different from that of any other flying machine, then it was not a good idea.

The Ace's big selling-point was its much-vaunted 360deg cockpit visibility. It was possible to see all around without obstruction. This was made possible by virtue of the short fuselage being equipped with a large and well-glazed cabin. Maximum occupant comfort meant that the cockpit was very wide. All of these aspects were to combine to generate some unexpected aerodynamic results that at low speed could create curious effects from the tail controls.

On the first flight, in September 1946, rudder control alternated alarmingly (depending on throttle-setting, speed and attitude) between 'snatching' and having no effect whatsoever. Reports that the aircraft flew off into the distance were not so much down to bravura as to the simple fact the pilot could not turn!

While the problem would have showed up easily with a smoke jet and a wind tunnel, the Chrislea company did not extend to such luxuries. Quickly it applied the belt-and-braces solution and fitted dual fins and rudders to produce one of the smallest twin-tailed high-wing cabin monoplanes on record. As expected this eventually cleared up the problem (after some trial and error) at the mere expense of money, complexity and weight.

The Ace still held the Joker when it came to sales. Its unconventional controls wholly negated any other claimed plus points and the company was eventually forced to incorporate a series of alterations to bring the controls more into line with conventional aircraft. The last version of the design, the Skyjeep, reverted to the tried and tested 'joy-stick and rudder-pedal' controls although even these were not your normal issue: the rudder was operated by 'harmonium'-type horizontally-hinged flap pedals provided with heel rests and toe-straps.

In the meantime, the costs of operating at Heston combined with the decision to shut down the airport completely (because of its proximity to the new Heathrow airport then being enlarged from Charles Fairey's delightful pre-war grass field) forced Christoforides and his little company to move. The shift to Exeter at the end of 1947 marked the beginning of the end for the company. And the M4 Motorway carved the heart out of Heston soon afterwards.

After several variations on the original design netted only minimal interest, the business was restructured about 1950 and Christoforides was out. The new owners laid down production lines but with the difficulty in both obtaining engines and putting money upfront for materials the business was wound up in 1952 and the work in hand scrapped.

So ended a brave attempt to make a light aircraft to rival the Auster. The company went wrong right from the start by trying to be too different and then lacked the courage to recognise early enough that all was not well with the Ace control system and bold action needed to taken quickly to remedy matters. Changes were made and the Ace (as the Super Ace) became a commendable light aircraft, but the old problem of long memories permanently tarnished its perception with ordinary pilots. This reputation fuelled by the natural reserve of the British people stifled sales.

Underlying the Ace, though, was the usual tangle of other problems, no single one of which was solely attributable to the aircraft's demise. The orders did eventually trickle in but by that time the company had undergone internal trials and tribulations associated with the two most difficult of obstacles to overcome – a cash shortage and an engine hiatus.

As early as the summer of 1945, Chrislea had submitted details of the Ace to the Ministry of Aircraft Production with a twofold request: first the company sought manufacturing assistance by way of factory premises and second it applied for sponsorship to produce 250 aircraft in its first year.

A confidential memo from the Sponsorship of Civil Aircraft Committee[2] reported on its examination of the aircraft and the firm's requests. This contained the following comments prefaced by a technical report by TD Plans:

Frenchman Claude Piel designed his CP.301 Emeraude side-by-side cabin two seater in the mid-1950s. Intended for amateur construction, this all-wood monoplane was rated as a complicated project because it had elliptical wings, meaning that every wing-rib was different, and a complicated wider-than-it-was-deep mainspar. However it was successfully modified and built in at least two distinct British varieties. First was the Garland-Bianchi Linnet of 1958 (pictured here) which was built at White Waltham by Douglas E Bianchi and P A T Garland. The prototype G-APNS was test flown by Sqdn Ldr Neville Duke on September 1st 1958. A second variety was known as the Fairtravel Linnet and this was the work of Don Bennett at Blackbushe. The main difference was that this had a one-piece sliding cockpit canopy replacing the doors seen on this example.

... further examination of the Chrislea Ace shows that this aircraft is similar to the Auster with a Lycoming engine, except for the slightly lower power. The figures in the brochure are all on the optimistic side but not unduly so except possibly for the specific consumption of .45 pints/BHP/hr. Our experience on light engines indicates that .6 pints/BHP/hr is a more likely figure, and a rough indication of what we should expect from this aircraft carrying 4 passengers is set out beside the firm's claim for the Monaco [engined] version.

All-up weight in lb. Firm's claim 1650; MAP [Ministry of Aircraft Production] estimates 1750: Take-off run heavy in ft. Firm's claim 430; MAP estimates 600: Cruising speed 85% power in mph. Firm's claim 110; MAP estimates 102: Stalling speed in mph. Firm's claim 43; MAP estimates 50: Range in still air on 17 galls in miles. Firm's claim 390. MAP estimates 275.

The alternative engine (85 hp Franklin) is not regarded as a really practical proposition as the aircraft even with a Monaco engine is really under powered.

On technical grounds therefore there seems no strong case for not sponsoring the Monaco engines version of the Chrislea Ace.

The Committee is asked to consider whether, in the light of this report, they are prepared to sponsor the proposed production of 250 aircraft in the first year. In this connection, the firm expect to export all their aircraft, but are unwilling, very reasonably, to formally undertake to do so. They are, however, prepared to give a guarantee to devote 90% of the output to export.

The outcome was the rejection of the company's plans and the necessity to find larger production facilities resulted in the move to Exeter. Inability to secure the planned engines and then the refusal of an application for the necessary permit to buy materials paved the way towards the inevitable, for the necessary volume production combined with market resistance precluded any possible chance of the company entering a profitable volume production.

The company felt that the Ministry, in blocking its plans, was preserving Auster's virtual monopoly of the market. Nobody can say for certain, but hindsight suggests that there was more behind the official attitude than that as this document implies.

Chrislea's contribution to the post-war light aeroplane was curious in the extreme. On the plus side, it was the first post-war light aircraft planned to take the 'flat-four' format engine being designed around either the 85/90 hp Franklin (a popular pre-war American engine) or, ideally, the new British Monaco motor to be built in Watford. As the Ministry report concluded, even assuming the engine might have been available, the Franklin would have been a poor choice for a four seater and even the Monaco was still a little on the underpowered side for comfort. Another problem was the availability of the US engine and the restrictions on foreign funds for its purchase.

Forward thinking dictated a tricycle undercarriage, still a very new concept for a small private aircraft, resulting in an attractive-looking machine that was then hampered by an eccentric and unique control system. With shades of the pre-war Sykes Monoplane [37], the aircraft was supposed to bridge the gap between

---

2. Committee set up to consider Sponsoring of Civil Aircraft: Agenda of meeting held on Thursday December 13th 1945, Item 2(e), Memo SCA/45/18 "Chrislea Aircraft Ltd. Heston". The company was seeking factory space at Aldenham (Elstree), presumably to be close to its engine-maker, Monaco, 'or some other airfield'. Documents in author's private collection. Monaco, remember, maintained its engine test facility at Elstree.

private motoring and private flying by making an aeroplane that was easy to enter and, in the minds of the designer, logical to fly. Logic, in this case, extended to a control system that was almost as idiosyncratic as that adopted by Henri Mignet for his 1930s *Pou-du-Ciel* while retaining the steering wheel as commonly found in the family car.

Of course, to change the fundamental manner in which an aircraft is controlled calls either for a system better than that already in use by every other aeroplane, or the confidence that the new idea will catch on and operate seamlessly alongside existing systems. As time would tell, neither path was feasible and the designer and company chief, Richard Christoforides, was oblivious to criticism and went on paddling his own canoe until all around forced him to give in. But even his eventual concession (those harmonium-type pedals for the Super Ace) was only grudgingly conceded.

Several examples of the Ace remain airworthy to this day and are the pride and joy of their owners suggesting that the aircraft could have had a much larger market had its designers listened to their critics early enough.

5. Elliotts of Newbury Ltd

If the builders of the previous aircraft turned an expensive deaf ear to criticism, then the people behind the Newbury EoN positively sought and encouraged outside critical comment at every stage and from all and sundry.

The Buckingham family had been in the woodworking business since the First World War with the old-established furniture-making firm of Elliotts. The brothers Horace and Cecil de Vere Buckingham became joint managing directors in 1921, Horace also becoming chairman in 1938.

Involvement with Chilton Aircraft through Alexander Reginald 'Reggie' Ward and The Hon Andrew W H Dalrymple introduced Elliotts to aviation and aircraft woodwork. This was experience that the business turned to national benefit during the war with aircraft work in the form of sub-contracts from Airspeed among others.

Horace Buckingham was also a gliding enthusiast: in 1946 Elliotts began production of a Chilton-modified version of the Meise sailplane and more than 150 examples were built; this became the Olympia, later taken over and successfully manufactured by Slingsby Sailplanes.

While the company possessed both genuine interest and outstanding capability in wooden aircraft, the real reason that it made the leap of faith into light aircraft construction was really though desperation. During the war it had built up a highly-skilled workforce and fully-equipped premises in which it had honourably completed contracts for both wooden and metal-component airframes to the value of £2,500,000.

Once the war was over, the firm wanted to return to its core business of quality furniture-manufacture but for some reason the Board of Trade steadfastly refused permission. It is perhaps hard today to realise how restricted life was in 1946 and that without the proper approval a company could not simply go back to its old ways. As it was, official interference and misdirection was not uncommon in the early days of peace. Elliotts had 200,000 sq.ft of modern factory plus 550 skilled employees and no work. No alternative contracts or even suggestions were forthcoming and from being engaged in work of vital national importance, the firm was now totally ignored by the authorities. A skilled workforce faced a bleak future.

Horace Buckingham wrote at that time: 'The Board of Trade harshly deprived Elliotts of their legitimate livelihood: they have offered no advice or guidance for a replacement production.'

Declining the opportunity to accept defeat, the firm frantically cast about for other work and for a time made prefabricated houses, a project that ended in disaster through official ineptitude between various rival ministries.

Glider-building just about enabled the firm to stay solvent. Still striving to do the best for his country, Buckingham's gliders were demonstrated in America (at his own cost) and earned many sales helping to bring valuable dollars into the nation's coffers. It was at this point that Horace Buckingham looked at powered aircraft. Like so many other small firms of that era, he was aware that the interests of the light

The Miles M.65 Gemini 1A was so-named because it was little more than a twin-engined version of the Messenger fitted with a retractable undercarriage. This dramatic night-time photograph of G-AKHP reveals details of the flaps and ailerons that would be lost in daylight. It gained its C of A on December 11th 1947.

From the original Gemini, F G Miles developed the 'ultimate' model – the M.75 Aries which was flown at Redhill in February 1950 under the markings G-35-1 and later demonstrated at the Fifty Years of Flying Exhibition staged by the *Daily Express* newspaper at Hendon the following July. The Aries had a pair of Cirrus Major 3 engines and larger tail surfaces in order to cure the Gemini's one major weakness – marginal directional control under single engine flight conditions. Later this machine became G-AMDJ. On March 1st 1955 it was sold to Australia where it became VH-FAV.

aircraft market were vested in just one firm – Auster – or two if you included Miles. Believing that there was a need for a new type of British light aeroplane, Buckingham sought the necessary expertise that was crucial to the development of such a project.

Such expertise was available with a business called Aviation & Engineering Projects Ltd of Feltham and so Elliotts collaborated with them to create a new all-wood machine. Heading this design-consultancy organisation was none other than Carl R Chronander who, with James I Waddington and J A Heron had designed the CW (later General Aircraft) Cygnet in 1936. They had also produced the design (and a mock-up) of the larger Swan previous to their bankrupt business being taken over by General Aircraft Ltd immediately before the war.

The outcome of this fresh partnership was the Newbury EoN light four seat monoplane. It was initially planned as a twin-engined design to be powered by the new Monaco flat-four and promoted to sell at under £2,000 but, following publication of the first post-war British Civil Airworthiness Requirements by the Air Registration Board, it was discovered that the projected twin would not be able to meet the minimum single-engined climb requirement in the event of an engine failure on take-off. The answer, then, was a single-engined aircraft.

It was then realised that this sort of aircraft really needed a minimum of 125 hp and the only suitable engine of this power and flat-four layout was the American Lycoming. Owing to currency restrictions it was pretty certain that government sanction would not be forthcoming for an engine from a dollar area. The company thought afresh. Aware that the projected Nuffield engine was likely still to be some way ahead, the prototype was fitted with a 100 hp Blackburn Cirrus Minor II inline with which it proved, as suspected, underpowered. This was soon replaced by a DH Gipsy Major 10 (and a lengthened nosewheel).

Aware of his company's lack of experience in the world of powered light aircraft, Buckingham arranged to display and demonstrate the Newbury EoN at the SBAC's show held in 1947 at Radlett. Here he encouraged others in the industry to examine, comment and criticise. It was a frank and honest approach that earned him the cautious respect of his peers to whom this sort of honesty was, to say the least, uncommon.

Again Horace Buckingham, writing in 1947, takes up the story in what has to be the most unusual aircraft sales brochure ever produced; it is on the one hand an exposure of the problems endemic throughout the aircraft industry while on the other it shows a frankness and sincerity that borders on the naive:

> The company feels the aircraft is highly satisfactory as an aircraft, but wish to satisfy itself that it fills a need, and that it is an exportable machine. It is suggested that after a satisfactory production in timber and plywood and the finest possible machine evolved that the same machine should be changed to all-metal.
>
> In addition it is felt that if orders were accepted and deliveries promised prior to a production type machine being established, and also satisfying ourselves that the machine decided on was as perfect as possible, then the sales so obtained and the pressure for delivery would hamper the satisfactory production of the "Newbury EoN".
>
> Further, our opinion is that in order to economically produce a machine of this type it is necessary to have a minimum output of 200 machines per year. We are informed by experienced members of the aircraft world that the disposal of this quantity in this country and abroad is impossible without Ministerial assistance. From time to time officially such assistance is quoted as likely to be forthcoming in the future, but if promises are unsupported by actual developments then it would appear that this Company's difficulties would only be added to by commencing a production of the "Newbury EoN".
>
> We therefore apologise to all prospective interested parties who would wish to discuss sales with us for our inability to talk on definite lines, but assure them we welcome their criticism, advice and propositions. After hearing these if we decide on a standard model and commence production we anticipate deliveries will commence prior to Radlett 1948, and orders will be accepted and definite delivery dates promised six months after decision to produce.[3]

Development of this aircraft was planned but although it offered attractive features and specification, sales were not forthcoming. It was widely demonstrated (notching up more than 300 hours of flying) and all those who flew it spoke glowingly of its handling qualities. Peter Masefield was so impressed that he told Elliotts: 'I want you to know that, in my opinion, you have an extremely promising little aeroplane which may well prove most attractive to the whole of the light aircraft movement.'

With a selling price of under £1,750, the EoN was still more expensive than an Auster which weighed heavily against a company that, as far as the flying fraternity knew, had never before built a powered aircraft. What most did not know was that Auster Aircraft Ltd consistently sold its aircraft if not exactly at a loss then certainly too cheaply and that prices would soon rise. Hindsight thus reveals that Elliott's price was actually competitive.

The final nail in the EoN's coffin, though, came from the Air Ministry which began to release increasing numbers of surplus trainers at prices well below that being asked for a new EoN. As one observer commented at the time, why spend that amount of money for one new aeroplane when for rather less you can buy half a dozen Tiger Moths or Magisters. Sadly, of course, he was right.

In October 1948, Elliotts officially announced that it was abandoning development of the EoN and its projected EoN Mk.II. Stanley Orton Bradshaw, on learning the news, wrote: '[it] is the epitome of frustration and this machine stands symbolically as a mute protest against the general conditions which today mitigate against our light aviation.'[4]

The EoN almost had a military spin-off: the company submitted a side-by-side two seater all-metal version as a RAF trainer to Spec T.16/48. However, the successful candidate was Percival with its P.56 design submission which became the Provost.

In the end Elliotts' beautifully made – perhaps too well-made for it did have a detail-rich structure – and was relegated to spending most of its time aero-towing Elliott gliders to customers while engaged on one of these tasks, an unfortunate (and avoidable), accident wrote finis to the whole enterprise.

While readying at Lympne to tow the second of three gliders to Denmark on April 4th 1950, the engine was started without there being anybody in the cockpit. The runaway aircraft, hotly pursued by its hapless towline-drawn glider, ended up wrecked in a hedge. Even that, unfortunately, wasn't the end for

---

3. This is extracted from what would normally be considered a sales brochure presented at the 1947 SBAC Show staged at Radlett – hence the suggestion of the following years' show 'at Radlett'. The brochure, hand stitched between printed boards, is in the form of duplicated sheets which, from their irregular and uneven purple-blue images, suggest they might have been produced on a jelly mimeograph rather than an ink duplicator.

4. *The Light Plane*, November 1948, p.17. Stanley Orton Bradshaw was a well-respected pilot, aviation journalist and co-editor of this splendid, yet short-lived, magazine. His initials at the end of an article, 'SOB', were almost as well-known at one time as those of his illustrious contemporary, 'CGG'. He was killed with Edwin J 'Eddie' Riding and another in the crash of an Auster Autocar on April 7th 1950.

that August 3rd everybody involved found themselves invited to attend Seabrook Magistrates' Court. The EoN's erstwhile pilot, who was a qualified glider flyer and instructor but had no powered aircraft licence, was fined for operating a powered aircraft without a licence, while the glider pilot, who was normally the EoN tug's pilot but on this occasion was hoping to be a glider pilot, was fined for aiding and abetting. It is merely coincidental that the unqualified pilot of the now-defunct EoN enjoyed the name of Towgood.

This brought to an end the unfortunate tale of the Newbury EoN. To analyse why is pointless: the Air Ministry had refused to decommission surplus light aircraft in 1946, but had changed its mind two years later. And that was it.

Early in the 1950s the company produced the outstanding Olympia 4 series of sailplanes, a later development of which won events at the 1963 British National Championships. In the spring of 1966 Elliotts, second only to Slingsby in glider manufacture, gave up manufacture and concluded an agreement that saw all servicing, spares and any future manufacturing rights of the EON Olympia 463 sailplane handed over to Kirkbymoorside. A second incomplete Newbury EoN was stored for a while but later destroyed. Horace Buckingham died in 1965 in his 65th year.

6. Portsmouth Aviation Ltd

Originally an airline operator (as Portsmouth, Southsea & Isle of Wight Aviation Ltd founded in 1931 and starting operations the following year), this business had spent all its original capital by the end of 1938. From that time onwards, though, it managed to show increasing profitability.

Reformed as Portsmouth Aviation Ltd, it undertook lucrative wartime contracts but never directly lost sight of the fact that it had an effective monopoly on the Portsmouth-Ryde (IOW) air route. It was largely this fact that offered incentive for the business to design its own small airliner that could fulfil the needs of the executive and private pilot as well as charter and feeder-line work. The outcome was the Aerocar, an unconventional, advanced aircraft that did not make the same mistake as, say, Planet, and go for a radical or 'quantum leap' machine.

Portsmouth Aviation's Aerocar was an eminently practical and attractive twin-engined twin-boomed design that fitted neatly in the category of private owner and light-commercial feeder offering considerable comfort and economy. It introduced a handful of novelties – sufficient to make it attractive to the purchaser, yet not so many as to dissuade those with a more conservative outlook. Above all, it flew well.

Curiously the Aerocar was designed by a man who had no aircraft design experience. Francis Logan Luxmoore was born on August 4th 1897 and educated at Eton subsequently joining the Royal Flying Corps, transferring to the Royal Air Force and gaining a permanent commission in 1919 as Flt-Lt. A practical man and a good designer he was, nevertheless, no detailer or stressman and his drawings for the Aerocar were independently stressed by Frank Wilkinson, Noel Nash and Joe Doley. Even so, many features of the Aerocar airframe highlighted the designer's unfamiliarity with his medium – not, as we shall see, a wholly bad thing.

The Aerocar originated from an independent wartime submission made to the Army by Portsmouth Aviation on March 23rd 1943. This was for a 'general purpose aircraft for [military] requirements' capable of carrying up to four personnel, a motorcycle dispatch rider (who could start his machine in the air and, immediately on landing, ride out through a hatch in the back of the aircraft), nurse and stretcher case, light goods and so on.

Aviation lends itself to inspiring trick questions of the 'pub-quiz' type. One favourite is 'what's the oldest jet plane in the world?' with, as a corollary, 'when was the first private jet first registered?' They are trick questions because the answer is the Miles M.5 G-ADNL built as a personal mount for F G Miles to enter in the King's Cup Race of September 7th 1935. This single seater was built of standard Hawk components but the fuselage was shorter. It flew the 953 mile course around Britain at a speed-winning 165·74 mph. There were five Sparrowhawks in all and this example, pictured near Woodley in 1935, went on to become that curious first-ever private jet.

In December 1950, G-ADNL the Sparrowhawk was sent to F G Miles' workshop at Redhill in Surrey where the fuselage was cut in two and the wings severed at the centre-section. A new front fuselage containing a new single seat cockpit was built together with a centre-section into which could be inserted a pair of Turboméca Palas gas turbines. At the same time a different tail unit was built. Construction was completed at Shoreham after the firm moved back to its roots in 1952. Now christened the M.77 Sparrowjet, G-ADNL became the racing mount for Fred Dunkerley. After several years of uncertain luck, Dunkerley managed to win the King's Cup Race staged at Baginton on July 13th 1957 with an average speed of 228 mph. The machine was plagued by starting problems plus the fact that the 330 lb st engines were insufficient to overcome the rolling resistance of other than a very smooth runway. Tragedy robbed us of this unique veteran when it was lost in a hangar fire at RAF Upavon in July 1964.

101

Called the Type 107 and powered by two 130 hp Gipsy Major engines, the machine would have had a 3,600 lb all-up weight, a 152 mph top speed, 132 mph cruise and a stalling speed of 56 mph.

That the project was not so much rejected as ignored by the powers-that-be should have come as no surprise: military requirements were not contracted to operators outside the unofficial coterie of suppliers set up and monitored by the minions of Whitehall.

Once the war was over, Portsmouth Aviation lost no time in resurrecting its design, work on which seems to have progressed at some level since the time of the unfruitful Army submission. The outcome was the Type 109 (with Cirrus Minor Series II engines) and the Type 110 (with Cirrus Major motors). In the event only the Type 110 was built.

The novelties (for the time) included a pneumatically retractable tricycle undercarriage that allowed sufficient protrusion so that, in an emergency, a wheels-up landing could be effected without damage), engines aspirated through cowling sides and exhaust venting from the top of the wing cowling to reduce cabin noise, plus a cabin that could quickly be converted to carry freight or a motor-cycle.

The Aerocar was built like a battleship. Small wonder that its proposed weight estimates were not met in the prototype. For a start, the fuselage pod was built around a metal fabricated and riveted 'egg-box'-type keel structure of unnecessary complexity and immense strength. Ever aware of the risk of undercarriage problems, retraction failure, or some other breakage, it was intended that in an emergency the aircraft could be landed in perfect safety without the formality of extended wheels: the retracted nosewheel leaving a useful portion of its periphery projecting, while the aft fuselage had two sprung skids permanently positioned at each rear side.

Cabin accessibility similar to that of a saloon car was provided with large, unstressed access doors each side. Upholstery and interior design extended to independent umbrella-holders – surely a first for a small aircraft – although these were the first things to be removed when subsequent attempts at correcting the excess weight problem were addressed.

Luxmoore's first flight of the Aerocar took place on June 18th 1947 and the marketing machine rolled into action. The success of the Aerocar – it needed but little post-flight adjustment – inspired the company to exhibit at the SBAC's show staged in 1947 at Radlett and the following year at Farnborough. With an impressive display and exhibition stand at the 1948 show, the firm promoted versions fitted either as a twin-float seaplane (talks were advanced with the American Edo float company[5]) or a ski-plane. Any hint of things going wrong was masked by a growing order-book as despite its radical approach, Aerocar customers apparently clamoured to buy.

An extensive evaluation of the Canadian market was undertaken by director Lionel Balfour with the Canadian Car & Foundry Company with a view to North American production. In regard to arctic territories flying a curious argument was put forward based on Canadian market intelligence, namely that operators were uneasy about having two engines. The reasoning quoted was that 'it was bad enough trying to start one engine [in the cold]: with two the first might well have stopped again before the second was got going'.

One of the last independent projects of F G Miles was the M.100 Student, a private-venture side-by-side two seat jet trainer-cum-tourer. Built at Shoreham and powered by one 880 lb st Blackburn Turboméca Marboré 2A turbojet, the Student was initially marked G-35-4 as seen here.

An elegant and surprisingly small machine, the Student is seen here in flight. Only one aircraft was built although it underwent numerous developments and was the prototype for a range of derivative aircraft. Registered G-APLK, the maximum speed was 298 mph. Later, on October 26th 1984, it was re-registered G-MIOO. Attempts to interest anybody in the machine came to nought and the aircraft was destroyed in an unnecessary accident. Fragments of the aircraft survive in the Berkshire Aviation Museum.

---

5. The Edo Aircraft Corporation of College Point, Long Island, New York, USA, established a new standard for light aircraft floats. The company took its name from the initials of its founder, Earl D Osborne, and its chief engineer was the talented B V Korvin-Kroukovsky. It was founded during 1925 to develop seaplane floats for light and commercial aircraft and by the spring of 1926 had become specialists in the design, construction and repair of Alclad seaplane floats and enjoyed a worldwide market. Although the EDO company has sold its name to others, its products are still available.

Nevertheless, orders flowed in and the company had to find manufacturing space, leasing a 34,000 sq.ft Ministry of Aircraft Production factory at nearby Christchurch. Besides space, the business also needed £50,000 to move forward. It assumed that it would be able to restart its Portsmouth-Ryde air service which, on profit estimates, would help subsidize the production. It even made contingency plans that if it were prevented from operating the Isle of Wight Air Services itself, then it could lease its Ryde Airport property profitably.

Portsmouth Aviation confidently predicted the annual production of 50 Aerocar Majors and the same number of Minors and suggested that the output of two aircraft a week was well within its capabilities. A most thorough budget statement was produced.

All, then, was contingent on the Labour Government permitting the company to resume its pre-war flying activities either independently or in conjunction with some other body such as BOAC. It was expected that re-starting services between Portsmouth, Shoreham, Bournemouth and Southampton to Ryde would happen in April 1946. It even planned to use twin-engined Bristol Wayfarers each with 55 to 60 passengers on the Portsmouth-Ryde route, so great was the anticipated demand.

Had all gone well, the business would have enjoyed nineteen profitable seasons before the hovercraft offered any competition in 1965.

Back in 1947, though, Portsmouth Aviation, a small company financially over-stretched, was now in something of a cleft stick. It did not have the money for the next and crucial move which was to finance production together with the necessary jigs and associated tooling. Whether the *Flight*-quoted figure of 288 machines ordered was correct and how many of those orders might ultimately have been converted to cash deposits one cannot say. The path from a bulging order book to an apron line-up now represented a journey of Biblical proportions. A massive additional investment was needed on top of the expenditure on research, development and prototype-building.

Had it been able to persevere there is every possibility that the Aerocar would have succeeded, perhaps generating a useful home and export market. But Portsmouth Aviation's mainstay business was in aircraft servicing for which it still had useful military contracts for Airspeed Oxford and Slingsby Kirby Cadet rebuilds. Additionally it was preparing a charter service while hoping to restart the Isle of Wight air ferry and develop Ryde Airport by re-siting the Ryde-Brading main road and extending the airport to the west.

On top of all this, negotiations were at an advanced level for production in India under manufacturing licence and a company – Portsmouth Aviation (Nawanagar) Limited – was actually formed. At the last moment a change in the political climate there withdrew expected financial support. It was now inevitable that the project was doomed.

This was not the only fly in the ointment, though, for the new Labour Government under Clement Atlee imposed crippling credit restrictions on British banking institutions. As money became more expensive and imports were restricted, so exhortations to export were not matched by any form of government support. This was particularly the case concerning steel tubing which was in limited supply and then only available to 'preferred users'.

It was this final hurdle that secured the failure of measures to shift construction elsewhere. Consequently last-ditch efforts were made in October 1949 to try to sub-contract manufacture either to engine-makers Blackburn-Cirrus or to Auster Aircraft at Rearsby. Both approaches were most kindly rebuffed — and the only airworthy Aerocar was scrapped in October 1950. There are stories that the second Aerocar cabin nacelle that had been shipped out to India may have fallen into the harbour following a dockside crane cable slippage while unloading. And Auster, intrigued by Portsmouth Aviation's impressive order-book, decided to try its luck with its own twin but the outcome, the twin pusher A.7 of September 1949, was, for the firm, a leap too far and it remained a mock-up project.

An outstanding design was thus crippled by national political failure to provide any aid whatsoever to a small but established firm that happened to be onto a winner and be holding a full order-book. This was rendered all the more scurrilous by the way a later government handled the Beagle business – a firm so mired in indecision that its ultimate defection to the land of insolvency was inevitable. Had but a fraction of the aid given to that outfit been available to Luxmoore and Balfour, then the Aerocar would have returned its investment by way of rich earnings.

Portsmouth Aviation's Aerocar was thus a victim of its own success combined with a goodly dose of government indecision. The Aerocar vanished — and Ryde Airport faded away eventually to become the site for another nondescript out-of-town supermarket.

7. Planet Aircraft Ltd

If ever success were to be guaranteed merely by the sheer weight of boardroom importance, then we would probably still have Beagle today. By the same token we would, unquestionably, still have Planet Aircraft Ltd.

The board of Planet read like the gilt-edged prospectus for a Royal Command Performance. It brought together every contemporary significant growth industry in the land from ICI Chemicals, giants in the business of petrol and oils, the enormous wealth of the Distillers Company – and Blackburn aircraft. The head man was none other than Charles Ball. In those immediate post-war years, he was one of Britain's top industrialists known to most, respected by all and possessed of the sort of financial judgement that probably suggested that walking on water was merely dependent on the provision of sufficient investment.

Major Charles James Prior Ball, DSO, MC, was born on February 15th 1893, the son of a prominent JP, and went on to serve in the Royal Artillery throughout the First World War. He distinguished himself on the Military Inter-Allied Commission of Control, the body set up to organise the disarming of Germany. This meant that he was well-connected, knew the right people and, above all, had a splendidly mixed bag of experience.

Nothing, though, could have prepared him for the Satellite, a project that he would learn to his cost needed more than money and top brass to make fly. Like the love of a beautiful woman, aerodynamics and radical ideas cannot be bought merely on the strength of a bank balance. As we shall see, though, Charles Ball's real skill was in survival and he ensured this by thoughtfully spreading the costs (which ended up as losses) across a wide spectrum of his companies.

As with the Chrislea Ace, the butterfly-tailed all-magnesium Satellite had no rudder pedals, control being by push-pull spectacles protruding from the instrument panel. Unlike the Chrislea, the Satellite was a true two-control machine, technology it replicated from the American Beechcraft Bonanza. Fitting the engine in the middle of the fuselage and driving a pusher propeller behind the tail was also not new (shades of the French inventor Victor Tatin and his work with

Louis Paulhan) but was at that time enjoying a revivalist fad in the States: Douglas had used it in the Cloudster in 1946.

That the Satellite should embrace both these features was not all that surprising since Major Heenan of Heenan, Winn and Steel, the consultant engineers responsible for bringing the design into being, had toured extensively in America where he found, among other things, that a four seater aircraft would fulfil 60 per cent of the potential market if it could be built to sell at a low cost. He also shrewdly deduced that the major market for an aircraft fulfilling this criterion would be outside England. In this aspect, the Satellite was designed from the outset as an export-earner. Heenan also proudly acclaimed that this was the first aircraft he had ever designed. He might just have thought better about owning up to that fact although it did nothing to deter investors.

The choice of magnesium as the principal material of construction was revolutionary since, being 35 per cent lighter than aluminium, it allowed the use of far thicker sheets of material to be specified. The main drawback is that magnesium is highly susceptible to corrosion and is also a fire hazard. Heenan deduced that pure magnesium is virtually inert to the action of salt water but if even very small traces of impurities are present such as nickel or iron, then electrolytic action automatically causes corrosion. As regards fire, Heenan concluded that because heat is dissipated quickly through thick metal, risks of combustion were no greater than with normal aircraft construction materials and probably less so.

A high-quality refined magnesium alloy – magnesium-zirconium – was developed by specialists F A Hughes & Co Ltd (a business of which Charles Ball happened to be managing director) which met the purity requirements and the potential for a strong, durable and very light aircraft seemed attainable. Figures were suggested to support claims that the then-current average payload of about eight per cent of the aircraft's all-up weight could be doubled.

Throughout its troubled development it was supported, rather curiously, by the aeronautical press, both *The Aeroplane* and *Flight* devoting considerable space to reports on it. The latter actually published what was probably the most uncharacteristically sycophantic article ever seen in the entire trade press almost suggesting the work of a junior journalist who had been very well entertained beforehand.[6] If words alone could make a project fly, then this should have done it!

While tests in structural strength were carried out at the Engineering Division of the National Physical Laboratory, nobody thought to follow these up with equally-important wind tunnel tests. Flight, it seemed, was eschewed the inevitable conclusion of building an aircraft using strong materials.

Construction took place in the Redwing works at Thornton Heath and the finished aircraft was taken to Redhill by road for erection in 1948. It was then trucked to Farnborough where it was a static star of the September 1948 SBAC show, drawing much probing speculation, in particular from those of us who, being aerodynamically aware, could not quite work out how it would fly.

From the limelight of Farnborough it was taken by road to Blackbushe for flight trials. Here it came under the dedicated scrutiny of the Air Registration Board which expressed itself as being rather uneasy regarding a number of design and construction points. The crunch came when it was found that the nine-inch wide undercarriage leg root-end attachments flexed alarmingly during fast taxiing trials. They also acted as the retracting pivot for the leg. This was, as it turned out, the least of the problems experienced for regardless of the speeds attained on the ground, there was no hint of rotation.

So what was wrong with the aircraft? Insufficient pitch control and insufficient tail moment seem only to have been part of a problem that began by the failure to carry out basic wind tunnel trials on a model. Carried away by the excitement of new materials and revolutionary but untried and unproven aerodynamics, the designer's concentration on construction methods rather than basics contributed to an expensive failure that did nothing for our light aircraft image.

The simple fact was that when on the ground there was limited angle of attack available and pulling back on the stick banged the ventral fin into the tarmac long before even oleo extension offered an increase in incidence. And shortening the central, ventral fin only allowed the propeller to hit the ground.

High-speed wing sections such as that used on the Satellite (said to be the docile NACA 23012 but looking horribly like the high-stall 10 per cent variant) perform extremely well at high-speed, but have a distinct tendency to produce limited lift at low speed and small angles of attack. Makers of model aircraft appreciate this well-known fact: it seems that certain designers don't. This means a high stall speed and low rate of climb.

In *Flight's* curious article, already referred to, is the comment that in every cubic mile of sea water there are over four million tons of magnesium. This fact was presented as an example as to how important the Satellite would be to our future economy. Was somebody really suggesting draining the oceans and building millions of non-flying Satellites, or were we all missing something? *Verb sap.*

The Newbury AP.4 EoN coming in to land. First flown from Welford, Berkshire, on August 8th 1947, G-AKBC was the sole example of this attractive four seater. It was destroyed in a pilotless take-off at Lympne on April 14th 1950 and the builders, Elliotts of Newbury, subsequently abandoned aircraft construction.

---

6. *Flight*, July 15th 1948, article 'Design in Logic' (five full pages in length).

8. Beagle Aircraft Ltd

The creation of British Executive and General Aviation Ltd was announced on Friday, October 7th 1960. The new firm, not yet officially known as Beagle, was solidly guaranteed by the Pressed Steel Co Ltd, makers of motor car bodies, railway rolling stock and refrigerators. Earlier that year the business had taken over the lease of Oxford Airport at Kidlington. The entire share capital of Auster Aircraft Ltd at Rearsby had been acquired and with it that maker's experience of more than 20 years of light aircraft manufacture. In due course a technical and manufacturing liaison arranged with F G Miles Ltd at Shoreham offered a virtual guarantee to the forward-thinking of the tiny but immensely talented design team.

Described as a subsidiary of the Pressed Steel Co Ltd, the business was created to design and manufacture a new range of executive and light aircraft for the home and export markets. It also promised to demystify some of the old aircraft construction philosophies, suggesting that we were about to see the use of other than expensive aviation components. After all, there were often cheaper alternative components available in the motor industry that were no less reliable than those demanding expensive paperwork. Pundits forecast aircraft that would share some of the pricing attributes of the family car.

Leading the business as managing director was Peter Gordon Masefield, the former MD of Bristol Aircraft Ltd. While no designs were immediately revealed, there was no doubt that the new firm would be challenging markets presently dominated by makers based in Wichita, Lock Haven and Bethany. Masefield foresaw 'a good opportunity of being able to sell into the States'

In mid-October 1960, the chairman of Pressed Steel Co Ltd, Alexander Abel-Smith, claimed that the BEAGLE Group intended to produce a 4/5 seater executive aircraft to sell as 'around £25,000'.

Recognising the confusing design numbering system used by Auster at Rearsby and accepting Miles' strict sequential order of designs, Masefield was keen to regularise the numbering system that the new business would use. In December 1960 he produced his recommendations[7] He proposed that Auster should have the prefix 'A', Beagle 'B' and Miles 'M'. Aircraft model

Developed from the successful pre-war Vega Gull, the Percival Proctor Mk.I appeared on the civil register in the immediate post-war years. This example, G-AHNA (R7486) gained its C of A on May 9th 1946 and enjoyed 21 years of life before being destroyed in an accident at Tolleshunt D'Arcy in Essex on December 27th 1967.

numbers should form a group the first of which showed the number of engines. The next two numbers represented the type number based on odd numbers for single-engined designs, and even numbers for twin-engined aircraft.

Masefield brought with him from Bristol two designs. First was the twin-engined Bristol 202 which became the Beagle 204 and was developed into the Beagle 206. The second Bristol design was the Bristol 219 single-engined five seater which ultimately became the Beagle 105. Bristol's twin-engined four seater design, the Bristol 218, was not taken up by Beagle and died with its parent company.

While the business had discussions with Rolls-Royce with a view to the production of a series of power-plants, these were all to be of American origin. This had the curious result that despite being a full member of the SBAC, Beagle's dependence on American-made engines rather than wholly-British motors would debar them from giving their usual Farnborough flying demonstrations.

On May 10th 1962 British Executive and General Aviation Ltd formed a subsidiary company called simply Beagle Aircraft Ltd which absorbed the two subsidiary companies, Beagle-Auster Aircraft Ltd, and Beagle-Miles Aircraft Ltd. It still had two factories separated by expensive land communications (trucks) and all the system duplication that such circumstances dictated.

Beagle's rate of expenditure soon outstripped its funds and on Friday February 12th 1965 Parliamentary Secretary to the Ministry John Stonehouse announced that the government had stepped in with a grant of £600,000 to assist in the development of the Beagle 206 and 242.

On December 12th 1966 it was announced by the then Minister of Aviation, Frederick Mulley, that the government was to acquire the assets of Beagle for £1m. He told Parliament that: 'Pressed Steel Fisher Ltd, on account of their other commitments, do not wish to retain their interest in the light-aircraft field'. The new development, Parliament was told, should enable Beagle to command an increasing share of the world market.

The magazine *Flight* (December 23rd 1966) suggested that 'the country has got a bargain for its £1 million' but it was one of those rare moments when editor John Ramsden got things wrong.

The rosy prospects for the Shoreham company soon evaporated (as did the taxpayers' million). Things were not going right for Beagle when, at the end of 1967, its attempts to sell fleets of B.206-S aircraft were scuppered. Initially, it seemed certain that substantial contracts had been secured but this was not to be. The first was from the South African Government which had ordered eighteen aircraft for air-sea rescue duty as well as fishery protection duties. This contract was blocked by the American State Department because the Beagles, powered by US-built Continental engines, would be flown by quasi-military pilots and might then be used for internal security operations to enforce apartheid regulations. Britain appealed against this on the grounds that the South African security forces already used fleets of Cessna 182 aircraft. The second hiatus concerned an order for fourteen aircraft for the Argentine Air Force. Here the problem was 'tit for tat' in that we had placed a ban on beef imports because of an outbreak of foot and mouth disease.

---

7. Masefield, P G: 'Beagle Group Aircraft: Suggested Related Numbering System', December 13th 1960.

This came at an unfortunate time as Beagle was expanding its facilities at Shoreham. As January of 1968 began so did work on a new factory for the production of Pups. The 60,000 sq.ft extension was to be completed by the summer. Its jokey nickname, 'the kennel', did not mask the high costs incurred in setting up and running this building.

In an exercise intended to take the fight into the enemy's camp, an agent had been appointed in North America. But Butler Aviation saw it all as an uphill struggle and, despite a useful currency devaluation at the end of 1967 (which made competition at home more costly), sales were very small. By the start of 1968, Miami Aviation Corporation of Opa-Locka, Miami, had been appointed Beagle's distributor for the south-east USA and the Caribbean area. It took three B.206.S aircraft as demonstrators.

Norman Jones, chairman of Rollason Aircraft & Engines Ltd, wrote at that time that:

> I do not believe that, just because up to now the Americans have succeeded in winning the lion's share of the world market [for light aircraft], there is any reason why we should even attempt to copy their type of machine. To try to imitate them must be a short cut to the bankruptcy court for a private firm, and an enormous waste of public money for a nationalised one.
>
> If we are not prepared to accept the permanent dominance of the United States in the world market for light aeroplanes, we must do just what our car manufacturers have done and strike out on a path of our own. To compete with foreign light aircraft, the British industry must produce aircraft that are intelligently different and are very good value for money, not only in terms of initial price but also in terms of maintenance and repair costs, and which command a good secondhand value.

Clearly a man who should have been running Beagle rather than the business that hand-built Druine Turbulents for the Tiger Club and others, Norman Jones was just so right when he said; 'If we do this, we are laying the foundations of an industry in light sporting aircraft that will certainly enable us to export to most countries of the world… We shall also be better able to adapt our models to the different demands of particular markets and climates.'

It was at this time that questions were being asked in Parliament as to how much actual money the government had advanced to Beagle and whether such sums were in the form of grants or loans and if the latter whether interest was payable.

The eye-catching twin-boom layout of the Portsmouth Aerocar Major which, with its two 155 hp Blackburn Cirrus Major II engines and over-boom exhausts made for a sleek and fast transport for its passengers. Emanating from a wartime design for an aeroplane that could transport a mounted motorcycle messenger (who would ride out the back of the pod fuselage on landing), the Aerocar was a brilliantly-engineered concept that attracted plenty of orders. It should have been an outstanding success, but its builders could not afford the leap of faith from prototype to production line. Of course, nobody would back them either. G-AGTG gained its C of A on September 10th 1945 but in the end this fine aircraft was broken up in despair in October 1950.

The Minister of Technology Mr Wedgewood Benn gave a written Parliamentary answer on February 2nd 1968 to questions from Mr Nicholas Ridley who had asked whether the £2.4 million advanced to Beagle as part of the company's capital was a grant or a loan. He stated that the sums were as grants, not loans and therefore no interest was payable.

Meanwhile Peter Masefield spoke at the British Light Aircraft Centre dinner held in London on February 9th. In a speech responding for the guests, he let it be known that the Pup was attracting great interest and that the first 115 examples would be delivered by the end of the year and that the first production Pup-100 was 'being painted at the weekend'. The Shoreham School of Flying, we learned, was taking delivery of this example so that the makers could check its use in service.

Early in 1970, Beagle was unable to raise any more cash and, despite increasingly urgent pleadings to the Exchequer, found its ability to continue in business to be seriously compromised. Its inevitable closure marked the end of Britain's last opportunity at regaining any vestige of world market share in the light aircraft business. This was now thoroughly sewn up by the Americans, the French and, to an interesting degree, the Germans.

Auster history authors *Preston and Ames* [46] comment thus on the Beagle fiasco:

> Throughout its existence Beagle was subjected to ever increasing under-capitalisation, despite changes in owners and being financially underwritten by the Government. In 1968, the company was placed in the hands of the receiver and, despite attempts to sell the Company, the assets were gradually disposed of and the Rearsby employees were made redundant. Some obtained employment with local companies, some diversified and others moved further afield, remaining in aviation, to the likes of Westland. A local trade union official summed [it] up by saying: 'I am disgusted that the Government is prepared to allow Britain's only long established light aircraft factory, which has served the nation in peace and war, to shut down, and skills and know how acquired by generations of craftsmen to be dispersed'.[8]

Without doubt, the Pup 150 was a fine aircraft: after an extensive air-test *Air Pictorial's* then managing editor wrote of it in his curiously pedantic 'third-person disassociated' manner:

> By the time we landed we were genuinely and honestly convinced that this really is the one aircraft we have flown which is not only as good a tourer as any foreigner, but which is also as good an ab initio trainer as the Tiger Moth.

---

8. Quoted from Austers *Nearly all you wanted to know* page 110; spelling, capitalisation, punctuation and grammar as printed.

So if it was that good, why didn't other companies clamour to take it on or build a better version? The simple answer is that the only likely candidates for such a job were the major manufacturers and, because they were major manufacturers, they would be quite unable to be competitive. Geared to the design and production of high-value military and commercial aircraft, little of their production equipment would be suitable for light aircraft manufacture. In other words, their whole ethos had progressed so far beyond the regime of the small aeroplane that it was now totally outside their reach.

When, during a design meeting held at Hatfield back in 1952, I asked de Havilland why it did not put the Tiger Moth back into production, the answer was both assured and shocking[9]. Because, I was told, with then-present labour costs and overheads the firm would have to produce a minimum of 500 aircraft and these would have to sell at £40,000 apiece at 1952 values, and the company was intelligent enough to know that it didn't stand an earthly of achieving that! It was with this in mind that de Havilland held exploratory talks with Phoenix Aircraft Ltd to consider 'sourcing' a suitable light aircraft design.

In the end, it was Scottish Aviation that took on Beagle Bulldog production not just because it had the enterprise and the initiative, but because it was *the right size* of business.

So much for the sorry saga of Beagle, brought to its knees by over-estimating its markets and undertaking expansion on the strength of a current order-book.

It was not all heartache, though, for there was one extremely successful light aircraft design that so far we have merely skirted around. This was the Chipmunk, de Havilland's brilliant Tiger Moth replacement designed in Canada in 1946. Production of this delightful metal monoplane was shifted to Hatfield in 1948, later to Chester, and it proved one of our most successful light aircraft.

The problem was that it was intended as a military trainer and although made in large numbers, few were to be civilianised. Then, in 1953, the RAF Basic and Reserve Flying Schools were closed and hundreds of these aircraft became available. Stored around the country, predominantly at Cosford, Aston Down, Hullavington and Silloth, they could be bought very cheaply. All, though, was not straightforward, and trying to satisfy ARB requirements for a C of A was an expensive, time-consuming and frustrating affair. Elstree Flying Club's then CFI David Ogilvy relates some of the problems:[10]

> When the surplus military [became available] many of us hoped that at last our chance had arrived to re-equip the clubs and schools with something more complete and advanced than the Tigers, Austers and Magisters....
>
> The Chipmunk 10 is a Service aeroplane and therefore, it seems, dangerous. The fuel capacity of 18 gallons, giving a safe endurance of about 2¼ hours, was considered inadequate – yet is it as bad as that of the Lycoming-Auster, whose 15 gallons tend to give rise to fear of failure and forced-landing long before two hours have been flown? That boiled down the initial excuse to rather weak reasoning, so after hours of dispute and desk-hammering we were permitted to retain the pair of nine-gallon tanks – into which, incidentally, ten gallons can be poured quite easily.
>
> That was one stumbling-block overcome, but... that was only the start. The propeller must come off and be sent away; and to get it back with the necessary tag of approval one must hand over a sum considerably in excess of twenty pounds. The instruments, too, must be pulled out to be overhauled and released; and with two complete blind-flying panels and a pair of compasses, as well as a number of ancillary dials, we find ourselves confronted with a three-figure bill before they can be re-installed.
>
> Even our old friend the Gipsy Major 1, surely the most rugged and reliable little unit ever produced anywhere, now comes under fire and fear of suspicion. The high-compression Major 8 in the Chipmunk is viewed with such official apprehension that any surplus military specimen that has run for more than 500 hours of its 1,000-hour life must be thrown away or returned for reconditioning. An engine that has completed a figure under this artificially prescribed amount may be retained for use – subject to its being partially pulled down for examination by a representative of the makers – who, incidentally, is not permitted to accept responsibility for its re-assembly and final clearance. For this an independent D-licensed engineer must be called in…
>
> Despite all this we still have basically a Chipmunk 10 – but this [marque] has never been approved as a civil aeroplane; so, in addition to hauling everything apart and putting it all together again, we must take great care not to put back all the parts in their original homes. By so juggling with what is established and what has been proved safe through experience, we eventually convert our Mk 10 to a 22, the later a new number concocted for the purpose, enabling us to apply for a C of A. But what of those parts that we must move? As an example, the hydraulic-fluid reservoir was originally mounted in a safe, easily accessible and easily checked position just inside the port cowling and on the

The SK-1 all-wood two seater jet racer designed by Hugh Kendall and built for John Nathaniel 'Nat' Somers to race. Constructed at Woodley 1954-55, G-AOBG was a remarkable small aircraft with a wingspan of just 22 feet 9½ inches.

---

9. Admittedly by this time de Havilland had successfully introduced the Canadian-designed Chipmunk as a British production aircraft and in so doing had moved itself well beyond the realms of 'cheap' fabric-covered biplanes.

10. This is an edited extract from an article by David F Ogilvy, manager and CFI of Elstree Flying Club, published in *Flight*, November 16th 1956, under the title 'Chipmunk Conversion'. While the club's example, G-AOSY, was not the first such conversion, Ogilvy was by far the most outspoken regarding what he (and many others) rightfully considered to be the obstructionist attitude of the then civil aviation system and the Air Registration Board in particular concerning making this proven military trainer into a private aeroplane.

forward face of the firewall, where it has functioned satisfactorily for thousands of airborne hours. Just to tempt fate and to ensure that any leak would have dangerous results rather than drip casually on to the bottom tray and thence to eternity, we must now position the tank immediately above the voltage regulator. Without this element of danger installed, we cannot so much as ask for a C of A, and the aircraft's activities must apparently be restricted to the teaching of Service pupils (who have included, it may be remarked, the Duke of Edinburgh).

And so on. We could write page after page of the troubles, setbacks, delays and expenses of converting our first Chipmunk for use as an instructional aircraft, but at last we now have it in service and it is earning belated doses of fuel and oil and proving more than popular with all who fly it. Unfortunately, business is business and all the cost of conversion, maintenance and operation must be passed on to the user, so no club or school can hope to operate this most useful machine at Tiger or Maggie rates. By club standards, however, it is a special aeroplane and its value is wrapped up more in its potential as an advanced trainer for instrument flying, aerobatics and radio work than as a counterpart or replacement for the earlier types.

In this overview of the post-war British industry, there remains another contender that, in fairness, ought to be mentioned and that was Britten-Norman's 1969 attempt at the light plane market. This one, however, was neither well-judged nor confidently executed. Created more out of unbridled enthusiasm (or boredom) by John Britten and Desmond Norman, the all-metal four seater Nymph was an overt challenge to the hitherto American-dominated market. Incredibly it was designed and built very quickly while the company's main production of BN-2 aircraft proceeded apace.

When Britten-Norman Ltd unveiled its handiwork, it was truly one of the best-kept secrets in the world of aviation. After all, the firm was hard at work building twin-engined Islanders and the triple-engined Trislander as fast as it could and there was surely no room for another project in the company's portfolio. As it was, nobody guessed or even suspected what had been going on behind the closed hangar doors at Bembridge until the curiously-painted light mauve and red BN-3 was wheeled out and first flown at dusk on May 17th 1969.

The story was that the machine had been built in 53 days, start to finish. So confident were its creators as to its likely success that all three – John Britten, Desmond Norman and flight engineer Andy Coombe – piled into the four seater for its maiden flight! One might have felt that putting virtually all the little company's precious eggs into one untried basket was tempting fate, but Norman for one had no such qualms: he frequently flew single-engined aircraft from Southampton to France the direct way rather than the more prudent land-predominant route.

The Nymph was an all-metal high-wing tricycle undercarriage machine with an optional (but not installed) folding-wing facility designed as an exportable product for local assembly from kits of Bembridge-supplied parts. In that respect it was planned as a foreign currency-earner.

True, *Air Pictorial* waxed lyrical about 'long slender wings and a shapely streamlined fuselage', but that could not alter the fact that the Nymph was an expensive but poor copy of an American light plane that was effectively untried and had no market pedigree. The same source went on to extol the Nymph's advantages and even its alleged benefits. None was there, though, as time would tell.

The company had neither the resources nor manufacturing facility for a second-string production line, even if only of kits. Already the company was overstretched and the concurrent developments that had evolved the bigger Trislander had put the business on the path to insolvency leading, two years later, to acquisition by the Fairey Group.

This, though, was not all. The Nymph was an overt, even downright blatant attempt, to design something that looked American. While it would be unkind to call it a Cessna derivative, it was more transatlantic in appearance that its contemporaries from the stables of already-bankrupt Beagle.

The problem was that if one was going to go for copying the Yanks, then this was a bad copy. A skin displaying rows of domed rivets and general lack of attention to external detail, even for a 1960s low-cost kit aircraft, were already points that customers watched out for. In short, the Nymph just was not good enough.

Shades of Auster's unfortunate Atlantic (which, close up, was a better-looking Yankee lookalike from a dozen years earlier) Britten-Norman's 53-day-wonder was left gathering dust at the back of the workshop for some years until it was quietly moved to a new hangar at Sandown Airport by Desmond Norman, now disassociated from the company he had co-founded

On June 20th 1984 the Nymph reappeared with a brand new paint job and some minor modifications as the claimed prototype of a 'new design' solely by Desmond Norman and called the Norman NAC-1 Freelance with a brand-new registration. That could not hide that it was already a 25-year-old outmoded imitation US light plane.

Looking back over this period shows an

Four seater Tiger Moths ought to be the stuff of bad dreams. Thruxton Engineering brought them into the real world with the so-called Thruxton Jackaroo by converting the elegant lines of the Hatfield biplane into the rather misshapen lumpiness of this four seat conversion. A number of examples appeared between 1957 and 1959. Three were tried out as crop-sprayers but the majority served with the Wiltshire School of Flying based at Thruxton.

extraordinary catalogue of lost opportunities and wasted effort and money. It would be nice to say something in favour of the Chrislea designs, but the best aircraft of what was at most a poor bunch – the Skyjeep – was too late to succeed. Auster was pre-eminent, but in the final analysis produced too many models that were merely derivative rather than innovative. Elliotts had the right idea, but nobody helped them when they needed it most. Portsmouth had a brilliant design but simply could not raise the necessary finance or external support. Nevertheless, had they been given the right backing, all three might have been world-beaters.

But perhaps the real loss was the potentially pre-eminent position of one company that so far has received barely a mention – Folland. This company's thinking was so far ahead of its time that, like Martin-Baker, its failure was almost inevitable, yet had the company been able to produce its FO.124, designed as early as June 1946, the course of British post-war light aviation might have been changed dramatically.

This one design had the potential to lead the market. The Beagle Pup of fifteen years later was only marginally better than that original Folland design, the development of which would surely have made Beagle virtually redundant. And the same company's thoughtful FO.127 and 130 would have spearheaded an early replacement for the already ageing Rapide and stolen a march on other light transports such as Britten-Norman's Islander and even DH Canada's Twin Otter.

Bright lights were few and far between at this point in our post-war private flying scene. The aircraft so far mentioned were well-known. There were others that never quite made it to the headlines although they deserved to. David Lockspeiser's extraordinary Land Development Aircraft was built and flown yet nobody took up the challenge and capitalised on the enormous potential of this design for use in under-developed and more rugged terrain. This machine could have proved as useful and utilitarian as Junker's G.14 rugged transport of the 1920s.

A casual observer will conclude that the government showed no real interest in our light aircraft industry and that in failing to facilitate financial assistance for Beagle in time of need, or in backing other potentially worthwhile projects, it behaved counter to the overall public interest.

This is true, but only in part, for it has to be said that the British Government (and the tax-payers) had already been caught out a few times as had the big investment banks. Fear of letting themselves in for more press and public knockabout made them a canny, if uninspired, bunch. From the Labour Government's ill-fated Ground Nuts Scheme in Kenya in the late 1940s to DeLorean Cars in the 1980s, financial institutions merely demonstrated they had learned to be wary of bright-eyed men toting portfolios of ideas.

In adopting a blanket approach to these people it was inevitable that the good would be thrown out alongside the bad.

Experimental aircraft tended to be merely military or, increasingly, commercial. One project, though, successfully bridges the divide between military, commercial and light aircraft and this was the extraordinary Youngman-Baynes high-lift machine. Often described by lay observers as 'a modified Proctor', this wholly-new design (which made use of small Proctor components such as windscreen, tail and undercarriage parts) was financed by the Ministry of Supply and built on the wartime success of R T Youngman's lift-and-drag enhancing flaps as used so successfully on the Fairey Barracuda, Fulmar and Firefly.

All of this owed its origins to something that had taken place long before the war. In fact, the inspiration had been that great pre-war challenge to aerodynamicists – the Warsaw *Europa Rundflug* or *Challenge de Tourisme International* of 1934 – an event to which Britain was to be excluded. Eight participating aircraft pushed the bounds of low-speed high angle-of-attack flight to new levels. The winner was the Polish RWD.9 with a lift coefficient of 3.53. This had a maximum of 306 hp giving a top speed of 173.5 mph and a minimum speed of 33.7 mph.

Other contestants included the BFW Me.108 (lift coefficient 3.18); the Fiesler 97 and the Klemm 36 with lift coefficients of 3.53 and 3.36 respectively. Of the Me.108, observers commented that the flaps extended almost the whole length of the trailing-edges and that lateral control was by small but long-chord ailerons working in conjunction with interceptors or spoilers behind the leading-edge slots.[11]

The extra wide centre-section is seen in this picture of a Jackaroo showing how the normal narrow Tiger Moth tank was retained and mounted on new longer centre-section spars. The extreme width of the cockpit door is also seen which effectively prevented any attempt at opening in flight or even starting the engine with the access open. Note also that this example has an unusual exhaust system with an expansion collector leading into an extended tail pipe. One-time actress, racing pilot Sheila Scott (1922-1988) used a Jackaroo for a while in the 1960s. As a four seater it was certainly a cheap machine to operate and acquire.

---

11. Shrewd observers commented that the German designs all drew heavily on the work of Gustav Lachmann of Handley Page whose valuable paper *Control beyond the Stall* had been presented at the Royal Society of Arts on December 17th 1931 and published under the same title by the Royal Aeronautical Society in 1932. The original lecture was attended by, among others, Dr Wilhelm Pleines, one of the principal assistants to the renowned aerodynamicist Professor Wilhelm Hoff (1883-1945) who was in charge of the Deutsche Versuchsanstalt für Luftfahrt (this was the German Aeronautical Research Institution or DVL) in Berlin.

That same event produced one aircraft that had the highest lift coefficient of the whole eight – the Czechoslovakian Aero A200 with a figure of 3.82. Almost all of the aircraft were fitted with Handley Page's patented leading-edge slots.

This had spurred on research in Britain, first with our own entrant for the 1935 *Challenge de Tourisme International* (which in the end did not take place) – a heavily-modified de Havilland Puss Moth (G-ABMD) created for W D Macpherson by Airwork Ltd at Heston. Leading aerodynamicists of the age (Handley Page's Gustav Lachmann, Martin-Baker's James Martin and Herr Hoeffner) joined forces to build a wing with full leading-edge slots, drooping flaps and ailerons and so on.

This work was followed up by tests on double Fowler flaps developed by the Royal Aircraft Establishment at Farnborough. These tests gave a maximum lift coefficient of 3.5 while the addition of a leading-edge slat increased this to almost 4.5. These were the highest figures attainable without the use of increased power and before the advent of boundary-layer control and blown flaps.

Development work disappears underground during time of war and so the research into high-lift was one project that did just that. Fairey's pre-war head of technical development was Robert Talbot Youngman who had produced the first amorphous flaps. Fairey's new FC.1 four-engined commercial airliner was to be the first machine to carry them but in the end they served well on the military machines listed earlier.

When peace was restored, further work on Youngman's flaps could no longer be justified at taxpayers' cost, so the designer had to form his own business in order to move forward. A definite need to improve take-off distances for military aircraft, especially for carrier-borne machines, succeeded in earning a Ministry of Supply backing and the little single-engined aircraft was built at Heston.

Those that either took part in the project or merely watched the machine fly knew that they were participating in the making of history for Youngman's amorphic flap gave the curiously tubby, square-winged aircraft a speed range from a little over 30 knots to 138 knots flat out; such a range (4.6) was at that time unheard of. After the principle had been proven, the cash ran out and the project was shelved. This simple but amazing aircraft was given to an aeronautical college where, in the interests of conservation and progress, it was broken up in 1954.

The people who really went ahead with Youngman ideas were not in the world of full-sized aircraft but in the world of aeromodellers who to this day are at ease with things that, 55 years ago, we thought were sensational. Of course, at that time they were and, naturally, they could have had enormous benefits for light aircraft. The problem was then, as now, that an industry without money or encouragement can seldom be expected to invest funds it does not have and, as far as its bankers are concerned, cannot secure.

In a similar vein, reference must be made to F G Miles' association with the extraordinary ultra-high aspect ratio wings of French designer Marcel Hurel and his company Hurel-Dubois that led to the creation of the Miles HDM Aerovan. This is covered elsewhere and, regrettably, proved to be something of a dead-end as Miles lost its identity to Beagle soon afterwards. Paradoxically, the design ended up with Shorts who noticed that the huge wingspan was an operational disadvantage. It generated the ugly but extremely practical Skyvan series.

To sum up Britain's post-war light plane industry, it was a gallant attempt at reviving the rich decades of the 'twenties and 'thirties but operated in a hostile economic environment. Conditions that demanded a rigorous adherence to a practical business plan were ignored as a talented and highly capable industry that was motivated by enthusiasm and a Micawber-like approach to prospects of financial security uncertainly probed unprofitable avenues.

Chris Paul had wondered if we were really air-minded. Whatever the answer, wise people were right to accept that Britain was both populated and governed by a monopolistic flat-Earth brigade that believed Man and bumble-bees could not fly, and therefore they should not be encouraged from the public purse.

Without doubt, Auster at Rearsby was the largest exporter of new light aircraft in the immediate post-war years and various Auster models were to be found in virtually every corner of the world. D-EFEP was a J/5F Aiglet Trainer exported to Germany in the 1950s and this picture was taken in 1959 by Mike Hooks.

CHAPTER FIVE
The Home-Made Aeroplane Triumphs!

Amateur-built aircraft are no recent phenomenon: they've merely come round full circle. After all, every one of the pioneer flyers was an amateur. The first factory-built aircraft were no more than an amateur builder making a machine to sell to somebody else. In the beginning, all aircraft were 'home-made'. The change to commercially-built aircraft did not necessarily alter the status of the homebuilder although he soon recognised the commercial advantages in distancing himself from classification with the raw novices amongst his fellow men. After all, 'A V Roe & Company' sounded much better than plain 'A V Roe'.

There was the added advantage that if you had the money you could hire somebody to help you build your aeroplane. You thus became an employer. This is how all aircraft manufacture – without exception – began and it was not really until time of the First World War that the individual makers began to be outnumbered by the aircraft manufacturing companies that were being established up and down the land.

For a while, the preferred source of aeroplanes for military use was the Royal Aircraft Factory, a matter of concern to those builders that were becoming properly established.

After the First World War had run its course, what official circles referred to rather disparagingly as 'the Trade'[1] received an increasing share of the business as aircraft manufacturers came to be favoured as the proper, correct people to engage in the arcane practice of designing and building aircraft, be they military fighters or flying club trainers.

Despite this, the amateur aspect of aircraft creation never actually went away. It certainly diminished in size and, in many cases, turned to building machines for the new sport of gliding. Every once in a while, however, a 'proper' powered aeroplane would appear that emanated from the garage workshop of somebody outside the now-established coterie of aeroplane-builders.

Home-built aircraft represent a fascinating and logical extension of a form of 'industrial revolution' that strongly influenced the industrious male as far back as Victorian times. While the upper classes had their huntin', shootin' and fishin' as means to occupy their time, the ordinary man in the street was encited to employ his spare time in a constructive way. The publication of several practical magazines such as *The English Mechanic* and, more in particular, *Work*, spurred the male of the species to use his hands to amuse and better himself. The upper classes still had their grouse-shooting, but the man in the terraced house now had his woodwork! The formation of Mechanics Institutes up and down the country at the end of the 19th century set in motion a new respect for practical work and encouraged amateur craft.

By the start of the 20th century all manner of handicrafts, cabinet-making and the ubiquitous fretwork were being practised by many. Meanwhile, women had their own publications to foster advanced needlework and those associated crafts considered more suited to the lady of the house at that time.

As the spare-time mechanic, who was possibly an office-worker in his breadwinning capacity, gained in confidence, miniature steam locomotives, boats and even motor cars emerged from little workshops across the land. When in 1933 the monthly magazine *Practical Mechanics* became one of the earliest of a dedicated tranche of 'practical' periodicals to hit the British bookstalls, the amateur realised that the world (meaning his capacity for making things) was something of an oyster now within his grasp.

These magazines moved a significant distance away from simply making bedside cupboards and decorative pipe-racks: they instructed how to make machines such as clocks, motor boats and wireless sets. Over the years that followed no subject was deemed too arcane for its readers. Except, perhaps, for splitting the atom, readers were encouraged to make looms, printing machines, steam boilers, lathes, cameras, telescopes, boats and even light cars. Telephones, the magic of the electric door-bell and elementary science subjects stayed with the boys' magazines. *Practical Mechanics* was aimed at the man who wanted a serious engineering challenge and, presumably, had the money to spend. And so came the flood of projects from single-cylinder gas engines to sash windows and X-rays, infra-red photography to touring caravans, radio controlled boats, underwater photography, a tea-making alarm-clock…

A major boost to the development of these skills had come right at the start of the century with the introduction of Frank Hornby's Meccano, promoted as 'engineering in miniature', which encouraged boys to assemble gearboxes, working models of fairground rides, cranes and industrial machines. This sowed the seeds of practical hand-work right from an early age.

It was much, much more than that which today is called 'do-it-yourself'. It was the fostering of engineering not so much for a practical purpose as for the love of using your hands and brain. And a young mind so stimulated so often became that of a next-generation career engineer and designer.

Craftwork became an extension of the urge in all thinking men to be *self-sufficient*. It was an urge to create. It cultivated an innate desire that had hitherto lain more or less dormant in many of us to do what Lilienthal and the Wrights had done.

And when *Practical Mechanics* magazine described how to build a glider readers clamoured for powered flight. It coincided with the arrival of Henri Mignet's Flying Flea and the magazine duly produced a multi-part article on how to make one at home. While based on the books written by its designer (and thoughtfully translated into English by the Air League of the British Empire), it was a fresh and artistic series which got many men (and boys) Flea-making.

By the second half of the 20th century, the very thought of amateur-built planes and weekend flyers was anathema to some people. All that was back in the untutored

---

1. For the story of 'the Trade' and its uphill struggle to beat the official monopoly see Ord-Hume [35].

days of the 1930s! It was in those bad-old days when America's leading monthly aviation journal, the Chicago-based *Popular Aviation*, followed the UK example and serialised instructions for building the Flea. In May 1937, editor John B Rathbun penned a gem of a story which had trans-Atlantic ramifications:

> Unregulated amateurs, or call them bootleg flyers if you will, have a surprisingly small number of accidents either as a total or as a per centage. On the other hand, licensed pilots flying licensed ships are standing and prominent proof that the regulations and laws governing these men are not effective in reducing accidents. Keeping the top speed down to 100 mph, or lower, is a more effective safety measure…

But we are slightly ahead of ourselves. The subject remains home-built aircraft in post-war Britain.

Maybe a classic example of a light aircraft that first saw the light of day in this manner and one that everybody knows was the Simmonds Spartan two seater biplane of 1930. This was built by its designer in a bedroom of his Southampton house. It went on to become such a success that a factory was set up to produce it 'legitimately' and it sired a small series of successful variants such as the Spartan Arrow and Spartan Three Seater.

A good handful of other very successful designs started out as the products of that grey area between 'one man and his dog' and the proper factory (whatever that may truly mean). The Miles Satyr, the Foster-Wikner Wicko and the Percival Gull are among those that fit into this category.

But things had been tightened up and in 1930 *The Aeroplane* weekly magazine was inspired to publish a news item in which it stated that 'the home-made aircraft is now virtually illegal' and that recent legislation effectively prohibited amateur construction of anything that might fly. This was concurrent with a contemporary belief that aircraft were expensive luxury items that were far beyond the reach of the 'ordinary man on the Clapham omnibus'.

It was to fly directly in the face of this belief that the Frenchman Henri Mignet launched his *Pou-du-Ciel* or Flying Flea first to a French, then the British market and, eventually, to the whole Western world. Here was a simple single seater that the inventor had not even built in a house, garage or garden shed, but in the confines of a city-centre apartment! Small, cheap

The establishment of a proper home-built aircraft movement in Britain really began in the mid-1930s with the HM-14 Flying Flea, the first British example, G-ADMH, being built, flown – and first flight crashed – at Heston Airport by Stephen Appleby. His machine, pictured here under a de Havilland DH.86, (G-ACZP *The Belcroute Bay* of Jersey Airways Ltd) was powered by a single-ignition Ford 10 car engine with its radiator placed behind the cylinder block right in front of the pilot's face. Here we see Sir John Carden (in trilby hat) looking at the engine. He would subsequently redesign the motor to produce the reliable, if heavy, Carden-Ford motor initially for the Flea and later for other small aircraft such as the Baynes Bee, the Taylor-Watkinson Ding-Bat and the Chilton Monoplane. G-ADMH was later rebuilt and fitted with the first Carden-Ford motor with which it did a fair amount of flying.

and simple to fly, the Flying Flea was now the answer to everyone's dream of getting airborne.

But, despite the pious words of John Rathbun in Chicago, there were many Flea-related accidents and some fatalities. Not the 'hundreds' that myth has handed down to us today, but several dozen, three of which were fatal in Britain (the fourth, often linked with the other three, was as the result of a ground taxiing accident).[2]

These accidents were thoroughly and expensively investigated using wind tunnels in both France and Britain. These tests quickly found that the problem was due to the design formula's aerodynamic sensitivity. The potential performance envelope of most normal aircraft has a wide operational 'hump' (a definable latitude involving the relationship between centre-of-pressure, centre-of-gravity and angle of attack) within which the aircraft can operate safely: the Flying Flea flew very well but its performance latitude was virtually nil: it was rather like sitting safely yet atop of a church spire for there was no room for error or deviation to either side. The designer, self-taught through empirical learning and consequently not aware of this anomaly, forgot to instruct his followers to adhere exactly to his plans or face consequences that were potentially dire.

The demise of the Flying Flea – the authorities refused to issue any more Permits to Fly for new examples or authorise annual flight renewals of existing ones on expiry – was a great disappointment to those who had been exposed to the euphoria of the availability of easy and affordable flight. It led to the appearance of a small cluster of 'substitute designs' intended to sate the appetites of those who had been bitten by the bug. Some of these were very successful while others were much less so.

The problem, that is as far as it could be seen as a problem, was that the ordinary man had tasted aeronautical freedom and was now filled with the enthusiasm to build his own aeroplane. Meanwhile the Air Ministry, with its responsibility for all aspects of aviation both civil and military, was unsure how best to cope with this rush of amateurs and their inability to understand the importance of paperwork… The Permit to Fly scheme, applicable to the Flying Flea, was ultimately extended

---

2. See articles by Ord-Hume: 'Those Killer Fleas', *Aeroplane*, August 2004; also article 'The Seventy-year Itch', *Popular Flying*, January 2007, pp.23-30.

to include the new breed of small amateur aircraft that operated without a proper Certificate of Airworthiness.

Amateurs, though, were by nature great experimenters and a flurry of motorcycle engines, converted car engines and occasionally downright poor engineering worried those in high places who realised that ministerial policing of the amateur side of aviation was no sinecure.

The effect of all this was to give the home-made aeroplane a decidedly bad name. The outbreak of war more or less at the height of the late 1930s resurgence of home-made aircraft not only stopped all work but it effectively froze a moment in common memory so that in the immediate post-war years people still talked of Flying Fleas as being current and with the received belief that they were all dangerous. Expressed simply, the popular image, built on half-truths and hearsay, was that all home-built aircraft were Flying Fleas and, since all Flying Fleas were dangerous and banned, there was something that was unsavoury and risible if not downright illegal in the whole process of trying to build your own aeroplane.

Unfortunately this impression was not just that of the uninitiated public but, as we have seen earlier in this story, extended to many in high places. Some aircraft engineers were anxious not to be associated with home-built projects just in case it might be interpreted as a sign of recklessness akin to dereliction of duty. There was also a hint that the amateur aeroplane-builder must be abnormal, unstable, deranged. The Flying Flea had given and it had taketh away…

The Air Ministry's refusal to renew any Permits to Fly or issue fresh ones for Flying Fleas in 1938 remained 'on the books' when the responsibility for post-war civil aviation matters passed to those now concerned with civil aviation. The real problem was in the wording. Incredibly the Air Ministry record passed on to the Ministry of Civil Aviation referred to 'the Flying Flea (home-made aircraft)' as being prohibited. This was interpreted in literal manner by the new regime of civil servants, not that 'the Flying Flea, *which is a home-made aeroplane*, is prohibited' so much as '*home-made aeroplanes*, collectively known as "flying fleas", are prohibited'!

At the start of the 20th century in the world of player-pianos, the trade-name of one maker (Aeolian's Pianola) became the generic term for the whole genus; then 'Hoover' (another trade name) became both a verb and a generic name for suction cleaners. And 'Flying Flea' meant *all* home-built aircraft!

Earlier I told how the Ministry of Civil Aviation was created in 1944 as a conjunction (but not fusion) of the old Ministry of Aircraft Production (whose Minister was newspaper proprietor Lord Beaverbrook) and the Ministry of Aviation. The first Minister for Civil Aviation was Lord Swinton who took up his appointment on October 22nd 1944. In the following April a Bill to establish a separate Ministry of Civil Aviation was introduced in Parliament and received the Royal Assent on April 25th 1945. As already related, that July, Lord Swinton was succeeded by Lord Winster after holding office for a mere six months.

Amateur aviation now stumbled around in that widening gulf between larger light aircraft and commercial/military aircraft. While there was nothing ever in print, it was soon obvious that the new authority, while tolerating private aircraft with full Certificates of Airworthiness, would prefer to rid itself of the genus *home-made aeroplane* regardless – and that meant Flying Fleas and everything else. Again nothing was formalised, but the clear indications were that legislation should be formalised and all aircraft that were intended to fly ought to have a full C of A. And this was a nicety denied to home-made aircraft because of a multitude of reasons that extended from lack of suitable approved manufacturing facility, lack of a full-time inspector, lack of a bonded materials store, quality-control minion, paperwork filer, paperwork creator and so on. To be 'approved' meant to have staff and paperwork. The man in the street operated as a one-man band and treated paperwork (whether perceived as probably unnecessary or understood to be *actually so*) with deserved contempt.

It would have been interesting to see just what might have happened had an amateur been able to throw sufficient money at the problem to build a 'regular' and conformist aeroplane. It was, of course, unlikely to happen. The story of Shapley Aircraft, a tiny company that was barely distinguishable from amateur status, tried that and, as told elsewhere, was stone-walled out of business. And other non-conformists, although better financed and organised, stood little chance of cracking the system (Chrislea, Elliotts, &c, &c).

One cannot say that the amateur aircraft movement died with the outbreak of war, only that it became, like so many other aspects of life, moribund 'for the duration'. Once the war ended, those with the latent or suppressed urge naturally began in earnest on the practical side of amateur aircraft. While most of these efforts were associated with the restoration of pre-war light aircraft, there was a strong group of enthusiasts that assumed the rules and regulations (meaning dispensations) that had reigned pre-war would be re-introduced.

In earlier chapters the birth of the ULAA was outlined. A little of this ground must be retraced and summarised to explain its creation and early operation, both of which are interesting and unusual. It was unusual in that it began as what the Americans might term a 'ways-and-

The concept of the home-made aeroplane was already established in America in the early 1930s with aircraft such as the Corben Baby Ace and Heath Parasol. Instructions for making these were published in mechanical engineering magazines. Several Parasols were built and apparently flown in Britain – unofficially. G-AFZE was started in 1939 but Robert H Parker did not complete it until 1947. Powered by a 696 cc Blackburne Tomtit inverted V twin, the red and silver machine made its first flight at Elstree on January 9th 1949 in the hands of Colin H Debenham. It was, though, grossly underpowered and most of the circuit was flown below hedge-top height. Re-engined with a 32 hp Bristol Cherub II and later fitted with larger tail surfaces it survived until April 1st 1966 when it crashed at Luton.

means' committee but swiftly changed to a lobbying group that realised its future depended not just in acting as a representative body, but in fighting (one way or another) the bureaucracy that was stifling amateur aviation.

At this particular stage in private flying, nobody could have foreseen how increasingly important the home-built aircraft movement would become over the next half century. Indeed nobody could imagine that our real light aircraft industry was approaching its end having been effectively wiped out by overseas competition, mostly from the west.

It all began in the issue of *Flight* magazine for August 22nd 1946. In it was a provocative article by one Irish-sounding 'Risteard Mac Roibin', the true identity of whom has never been revealed (but is known to the present writer), that was to change everything. This article, entitled *Encouragement for Fools*, posed the question 'What of the True-blue Amateur?' and offered 'Some Serious Suggestions in Light-hearted Manner'. The thrust of this two-page text urged a return to 'fun flying', citing the work of Henri Mignet and others. The author looked at different types of small aeroplane, coming down on the side of the small autogyro. It threw down a large gauntlet urging a resuscitation of amateur aviation and making a tranche of suggestions. In opening people's minds to unthought-of possibilities it became a sort of 'Rosetta-stone' of post-war private and amateur flying. The question concerned the conversion of pure possibility into practical opportunity from which reality might emerge.

This amazing article was written with a purpose in mind: to seek fellow enthusiasts and encourage them out into the open. It brought forth a small but significant flurry of correspondence. The first, published on September 5th, came from Ron W Clegg supporting the concept and urging that all interested people should get together and form 'a club, society, association – call it what you like' to promote sport-flying and amateur aircraft design and construction. On September 19th a letter from Sqdn-Ldr Alan H Curtis (who had worked with Alfred R Weyl in the pre-war days on the Dart Kitten) added his weight to Risteard Mac Roibin's words but adding that the minimum engine requirements ought to be a four-cylinder of 40 hp. He also identified Mignet as a genius adding that he 'couldn't agree more' with his philosophy.

More was to follow! Graham K Gates' letter in the September 26th issue favoured the economy of the light aeroplane and referred to the series of articles in the pre-war *Practical Mechanics* magazine that provided instructions on how to build the Luton Minor.

Further letters of support followed on October 17th and 31st (which sung the praises of the auxiliary sailplane) while on November 7th came a plea for the reintroduction of the Luton Minor from one E J Pope, later to become both a Minor constructor and a flying instructor at Denham.[3]

It was Ron Clegg's letter, however, that attracted correspondence from a number of like-minded souls. These were invited to a meeting at 15 Westbourne Park Road in West London October 26th 1946. The upshot was the formation of the Ultra Light Aircraft Association and an executive committee that included F/O Maurice Imray, Grp-Capt Edward Lucas Mole and several others including myself – the youngest by a good margin. The announcement of formation appeared in the correspondence pages of *Flight* on November 14th and this attracted even more potential members to the neophytic group.

Clegg's statement revealed that the objects of the association were 'to encourage the design, construction and ownership of all types of ultra-light aircraft; that is, of powered machines with an all-up weight not exceeding 1,000 lbs and an engine not exceeding 75 hp.'

All did not go well in the first months of the ULAA and some of those who had promised support were more interested in arguing design specifications of aircraft than in securing the future of a good and well-organised body. As told in an earlier chapter, Maurice O Imray wrote (*Flight*, November 28th) they were showing concern for aircraft minutiae rather than attempting 'to get down to the admittedly hard and unspectacular business of founding an organisation'.

Over the following months, countless representations were made through proper channels to the Ministry of Civil Aviation, the general thrust of which centred on the simple fact that a growing number of enthusiasts wanted to fly ultra-light aircraft (or anything else, come to that) without the need for costly Certificates of Airworthiness. In other words, the plea was for the reinstatement of the pre-war Permit to Fly system.

Several pre-war aircraft had been found and these became the test cases upon which the ULAA built its case and the MCA did its best to demolish it. Continual pressure from the ULAA was stoically and effortlessly resisted by a ministry that could not imagine the tenacity of a few ordinary people bitten with the aviation bug.

The problem continued to be aired in the correspondence pages of *Flight*. The well-known 1930s Yorkshire glider designer and Flying Flea builder Erik T W Addyman wrote (December 5th 1946):[4]

The letter from Mr E J Pope is typical of the troubles experienced by many other enthusiasts who are building their own low-powered aircraft and those who wish to fly them. It would seem that obstacles are deliberately put in the way of those who should receive encouragement and help.

I am afraid that the ATC and the RAF won't receive many volunteers when it is realised that they won't be able to make and fly their own little aircraft later on.

'The Magna Charta' [sic] of low-powered aircraft building and flying is the Gorell Report, and any attempt by Ministries to infringe the rights then granted should be faught tooth and nail in Parliament... The whole matter was most thoroughly investigated at the time and a safe arrangement made.

In the same issue there was also a letter from a Mr T N Walker who wrote:

With reference to the letter of E J Pope it may interest him to know that I, also, built a Luton Minor just before the war finishing it in fact too late to receive permission to fly. Since my return to 'civvy street' from the RAF I have been in communication with the Air Ministry regarding a 'permit to fly' but have been given to understand that '...it is by no means certain that it will be possible to reintroduce this pre-war practice'.

I take it that this must apply to all ultra-light types and wondered just how many enthusiasts have been similarly grounded by this edict. I have flown the machine twice – permit or no – and found it very sweet to handle, though a bit underpowered with the Carden engine. A 'permit to fly', even with all the pre-war restrictions, is all that I want – C of A is too expensive – but I want it now, not at some vague, very future date, and I can see no sound reason for its refusal.

---

3. E J Pope built his Luton Minor in a fourth-floor attic bedroom of his house in Ealing, West London. Despite the extreme difficulty of getting the materials up into the attic, he did not foresee the problems of removing the aircraft as it progressed. In the end, the fuselage had to be sawn in half to turn it sufficiently to lower it out of the window. At weekends he lived in a caravan on Denham Aerodrome where he was an instructor: he died there after a stroke one weekend lunch-hour.

4. For details of the Yorkshire pioneer Erik Thomas Waterhouse Addyman (1889-1963) see Chapter 1.

Something of an anachronism was presented by this machine. Built at Sandown on the Isle of Wight in 1962 as a development aircraft, this brand-new non-standard Luton LA.4 Minor G-ASAA was powered by a new 37 hp Aeronca-JAP engine from the Popular Flying Association's stock of unused engines made for the Aeronautical Corporation of Great Britain in 1937. Pictured on September 6th 1963 at the PFA Rally held at Rochester, Kent, its striking 1930s décor attracted considerable attention. It was all white with light blue lined in yellow, polished and clear-lacquered while the cockpit was fitted out with white quilted upholstery with blue piping. It won its owner/pilot a *concours* commendation.

The redesigned Luton LA.4A Minor was initiated under the aegis of Phoenix Aircraft Ltd. Sets of plans were marketed worldwide from 1962 onwards. Among the many builders was Donald Peacock of Colchester in Essex. It took him 2,000 working hours and £450 to construct the JAP-engined G-ATCN pictured here during construction on July 7th 1965.

Mike E Vaisey built this Luton LA.4A Minor G-AXKH at Hemel Hempstead in the early 1970s. The engine is a 1600 cc VW and the first flight took place at Panshanger on June 22nd 1974.

British Light Aviation – A Shifting Emphasis

Home-building was effectively restricted to re-worked pre-war designs until the happy invasion of the French! It began with rumours of a young Frenchman called Roger Druine who had designed and built a successful single seater powered by a modified VW engine. The aircraft was called the Turbulent and this photograph, taken by Harold Best-Devereux of an example built by Léon Clochez, was widely published in the amateur aviation press in the early 1950s. This example earned the Concours d'Élégance at the RSA meeting two years running.

Below: Harold Best-Devereux, then an ARB inspector and later to become chairman of the Popular Flying Association, was both a great Francophile and believer in home-built aircraft having served some time when he was a boy as an unpaid apprentice to the old Luton Aircraft Company at Tatling End, Gerrards Cross, and the close by Denham Aerodrome. He managed to borrow one of Roger Druine's Turbulents, F-PHFR, and secure permission to bring it to Britain and fly it around the country on a demonstration tour. Here it is at Elstree on its arrival in Britain. Thanks entirely to 'Dev's' persuasive abilities, the Popular Flying Association secured not just the UK selling rights to Druine's design, but got the authorities to accept the French type-certificate as precedent for a British airworthiness equivalent. The home-building movement was really under way at last.

Above: Besides the single seat Turbulent there was another French design – the single seat Jodel D.9. It was one of these that came to an early PFA Rally and as a result it became the second French design to be approved for amateur construction in Britain.

The spirit of amateur aircraft portrayed by a Druine D.31 Turbulent pictured with a Tiger Club member at Redhill. The Ardem VW conversion is pictured with a Hoffmann propeller having squared-off tips and blade terminal fences. Druine the designer, avid pilot and flying instructor, died at the age of only 37 on March 19th 1958 following a long battle with poor health.

A pre-war design that had captured the imagination of aviation enthusiasts was the single seater aerobatic biplane designed and built by a pilot and lecturer at the Chelsea College of Aeronautical Engineering, John R Currie. Called the Currie Wot, two examples had been built in 1937 at Lympne and, paradoxically, both shared the same engine – a single-ignition Aeronca E.113C (not, as reported widely elsewhere, an Aeronca J.99 JAP) removed from a crashed Aeronca C.3, G-ADZZ. After the war, Currie became chief engineer at the Hampshire Aeroplane Club, Eastleigh where, under persuasion from John O Isaacs and Vivian H Bellamy, he redesigned the aircraft and, financed by Bellamy, built a new prototype, G-APNT. The second machine was G-APWT first flown on October 20th 1959 powered by a 62 hp Walter Mikron II. This aircraft spawned a number of variants and soon amateurs were making Wots up and down the country.

This letter expressed in a nutshell the official attitude towards home-built aircraft in the immediate post-war period.

Several amateur builders received the same treatment at the hands of the Air Ministry and its civilian quango the Ministry of Civil Aviation.

The ULAA was not the only 'amateur' or private flying association although, at a few months, it was unquestionably the youngest. More influential was the Royal Aero Club with its committee of men in high places such as Colonel Rupert Lionel 'Mossy' Preston who was just one person whose circle of friends and acquaintances took in Royalty, nobility – and government ministers. In other words, people like Preston were better equipped to 'lobby' support than most.

Besides the Royal Aero Club there was the British Gliding Association (BGA). Despite its grand title, it, too, was newly-founded but it did have as president the Viscount Kemsley. As a newspaper baron and overt supporter of civil aviation, Kemsley was a powerful force. In the closing months of 1946 news broke that the authorities were planning that all gliders should have full Certificates of Airworthiness and be maintained by as-yet-to-be-appointed M-licensed (glider) engineers, this imposition served to unite the efforts of the RAeC, the BGA and the ULAA against the ministerial campaign against sporting aircraft and recreational flying. Kemsley added respectability to the protests that followed.

As related earlier, the Royal Aero Club had as its headquarters 119 Piccadilly while the BGA had an at least equally prestigious headquarters address – Lord Londonderry's magnificent former home Londonderry House, 19 Park Lane. The Marquess had generously placed his home at the RAeC's disposal for 21 years at peppercorn rent and by the end of 1946 this would become known as The Aviation Centre: nobody could have foreseen that within a short space of time this fine house would be swept away to be replaced by an architecturally and spiritually bereft modern hotel.

From its rather more lowly address at 24 St George's Square, Victoria (Ron Clegg had gone abroad with his job and the Association's address was now that of Maurice Imray), the ULAA's cause was promoted and, thankfully, received the full, sustained and sincerest backing of both the BGA and the Royal Aero Club. The Ministry shuffled its feet. By this time, several ULAA members had aircraft that they were hoping to fly on a Permit system.

The MCA then came up with its trump card. Yes, it would reintroduce Permits to Fly, but they would only be issued to aircraft that had previously (*i.e.* pre-war) been operated on the Permit system and could be proved so, meaning the survival or the original Permit and all logbooks. Furthermore, the aircraft would have to be identical to its pre-war original, meaning the same airframe-engine combination.

Then there was a great confusion about what degree of 'repair' or 'restoration' was possible before an existing (meaning pre-war) ultra-light fell outside the category of a 'rebuilt pre-war Permit holder'. An arbitrary twenty per cent was put forward. Anything more than that and it would be classed as a new aeroplane even if it had a pre-war registration.

The story of the present author's battle with this restriction which turned into sheer farce is related in the book *On Home-Made Wings* [35]. It was the ultimately successful outcome of a war of attrition rather than mere battle with the Ministry that ultimately forced the authorities to re-instate the Permit to Fly system, but not without a mountain of obstructionism that had to be eroded relentlessly over the following years.

There was a prime problem with the MCA interpretation of 'ultra light' and this was a restriction which coloured the development of the movement for many years. This defined an ultra light aircraft as a machine with a stalling speed of less than 45 mph whose all-up weight did not exceed 1,200 lbs and whose power was less than 75 hp.

Over the years that followed, a shift of balance took place, first away from the amateur aircraft, and then back towards it again in a very big way. Earlier on it was explained how the Permit to Fly system had been a product of 1930s Air Ministry thinking. With the Air Ministry now nothing to do with civilian flying, the field was open for some new legislation or, if not exactly that, then a new interpretation of all that had gone before. In the fullness of time, that is what happened.

Through the efforts of the ULAA and its successor the PFA, Permits were reintroduced and designs for amateur aircraft construction approved. It should be remembered that the PFA itself was an amateur organisation and none of its executives received any remuneration, giving freely of their time and expertise. No charge was made for PFA services except for the acquisition of paperwork where money had to be exchanged 'up front'.

Time has shown that as the PFA became larger and larger it was forced to employ regular staff and to levy charges for its services. Today the PFA is named the Light Aircraft Association (LAA) and is a business which has to operate along the same economic guidelines that frame any such commercial enterprise. This is one of the hazards of an organisation that starts as a small and friendly society to help others, and ends up as a large and impersonal body the aims and objects of which have become obscured, or changed, with the passage of time.

An interesting aspect of the reintroduction of the Permit to Fly is that the Ministry conceded that certain light aircraft that normally operated on a full certificate of Airworthiness, could safely be down-rated to operate on the less-demanding (meaning less-costly) PtF system. As already explained, there were strict limitations on the size, power and performance of these machines which, for instance, ruled out the larger Austers but allowed in British Taylorcraft Model A and C, and some American Piper Cubs. It also excluded 'heavies' like the Tiger Moth, Moth Minor and BA Swallow.

The principal service for which the ULAA and PFA was created was to foster cheap flying and home-built aircraft. The difficulty lay in finding suitable designs that would meet post-war requirements as regards airworthiness expectations in terms of engine reliability, safety in the hands of the novice pilot, and a necessary short and possibly rough field performance.

The first aircraft to gain approval was the Luton Minor, initially in its pre-war form as described in *Practical Mechanics* magazine for 1938. It was the present author's work to revise this aircraft, initially as Light Aviation Supplies, then as Phoenix Aircraft Ltd, that produced the LA.4A variant, essentially a wholly-restressed and re-worked design to take engines up to 65 hp including the 'new' VW car-engine conversion.

Besides this, a similar redesign and restressing was undertaken for the Currie Wot single seat biplane which was revitalised by John O Isaacs and the original designer, 'Joe' Currie.

There is an unsung debt of gratitude that post-war amateur aviation owes to the French. Were it not for the enthusiasm and the camaraderie of our fellow aviation enthusiasts across the Channel, then the amateur side of post-war British private flying might well have been set back further. The immediate (so it appeared) availability of home-built aircraft to the French enthusiast at the end of the war was an inspiration to

Currie Wot G-ARZW, below, was built by Dr John H B Urmston of Botley near Southampton who, like John Isaacs, was a member of the Hampshire Aeroplane Club. He began work in 1961 and it made its maiden flight at Eastleigh on April 18th 1963. Another Mikron-powered model, this time with a Mk.III, these were dubbed 'Hotter Wots'. This aircraft and its companion G-APWT both flew across the Channel to France. Here Mike Hooks has captured a fine image of the Hotter Wot in a low turn.

The rather archaic yet nevertheless attractive lines of the Currie Wot G-APWT with its Walter Mikron II inline engine captured at take-off from Elstree Aerodrome by Richard Riding. The refinement of the long exhaust pipe kept cockpit noise down to acceptable levels in this practical little single seat sporting aeroplane for the amateur aircraft builder.

Given the name ¿Que mas? (Spanish for 'What else?'), E H Gould's Hotter Wot G-AYMP was built in Sussex and also powered by a Walter Mikron III which developed 65 hp. This gave the machine a top speed of 95 mph with a comfortable cruising speed of 80 mph. Notice the revised fin and rudder profile.

Styled the Super Wot, the most powerful of the piston-engined Currie Wot biplanes was G-AVEY built at Wolverhampton by K Sedgwick and A Eastlow. With a taller undercarriage to provide adequate propeller clearance, this was powered by a Pobjoy R geared radial engine. It was registered on January 31st 1967 and first flew four years later.

Following on the success of his Taylor Monoplane, John Taylor went on to design the smaller and faster Titch so named after his friend and PFA executive committee member, Wing Cmdr O V 'Titch' Holmes. With a span of 18 ft 9 inches and a top speed of 180 mph, the 85 hp Continental-powered Taylor Titch prototype G-ATYO first flew at the hands of its designer on January 4th 1967. On May 16th that year it crashed and killed Taylor. Other examples have been built since.

THE HOME-MADE AEROPLANE TRIUMPHS!

Amateur flyer John O Isaacs had always admired the lines of the Hawker Fury so set about designing and building a seven-tenths scale replica based on the Currie Wot. This, he claimed, reduced the detail design and stress work needed. The all-wood machine was designed and built at Southampton between 1961 and 1963 with a 65 hp Walter Mikron III as power plant. Registered G-ASCM it was first flown at Thruxton by John Heaton on August 30th 1963. This little home-built with a wingspan of just 21 feet cruised at 75 mph. It was later re-engined with 1 125 hp Lycoming O-290-D and painted in the colours of 43 Sqdn, RAF. In this form it was called the Isaacs Fury Mk.2.

The sole Coates Swalesong SA.2 made its first flight at Rush Green on September 10th 1973 and was the precursor of Swalesong SA.3, a somewhat simplified version for amateur construction.

Eric C Clutton and E W Sherry designed the FRED as a very simple, easy to fly home-built. FRED, asserted Clutton, stood for Flying Runabout Experimental Design where 'experimental' is used in the context of the American equivalent of the Popular Flying Association, the Experimental Aircraft Association. Designed between 1957 and 1963, the prototype G-ASZY, has flown with a variety of engines, the first flight being at Meir, Stoke-on-Trent, on November 3rd 1963 with a 27 hp Triumph 5T. It subsequently flew with a Scott A.2S and then a 37 hp Lawrence L-5 radial. Modification of a 66 hp Volkswagen engine produced the version pictured here.

everybody. And the willingness of the French to attend our puny air rallies was on the one hand a tremendous boost and on the other an acute embarrassment. One notable ULAA rally brought three French home-built aircraft all the way across the water and well into mainland Britain while all we could muster was one rather dilapidated-looking Tipsy. In so many ways and by example, the French taught us to fight for our rights!

Even more importantly, it was the example of the French and the French legislation in particular that lifted the ultra-light aircraft movement in Britain and allowed more powerful two-and three seater aircraft to be considered for Permit to Fly operation. In the 1960s, the French legislative form became the pattern for the updated British rules.

But the French were an inspiration and thanks to the unstinting work of a few stalwarts of which Harold Best-Devereux (1919-1985), then working as an inspector with the Air Registration Board and much later to be PFA President, was the leader, the Druine Turbulent became the first foreign design to be approved for amateur construction in Britain. This was followed shortly afterwards by the Jodel; D.9, then the Druine Turbi two seater, the Piel Emeraude and the Druine Condor. Marcel Jurca's racy-looking Tempete suggested that the French were maybe a bit braver than our own potential home-builders but at least that design was also available.

Of these, the Turbulent was by far the most popular and entered production here as the Rollason Turbulent. The Emeraude, a rather challenging design for the home-builder on account of its complex elliptical wing and attendant double-tapered mainspar, was also taken up by the Garland-Bianchi organisation as the Linnet, later to be known as the Fairtravel Linnet. The Bearn GY-20 BabyClub, amateur built in France as the Gardan GY-20 Minicab, also became a British builders' favourite, the design having been acquired, improved and fully redrafted for British requirements and amateur constructors as the Ord-Hume GY-201 Minicab.

Even so, there was still no new and original all-British design for a home-built aeroplane. The first was John Isaacs' Fury I, a seven-tenths scale single seater based on the Hawker Fury biplane fighter of the 1930s and using the Currie Wot as a starting-point. This was followed by an improved version, the Fury II, after which Isaacs made a three-tenths scale Supermarine Spitfire.

The first wholly innovative home-built design after the war was John Taylor's Monoplane and he, too, followed this up with his own single seat scale model of the Spitfire.

Here I am discounting the Britten-Norman BN-1F G-ALZE which, while technically it was the first new post-war amateur design, proved an unsuccessful flier and was sadly relegated to has-been status.

Another significant development was the revival of interest in the autogyro but only as a very small personal runabout. Thanks to the enterprise of an American of Russian descent, Igor Basil Bensen (1917-2000), the interest in tiny rotary-winged aircraft was re-kindled in Britain. Besides building Bensen-designed machines, amateurs developed the original American design producing a whole raft of individual and derivative machines each improving on the US original.

Most notable among these has been the work of Kenneth Horatio Wallis, a retired Royal Air Force officer who devoted considerable time, effort and research to producing a wholly-British small autogyro. His work was immortalised in a well-known James Bond film that did more to promote the small autogyro in Britain than any other post-war rotary-wing development.

As the 1970s approached, it became increasingly apparent that Britain had a strong and viable home-built aircraft movement which, with its increasing tendency to explore the technicalities of new design and modern materials and technology, bordered on the new-age industry.

Many of the new designs that have appeared since then have gone into production as kits, complete aircraft and plans for amateur-building. This produced a situation where Britain at the end of the 20th century had more aircraft manufacturers than in 1950 – albeit smaller and, one has to say, more vibrant outfits.

If Britain has lost her light aircraft industry, then it has been more a loss of tradition than actuality, for what has really happened is that the high ideals of the aspiring manufacturers have been replaced and subsumed into a large number of very active enthusiasts.

In the final analysis, then, it is the long-derided amateur aircraft builder who now shoulders the responsibility for sustaining Britain's light aircraft industry. In truth there can be no better people to carry that responsibility. And the illustrious ghost of 'Risteard Mac Roibin' and his colourful pen may be laid to rest once and for all…

Mitchell-Proctor Kittiwake II designed by Roy Proctor and R 'Kit' Mitchell between 1966-67 was a two seat all-metal low-wing amateur-built light aircraft for use as a glider-tug. Fitted with a Rolls-Royce Continental O-240-A engine. Prototype G-AWGM was built by Robinson Aircraft at Blackbushe and first flown there on March 19th 1972.

Peter C Lovegrove's much-modified Bensen B-8 G-AXII dates from 1969 which was when interest in small autogyros escalated.

Aerobatic pilot Tom Storey designed a small single seat Formula One racing aircraft which he called the TSR.3. Construction took place at Redhill Aerodrome in Surrey and made its first flight there on July 25th 1968. Powered by a Continental C90, G-AWIV, the 'TSR' in its name stood for Tom Storey Racer and the numeral '3' was to distinguish it from the infamous fiasco surrounding the British fighter known as the TSR.2.

CHAPTER SIX
Engines:
the Chicken-and-Egg Situation

One positive outcome of the Second World War was to be found in aircraft engines. There had been considerable advances in research and development in the sphere of high-powered engines and their operation. Britain and America were not alone in this and so great interest was aroused when the opportunity arose to examine in close detail German engines from captured or shot-down machines. Some of these innovations were good, others less so in ways of impracticability or cost.

The adoption of fuel injection for almost all the Luftwaffe's internal combustion motors, while considered a surprising advance, was actually not a German invention. Again, the Daimler/Mercedes-Benz DB 601A 12-cylinder inverted 'V' type pioneered the aeronautical use of a hydraulic coupling to drive the supercharger. Operating on the 'fluid flywheel' principle known in the motor industry since at least 1929 and popularly used on pre-war Daimler and Lanchester motor cars, the adoption of this to the aero-engine was, though, a stroke of genius. The same engine, however, had another unique feature – a simple and cheap clockwork boost control. This allowed the boost to be increased automatically for one minute only at take-off.

In 1940, America saw a revival of interest in steam-driven aircraft and some fairly extensive theoretical design work was carried out with the goal of producing a turbine that would develop between 3,000 and 5,000 horsepower. This was not the first, of course, and in 1934 an inventor named LaMont had tried to interest the US Army in an aircraft motor that used a central high-pressure boiler in the fuselage with two 18-inch by 36-inch turbines in the wings developing 1,500 hp each. The condenser, operating with a 21-inch vacuum, was behind the airscrew. It was the condensing system that the Air Corps did not like, and the project had been dropped. And that followed trials back in 1929-30 of the Besler Brothers' steam-powered biplane in California[1].

Steam for aircraft was not merely the province of crackpot weirdo inventors and there were still many engineers that saw steam as a distinct possibility, in particular for the light-to-mid-sized private aircraft. These few, but vociferous, steam fanatics were boosted in their beliefs by the simplicity of drive and the inherent 'flat' power curve of the steam engine. The drive simplicity and that shallow power curve together meant that an engine could operate at any speed that was convenient and still produce almost maximum power. Furthermore by putting the engine effortlessly into reverse gear, the aircraft fitted with a steam motor could perform short landings by using 'reverse thrust' without any of the expense, complexity and weight of a variable-pitch propeller and its operating gear.

Besides steam there was the diesel or compression-ignition engine. Although long-credited to patentee Rudolph Diesel (February 1893), the compression-ignition motor was actually an English invention. Herbert Akroyd Stuart (1864-1927) built his first successful oil engine at Bletchley, Buckinghamshire, six years before the German ever made an engine.

Long Beach Municipal Airport was the site for an unusual flight in May 1946 when the Austrian-born Fred A Thaheld flew his Stinson Model 10 Voyager fitted with a home-made motor. This 125 hp horizontally opposed air-cooled four-cylinder compression-ignition engine was of 290 cubic inch capacity and weighed 235 lbs or 1.88 lbs/hp. Performance was claimed at least up to that of an conventional petrol engine but with a better climb. Thaheld had pioneered radial diesels with Guiberson of Dallas back in the 1930s.

It comes as a bit of a shock to discover that, despite the immense advancement made during the war with high-power engines such as the Merlin and its sisters, as well as the amazing Bristol radials with their sleeve-valves, unlike the Americans we had made absolutely no progress whatsoever with small engines. True there had been little demand for them in time of war, but it left us with what was essentially 1920s technology – and then an enormous gap to high-power military engines.

A handful of progressive designers and manufacturers were quick off the mark, though, and within months of the end of hostilities, the early flowerings of a post-war revival made their hesitant appearance. Indeed, the early months of 1946 saw a veritable fluster of new-motor announcements foremost amongst which were the Jameson and the Monaco.

The first new British low-power engine to be announced was the 100 hp Monaco flat-four, which was actually designed before the war. In this respect it pre-dated the Jameson. The Monaco was a smart, compact-looking unit that was a harbinger of things to come (in the main from America). It was only the second original flat-four motor to be developed and built in Britain, the other being the pre-war Coventry-Victor Flying Neptune. All of these were air-cooled conventionally-aspirated motors.

The Monaco made its successful maiden run on March 14th 1946 and it seemed merely a matter of time before it completed its ground-testing and then type-testing which was proposed to be conducted in the new Chrislea Ace at Heston. In fact Chrislea had gone so far as to specify the Monaco as the power-unit for its production aircraft, announcing the fact in *Flight* as early as April 25th. A version for use in helicopters was explored, as was another for internal wing-mounting in multi-engined aircraft with drive using an extension shaft for a pusher propeller. Clearly the Monaco and its designers were filled with potential.

---

1. William J Besler successfully flew a biplane whose original Curtiss OX-9 motor was replaced by a steam engine. The event took place on April 12th 1933 at Oakland Municipal Airport, California. A two-cylinder compound double-acting Vee type, the high-pressure cylinder had a bore of three inches and the low-pressure one a bore of 5¼-inches. The stroke was 3 inches. The boiler consisted of a single tube 500 feet long and heating was by oil-burner to release 3,000,000 BTU per cubic foot of firebox area. With a total water consumption of 1,500 lbs/hour, the condensing system allowed a recovery of 99 per cent. The engine developed about 150 hp at 1,625 rpm with a boiler pressure of 1,200 lbs/sq.inch. The engine weighed 180 lbs and the full installation including boiler, water and fuel oil weighed 485 lbs. The engine proved remarkably quiet in the air and featured one aspect achievable by no other type of motor – reversibility which enabled the propeller to be used as an air-brake for reverse thrust on landing.

While America transitioned from radial engines to flat-four and flat-six engines, at the end of the war Britain still favoured the inline format. It was thus a bold move when Watford-based Monaco revealed its horizontally-opposed engine. This underwent prolonged running in a test-facility at Elstree Aerodrome during 1946 and 1947. A well-finned and compact design, this 75 hp motor and a 100 hp version largely represented the hopes of the British light aircraft industry at that time.

Chrislea, then of North London, promoted the Ace as a 'full four seater or freighter with 85/90 hp Franklin air-cooled engine, pay load 550 lbs, 360 deg visibility, take-off 105 yards, cruising speed 105 mph, safe range 380 miles' at an 'approximate' ex-works price of £475 as early as February 5th 1945 – the war did not end until that May. From whence it thought it could source Franklin engines was unclear but by March of 1946 it was advertising that production aircraft would be powered by the 100 hp Monaco with 17.5 gall tank giving range of around 400 miles. In the end the aircraft was ready long before Monaco could even suggest a delivery date. Chrislea, now at Heston, changed to the 125 hp Lycoming.

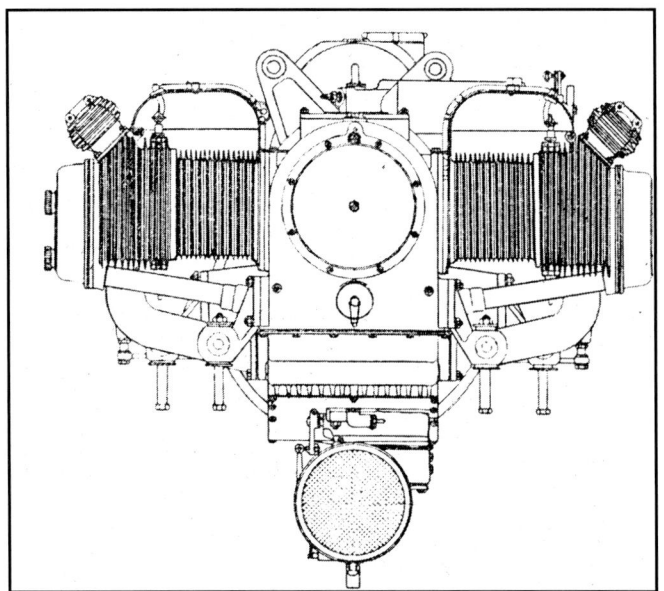

Narrow frontal width was one of the more attractive selling points of this well-designed and practical little motor. Although at least one test-engine existed, no original photographs have survived.

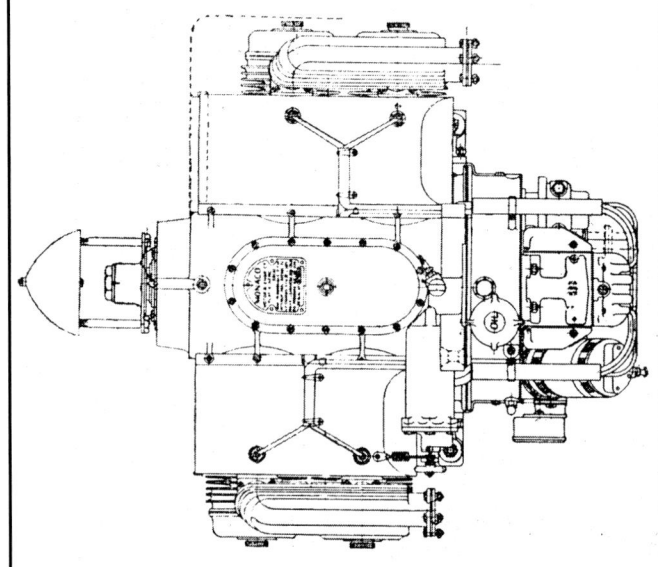

The Monaco in plan view shows the simple layout with the twin magnetos mounted side-by-side on a rear cover which housed linear-mounted gears to drive these and, below them, the fuel pump.

Mounting for the Monaco was unconventional although perfectly adaptable and simple. There was a pair of lugs for fore-and-aft bolts at the top and two more at the bottom for vertical bolts, all of which passed through rubber Silentbloc shock absorber bearings.

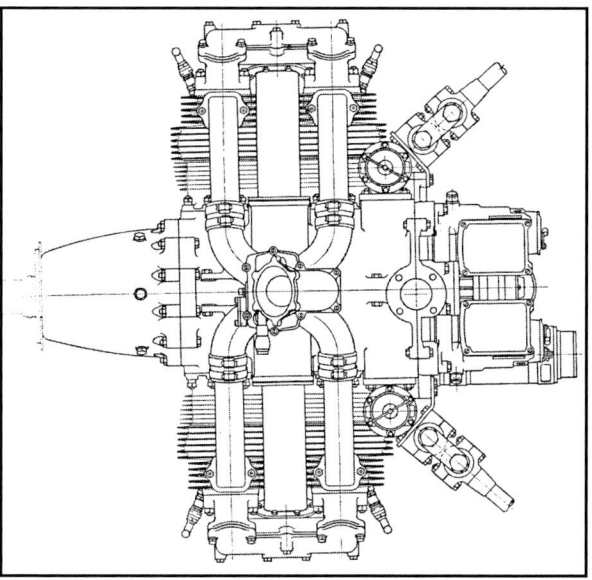

Another new engine was the Jameson FF-1, a short-stroke motor with a high compression ratio of 7.4:1. Prolonged running on a test rig had indicated an average power of 96.5 bhp with a maximum of between 102 and 106 hp for a ready-to-run dry weight of 291 lbs. Although way outside the 'sweet-spot' of under 2 lbs/hp, the Jameson was nevertheless a small, compact unit initially intended for use in helicopters and the first use was in the Cierva Skeeter prototype.

As time would sadly tell, like the Nuffield engine announced shortly afterwards, it would never fly. Unlike the Nuffield, it virtually completed its tests and was earmarked to take to the air in at least one aircraft type if not two – the Essex Aero Sprite was to have been another vehicle for this attractive-looking power-unit.

Monaco's problems seemed to stem from the age-old problem of cash-flow, although it has to be said that lack of sales linked to a suitable airframe combination probably played a sizeable part in the company's difficulties. A chicken-and-egg situation existed because airframes could not really be designed without engines – and engines could not be produced until a market existed amongst airframe-makers!

As it was, the old Monaco Motor & Engineering Co became Monaco Engines in 1947 and moved from Watford to Kings Langley. Two years later the business was sold to Associated Equipment Co Ltd and the development of aircraft engines ceased.

Next on the scene was the Jameson, also a child of the opening months of 1946. Designed by Joseph Lambert Jameson (b. April 8th 1902), it was conceived in 1943 as a technically advanced four-cylinder air-cooled horizontally-opposed unit. Built at Ewell, Surrey (and with the tacit encouragement of Miles Aircraft Ltd), this motor was lauded by the technical press for its radical design features and innovative construction.

A curious induction system provided an extremely weak mixture near the piston crown becoming richer further out until the richest mixture was located at the sparking-plug. On firing, the theory was that the rich mixture would combust and so bring about a pressure-propagation through the weaker strata, allowing them to be ignited, the rate of pressure-propagation always being in excess of the flame rate. The effect would be for the engine to be capable of adjusting its own rate of compression to suit the mixture as it burned. This process was said to induce very smooth running characteristics.

Singular measures taken to simplify design and construction meant that all valves were operated by 'ganged' push-rods which ran from overhead camshafts through a rectangular-section push-rod passage between each pair of cylinders.

With a bore of 105mm and a stroke of 95mm, the 3.28 litre engine had a quite high fundamental compression ratio of 7.4:1 and had a maximum take-off power output of between 102 and 106 hp at 3,050 rpm and a maximum continuous of 88-92 mph at 2,800 rpm for a weight of 280 lbs. The power/weight ration was 2.542 lbs/hp. Extensive use was made of magnesium castings and the propeller drive was via spur reduction gearing with a ratio of 0.619:1. A 12-volt electric starter was mounted direct on the crankshaft.

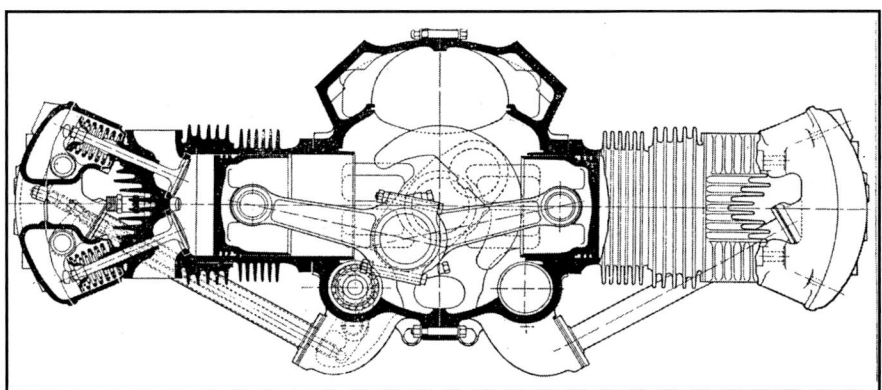

A cross-sectional drawing shows some of the Jameson engine's unusual features. The straight (not offset) cylinders had a domed cylinder-head and employed pistons of an unusual shape designed so that running on a very weak mixture resulted in a piston-crown temperature gradient which was remarkably shallow. This contributed to a high cruising power output for maximum fuel economy while lower than usual oil temperatures dispensed with the need for a large oil cooler.

A prototype Jameson engine completed a 100-hour Ministry of Supply development test in 1946 and two years later it was submitted for type test under both civil and military conditions. Due to the failure of a valve spring before completion of the tests, only a 100 hours' civil flight clearance was obtained. In this form it was used briefly in one of the prototype Saunders-Roe Saro Skeeter two seat developments of the Cierva W.14 helicopter and also – again briefly – in the Miles M.18 Mk 1, G-AFRO/U-0222.

All in all then, the Jameson was little more successful than either the Monaco or the Nuffield, this latter being an attempt to revive the efforts associated with the Wolseley engines before the war.

Wolseley Motors' aircraft engines had gone through a very difficult time in the 1930s partly due to the uncertain relationship between Sir William Morris and the authorities. Treated as a car-maker (which of course he was) as distinct from an aircraft-engine maker (which he was also) meant that Wolseley's fine range of pre-war radial engines, although successfully flown in many types, received neither proper recognition nor military contracts. Although championed at every opportunity by C G Grey in *The Aeroplane*, Morris himself was pointedly excluded from the aviation circles to which he had every right of inclusion. It was suggested that 'legitimate' aircraft-engine makers thought him at best an outsider, an interloper and an opportunist, and at worst a mere amateur. Those that knew Sir William knew him as a kind man and a true enthusiast, ingredients that were different from those found in most hard-headed businessmen and consequently making for a person who probably rubbed the authorities up the wrong way.

Effectively prevented from supplying aircraft engines to the national defence, Morris, now Lord Nuffield, remained an enthusiastic supporter of aviation and light aviation in particular. In 1947, realising that there would be a light plane market once a suitable engine was available, he took a characteristic gamble and backed his undiminished faith in aviation by putting the weight of the engine division of the Cowley-based Nuffield Organisation behind it.

The Nuffield motor, announced in 1947, was specifically intended for light personal aircraft and was the work of youthful engine genius Tom Brown. Design occupied the latter part of 1945 and most of 1946 and it quickly became a talking point within the industry. Like the Monaco and following the trend in the best of American light engines it was to be an air-cooled four-cylinder horizontally-opposed direct-drive engine. Sensibly it also followed the growing fashion for making high-compression short-stroke motors and this 3.82-litre motor had a bore of 111mm with a stroke of 98.4mm along with a compression ratio of 6.3:1. The projected maximum power was 100 hp at 2,600 rpm with a cruising power of 70 hp at 2,300 rpm. Overhead valves, extensive finning of cylinders and crankcase sump were combined with an interesting ability to be used either in tractor or pusher configuration. It was also equipped as standard with a 12-volt electrical system and starter motor.

Projected developments included possible fuel-injection and the belief that this would be the first of a whole new family of Nuffield aircraft engines. Unfortunately in spite of strong encouragement from both the Royal Aero Club and the Ultra Light Aircraft Association (despite the fact that at that particular time the Nuffield was well outside the ultra-light limit as regards power), William Morris's motor never materialised and within two years all reference to it had been expunged from the records.

The reason why has never been revealed but it is strongly suspected that despite the virtual certainty of its success, the state of the light aircraft market and the need for high-volume production alarmed the shareholders and frightened the accountants. Had one production airframe-maker the confidence to call for just 50 engines, I personally know that Nuffield would have gone for it. As it was makers of new airframes were not exactly thick on the ground. And they could be forgiven for preferring existing 'approved' motors.

There is also some evidence to suggest that established engine makers Blackburn and de Havilland brought pressure to bear on airframe-makers with whom they enjoyed a symbiotic relationship as suppliers. The inference was that they were not to encourage any new motors otherwise 'existing supplies of engines could not be guaranteed' – a bit of bluff-calling and probably on both sides. Shades of the pre-war Avro Alpha engine saga all over again!

In the years that ran up to the outbreak of war, one of the great promises appeared to be the Aspin engine. The aeronautical press was regularly filled with glowing reports of the development of this technologically advanced four-cylinder motor which had rotating conical valves and a host of other novel features, not the least of which was an extremely high compression ratio: in excess of 20:1 was claimed for one motorcycle engine used to evaluate the principle.

Designed by Frank M Aspin of Bury in Lancashire, this motor seemed well on the way to becoming the light aircraft power-plant of the future. Some development work even continued (at a reduced pace) throughout the war and press reports

It was hoped that the British Nuffield engine would rival any flat four that the Americans could produce. Intended to be the motor for the future and capable of expansion to a six or even eight-cylinder variant, the engine was a brilliant proposition from a brilliant young designer. But Nuffield, like Wolseley before it, was a cursed name in the aviation world where a heavy-gang of established makers knew just how to keep new boys out of their patch. Britain's greatest loss in 1947 was the decision by Morris Motors to abandon this fine motor. With a compression ratio of 6.3, a maximum output of 100 hp and a comfortable cruise of 70 hp at 2,600 rpm, the mouth-watering part was that the selling price was expected to be no more than £200.

continued to suggest that its arrival was always 'still imminent'.

Frank Aspin was another of those visionaries who cast his gaze initially at high-performance motorcycle engines. Like Roland Cross and others, he believed that he was on the right path. Over the years he invested heavily in this development work through his chain-saw manufacturing business. However, although at least ten prototype or development engines were hand-built and run (in cars and motorcycles in the main), the Aspin aircraft engine never did materialise and during the 1960s Bury Engineering Co was forced into liquidation through cash-flow problems which, one may assume, were at least in part due to the huge investment sunk into the aero-engine dream.

Many other projects had come, gone and been forgotten – and many recalled with a sigh of regret the extraordinary design of talented young L B Stedman as far back as April 1924. Stedman's two-stroke was revolutionary in that it was proposed as a four-cylinder 'squashed X'-format. Alternate cylinders drew their mixture from the crankcase while the others were fed from a chamber around the crankcase. Claiming even mixture distribution and extremely light weight for high power, Stedman appealed for criticism of his design. Despite trying hard, the bigger engine boys failed: nobody could fault his proposals. As the years passed it became clear that Mr Stedman had chosen to sit on his formula – for good. Why? Nobody would build it and he had no money.

Which was not the case with Helmuth John Steiger's lovely side-valved inverted V four-cylinder 85 hp motor built as early as 1934 by General Aircraft. Called the Monarch and flown in a Moth, this was almost as fully developed as Avro's Alpha 90 hp radial of 1927 mentioned just now and flown in four aircraft and about to enter production when ordered to be scrapped by Armstrong Siddeley upon that firm's investment in Roe's business.

But there were other and much later engines that tried hard and expensively to rival the two bastions of post-war private aircraft – de Havilland and Cirrus. Take Coventry-Victor, for instance. The pre-war Coventry-Victor engines were described in *British Light Aeroplanes* [37]. The Neptune was the company's best-known industrial motor, a workmanlike air-cooled flat-four of conventional form and layout which was used in a number of applications including agricultural hay-balers. A variant for aircraft use called the Flying Neptune was produced and flown first in a Piper Cub (G-AIYX) by BKS Engineering of Southend, and secondly in a Druine Turbi (G-APFA). Apart from annoying problems with cylinder cooling this was a good smooth and reliable motor spoiled only by its horrendous weight. Although flown extensively by the present author and thoroughly tested, it, too, disappeared from the scene.

Somewhat larger than the motors so far mentioned was Roy Fedden's quite amazing 185 hp horizontally-opposed six-cylinder engine introduced in 1946. A wholly-unique concept, this ultra slimline unit was a mere 14¾-inches from top to bottom and was intended to be buried in a wing leading edge. Inspired by the De Havilland Albatross-type of aircraft power-unit installation and with designs such as the pre-war Armstrong-Whitworth airliners in mind, it was a sad fact of life that by the time the Fedden motor was up and running the idea of buried piston engines had been superseded by the era of the early jet engines. Fedden's motor, despite being overtaken by other technology, remains nevertheless a unique concept for a flat six – it was a sleeve-valve engine fitted with cylinder barrels of low-expansion silicon alloy.

As regards larger motors for fledgling commercial airliners, the position was very different. We had a superfluity of engine makers, all turning out (or offering) first-rate motors. Following the 1946 Paris Air Show, the magazine *Flight* lamented that it was ironical that 'every country with the exception of Britain is handicapped by the lack of suitable power units for its latest aircraft,' to which Ron Clegg of the newly-formed ULAA promptly responded saying that the real irony lay in the fact that 'this should be the one country in which the development of amateur flying is seriously hampered by lack of a suitable low-powered engine around which could be designed a popular ultra-light machine?'

Immediately the war ended, those with an interest in light aircraft production were well aware that the availability of suitable engines was going to be the primary stumbling-block to their successful restitution of the light plane industry. Unlike the years following the First World War, government surplus was unlikely to present either option or opportunity.

Certainly by 1948 those who explored possibilities for the ultra-light aircraft knew their goal was never likely to be realised unless there was a suitable engine. Supplies of pre-war light engines had virtually dried up (although a batch of undelivered 1938-built JAP J.99 engines and spares for Aeronca aircraft offered a small and specific glimmer of hope for owners of pre-war designs) and the revival of motors such as the Carden-Ford and Scott Flying Squirrel was deemed impractical.

It was in this atmosphere of frustration that the design committee of the Ultra Light Aircraft Association, under the guidance of Grp Capt Edward Mole and the present writer, proposed a list of requirements that formed a design specification for two categories of ultra-light aircraft engine. These specifications were published in the early part of 1948 and, to our delight, drew a number of designs and proposals from industry and amateur engineers alike. Some of the ideas submitted were workable, others were not without merit but for one reason or another were impractical.

Roy Fedden's ultra-slim six-cylinder was for burying in wings or replacing Gipsy Queens in a stylishly-recowled Rapide. It was, though, a case of a motor that was obsolete before it was even introduced which was such a shame for it was one of the cleverest and smallest mid-power piston engines ever made. By the time it was ready, the world was viewing the lighter and more powerful turboprop engine as the answer to that particular power-range.

British Light Aviation – A Shifting Emphasis

Below: This is a production Cirrus Minor viewed on its starboard side and revealing its simplicity. The horizontally-divided crankcase gave easy access to crankshaft bearings and connecting rods.

Right: The most prolific British engine maker remained Blackburn Cirrus with its Minor and Major inlines and, launched in 1948, its larger 180 hp Bombardier. The origins of the Cirrus go back to the earliest days of Frank Halford and the Gipsy engines of de Havilland. That they remained perfectly adequate motors well into the second half of the 20th century is indicative of just how good they were.

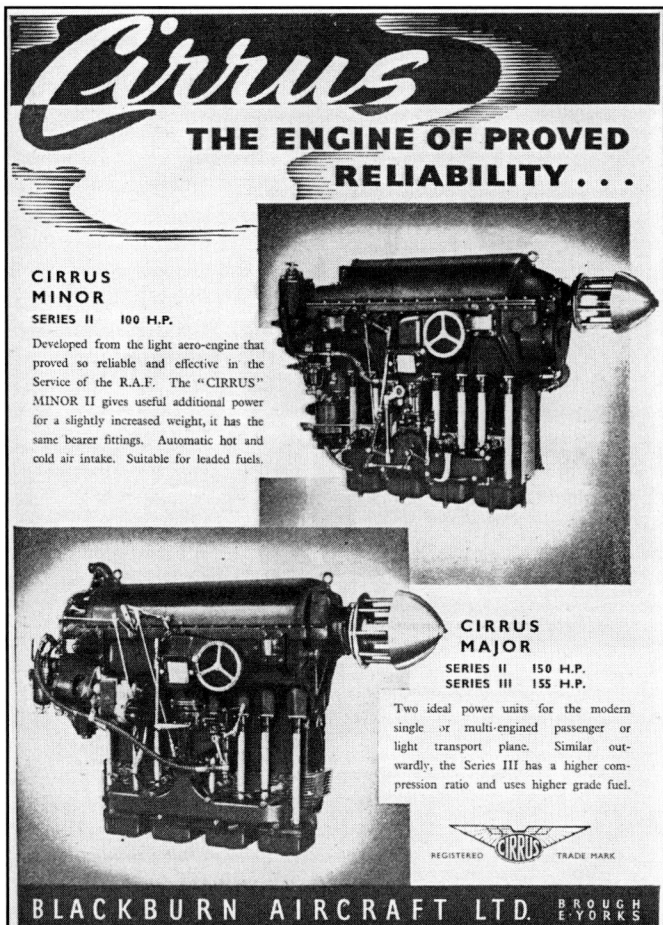

Left: Similar in layout, the Cirrus Major offered a simple and convenient power upgrade from around 100 to 145 hp (depending on the Series number) for a weight increase of up to 100 lbs.

Below: The big four-cylinder Cirrus Bombardier was the first of the company's engines to incorporate fuel-injection. This, it was said, gave a 25 hp increase in power over the similar-sized Cirrus Mk.III which had normal induction via a carburettor. It was a long motor being almost 41.5 inches from front to back as can be seen from this prototype installation in Miles Messenger 5 G-ALAC. This motor was to have been the start of a whole new range of Blackburn motors the second of which would have been the 265 bhp six-cylinder Musketeer and the 32- hp six-cylinder supercharged Grenadier, neither of which came to pass. The test aircraft was destroyed in a crash only a few days later.

It is an unfortunate fact of history that of all the ideas proposed and despite all the encouragement given, none of these propositions ever came to fruition and the sum total of the time and effort expended by the ULAA's design and technical executive committee ultimately proved wasted.

Useless though it ultimately turned out to have been, the ideas that were presented gave plenty of inspiration and that, in turn, nurtured hope. True, it was precious little, but better than nothing!

The so-called ULA (Ultra Light Aircraft) engine attracted the attention of one of the best-known motorcycle engine designers who rashly promised not just to design but also to produce an engine for the ULAA movement. He proposed a flat twin of 1,700 cc that would develop 40 hp at 3,000 rpm. If the propeller-designers could accept 3,500 rpm, he felt the engine could easily be up-rated to 50 hp. For simplicity and cheapness (not to mention weight) an ungeared propeller drive was essential.

Many hours were spent in discussion over this engine and the extreme novelty and robustness was, at that time, unparalleled. To reduce manufacturing costs, there was no offset in the cylinders, each directly opposed the other and sophisticated balancing allowed in effect a 'one-piece' connecting rod/crankshaft. By April of 1948 plans were afoot to place an order with a manufacturer to produce 'a few' prototype engines for trial within the year.

The go-ahead could not be given because there were no suitable aircraft in which to test the engines and, even if there were, there was no possibility of gaining any sort of airworthiness-certification to allow tests to proceed. No aircraft – no engine, and no engine – no aircraft. In years to come this would be described as a 'Catch 22' situation.

Other designers came and went, amongst them Roland C Cross who ran a manufacturing business under his name at Bath. He was no novice designer having been responsible for the design of the Cross Rotary Valve. This valve, by permitting a symmetrical cylinder head and by the avoidance of hot spots (such as occur in the case of poppet exhaust valves) enables extremely high compression ratios to be used without the risk of detonation. This allows much increased volumetric and thermal efficiency which in turn produces greater power and fuel economy.

Cross's ideas had been tried and tested in experimental motorcycle engines and these caused some excitement from the 1920s onwards. He was apparently always improving his designs, but never finalising anything for production. Mr Cross made much of the fact that an experimental engine with his rotary valve had been used successfully at a compression ratio of 11:1 – and that while running on wartime 'Pool'. For the uninitiated, Pool was a brandless petrol marketed to those motorists who had earned, by way of their occupation or service duties, a wartime fuel allowance: it was a pretty mediocre fuel as regards quality and had a low octane rating.

Cross produced a preliminary design for a three-cylinder radial intended to comply with our objectives for simplicity and low-cost production. He paid great attention to ensuring smooth torque and the engine, intended to have a capacity of 1,500cc, was very compact. Versions were projected that would be both direct-drive and geared, the ungeared motor to produce 45 hp at 3,000 rpm or, in a racing version, 55 hp for a weight of 140 lbs (3.11-2.55 lbs/hp). The geared version would be run at 4,000 rpm and produce 60 hp nominally or, in a souped-up version, 74 hp for a weight of about 150 lbs (2.5 – 2.03 lbs/hp). Most interesting of all, though, was the projected power-consumption of only 1.6 gallons/hour.

One drawback to the Cross proposal was that the geometry of the Cross Rotary Valve made the overall length of the cylinder and its head much greater than, say, a conventional poppet OHV cylinder because the Cross valve was cylindrical in form and placed parallel to the crankshaft. Unlike, for instance, the sleeve-valve engine which made for a very shallow head, the Cross was appreciably longer or taller.

Embarrassingly, certain members of the ULAA executive were somewhat flattered that a man of Cross's genius should be interested in the ULA engine quest. Undoubtedly Cross was a clever man, but his many years of invention had yet to secure him a production motor. He was thus little more than an inveterate tinkerer who had neither capital nor backing. His engine, we were assured, could quickly be a reality so long as the ULAA could raise a development order and provide a favourable market outlook. There was also the assumption that the ULAA was financially able to back Cross's project. And so Mr Cross's marvellous motor joined others doomed to the folder marked 'projects unfulfilled'.

There were others such as Mr Scott Mackirdy who favoured a high-speed diesel two-stroke of the type used successfully in model aircraft and suitably enlarged. A study of these model motors revealed that their high power/weight ratio is attributable to their extremely high operating speeds and if scaled up to ULA size the mass of reciprocating parts would demand their fabrication in then-very-expensive new high-strength alloy steels. Furthermore gearing would be essential with its associated weight and cost penalties while the large pistons would pose heat-dissipation problems. Consequently it was felt that a diesel of the type suggested would, if scaled up to ULA size, be difficult to cool adequately. Furthermore very heavy bearing loads would combine to negate the otherwise extreme simplicity of the diesel principle.

While inviting comments from others, the ULAA placed this suggestion to the bottom of the pile where, as time was to tell, it was no less successful than any of the other suggestions!

Many were the suggestions that flowed into the ULAA Design Sub-Committee's office. Some were a bit far-fetched like one from a member in Harpenden who proposed doing away with an engine and using a rocket-driven propeller. Others were eminently practical. One of these came from H R Mayes who had been chief designer of the Monaco Engine Company until the business had changed hands in 1948. During the summer of that year he became very interested in the potential of the ultra-light aircraft and its engine. In that August he revealed his plans for a really attractive little motor that appeared to offer an ideal solution so long as its manufactured price could be kept below £150.

A push-rod operated overhead-valve flat-four design which was not unlike the earlier Monaco motor was proposed. With a capacity of two litres it would develop 50 bhp at 2,600 rpm. The design was particularly neat and compact, while adequate cooling and accessibility had been carefully studied based on the considerable test-bench experience gained on the earlier motor. A simple form of 'dual ignition' was used via a single 'duplex' magneto so saving weight and complexity. Pressure lubrication was used along with a wet sump of two gallons in capacity.

Perhaps a hark-back to earlier times and to Pobjoy in particular, as an alternative to the electric starter, Mayes proposed a hand starter that could be operated either from the side of the engine or from the cockpit. This last aspect was warmly applauded by those on the Design

Sub-Committee that saw no future in prop-swinging in the second half of the 20th century. Others, the Author included, knew that for every extra feature the ultimate penalty was always weight and cost – and we wanted an engine that would cost no more than £150. Heaven knows that was expensive enough!

Mayes' motor was the fourth engine design considered to be 'in the running' for the competition to create the ULA engine as that autumn turned to winter. There was, though, the insurmountable problem of making an engine. Designing it was one thing, but finding a manufacturer who was prepared to sink the necessary investment for production without an immediate market prospect was another. Nobody could be blamed for there was no surplus of money floating around. Companies did not need to consider work as a tax-loss for they were already having trouble maintaining their core business activities let along expanding it.

In an endeavour to reach some sort of solution there were many meetings with companies and engineers but there was no way of hiding the fact that the cost of development, certification and production of a new engine was heavy. The Air Registration Board, in a rare moment of benevolence to the ultra-light aircraft movement, even issued dispensation to allow the use of commercial materials and manufacture by non-approved manufacturing sources. The benevolence was sustained to the extent of agreeing to a new type-test of greatly reduced severity for the newly-introduced ULA category Certificate of Airworthiness – we had no Permit to Fly system at that time and the C of A, even the ULA category applicable to aircraft with a stalling speed below 40 mph, was very expensive to obtain, maintain and renew.

The Ultra Light Aircraft Association was thus in a stalemate position. Having fostered the design of engines it had no means of taking the project any further. The Design Sub-Committee now began exploring the possibility of arranging a development contract for one of the four successful designs, selected by tender, either from the government authorities or from some far-sighted, public-spirited patron.

Unlikely though the success of such action might sound today, at that time the whole future of the ULA movement and cheap flying was dependent on there being a suitable engine. As far as the chicken-and-egg problem over the non-existent market, the ULAA was convinced that once an engine was available as a production item the growth of the ULA movement would accelerate and a useful market emerge both at home and overseas.

Of the many meetings we held and the numerous miles we travelled to talk to companies, the dreaded bit was when the prospective manufacturer asked that key question: what was the market forecast for the finished motors for the first five years? Once this stage was reached, we knew the meeting was at its end for we had no suitable aircraft, no suitable design, and no strategic business plan beyond our enthusiasm.

This was also tough on the engine designers who mistakenly believed that the ULAA was rich enough to underwrite manufacturing contracts and possessed a marketing department to promote and sell the final product. One well-known manufacture was extremely helpful and encouraging and came forth with the positive news that the proposed motor could be produced for under that magic £150 so long as output in the first year topped 500 and could be doubled in two years... We were dabbling in another world!

Earlier I mentioned the fellow in Harpenden who had suggested a rocket-propelled propeller as a cheap alternative to an expensive engine and propeller. While the more practical of the engineers on the ULAA Committee rejected this idea, others didn't, among them Alfred R Weyl who was then chairman (and only member!) of the robustly-named ULAA's Research Sub Committee. The jet-propelled airscrew arose from the revelation that an Austrian engineer, one Josef Reder of Wiesloch (Baden) had already gone a long way down this path. A former technician with the Junkers company, Herr Reder conceived an airscrew that was jet-propelled at its tips.

While it was not exactly a new idea and savouring more than a little of the infamous Brannen helicopter at Farnborough in the 'twenties, it appeared to offer a simple solution to the apparently inherent limitations of the concept. Whereas a simple ram-jet is hopelessly inefficient when operated at a speed below about twice the speed of sound, the airscrew itself is efficient at low speeds but experiences a considerable loss of efficiency the closer the speed of its tips approaches that of sound.

Reder overcame that difficulty by using pulsating ducts for his jets, the principle being identical to that used in the engine of the V1 flying-bomb. He called the principle the 'Re-jet' and estimated that a propeller of one metre disc diameter could produce (not absorb, note!) 28 bhp at 40 mph forward speed, raising to about 90 bhp at 200 mph. Were the propeller disc to be two metres in diameter (which, by the way, would be outside the then ultra-light aircraft category), it would generate 115 bhp at 40 mph increasing to 400 mph at 200 mph. Although the fuel consumption was estimated to be double that of a normal aircraft engine, economy was possible because it could burn cheap, low-grade fuel. It was also extremely light as a power source there being very little ironwork other than a thrust bearing and firewall mounting.

The jet prop scheme was, like the Cross engine and all the others, no more than an idea, but it was a curiously attractive one the more one thought about it. A very light weight power source, it really needed no more than a hub and a pivot plus some sort of spark-magneto driven from the rotating airscrew in order to get the pulse chambers going. The lack of a regular metallic engine unit reduced aircraft tare weight, increased payload and cut servicing.

While the ULAA's Weyl and Mole excitedly submitted Reder's Re-jet as a serious proposal for development, there were those on the committee who were looking at other and more conventional motors such as the three-cylinder inline allegedly invented by Marendaz.

Donald Marcus Kellway Marendaz had already made something of a reputation for himself in the pre-war days through his

De Havilland's Gipsy Major has been the bastion of British light aircraft since the mid-1920s and the number of models has only gone to confirm the durability and utility of the basic design. This is the 130 hp Gipsy Major Series I which, like, the Cirrus, were the last of the long-stroke engines. This motor had a stroke of 140 mm for a bore of 118 mm giving a cruise power of 120 hp at 2,100 rpm. These relatively low speeds gave the engine a long life and extended times between overhauls.

exploits in light aircraft design and manufacture. These are described in *British Light Aeroplanes [37]* and need not be considered here. Suffice it to be said that Mr Marendaz and some sort of controversy were never all that far apart.

It transpired that during the war Marendaz had produced (or been involved in producing) a compact motor for sustained and heavy use in small tractors and lighting plants. A 650cc upright unit, it had a chain-driven overhead camshaft and developed 18 bhp at 4,000 rpm for a weight of 54 lbs – 3lbs/hp. The idea he now proposed was that with some small modification this would make an ideal ULA engine.

The Marendaz had a deeply-finned cylinder block which, with the crankcase, was produced as a single casting in light alloy into which centrifugally-cast liners were pressed. The cylinder head was also of light allow with bronze inserts for valve seats and sparking-plug bosses. A triple-throw crankshaft was carried on two large plain bearings of white metal, pressure lubrication with a dry sump being used. There was provision for the incorporation of an oil cooler if required. Ignition could be by coil or magneto, the drive being taken from the free end of the overhead camshaft.

While an attractive idea, Marendaz himself proved to be not the easiest of people to deal with and it was ultimately impossible to establish beyond all reasonable doubt who exactly owned the rights to the engine that he called 'the Marendaz' since it seemed to us unlikely that he had designed it himself. His replies to technical questions often seemed naive.

An unfortunate pre-war track record in business that culminated in a mysterious fire which destroyed his factory along with a new aircraft for which a replacement miraculously appeared Phoenix-like from what were supposed to be its insurance ashes, inspired careful treading. Years later it turned out that the Marendaz motor was merely a third-party product of his engineering works. And it could not have been readily converted.

In the background all this while, the Coventry-Victor Motor Co Ltd of Coventry, in the form of the Major Weaver and his team, maintained a low-key presence in ULAA circles, offering advice to the Committee if and when needed. The company chief engineer was a Mr E W Wright and the young director (son of the founder) was diplomatic Alfred N Weaver who had a London address in Brendon Street. Alfred Weaver was the calming influence to the Design Sub-Committee for while A R Weyl and Edward Mole tended to pursue every avenue with equal enthusiasm (although most of them were obviously dead-ends), Weaver was a fine diplomat and did not stop them, but consistently avoided over-encouragement! The quest for the ULA engine was too serious a matter, particularly when (and if ever) it got to the investment stage.

Coventry-Victor had actually produced a small number of aircraft engines before the war. It is not thought that any of them ever actually flew, but they were available. In this respect they were even less successful in the aero-engine business than Sir William Morris and Wolseley!

Head of the firm was Major Weaver, a one-time military man who very much looked the part. Unlike his son, he was outspoken and never pulled punches for the sake of tact. We only saw him occasionally but he nearly always had something pretty strong to say regarding the quest for the ULA. But Major Weaver had an ace up his sleeve. It wasn't a ULA engine, but it was almost a light aircraft engine. This was an aeronautical variant of his firm's Neptune, a four-cylinder air-cooled flat four that was widely respected for agricultural use. It was called the Flying Neptune.

The Flying Neptune was to be flown in at least two aircraft and is found fully described in Chapter Ten. In the end, though, it did not alleviate the problem of the true ULA motor. Even the discovery of the astounding German Zundapp four-cylinder inverted inline of 51 hp was, at that time, too powerful for the ULA category. The Zundapp did, however, occupy the Design Committee for some while for it was so amazingly small and light (like a scaled-down Gipsy Major) that there were plans afoot to try to get it into production de-rated to 45 hp. Even with a reduction in power it would still show a very attractive power/weight ratio. But negotiations with the German company were neither easy nor straightforward, in particular since they had to go through the Air Ministry and the Board of Trade – as unwieldy a process as one might ever imagine.

Before leaving the name of Coventry, one other business should be mentioned – that of Coventry Climax which was based

Left: The Coventry-Victor Flying Neptune horizontally-opposed flat four air-cooled engine first flew in Piper Cub G-AIYX which was converted as a flying test-bed by BKS Engineering Ltd of Southend. Although it was a big and heavy motor it cowled quite neatly, save for a rather ad hoc port-side air-vent as seen here. The Cub was only ever flown 'one-up' with this heavy motor. After extended evaluation flights, the engine was removed, the Cub restored – and the engine passed on to the present author for fitting into Turbi G-APFA.

Right: The Flying Neptune fitted to the Druine Turbi G-APFA. While the BKS Cub installation had taken the engine unchanged and flown it, it was a heavy motor. Faced with tighter constraints in the light weight Turbi, the engine had to be lightened considerably by replacing some heavyweight steel studs and brackets. Because the mounting lugs were the same as those for the original used in farm machinery, namely horizontal under the crankcase, a 'chair'-type of mount had to be designed which was neither ideal nor lightweight. The heavy magneto is seen at the top of the motor. This engine had one saving grace: it ran very smoothly and its agricultural origins meant that it could run without lubrication if necessary. This novel attribute was confirmed when an in-flight oil-pipe failure unexpectedly drained the sump during a test-flight.

British Light Aviation – A Shifting Emphasis

Here the Flying Neptune-powered Cub is seen on an early air-test by John Fricker. He reported the machine handled very much like the ordinary Cub but with just 55 hp up front – and rather small, heavy horses at that – it was not quite so fast.

Coventry Climax was founded in 1903 by H Pulham Lee, a one-time Daimler engineer, who saw a market opportunity for an independent engine-maker. Originally called Coventry-Simplex, the firm became associated with stationary power units but shortly before the war it entered into an arrangement with Continental Motors Corporation of Detroit, planning to offer 40, 50, 65, 75 and 85 hp engines. Engines already well-established in America and capable of a useful 2.28 lbs/hp, the option to handle them in Britain would be thwarted by the war. In 1945 the company chose not to proceed and so it fell to Rolls-Royce to pick up the Continental agency for the UK – but not until 1960. This somewhat premature notice for Coventry Climax/Continental engines comes from the 1941 edition of *Jane's All the World's Aircraft*. In 1963 Coventry Climax was taken over by Jaguar Cars and thus, five years later, became lost in British Leyland.

at Newbold-on-Stour, Stratford-on-Avon. A long-established company (it had been making internal combustion engines since 1903), this business had negotiated the manufacturing rights for the American Continental range of four-cylinder horizontally-opposed air-cooled aero-engines in Britain. The deal with Continental Motors Corporation of Detroit, Michigan was concluded just weeks before the outbreak of war in 1939. Coventry Climax went on to produce vast quantities of light engines for generating sets for airfields during the war. By the end of the conflict, Coventry Climax, no doubt wisely, failed to see sufficient of a market for a 'new' light engine, in particular as Monaco was, to all intents and purposes, a long way down the road towards production while Nuffield had the clout to put an engine on the market speedily. The firm concluded there was too great a risk to warrant picking up the Continental licence deal. That would be left to Rolls-Royce.

Another source examined was the Briggs & Stratton made by a company famous for its small stationary engines but at that time the company had no interest in 'high-speed' motors.

And so it came to pass that no British contender for the low-cost light-weight ULA motor ever appeared. As late as 1964 the only light, low-powered engine available in Britain was the Rollason-converted Volkswagen producing between 30 and 40 bhp and costing from £275 ex-works.

Enthusiasts tried hard to embrace engine technology from abroad wherever possible, but were inevitably frustrated at every turn since they could offer neither contract nor surety of return to the inventors who were all, as might be expected, out to earn cash. One such motor was the Wankel.

Appreciating that rotation is always preferable to reciprocation, engineers have striven for years to replace things that go up and down ferociously with parts that merely rotate, ostensibly with less wear and tear and, probably, a reduction in noise and vibration.

In 1957 news emerged that a new type of engine had been devised by a German inventor and engineer named Dr Felix Heinrich Wankel (1902-1988). He had been credited with the first practical rotary internal combustion engine (1934-1956) and during the Second World War he had worked on the development of fighter aircraft, ending up being imprisoned by the French occupation forces. Wankel's rotary, as distinct from the rotary engines of the First World War, comprised a stationary outer casing within which the combustion chambers continually rotated thanks to an eccentrically-driven convex-shaped three-sided rotor. The eccentric drive meant that the rotor offered a charge space for its fuel mixture that varied from very small (exhaust phase) through a widening area (induction), a diminishing area (compression) and a reduced area (ignition) before reverting to the first position again. Because the rotor was in continuous and steady motion, loads on the engine were minimal.

The outcome was known technically as an epitrochoidal engine.

Like all things in life, its advantages were almost eroded by disadvantages. Paramount of these was that of sealing the combustion chamber. Because the rotor had a square cross-section, it called for two circular friction seals on the sides of the rotor, and a transverse rubbing seal on the peak of each of the three 'nodes' or 'lobes' of the engine.

It took seven years of post-war development before the first engine was available for commercial use: it was first marketed in a small car called the NSU Spider. The motor was never without its obstacles and the early years were dogged by reliability problems and high fuel consumption. Considerable expense was needed to develop the motor further but clearly the little NSU firm was too underfunded to undertake such a programme.

Taken on (by 1967) and developed by Daimler-Benz and the Japanese firm Mazda, the former built a car that was very troublesome and when, in 1973, the oil-price crisis reared its ugly head, the time was chosen to drop the motor. Back in 1963, Mazda had acquired a licence to develop the motor though its Toyo Kogyo development engineering arm under the leadership of its engineering head Kenichi Yamamoto. Mazda successfully launched several motor cars and then, in 1972. General Motors of America obtained a manufacturing licence from NSU.

Meanwhile the motor had generated considerable interest amongst budding aviators, for the engine was light in weight for its power which was developed at a rather high rotational speed. Several attempts were made to produce a lightweight aircraft unit but the inherent stumbling blocks of the engine were never truly solved.

Unlike most normal engines, attaching a propeller hub proved to be an engineer's nightmare. The central eccentric shaft (you could hardly term it a crankshaft although it was the central feature of the motor) could only cope with carrying the rotor turning under normal combustion loads and could not take any thrust load at all. This necessitated a gearbox of sorts – not altogether a bad idea to slow down the propeller speed.

The Wankel was still a good idea but it was not adequately developed at the time. With the aviation interests looking to the motor industry to complete the development work, it only took the motor industry to back off and that was effectively the end of it. What really killed it off were the stricter controls over exhaust emissions and the rising price of fuel.

Another motor of a style that became described as 'orbital' was the Bradshaw Omega. This was the brainchild of none other than veteran aircraft engine designer Granville Eastwood Bradshaw (1887-1969) who had been responsible for the design of the early ABC engines including the dreadful Dragonfly radial of First World War infamy.

The Omega was a strange motor that was, like its then aged designer, not bereft of charm and potential. It was clever in concept but if anything it was probably ahead of its time since, like the Wankel, it demanded special seals that were just not available. And like the Wankel, it had a rotary combustion chamber but there the similarity between the two engines ceased.

The Omega was an annular-shaped casing made in two halves and joined around the periphery. This created a toroidal chamber that was extremely difficult to manufacture within the necessary degree of accuracy. Contained within the engine were two 'connecting rods' that were pivotally mounted to a central drive shaft via a one-way clutch and a set of drive cams or eccentrics. The ends of each connecting rod terminated in a piston that was shaped so that it exactly fitted into the toroidal chamber – again a singularly complex piece of machining.

As the central shaft was rotated, both connecting rods reciprocated radially, 'clapping hands' at specific places around the 360 degrees of the toroid to create the cyclic stages of induction, compression, ignition and exhaust. A novel feature of the engine was that it could be said to have two complete combustion cycles per revolution.

The designer, a meticulous draughtsman of the old school, claimed that a 2-inch diameter toroid with a ten-inch pitch-circle diameter could develop the equivalent of 80 hp for a weight of under 70 lbs. It was thus ideally suited to use as a car engine, a scooter-motor, or a power unit for motor-boats, light aircraft and defence uses. There seemed to be no application that might not benefit from the Bradshaw Omega.

Bradshaw, spectacularly white-haired and living in retirement close to the seafront at Ryde, Isle of Wight, invited the London press to his comfortable Solent-view home and put on such a charming and convincing display that his engine was featured in most of the daily newspapers, business journals and technical magazines. The big feature of this beguiling concept was that, like that earlier project, *nobody could fault it* – on paper! And that included me! As director of a small engineering firm, I offered, with the carefree confidence of inexperience in such matters, to build the prototype in our Newport workshop.

The manufacture, while tricky, was not impossible and many hundreds of man-hours later we had the motor complete. With visions of fitting it into my light aircraft at Sandown Airport, we began the testing. Several months later, having got the motor to fire and run erratically under the prime moving power of a large electric motor, we concluded that an engine that required a massive electric motor to drive it before it would occasionally fire was somehow missing the point and thus was not on.

The tantalising thing was that the motor *almost* worked. Like the perpetual-motion machines of old, it seemed so close to working that surely it only needed the smallest extra labour to attain success. The real problem was that the compressed gases could not be held in the combustion areas long enough for the sparking plugs to detonate them because the seals around the connecting rods were just not good enough. We tried to get other and larger businesses interested in the project, in particular the car makers. Several came and looked: all agreed it was too expensive for results that were too uncertain.

After expenditure of many thousands of pounds on the project we abandoned work – and gave the elderly Bradshaw his engine as a memento. He remained trying to get somebody – anybody – to take it on right up to the time of his death. It was another motor truly described as a clever non-starter.

The struggle to find a lightweight low-cost motor occupied many people for a number of those immediate post-war years but in the end the sum total of all this effort was nil. Besides drawing-board designs, many car engines were considered for, if Carden had made so practical a job of the Ford in 1935, then surely the same was possible now. The most likely motor considered was the Daf, a small Dutch engine recalled as powering a small car of the same name and having a belt transmission and no gearbox as such.

Looking for a ULA engine gradually faded from the day-to-day activities of the Ultra Light Aircraft Association, by then reformed as the Popular Flying Association. It had ceased to become a goal of driving importance for, so long as conversions of the VW car engine were available, then we did not need to face the undoubted complex negotiations and potential high cost associated with a newly-developed and probably over-expensive new engine. We put up with the heavy VW for our small aeroplanes. After all, Norman Jones used them in his production-line Druine Turbulents.

Not that the inventors were deterred, for the creative spirit is a free one that does not conform to boundaries. And so, when a Hampshire firm of engineers and machinery merchants named William R Selwood Ltd of Bournemouth Road, Chandler's Ford, Eastleigh, opened its doors to all and sundry to view a brand new engine in 1961, the response was if not exactly muted, then tempered with reserve.

Welshman Selwood founded his firm in Southampton in 1946 and his 'orbital engine' was his private brainchild. It had what he called rotary pistons and was described as a 'kinematic inversion of gas-turbine fuel-pumps in which an inclined ball-bearing imparts a swash-plate drive to axial pistons'. Since most usable ball-bearings are spherical in shape and therefore may not be 'inclined', the designers obviously meant 'ball-race'. This revival of the swash-plate motor was interesting: a demonstration engine was 10-inches in diameter and had a swept volume of 700 cu.cm. It had six double-ended cylinders which were curved to maintain a constant radius from the centre of a spider (carried on that inclined ball-race) on which the pistons were mounted. The engine was a two-stroke with scavenging by a Roots-type blower.

The designers claimed all the usual features – simplicity, compactness, excellent dynamic and pneumatic balance, and the elimination of both oil lubrication and liquid cooling. Unlike too many other engine 'demonstrations', this event was marked by the successful running of a demo motor accompanied by the proviso that the engine needed a lot more development. Everybody present was impressed and went away with a spring in their step. But realists understood the comment about 'development' which is another way of saying 'money, investment, incentive, orders'. The sensational Selwood swashplate motor was soon sadly sidelined; its inventor dying at the tender age of just 55 in 1968.

So far we have been considering the small engines sector. There were others in the light plane sector. Significantly, though, although in pre-war years de Havilland dominated the scene with its

In September 1957 the Popular Flying Association was invited to be the star attraction at London's Do-It-Yourself Exhibition at Earl's Court. As featured 'bait' in the exhibition's publicity, we were given a large display stand and invited to fill it however we wished so long as we had a 'home-built' aeroplane on it. For the PFA this was excellent publicity. The author flew up the Flying Neptune-engined Turbi G-APFA which formed a dramatic centrepiece but we also showed other engines and here I am pictured explaining the workings of the ARDEM conversion of the Volkswagen car engine to racing driver Mike Hawthorn, right. The engine was developed for the single seat Turbulent by Rollasons of Croydon who, at this event, referred to it as the 'R.T.W.' engine. Hawthorn, at the peak of his Formula One career, was killed on the A3 Guildford Bypass on January 22nd 1959 three months short of his 30th birthday.

The VW engine, in the form of the ARDEM conversion made by designer Roger Druine in France and adopted by Rollasons at Croydon, made for a neat installation in the Turbulent. It needed no engine-mounting since the attachment studs were arranged on the back of the crankcase so they fitted holes in the firewall and could simply be fitted with washers, nuts and split-pins. Fitted with dual ignition (two spark plugs per cylinder) and a Solex carburettor the 1,192 cc engine was claimed to produce 30.7 bhp at 3,000 rpm for a dry weight of 133 lbs (a rather massive 4.3 lbs/hp). Several excellent alternative conversions were offered (that by Peacock being very good) and slightly larger capacity engines were tuned up to produce much more than 30 hp, but they were all heavy.

Gipsy series of engines, the only Gipsy motors to appear on the scene in post-war years were war-production (for Tiger Moth trainers) and otherwise civilianised units. De Havilland had ceased to have so much as a toehold in the market that was once its very core business.

That left Cirrus, by then a division of Blackburns. The range was limited to the Cirrus Minor and Major, and the later military-aimed Bombardier. The Bombardier was the first Frank Halford-designed motor to be fully-dimensioned and specified in the Metric system and was also the first to adopt fuel-injection. There was one basic model, the 702, but a derivative was the 203, the principal alteration being the direction of rotation from right-hand tractor to left-hand tractor. The basic post-war Blackburn engines are described in Chapter Ten. While the Gipsy Major underwent several stages of improvement in the 1940s[2], de Havilland soon concentrated more on its larger engines such as the Queen which had first seen the light of day as far back as 1933.

From all these engines in the 100-200 hp bracket, the only significant new entry was the Bombardier – and that itself was a derivative. It was, however, the first British direct petrol injection engine to gain Air Registration Board approval. While used by the Army AOP.9 Austers as well some civilian applications, the Bombardier was an impressive motor in many respects yet was directly descended from that very first light upright engine designed by Halford at Croydon in the 1920s – the ADC Cirrus.

Bereft of light engines of our own manufacture, it was not until Rolls-Royce Ltd secured a manufacturing licence for the Continental range of flat-four engines (so taking up where Coventry Climax had left off in 1938-39) that we had a British-made light plane engine again. Beagle's success, such as it was, depended on American-designed, Rolls-Royce-built motors.

If there has been one significant change to the light aircraft engine since the 1920s it has been the vast increase in crankshaft speed. From the long-stroke low-rev motors with their generally shallow power curves we have moved steadily into an era of 'over-square' short-stroke engines with double the crankshaft speed and peaky performance curves.

This is a mixed blessing since slow-running engines hold many advantages

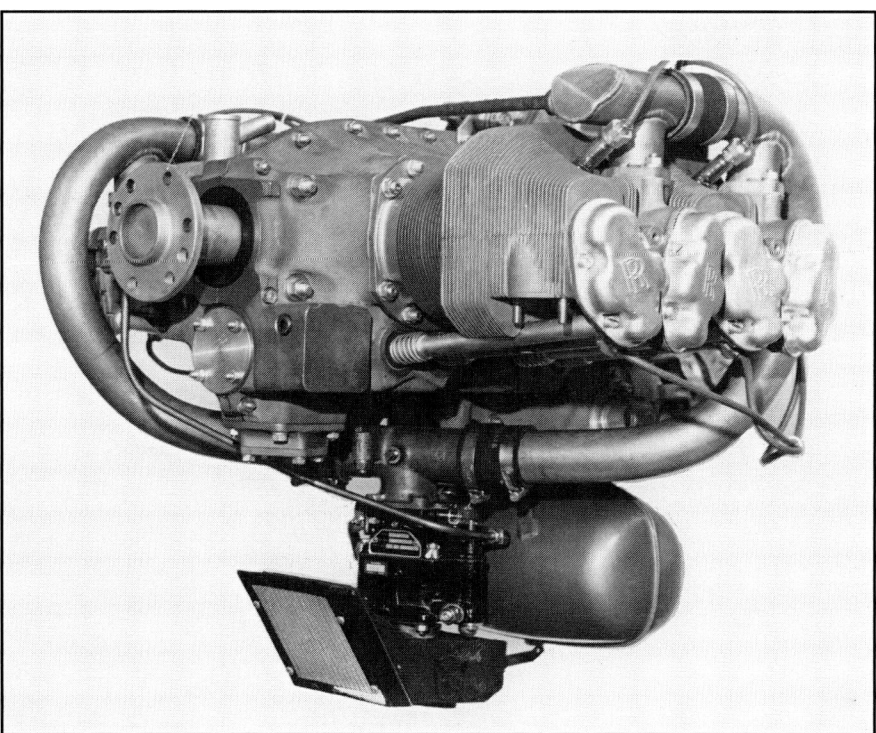

When, in 1960, Rolls-Royce secured a licence agreement with Continental Motors Corporation of Detroit it arranged that besides handling UK and European sales it would also licence-manufacture certain of the Continental range. Additionally, Rolls-Royce was to be allowed a degree of independent development of the Continental range. Here is a picture of the Rolls-Royce Continental O-240-A 130 shp flat four which features both improved fuel consumption and lighter specific weight than the original O-200 from which it was developed. The rocker-box covers reassuringly proclaim 'R-R'.

not the least of which are increased propeller efficiency and reduced wear. There must be few left now who may recall the deep, throaty roar of the Beardmore-powered Martinsydes at Croydon from the old ADC days, yet those 160 hp engines gave their full power at just 1,450 rpm. And the DH Cirrus Moth flew comfortably at 1,600 rpm.

Those that lament the days gone by are mere nostalgists except when their complaint relates to something tangible and useful which has been lost along the way. Nevertheless it seems that we let slip through our eager fingers at least a few opportunities that hindsight suggests would have proved their worth. It was ever that chicken-and-egg problem: we let them escape our grasp because the moment was wrong.

So if we did not have the design ability, then surely it might have been possible to put back into production some of our pre-war successes? Well, not really. The only two worth reintroducing might have been the Gipsy and the Cirrus, but they were already spoken-for by their original makers. That left one more possibility – the brilliantly-designed Pobjoy Niagara. The problem was that few people cared much for radials on the grounds of the difficulty of cowling them neatly and because they looked old-fashioned. Advantages such as superior cooling and structural concentration (short physical length for a lot of cylinders) didn't cut much ice. After all, we had nothing – but we could still be choosy if we wished!

So far we have looked, with a wry smile, at the considerations of the aerial steam engine and seen it discounted. We have looked also at diesel engines which, at the end of the 20th century, had already undergone something of a renaissance as more and more inventors experimented with light(ish) low-powered compression-ignition motors for small aircraft. We have also seen how pure jet engines (albeit foreign-made ones) have been used experimentally in the Sparrowjet and the Somers-Kendall racers.

In the course of this work, I have mentioned the only British contender, the Budworth engine developed at Harwich

---

2. The maximum permissible running time between complete overhauls for the Gipsy Major I was increased to 1,500 hours in May of 1945. The original 1,260 hours TBO (time between overhauls) was already higher than that of any other light engine and marked the latest milestone in the life of a remarkable motor that had originated in 1933 at 750 hours TBO and systematically climbed through the records.

At the top end for light aircraft as regards power output, the Rolls-Royce Continental TSIO-520-E was a turbocharged six-cylinder flat motor which produced 300 hp. Introduced in 1968 it went on to enjoy a distinguished career powering the Britten-Norman Turbosystem Islander light feeder liner. Its place as a more powerful successor to the de Havilland inline series of six-cylinder Queens confirmed the American succession to the Hatfield crown with the shorter, stiffer-crankshafted compact six-pot format motor.

Early in the 1970s, Rolls-Royce revealed that it was to handle the new Teledyne-Continental range of horizontally-opposed motors under the name Tiara and which offered power/weight ratios as low as 1.33 lbs/hp in models from four through six to eight cylinders. This news effectively sealed the fate of the British aircraft engine manufacturing industry. We would now become an American-powered nation – albeit one branded with the two Rs.

In 1960 the Gas Turbine Subsidiary of the Rover Company Ltd introduced two very small turboprop engines. Here is the TP.60 which produced 70 bhp for take-off and 60 bhp continuous. At just 30 inches in overall length and with a weight of 235 lbs, the motor cost some £1,500 – then rather too expensive for most users.

A candidate for the smallest turboprop aircraft in the world was the veteran Currie Wot G-APWT, first registered in October 1959. Built at Eastleigh by Vivian Bellamy, it was first powered by a 37 hp Aeronca-JAP flat twin, then a 62 hp Walter Mikron II inline four-cylinder and then a 60 hp Rover 1S.60 gas turbine from a naval auxiliary power unit and flown in this fashion by Bellamy on January 26th 1960. Later it became the flying test-bed for the 70 hp Rover TP.60/1 single-stage axial flow turbine as shown here. Subsequently it reverted to a Mikron installation having somewhere in between been fitted with floats and operated as a seaplane! G-APWT was thus probably the most versatile of single aircraft examples in post-war Britain.

but curtailed through the death of its designer. That the design was subsequently pirated and put into production by an American engine-maker (with whom he was negotiating rights when he was killed) merely confirms how advanced and worthwhile David Budworth's tiny motor really was – and how eager those Yanks were to capitalise on our ideas, officially or otherwise.

One other type of engine needs to be mentioned and this is the turboprop. It remains a curiosity of the British engine world that this form of lightweight transitional motor has received so little support. Amidst effete arguments of the 'it stands to reason' type that the engine is fuel-hungry, the gas turbine is small, compact, lightweight, simple to run and is vibration-free. In short, it offers everything the light plane owner could want – even the reassurance of a propeller.

During the quarter-century following the start of gas-turbine-powered flight, every category of powered flight quickly became dominated by this form of power with the notable exception of the aeroplane requiring less than 300 hp. True, for large commercial aircraft the domination was relatively short-lived until the pure jet took over, but the small aeroplane remained out on a limb until the early 1960s. In that year, Rover Gas Turbines Ltd of Holyhead Road, Coventry, produced a series of small gas-turbine engines that were eminently suited to light aircraft use. A small number of installations followed.

In the hands of enthusiast and engineer Vivian Bellamy, the first flight was made in a home-made Currie-Wot (G-APWT) – the world's smallest and lightest turboprop aircraft. This was followed, in 1965, by an installation in one of the earliest post-war Auster Autocrats, G-AGVI, which remained jet-powered for three years before reverting to its old power-unit. The most notable conversion, however, was Bellamy's Rover-powered Chipmunk (G-ATTS).

Why, then, did turboprops fail in the world of the light plane? An easy answer is that they used a lot of fuel per hour – something in excess of one pound weight of fuel per static horsepower per hour which, in the case of the Auster, worked out to a consumption of around 12 gallons/hour. Against that, though, was the fact that, at that time, turbine fuel was approximately half the cost of petrol. Because the engine was a lot lighter, however, some of the weight of any extra fuel could be written down without affecting the disposable load. The Auster installation, for example, despite having a massive Beech/McCauley constant-speed hub and a pair of cut-down Cessna Skymaster metal blades, actually turned in 5 lbs lighter than the old Cirrus installation – and that included electric starter!

The real downside, unfortunately, was cost. Rover's price for the engines was not cheap. The TP.90 used in G-AGVI was costed at £1,800. By the time the cost of alterations, full installation and revised cowlings had been taken into consideration, the price was up to around £2,500 for converting an existing aircraft. These costs could have been reduced by mass-production but we've already been through that hoop. Volume production numbers to engine-makers are usually between ten and a hundred times more than what volume-production numbers mean to aircraft-builders in reality.

In 1966 Peter Masefield, then chairman of British Airports Authority, spoke warmly of the future of low-cost fan-jet engines for light aircraft. Delivering the Louis Blériot Memorial Lecture in Paris before the Royal Aeronautical Society and its French counterpart (the AFITAE), Masefield said: 'I believe that as with major transport aircraft the days of the propeller turbine engine are limited and that instead we shall see relatively low-cost fan-jet engines capable of giving satisfactory take-off performance with improved noise levels'.

The lightweight pure jet engine is discussed further elsewhere.

Money has always been the governing factor in any serious engineering enterprise. Any firm can and will make you anything from a washer with a special hole in it all the way through to a finished aircraft engine so long as the finance is there. And while aircraft-builders frequently created aircraft without serious or adequate funds, engine-making has always been a different story.

Very recently, electric motors for light aircraft have shifted from being in the realms of 'nice but heavy' with durations thought of in minutes, to the realm of practicality. Extremely lightweight motors are now a reality and battery power in terms of life and endurance is expanding all the while thanks in the main to work on all-electric motor cars. While this medium augers well for a future in home-built aircraft, it was an unthought of excursion into a distant future in the period covered by this present study.

Reverting to the decades following the end of the Second World War, if one had to summarise the difference between a new engine from an amateur designer, and the comparable new aeroplane, the difference might justly centre on the probability that engine-designers are excellent theorists yet lack the extensive engineering facilities and financial backing needed to turn their designs into hardware. Aeroplane-designers, on the other hand, work with generally simple and low-cost materials that can be manipulated without costly tools and facilities. Despite these restrictions it is probably reassuring that there is no shortage of visionaries in either field.

Finally a demonstration that little changes politically with a story from beyond our proscribed dates. Chipmunk G-ATTS flew well with a Rover TP.90 but for a very fast and sleek non-standard Chipmunk one had to turn to G-ARWB demonstrated at the SBAC Farnborough Show in 1980. It was powered by a highly-tuned V-six turbocharged piston engine called Sapphire developed by a Shoreham firm, Aero Bonner Company. Masterminded by engine guru Bill Bonner, this 200 hp motor was liquid-cooled with a ventrally-mounted radiator. The constant-speed propeller was driven via a 2:1 reduction gear. In 1980 the RAF showed interest in revamping its Chipmunks with this engine. Prime Minister Margaret Thatcher vetoed it.

John Taylor of Leigh-on-Sea in Essex was a talented amateur designer. His first design was the diminutive 21-feet wingspan Aeronca-JAP-engined Monoplane. Registered G-APRT, it was constructed in his upstairs sitting room at his Leigh-on-Sea, Essex, home. Here the completed starboard mainplane is lowered to the ground. *Picture by Terry Taylor*

The designer seated in the cockpit of his Monoplane prototype prior to its maiden flight at the hands of Wing Cmdr Oswald Victor 'Titch' Holmes at White Waltham on July 4th 1959.

Many examples of the Taylor Monoplane have been built around the world. Here 'Titch' Holmes prepares for a take-off at White Waltham. It was in token of his appreciation for Wing Cmdr Holmes' assistance that Taylor called his second design the 'Titch'.

The fuselage of John Taylor's Monoplane emerges from his first-floor flat in Sunnyside Road, Ilford. It is obvious that he was able to complete all covering and painting in the comfort of his lounge. *Picture by Terry Taylor*

CHAPTER SEVEN
Our Aircraft Industry Suffers as Imports Grow

From its self-assured position on the world stage in pre-war years, the British light aeroplane industry faced its greatest challenge in post-war years, particularly between 1960 and '70 as imports increased in quantity. The entire aviation industry – it was just getting accustomed to being renamed 'aerospace' – was now on shaky ground. In business terms it was grim. In terms of management planning, it was blundering from one disaster to another. In terms of government involvement, it repeatedly created situations that, were they not of such awesome import, would have been laughable. Business analysts would today call it 'boardroom amnesia'.

Looking back on it now, it is to be a hard job to sort out the separate channels of military, commercial and private aircraft. All found themselves in pretty dire straits. Historically it becomes apparent that the fortunes and expectations of one were tied up with those of the others. In simple terms, what went on in the realm of defence and commercial aviation impinged almost equally on the light aircraft sector.

Remember that as late as 1945 we still had a worthwhile aircraft industry that was turning out machines as diverse as the Taylorcraft and Tiger Moth at one end of the scale, with the Spitfire and the Lancaster at the other. And in double-quick time. As an industry, aviation was highly-motivated, well-managed and possessed of some of the best designers and engineers in the world. In methods of production it had an established form that, while now mostly superseded by 'just-in-time' planning, worked astonishingly well despite continually bearing the brunt of enemy bombing raids that could take whole production sectors out of the equation in a moment. It was efficiently lubricated by large quantities of money, mostly, we can now see, American-sourced.

It took just 25 years to reduce this great capability and competent expertise to almost nothing. One short-sighted measure after another struck the industry like gigantic Atlantic rollers battering a ship in a storm. As each wave hit, the ship of industry heeled over a little further. And each strike was quicker than it took for the vessel to right itself. Consequently it was inevitable that the final blow would send the ship to the bottom.

For a long while there was acrimony and cries for heads to roll. The wise ones knew, however, that in the real world of politics and business where management is a term used to cover both good and bad administration, pinning responsibility onto an individual was like attempting to pin a jelly tail onto an over-frisky rubber donkey.

It all began, as so many things have a habit of beginning, far away from the topic we have in mind. It probably started with Duncan Sandys and his Defence White Paper of April 1957. This propounded the heinous policy that the concept of the manned fighter aircraft was outmoded and future defence reliance would be placed on missiles. Remember that this was still the time of the Cold War when America and the Soviet Union viewed each other as a time-bomb about to explode with disastrous consequences to the opposite side.

But there was more. Since 1951 we had had a Conservative government and by 1957 Prime Minister Anthony Eden was becoming concerned over the cost of defence. Over the previous five years it had absorbed ten per cent of our GNP. Material resources, the workforce and, in particular, large numbers of engineers and scientists, were engaged on military work[1]. And so, when Sandys wrote: 'Fighter aircraft will in due course be replaced by a ground-to-air missile system', the remaining vestiges of well-being that still permeated industry quietly drained away as the cold realisation dawned that it just wasn't wanted any more. No greater threat to security and job-certainty exists than the fear of unemployment.

In case this sounds too dramatic, just look at what happened in the next few months. The government decided not to proceed with the development of a manned supersonic bomber. The Avro 730, which was intended to replace the V-bomber force, was cancelled and the considerable amount of design and already undertaken (and paid for) was written off. Now all effort was to go into developing a ground-to-air missile system 'which will in due course replace the manned aircraft of Fighter Command'. Work on the next generation of fighters promptly stopped.

The original Chrislea Ace, G-AHLG, had a single fin and rudder (see page 49) but the wide cabin blanked the tail surfaces and made the rudder inoperable. The excessive wing dihedral only worsened things. After a hairy first flight the Ace appeared with this prototype twin tail but still with too much dihedral. The Ace was designed before the end of the war and was actually advertised nine months ahead of the declaration of peace. It seemed that nothing could hold back this fine little aircraft. Events conspired otherwise, though and despite revisions to better aerodynamics, following a shift from Heston to Exeter, increasing materials shortages finally forced the company into liquidation. A whole store of unfinished aircraft went for scrap. Around 21 examples of various models had been built and flown.

---

1. Reed, Arthur: *Britain's Aircraft Industry – What Went Right? What Went Wrong?* Dent, London, 1973, p.71

British Light Aviation – A Shifting Emphasis

In winding up his White Paper, Sandys dropped in a potent aside. 'The new defence plan involves the biggest change in military policy ever made in normal times. In carrying it through, a certain amount of disturbance is unavoidable'.

Disturbance, indeed! Destruction would be a more accurate term. As far as government investment was concerned, this defence plan was a final coffin-nail as it took cash from the British aviation industry and sunk it into the American Skybolt missile.

It was inevitable that the number of aircraft companies in Britain was going to require a downward adjustment. Companies coagulated creating essentially two airframe groups and two engine companies. Where once they might have resisted this identity-suppression, now they eagerly embraced it as a last-available lifeline to some sort of survival-in-numbers.

This was the British aviation industry's 'night of the long knives' and, when the Socialists came back to power after thirteen long years in the wilderness, they immediately made their mark by cancelling the HS.681 jet transport and the P.1154 vertical take-off supersonic fighter in January 1965.

The TSR.2, upon which so much of industry's activity hung, was quickly axed by the Labour government's Chancellor James Callaghan in his Budget statement on April 6th 1965.

Memories were still rather raw over the Panavia MRCA (Multi-Role Combat Aircraft, better known to aerocynics as 'Mother Riley's Cardboard Aeroplane') which had dragged on for such a long while changing its specification in tune with the parliamentarians of the day the way a chameleon changes its colour. Indeed, MRCA was so well-known as an aviation white elephant that could morph into something different every week that it actually became the nub of radio comic jokes.

The other aircraft that was in the forefront of our industry's thoughts was the Navy's F.111. This had been successfully sold by its makers to America's President John F Kennedy after he took office in 1961. The project was to survive a few years longer until it, too, was cancelled by the Labour government in January 1968. Not only did we lose this important American aircraft development work, but we demonstrated to the Americans our lack of industrial integrity.

Frederick G Miles had penned a particularly gloomy message regarding America's view of Britain back in 1947. He was writing in particular about the power shortage and enforced month-long industry shut-down, but his comments remained viable under the new regime of 1960s product abandonment[2]:

> …America has some very definite opinions about us. While I was there, I met many good and influential friends; every one of them was sure that England is finished and ended.

Grim as the situation was, government had already decided to fall back on that universally accepted panacea for troubled times – a committee and a subsequent report. The chairman of Tube Investments, Lord Plowden, was asked to set up this 'think-bag' for the purpose of considering 'what should be the future

The Buckingham brothers were immensely proud of Elliotts, their furniture-making business and were thus proud to join the ranks of aircraft manufacturing sub-contractors to speed the war effort in time of war. In 1945 with the cancellation of all military contracts and red tape that prevented them from going back to furniture-production, they found themselves with a highly-skilled labour force and no work. As a result they designed and built the all-wood EoN monoplane, the unconventional capitalisation standing for 'Elliotts of Newbury'. Widely demonstrated and with development plans, Elliotts needed some official interest to push the programme forward. None came. Too expensive as a new aeroplane in a market rich in cheap war surplus machines, this fine four seater, the Newbury EoN, became a project abandoned.

Portsmouth Southsea & Isle of Wight Aviation started out as an airline and aerodrome proprietor, providing an air service to the large grass aerodrome at Ryde on the Southern Vectis. During the war the company became Portsmouth Aviation and as peace loomed ever closer, the directors embarked on the design and construction of a practical twin-engined aerial taxi/feeder liner/freight transport/private owner aircraft. They called it the Aerocar and it performed perfectly. Everybody who flew it spoke glowingly of its handling and performance. High-mounted engines and over-wing exhaust ejection made for a quiet passenger cabin. The orders started rolling in but the company had no money to make the transition into aircraft production. Nobody wanted to help, the old excuse of the National Economy was used as the grout to fill the cracks in our aviation policy – and the Aerocar was scrapped.

---

2. Miles Aircraft Company Ltd: News, Vol. 6, No.2, 1947. A *Backs-to-the-wall* message.

Our Aircraft Industry Suffers as Imports Grow

This eye-catching design captured the imagination of many that saw it. The all-magnesium butterfly-tailed Planet Satellite emerged from a construction group comprising a finely-interwoven mesh of companies. In the firm belief that the organisation plus modern materials could overcome absolutely every problem including aerodynamics, G-ALOI was finished at Redhill and taken to Blackbushe for its first flight. As more than one pundit had suggested, insufficient tail clearance meant that the ultra-thin wing could not adopt a sufficient angle of incidence to make lift a likely by-product of the efforts of horsepower, pilot and 'brakes-off'. The Satellite was probably unique in being a project that succeeded in failing entirely without external (meaning government or ministerial) aid.

There's an old adage in business that you should never undermine your core business and diversification should only be attempted when all else has failed. For Britten-Norman Ltd on the Isle of Wight, it had already struck gold (or oil, if you prefer) with its Islander and Trislander series of Dragon Rapide replacement small airliners so the last thing it really needed was to launch another aircraft unless it was a variant on the successful formula that it had found. News that it had secretly been designing and building a four seat all-metal Yankee light plane-look-alike was therefore greeted with surprise. In May of 1969, the B-N3 Nymph G-AXFB was unveiled to an incredulous press at Bembridge where everybody was taken in a fleet of Islander aircraft to take happy pictures of the little Nymph as it flew around the spectacular Island coastline. The Nymph was aimed directly at a world market already being dominated by makers such as Cessna and Piper. Designed by the talented young John Britten who had already designed the B-N1F, the unbuilt B-N four seat low-wing monoplane, the B-N 2 Islander and Trislander, the Nymph was attractive from a distance but, as an American challenger it suffered somewhat because it simply wasn't good enough. Rows of dome-head rivets savoured of older Luscombes and Mooneys and would not pass muster in today's environment. Offered also as a semi-manufactured kit for currency-earning amongst third world nations, it also failed. John Britten died young and the Nymph languished for many years until Desmond Norman, 'revised' it (mostly involving a new coat of paint, new name and fresh registration as G-NACI). Death also overtook Norman and the Nymph, in any one of its guises, was forgotten.

Left: George Miles designed and built the advanced M.100 Student G-APLK as a private venture at Shoreham in 1956-57. A two seater with side-by-side seating, it was powered by one 880 lb static-thrust Turboméca Marboré 2A turbojet, a motor for which Blackburn had just secured the UK distribution licence. Superbly easy to fly, it would have been an ideal trainer for the RAF (it was marked, for a while, as XS941), an executive private owner jet or even an advanced machine for the flying club. But nobody wanted it or could see any use for it. It faded from the scene and today bits of it can be found in the marvellous Miles Aircraft Museum in Berkshire – a last resting-place for Miles' memorabilia near the once-hallowed ground of Woodley Aerodrome, today a housing estate.

Right: De Havilland produced the Canadian-designed DHC.1 Chipmunk in England, first at Hatfield and then Chester. Once in private hands, though, some examples were modified. One was G-ATTS, ex-WP895, which was a star turn at the SBAC Show staged at Farnborough in September 1966 when it appeared in flight powered by a 118 shp Rover TP.90 turboprop engine cowled extremely neatly. Behind this was that renowned forward-thinking man of the era, Vivian Bellamy who had flown the Currie Wot biplane with a similar engine. The installation was undertaken by Hants & Sussex Aviation Ltd at Portsmouth Airport. More that 100 hours of development flying was achieved without incident but no interest was shown in further conversions. The original Gipsy Major piston engine was put back and in October 1969 G-ATTS was sold to the Americans where it became N2247.

A genius ahead of his time was test pilot and engineer David Lockspeiser. He thought up the novel Land Development Aircraft, a multi-role light aeroplane for use in undeveloped parts of the world. A seven-tenths scale model was built driven by an 85 hp Continental C85-12 rear-mounted pusher engine. Registered G-AVOR it was built at Shalford in Surrey and registered on June 8th 1967. The designer ultimately made the first flight at Wisley. Initially it had a four-wheeled landing gear to enable it to straddle a cargo pannier which could then be loaded using an in-built winch in the cargo hold. However this was subsequently revised with a conventional tricycle gear as seen here.

The LDA-1, later renamed the Boxer, was made to be dismantled and packed into small crates. It could even transport spare component parts inside its cavernous fuselage. In a hark-back to the original pre-war Simmonds Spartan aircraft, wing panels, front and rear, were interchangeable as were all control surfaces. Utility was second only to ease and economy of operation. This scale model was widely demonstrated but nobody was really interested despite occasional flashes of encouragement. The cruel fate of the project came when the sole example, pictured here, was destroyed in a mysterious hangar fire. It was not insured. The designer later died and the project followed suit.

place and organisation of the aircraft industry in relation to the general economy of the country, taking into account the demands of national defence, export prospects, the comparable industries of other countries, and the relationship of the industry with government activities in the aviation field'. The committee was to make its recommendations on any steps and measures that it considered necessary.

In due course, Plowden completed his report, helpfully advising that it had cost £16,980 10s 0d to produce. He began by establishing that there were over 300 factories ranging in size from under 25 to over 17,000 employees. As of June 1965, 259,000 persons were employed, 17 per cent fewer than during the post-war peak of 1957 since when, the report added, there had been an almost continuous fall.

In the light aircraft scene, Plowden found that:

> of some 135,000 light aircraft active in the world in 1964, over 85,000 were in civil use in the United States. The principal users of light civil aircraft in Europe in 1964 were France with about 3,800, Germany with about 1,700, and Britain with about 1,300. For every licensed private pilot per head of population in Britain, there are just under two in France, four in Switzerland and six in the United States.
>
> American manufacturers also dominate the Western world in the production of light aircraft. The five main light aircraft companies in the United States produced over 8,500 aircraft in 1964, some 82 per cent of the world total for the year.

Looking at Britain's share of the world light aircraft market, it was easy to see how it had declined in recent years. In the early years after the Second World War, British manufacturers, especially the Auster Company, met with some success; the 610 British light aircraft produced in 1951 representing 16 per cent of the world total. During the rest of the 1950s, British light aircraft manufacture steadily decreased. The world market was growing and competition from America escalating. Britain's share of the pot was insignificant.

By 1959, when world annual production was double that of 1951, British production totalled only 30 aircraft. After the lifting of currency restrictions in the latter half of the 1950s and early 1960s a growing number of light aircraft, mostly French and American, was imported. At the time of the Report, imports amounted to about £1m a year.

As regards the prospects for light aircraft manufacture in Britain, Plowden was initially optimistic.

> It was represented to us that the manufacture of light aircraft ought to be well suited to the aptitudes and resources of British industry at the present time. The market is buoyant, the sums at risk in development are not excessive, and lower wage rates should give British manufacturers a marked initial advantage in costs over their American competitors.
>
> There is something in all these arguments. We endorse the Government's policy of readiness to provide launching aid for suitable light aircraft projects. We consider too that the Services should be encouraged to buy British light aircraft wherever possible.
>
> We do not believe that rewards from participation in light aircraft manufacture will be easily won. The major American companies are strongly entrenched in world markets. British aircraft will need to be more attractive than the competing aircraft in design, performance, and price, if our manufacturers are to regain a remunerative share of the market.

Crucially the Report commented that:

> Though the sums needed to launch a light aircraft are small compared with those required to launch large airliners, we doubt if the necessary funds can be raised wholly in the private market at the present time. We recommend therefore that, in suitable cases, a measure of Government financial assistance should be given towards the production costs, as well as towards the launching costs, of promising light aircraft. Suitable arrangements for recovering this expenditure through sales should be made.
>
> We see no reason why this branch of the industry, given the necessary Government assistance for a few years, should not become commercially self-supporting rather sooner than the rest of the industry. We think the Government should review progress from time to time in the hope that within a few years the industry will be self-sufficient. If on the contrary, light aircraft business were not approaching this objective by then, the case for continuing assistance would then be open to question.

The Plowden Report was flawed in many ways. Even as it was published, the belief was that it had presided over an industry already on its last legs and, in the majority of aspects that it considered, it had avoided some key issues. There was disapproval of the make-up of the Committee, critics being quick to point out that it was short on technicians skilled in the aircraft industry. It had also relied heavily on advice from those who had vested interests. One observes with interest, for example, that Peter Masefield, head of Beagle, had presented very fully to Lord Plowden's men on a number of aspects. After all, light aircraft played only a very small part in His Lordship's brief and, likewise, his conclusions.[3] It could also be argued that at that particular time, Masefield was about all that was left of the light plane camp. He must have been the inspiration for Plowden's 'promising light aircraft' observations.

Significantly, within fewer than five years, the government would allow both of Britain's only small aircraft makers to go into receivership when the short-term salvation would have called for a maximum of £10m of taxpayer's money. As it was, first the original Britten-Norman business collapsed, and second Beagle went under. In the case of Britten-Norman, the firm was saved from within the industry in the short-term before a further crisis forced it into foreign ownership. Reason? It was an attractive proposition with a unique product. And Beagle went to the wall, its key design – the Bulldog – being saved (together with a goodly portion of British reputation) by the timely intervention of Scottish Aviation. The rest of its lines, sadly, were

By the end of the 1950s, Auster Aircraft Ltd at Rearsby found itself in a tricky position. The enormous losses associated with the Agricola project had almost bankrupted the business and so, when the opportunity arose to join the newly-formed British Executive and General Aviation Ltd, better known as Beagle, and breathe some fresh life into its Tugmaster/Workmaster/Autocar designs, Auster at once 'joined up'. In company with George Miles, Auster reported for duty at the new company and soon had some development cash with which to embark on a new project involving reworked Auster Mk.6 and T.Mk.7 airframes. Because Beagle was a 'doggy' name, all its projects would have to be named after dogs. Here is the Auster-designed Beagle Terrier 2, G-ARRN registered on June 16th 1961. It was later sold to Germany.

expensive but not very good American look-alikes and consequently never in the equation.

I have already shown that I believe Beagle faltered thanks to the conviction that, as Pressed Steel had initially reckoned, you could stamp out modern aircraft the way the British Motor Corporation was stamping out Morris and Austin cars next door. They further supposed that many costly aircraft components could be replaced by off-the-shelf motor parts. Demystifying aircraft design and construction was one thing: high-volume low-cost production was another. Britain was indifferent to both.

Beagle demonstrated not so much how to approach aircraft design in the second half of the 20th century as how not to run a business. The government-appointed managing director took office early in 1968 and almost single-handedly demolished the company.

As one-time head of Singer's, it was no doubt correctly assumed that he knew just about everything there ever was to know about sewing-machine production: the only concern was that (a) he drew an impressive salary, and (b) he had at best a rather restricted knowledge of aircraft. There was still the avid belief in the company that the original Pressed Steel Company's brief was attainable.

As expected, the new MD instituted the 'resignation' of several senior men and carried out a heavy pruning among the non-productive departments in order to place increased emphasis on production. The 'new broom' policy was expected, but his limited aircraft-manufacturing experience prevented him from realising the importance of, say, a strong design and post-production team: several significant staff were swept up with the dross leaving key departments weak.

By a strange coincidence, a year after Keith Myer took up the reigns, Beagle (meaning Myer) appointed a new marketing director. Now one would expect the marketing director of a firm with the aspirations of Beagle to be a real high-flyer in every sense of the term. If not himself a qualified and respected

There were other hopefuls and just like the Essex Aero Sprite, the Planet Satellite and the Bianchi Survey, the Tawney Owl was somebody's dream for that hard-to-define private owner and club market. However, unlike the Essex Aero Sprite, the Planet Satellite and the Bianchi Survey, the Tawney Owl actually flew. The problem was that it didn't fly very far. Test pilot Angus J McDonald and his passenger-co-pilot Harry Radcliffe managed a couple of hundred yards in semi-stalled condition before making an inverted landing just outside the airfield at Stapleford on April 20th 1960. The reasons why are related elsewhere. Suffice to say that this marked a premature end to another project which might have been saved by some low-cost wind tunnel trials with a model before construction ever began. As it was the Porsche flat-four-powered twin-boom all-metal two seater became an exercise in futility. While the configuration of the Tawney Owl was fairly conventional, it suffered from having an inefficient wing with an aerodynamically-challenging centre-section cut-out. The wreckage is allegedly being rebuilt.

---

3. For a first-rate analysis of the Report and its impact on the aircraft industry, the reader is referred to Reed, *op.cit.*

Down at Shoreham, Beagle saw its future in making executive twin-engined aircraft and production of these was undertaken in the former Auster factory at Rearsby by 1963. Here an impressive line-up of Beagle B.206 Series 2 aircraft fills the one-time Auster shops. These pictures mark a last gasp of light aircraft building in England, although Scotland would continue a fraction longer when, later, it took over some of failed Beagle's orders.

A military version of the Beagle 206 was the 206R Bassett intended for RAF Northern and Southern Communications Squadrons. The first was delivered in May of 1965 while the first civil 206 sales began in the same month. Here the production assembly shop at Rearsby shows advanced construction in hand. Sharp-eyed observers will see unfinished Auster fuselage frames stored in the roof-trusses.

Pictured on March 28th 1966, Rearsby production of the Beagle 206-S suggests rather cramped conditions reminiscent of wartime aircraft production standards. Shame the output didn't match, though.

pilot, then he would be expected to have the sort of encyclopaedic knowledge of aircraft to enable him to debate the benefits (or otherwise) of Beagle products vis-à-vis competitive designs the world over. In truth, the new top man, upon whose shoulders, theoretically at least, rested the future of the company, was the former vice-president (Europe) of none other than that certain sewing-machine maker that had given us Myer. While the man appointed, D W Gray, was an Englishman, that in itself could cut no ice. Susurrations about looking after friends stirred through the corridors of most places except government who, besides owning Beagle, have never been strangers to nest-feathering and nepotism in high places.

Beagle had successfully 'sold' some 206s to the Argentine Air Force but an unrelated outbreak of foot-and-mouth disease resulted in an embargo on Argentine meat imports, so the Beagle deal was titted for tat in March of 1968. This came on the heels of the matter of a potential sale to the South African Government which was scuppered by an American government embargo on the Beagle 206's Continental engines. Nearer to home, the RAF was considering a revision of pilot training which would see ab initio recruits put through a training scheme on Pup 150 aircraft. The scheme, which would have taken several years to implement, could not be finalised in the time that the Shoreham company had left. Not all of Beagle's bad luck was of its own making.

At the end of 1968, questions were being asked as to when the first mass-produced aircraft might emerge from this very expensive firm with two factories and a lot of public money. Myer responded by saying that by that time thirty Pup-100/150s had been delivered, promising that production would 'definitely reach one per day by the middle of 1969'. He also said that orders, with deposits, had been received for more than 250 Pups. And when would Pup production start to break even? That, said Myer, depended upon the introduction of further Pup variants. More models were necessary because the competitive pricing policy of the market did not give enough profit on the cheaper models like the Pup-100/150. 'Break-even', he said, 'tends to be a receding target. At the moment I would say that it is several hundred Pups beyond our present order list'.

Speaking to *Flight* (January 2nd 1969), Myer said he was certain that both the Shoreham and Rearsby 'production centres' would continue to be necessary and that there was 'very little chance' that either of them would be closed. He did, however, suggest that he might well have to redistribute work between them.

There was a story doing the rounds at the time that reflected the profligate-expenditure approach of Beagle. It was said, undoubtedly mischievously, that if the firm's executives (they were looking at Masefield at the time but carefully avoided mentioning him by name) had been asked to build a shed for a lawnmower they would first have scoured the world for a source of Grade A platinum roof-tiles and, having bought them, would then build a roof and fix the platinum tiles in place. At this stage it would be found that the finished roof was unexpectedly heavy and it would now require great effort and manpower to lift up the roof with expensive cranes while gold-brick walls were separately built and then inserted beneath it. And in the end the lawnmower would not fit inside because the doorway was an inch too narrow!

This may well have been a malicious exaggeration of Beagle's business practices but the evidence remained that each aircraft produced cost the taxpayer dearly. On top of this there was an unfortunate problem with the first Pups. These had been delivered to the Shoreham Flying Club which was literally right on the factory doorstep. There were continual little problems and failure of systems. Particularly the wheel-brakes created high-maintenance problems. The club's aircraft spent much longer in repair than might be expected of new aircraft made in the premises next door. And the work had to be completed in the club's hangar.

The club was dismayed to find that its next-door neighbour Beagle – surprisingly – didn't want to know about the problem and apparently not only *would* not fix it but *could* not: the department that had been set up to attend to after-sales matters was one of those had been 'pruned' by the new management. And once a Pup had been sold, hand-washing was the order of the day.

Shoreham Flying Club, bending over backwards to 'buy British' and support Beagle, was in a nefarious position and, not surprisingly, they got rid of their early production Pups pretty quickly on the grounds of their being uneconomic to

Above: It was not immediately all doom and gloom, though, for the firm did make some sales. Here Beagle 206 G-ATYX was sold to Spain as EC-BJF. It seen here formatting on the prototype Srs.1 Pup, G-AVDF on May 23rd 1967.

Below: Beagles 206 Srs.1 G-ASOF flies in loose formation with a 206 Srs.2 G-ATYD. The first machine had been used as an Australian demonstrator but ended up with Cumberland Aviation Services Ltd of Carlisle in 1968. This was the design that encouraged the company for it was to produce quite large numbers of various models, 79 in total – a worthwhile batch run.

operate. The association with being 'sold a pup' now seemed uncomfortable apt.

Meanwhile Beagle continued to spend money and even bar-room economists could see that the losses on each aircraft built could never do other than accumulate. The present author, speaking to Sir Denning Pearson, chief executive of Rolls-Royce about the then-new RB-211 engine for an American airliner, recalls being told by this eminent authority that 'we lose a quarter of a million pounds on each engine we make – but we've got orders for 74 of them!' Which merely seems to demonstrate that the philosophy of the old perpetual-motionists (namely that friction was a constant force that could be beaten into submission merely by adding more gears[4]) remained alive and well in the high echelons of the 1960s business world.

As the 1960s drew to a close, Britain's only light aircraft producer was poised on the brink of liquidation. It would not be saved and its eventual closure put an end to Britain's hopes of recapturing any vestige of home market, let alone a world market. In the years that followed we would have contenders such as Slingsby Aircraft, interesting designs like the Optica and practical designs like the Firecracker and Trago Mills Sprint. None was destined to leave any lasting impression whatsoever.

By 1968 the private aircraft that were available to the purchaser had changed out of all recognition. Gone were the familiar names of Miles's, the Austers and the Percivals in a marketplace now strongly controlled by France and America with Italy and Czechoslovakia taking advantage of those gaps that suited them. All overseas manufacturers now had agents and distributors in Britain and availability was ex-UK. Here is a partial list of aircraft based on that published by *Flight* that March. All British aircraft are included:

SINGLE ENGINE SINGLE SEATERS

Type	Engine	Nationality	Remarks	Basic Price
Nipper Mk.3	45 hp Ardem 1500 cc	UK (Belgian origin)	Fully aerobatic, C of A	£1,650
Sportavia RF4	39 hp Rectimo VW	France	Fully aerobatic, C of A, powered sailplane	£2,180
Rollason Turbulent	45 hp Ardem 1500 cc	UK (French origin)	C of A	£1,450

SINGLE ENGINE TWO SEATERS

Type	Engine	Nationality	Remarks	Basic Price
Beagle Pup 100	100 hp R-R Continental O.200	UK (US engine origin)	Semi-aerobatic	£3,850
Beechcraft Musketeer Sport III	150 hp Lycoming O-320	US	Semi-aerobatic, occasional four-seater	£76,232 (inc radio)
Bölkow Junior	100 hp R-R Continental O-200	Germany (US engine origin)	Semi-aerobatic	£4,300
CEA Dauphine	115 hp Lycoming O-325	France (US engine)	Semi-aerobatic	£5,280
Cessna 150	100 hp R-R Continental O.200	US	Semi-aerobatic, occasional four-seater	£4,935
Fairtravel Linnet	100 hp R-R Continental O.200	UK (US engine origin)		£2,495
Laverda Super Falco	160 hp Lycoming O-320	Italy (US engine origin)	Semi-aerobatic, occasional three-seater	£5,800
Omnipol Zlin 526	160 hp Walter Minor 6111	Czechoslovakia	Fully aerobatic	£7,800
Piper Super Cub	150 hp Lycoming O-320	US	STOL utility	£5,430
Piper Cherokee 140	150 hp Lycoming O-320	US	Semi-aerobatic, occasional four-seater	£5,413
Rollason Condor	100 hp R-R Continental O.200	UK (French design, US engine origin)		£3,500
SAN D.150	100 hp R-R Continental O.200	France (US engine origin)	Semi-aerobatic	£3,900
Socata Rallye Club	100 hp R-R Continental O.200	France (US engine origin)	Semi-aerobatic, occasional four-seater	£3,995
Jodel D.120	100 hp R-R Continental O.200	France (US engine origin)		£3,540

---

4. See Ord-Hume, Arthur W J G: *Perpetual Motion: The History of an Obsession.* Allen & Unwin, London, 1977: 2ed. Adventures Press, Kempton, Illinois, USA, 2005.

Single engine Four/Five Seaters

Type	Engine	Nationality	Remarks	Basic Price
Aero Commander Lark	150 hp Lycoming O-320	US		n/a
Aero Commander Darter	180 hp Lycoming O-360	US		n/a
Beagle Pup 150	150 hp Lycoming O-320	UK	Semi-aerobatic	£4,700
Beagle Husky	180 hp Lycoming O-360	UK		£5,430
Beechcraft Musketeer Custom III	165 hp Lycoming IO-346	US	Four-seater	£8,395 (inc radio)
Beechcraft Musketeer Super III	200 hp Lycoming IO-360	US	Four-seater	£9,225 (inc radio)
Beechcraft Bonanza E33	225 hp Continental IO-470	US	4/5 seater	£15,465 (inc radio)
Beechcraft Bonanza E33A	285 hp Continental IO-520	US	4/5 seater	£17,050 (inc radio)
Beechcraft Bonanza V35A	285 hp Continental IO-520	US	4/5 seats	£17,900 (inc radio)
Beechcraft Bonanza V35ATC	285 hp Continental TSIO-520	US	4/5 seats, turbo-charged	£20,310 (inc radio)
CEA DR 250	160 hp Lycoming O-320	France	Private	£6,000
CEA DR 253 Regent	180 hp Lycoming O-360	France	Private, occasional 5 seats	£7,330
Cessna F172	145 Rolls-Royce Continental O-300	US	Occasional 5 seats	£6,810
Piper Cherokee 180D	180 hp Lycoming O-360	US	4 seats	£7,734
Piper Cherokee Arrow	180 hp Lycoming IO-360	US	4 seats	£9,111
Piper Comanche 260B	260 hp Lycoming O-540	US	4 seats	£12,780
SAN Excellence	100 hp Rolls-Royce Continental O-200	France	4 seats	£3,800
SAN Mousquetaire	180 hp Lycoming O-360	France	4/5 seats	£5,700
Soccata Rallye Commodore 150	150 hp Lycoming O-320	France	4 seats	£5,750
Soccata Horizon 160	160 hp Lycoming O-320	France	4 seats	£6,200
SIAI-Marchetti S.205-18F	180 hp Lycoming O-360	Italy	4 seats	£7,290
SIAI-Marchetti S.205-20R	200 hp Lycoming IO-360	Italy	4 seats	£9,165

The second production Series 1 Pup, G-AVZN, was delivered to the local Shoreham Flying Club on April 12th 1968 in a ceremony involving a lot of flowers. For the club, having the manufacturer of its new aeroplane just yards away must have seemed a reassuring situation. However, these early Pups suffered continual minor problems, the worst of which was a high incidence of brake problems. The problem was that by this time Beagle's management was deeply into a cost-cutting phase and first facility to be axed was its vital after-sales service section. The club suddenly realised that it had, so to speak, been sold a pup – four of them to be exact. In September the following year it was forced to cut its losses, sell its Pups and re-equip with new aircraft that came from slightly further afield than the hangar next door.

What everybody was really waiting for from Beagle was its much-vaunted Pup. By the mid-1960s there was great activity at Shoreham as Beagle began producing the Pup in quantity. It all looks satisfyingly busy and the impression is that once more we have a great light plane industry within our shores

The two seat Beagle B.121 Pup Series 1 G-AVDF was the prototype first flown by 'Pee Wee' Judge on April 8th 1967. It had been a long time coming and, despite all the factory activity, nobody seemed quite sure how soon production could be ramped up to profitable numbers. This nimble aircraft is seen in a vertically banked turn over the Sussex countryside. This aircraft still flies today.

Here we see final assembly of a Series 1 100 hp Rolls-Royce Continental-powered Pup G-AWEB. This was the first of two demonstrator aircraft for the US agents, Miami Aviation Corporation. It was fitted with long-range tanks and flown to the States in October 1968 via Shannon – an enterprising move indeed. Behind the scenes, though, the cash crisis that would finally kill off the company was looming ever larger.

Clear from this is the dominance of the American-manufactured light aircraft, not all of which have been included on the grounds of unnecessary repetition of the theme. Also apparent is the strength of the French industry and the evidence that it was already capable of building machines that suited a pan-European market.

Even at its height, British aircraft production seldom hit double figures, rarely three. By comparison, Aérospatiale's SOCATA division delivered its 2,000th Rallye light aircraft early in 1972. David Dorrell (*Air Pictorial*, June 1972) wrote:

> British firms have tried to break into [the light aircraft] field again… but so far any significant success has eluded them because of the scarcity of private fliers in their own country. But how can there be more private owners in Britain to give the manufacturer sufficient cause to try again? It's a vicious circle. Private flying in Britain is expensive. We still labour under the iniquitous petrol tax; landing fees and service charges in certain places are higher than they should be. The regulations governing the issue and renewal of private pilots' licences and certificates of airworthiness cause much needless expense.

There was a familiar sound to Dorrell's words. Well might there be, for they had been repeated at regular intervals since 1946 and would go on to be repeated for some years to come. But it was a fundamental difference between France and Britain that allowed the scenario that sparked this off to come about. The Popular Flying Association's then-president, Air Commodore G J C Paul, responded the following month:

> Ever since the Liberation in 1945 successive French governments have granted generous aid to flying clubs and amateur constructors and fliers, in the belief that this is the nursery of aviation and the source of many of the next generation of designers, constructors and aviation leaders. How right they have been proved is demonstrated again and again by the remarkable successes gained by the French aviation industry, the equipment of the French Air Force, and the expertise of French air transport.
>
> The Americans, whose aviation expanded out of all recognition in the period 1939-45, in contrast to the French which was decimated, had different problems; one especially important piece of US Government aid is the provision of air traffic services and controllers by the FAA at all approved airports; thus the great expansion of airports has been aided.
>
> In Britain the most notable change in Government policy has been to withdraw the petrol subsidy which formerly helped light and amateur flying. Quite possibly the administrative problems of continuing the subsidy make it impossible to expect any change of heart on this. However… one of our greatest needs is airfields. Could our own Government not follow the example of the USA by providing air traffic controllers and associated facilities at all airfields willing to have them, and pass on the benefits by insisting that where this was done, all landings by aircraft of less than 2,500 lb auw should be free.

Paul went on to point out that as late as 1972 we still had a sizeable success story in the aviation world about which to crow. Rollasons (a private and family-owned business) had built more than 40 Condors and promised there were more to come! In fact there would be more than 50 of these Croydon-built two seaters that were leased out by Norman Jones to some score of British flying clubs. But the Condor was a light aircraft for club use that was cheap to run and put speed and comfort a long way down the specification sheet. Splendid though the all-wood Condor was, it was no businessman's runabout. It could not be expected to compete with the likes of the Italian, French, German and American products in such terms. The Beechcraft/Cessna/Piper image was a marketing goal that eluded us.

We no longer had the ability to compete in those markets because we had neither the product nor the manufacturing incentive any more. The will to try was also gone.

The first production Pup Srs.2, a four seater powered by a 150 hp Lycoming O-320-A2B, was G-AWDY which went to Switzerland in August 1968 as HB-NAA.

Pup Srs.2 G-AVLN is pictured here flying by the Bernese Alps, probably thought more photogenic than the Shoreham seafront.

For military use, the Pup's big brother was the Beagle Bulldog powered by a 200 hp Lycoming IO-360-A1B6. Orders had been secured and it was a question as to whether or not Beagle had the finance to honour these orders, in particular from Sweden and the Royal Malaysian Air Force. Beagle's future effectively depended on the execution of these orders. In the end the company was dissolved before this could be achieved. The entire production of Bulldogs was shifted to Scottish Aviation (Bulldog) Ltd at Prestwick which made a success of the job. Here is the production line in full flow in 1970. Our last light plane factories at Shoreham and Rearsby closed for good. The final light plane production facility was therefore in Scotland and when it faded it passed quietly without even the skirl of the bagpipes.

CHAPTER EIGHT
Chronology of Light Aircraft and Engines

In this chapter, information is provided on aircraft and engines and showing the dates as to when each was introduced. This reveals clearly how the light aircraft industry was in steady decline even as it attempted its post-war revival. Only a few makers of aircraft existed and their production was, to say the least, hampered by parameters of economy and legislation. By collating these data into years, both comparison and interpretation becomes easy.

Aircraft are shown by date of first flight in the convention year, day, month. Throughout, the first column gives five pieces of information, e.g. M2/0/1F. The first letter of characters signify whether monoplane (M), biplane (B), triplane (T), or rotorplane (R). This is followed by numerals that indicate how many crew separated by a slash from how many passenger seats were provided. The second slash separates the third piece of information which is the number of engines. Finally is a letter that indicates whether the aircraft has a fixed land undercarriage (F), a retractable land undercarriage (R), if the aircraft is a flying boat having an immersed hull (B), a seaplane supported on separate floats (S), or if the aircraft is amphibious (A). The most common style gives preference, i.e. a seaplane later converted to fixed-undercarriage land use would be S-F, but a landplane altered to a seaplane would be F-S.

Where during its life there are changes in specification, these are indicated by characters separated by a hyphen. For example, an aircraft that might have one or two crew is shown as 1-2, and a passenger capacity of two or four is indicated as 2-4, while an optional retractable undercarriage may be shown as F-R.

The second column gives the date of the first flight. Where, other than the year, the precise date is unknown, the symbol '--/--' appears. Where the month is known but not the day, the symbol '--/x' appears (where 'x' equals the number of the month). Where some aircraft that are listed were never completed or, for any other reason, did not fly, the legend 'n/a' is used. Where, in some cases, the precise date of the first flight is unknown, the date shown will be followed by the symbol '¶' which is the date of issue of the C of A or the date of issue of the civilian registration in lieu of known maiden flight. In all cases, the date refers to the prototype, and not (unless specifically shown as such) to a different marque or model.

Where a design that was subsequently manufactured in Britain originated overseas, the symbol '*' follows the name of the aircraft, i.e. 'Druine D.31 Turbulent*'.

The fourth column offers the briefest information on the machine, its purpose or inspiration (where specified), and whether or not it was successful.

The engine information that concludes each list of new aircraft relates only to British-made engines introduced or developed between the years 1946 and 1970. Licence-built engines such as the Continental built by Rolls-Royce are included as are those British conversions of European-made motor car engines for aircraft use such as the VW used by Rollasons.

The dates given show the year in which an engine was developed, certified or first flown. Commercial practice sometimes dictated that an engine was well advanced in design and manufacture before it was first announced. This means that in some instances these dates may be later (by no more than a year) than the appearance of the first experimental specimen.

A word about power ratings. As explained later on in Chapter Ten, the method of ascribing the horsepower output of a motor often appeared to have been inspired by a process of random selection involving pieces of paper and a hat. Some makers quoted take-off power, some ¾-throttle power, others various cruise settings. The result is that we often find that different powers were ascribed to the same engine. I have followed manufacturers' convention where possible, taking figures from published data. It may not always be proven to have been the right choice.

The engines listed here are those used in light private and home-made aircraft. There were many others, of course, which only had military or commercial use: these are specifically excluded. What is interesting to note is that, unlike in the 1928-40 period when there was no actual shortage of different types of engine, the post-war years were extremely lean for the engine-makers. Indeed there were so few new engines built as to make it possible to single-out the key events not

The prototype Auster Autocrat G-AGOH was generated from various bits and pieces and the unfamiliar rear fuselage glazing is pure Auster 5. Nevertheless, this is the first three seat Autocrat complete with little 'secretary's seat' placed sideways behind the front two.

British Light Aviation – A Shifting Emphasis

just in the year but, virtually, the decade.

The irony is that throughout this whole period stretching from 1946 to 1970, there was only one significant new engine produced – and that was a direct descendent of the very first four-cylinder inline engine designed by Halford at the Croydon works of the Aircraft Disposal Company in 1924!

Because there is no purpose in viewing progress in any area of industry or commerce in isolation, and since it is only possible to equate progress in the light of other events that were taking place at the time that could, and probably would, impinge on matters aeronautical, I have provided an introductory annual overview of domestic economy, political associations and other factors that influenced industry.

The three decades that followed the end of the Second World War were curiously repetitive of the inter-war decades in that they were coloured by sustained periods of economic and political unrest. Concurrent with this were the extreme financial constraints that impinged on successive administrations. These conditions acted as a brake on almost all consumer activities and go some way to explaining Britain's sometimes painfully slow, hesitant support to industry and that of civil aviation in particular. True, successive government ministers with responsibility for civil aviation were, to varying degrees, favourably disposed towards private and club flying but their ability to actually do anything about it was very limited.

This annual summary therefore prefaces each year's list of new significant club and private owner aircraft. The commentary details the state of the market, the outside forces affecting it, and the effect that these affairs had on the aviation industry as a whole. To understand this interrelationship is to acquire a better appreciation of the narrow and specific history of commercial flight.

The reader will not find here all of the aircraft listed in Chapter Eleven because some of the machines described were not completed or did not fly until well after the 1970 cut-off point.

If nothing more, this chapter will indicate that far from being a great world leader at the head of the great British Empire, we were so financially crippled that we could barely survive. Had it not been for the continual assistance of America and also France both of whom loaned us great sums of money, we would have bankrupted ourselves on at least two occasions through mis-judged policy decisions. Britain's successive governments in those times reacted conservatively to the unfolding national problems and do not emerge as possessed of the strength they sought to project.

The post-war years marked the end of the British Empire as we knew it. In this respect, it also sounded the final trump to the great Victorian concept of empire-building and exploitation. We faced a time when those nations that we naively termed 'our possessions overseas' began to stand up for themselves and reclaim their birthright. Some, but by no means all, flourished outside the enveloping Union Jack.

One is left with the awful thought that our far-flung Empire was as much a financial hindrance to us as a cartographic benefit. Wisely we picked our countries with care (or was it cunning?) and the majority were ably suited to contribute produce and raw materials of various kinds that could in turn play a part in boosting the wealth of the Mother Country. It did not modify in any way the underlying truth that however great was our image, and how firm our stance; we were a poor nation financially overburdened and overstretched. While nationally we often paid dearly for the plundering of our empire, that money seldom if ever filtered down to the level of those upon whom we were dependent as a workforce. We were never 'good employers', however talented we were at exploitation.

It is with this concurrent sequence of events that we may make our assessment of Britain's position in post-war private flying. It may go some way towards explaining why our light aircraft industry capitulated to foreign expertise and investment and not only *didn't* make a serious attempt at regaining its pre-war position, but absolutely *couldn't*. It will also show just why we were so far behind the rest of the world, how our lead had been lost really early on like at the outbreak of war, and why our light aircraft industry was so underfunded for the rest of the time that it could barely keep its head above water, let alone compete in markets across the oceans be they to the west or south.

When civil aviation was able to start up again in 1946, we had far too many potential makers for the actual size of the market. The era of whittling-down was about to break.

1945

With the outbreak of war in September 1939, petrol to private motorists had immediately been rationed to 200 miles per month. However, as oil supplies were constantly under threat from enemy action, in particular resulting from the problems of the summer of 1942, private motoring was banned for all but essential users. Private flying, however, had been banned the moment war was declared on September 3rd. This state of affairs was sustained beyond the ending of the war in Europe marked by 'VE' Day on May 8th 1945. While restrictions on private flying remained in force, largely because of the difficulties of dismantling the wartime restrictions and partially because the bureaucratic mind-set was still on a war footing, several manufacturers quickly registered civilian aircraft in the certain knowledge that private flying was about to re-emerge. In a bold move that recognised likely future trends, the Helicopter Association of Great Britain was formed under the presidency of James George Weir (of Weir, also Cierva Autogiro fame) and with Cierva's manager and test pilot Henry Alan Marsh as chairman. The idea was to promote the interests of those keen on rotary-winged aircraft.

M1/1/1F	--/--	Auster J-2 Arrow	Taylorcraft Plus C replacement; 65 h.p. Lycoming G-AGPS sole example. Known also as the Sharp Special named after engineer Ken Sharp
M1/2/1F	19/April	Auster J-1 Autocrat	Prototype G-AGOH made from modified Auster 5
M1/1/2F	09/Jul	Reid & Sigrist RS.3	Development of the Snargasher named Desford
M1/3/2R	26/Oct	Miles M.65 Gemini	Twin-engined variant of the M.38 Messenger with retractable undercarriage

Engines: • None

1946

January 1st marked the end of civil and private flying wartime prohibition. Sporting flying could re-start. Already the first Auster Autocrat had been built and flown and the first actually delivered to a private owner (December 1945). Auster began production of the Autocrat immediately. The Air Ministry restarted its Airmet continuous weather reports on long-wave radio from Dunstable on January 7th. The first full year of Clement Atlee's Socialist government and former PM Winston Churchill signalled the start of the so-called Cold War. The government nationalised the coal mines and the Bank of England and, on July 15th, American President Truman agreed to lend bankrupt Britain $3.75 billion. Minister of Civil Aviation was Lord Pakenham, aka the Earl of Longford (b. 1905, educated Eton and Oxford), a scion of the Anglo-Irish aristocracy, banker, publisher, prominent Catholic and friend of Hugh Gaitskell. At the outbreak of the war, Britain had 2m cars on the road. Now the war was over, the estimated number of motor cars had fallen to around 1.8m. Petrol, both car and light aircraft spirit, cost 2/- a gallon of which 37.5% was tax. The first flying club to re-open its door on January 1st was Cambridge followed by London Aeroplane Club which shared Panshanger Aerodrome, still an operational RAF aerodrome. Third rebirth on March 2nd was Luton which was managed by the Hunting Group. Downside was the sale on January 7th of Brooklands Aerodrome to Vickers Armstrong. Wiltshire School of Flying opened up again with Taylorcraft Austers charging £3 per hour dual or solo. Some 50 aerodromes around the country were open to private and club flyers. While the years of war took their toll on industry and, just as important, human resources, and despite the great pressures of the war effort that occupied every man and many women for long hours, there were those that knew war could not continue for ever. These people had plans for the return of peace. As a result, a handful of projects were ready to 'get off the ground' the moment the conflict came to an end. The Chrislea Ace, for example, was designed in 1943-44 and construction actually began, in a small way, in 1944. Doug Bianchi, identifying a demand for a low-cost trainer, designed a monoplane four seater and launched details in April: but it was never built. Gordon Bedson had an idea for the light aircraft that he announced this year, but that, too, came to nothing and would not emerge for many years by which time the designer had emigrated to Australia. The Wren Goldcrest suddenly emerged, complete and ready to fly, but with no possible hope of obtaining the necessary paperwork that would permit it to take to the air. Both the British Gliding Association (BGA) and the Ultra Light Aircraft Association (ULAA) were formed. Meanwhile private owners were in uproar at the high cost of landing fees and hangarage at state-owned airfields. Miles Aircraft responded by offering all private owners free landings at Reading. As the year drew to a close, news of two great new light aircraft engines raised the hopes of a nation still in the grips of austerity. First, from Morris Motors, was revealed Lord Nuffield's flat-four of 100 hp. Then we heard that a wonderful engine was being designed by Roy Fedden that could be buried inside a wing. Amazingly, instead of being inverted inlines, both these engines were to be built after the American style of being horizontally opposed.

Chrislea CH.3 Super Ace.

M1/3/2F	--/--	Helmy Aerogypt Mk.IV	Experimental twin-engined tourer destroyed on flight at Northolt Nov 26th
M1/2/1F	1/Jan	Auster J-1 Autocrat	Prototype already flown but pre-production and production of this three/four seater started
M1/2-5/1F	31/Mar	Percival Prentice	Civilianised RAF three seat trainer
M1/2/1F	22/May	DHC.1 Chipmunk	Canadian designed but produced in Great Britain
M1/1/1F	Summer	Auster J-2 Arrow	75 hp Continental-powered production aircraft
M1/1/1F	10/Sep	Auster J-3A Atom	65 hp Continental-powered prototype G-AHSY
M1/1/1F	19/Aug	Chrislea CH.3 Srs 1 Ace	Tricycle landing gear with single tail. Directionally unstable: modified to twin-tail
M1/1/1F	--/Dec	Auster J-4	90 hp Cirrus Minor I-powered flapless two seater

Engines:
- 520 h.p. Alvis Leonides 501 Series 1, 2 and 3
- 135 h.p. Blackburn Cirrus Major III
- 100 h.p. Blackburn Cirrus Minor II
- 130 h.p. de Havilland Gipsy Major ID-IF (available 1945)
- 240 h.p. de Havilland Gipsy Queen 30 Series 1, 2, 3, 4
- 250 h.p. de Havilland Gipsy Queen 32/33
- 220 h.p. de Havilland Gipsy Queen 70-1 (formerly Gipsy Six SG)

1947

America's position as a 'world banker' to Europe quantified by Secretary of State George Marshall who proposed a 'European recovery programme' funded by the US. It came to be known as Marshall Aid. A sense of hollowness as the era of peace brought no alleviation of austerity. Ministry relented and allowed pre-war Permit-operated aircraft to qualify for fresh Permit to Fly so long as they were in original 1939 condition and with the same engines. Up to 20 per cent of the structure is the maximum that could be renewed to qualify. Whitney Straight led government-sponsored Special Advisory Committee on Private Aviation which recommended government sponsorship of clubs among other things. Despite being an excellent report totally sympathetic to private aviation, no action was ever taken on its main recommendations. The worst winter freeze-up for decades paralysed the nation in the year's opening months. The knock-on effects to both home and industry across the country were extensive and contributed to the bankruptcy of Miles Aircraft Ltd.

Portsmouth Aerocar.

M1/0/1F	--/--	Tipsy Junior	Belgian-designed single seater adopted by Fairey
M1/3/1F	--/--	Prestwick Pioneer Mk.1	240 hp Gipsy Queen 32 to AM Spec for STOL communications aircraft
M1/3/1F	--/Mar	Auster P Avis	First shown at September 1947 SBAC Show.
M1/3/2R	18/Jun	Portsmouth Aerocar	Private and executive aircraft with light freight option
M1/3/1F	8/Aug	Newbury AP.4 EoN	All wood tourer/trainer/glider towing low-wing monoplane
M1/3/1F	5/Nov	Prestwick Pioneer Mk.2	Mk.1 with 250 hp Gipsy Queen 34
R1/3/1F	7/Dec	Fairey Gyrodyne	Four seat experimental helicopter

Engines:
- 540 h.p. Alvis Leonides 501 Series 4
- 560 h.p. Alvis Leonides 502 Series
- 540 h.p. Alvis Leonides 503 Series 2, 4
- 250 h.p. de Havilland Gipsy Queen 34

1948

The road and rail systems of Britain were nationalised on January 1st with gas and electricity on April 1st. Marshall Aid Act passed by US Congress allowed Europe $5.3 billion for post-war recovery. We finally saw an end to bread rationing but some other commodities, particularly chocolate and sweets, remained on coupon. The Olympic Games came to London and the shabby Wembley railway station was lavishly rebuilt as the main access point for Wembley Stadium. America took 38 gold medals: we won three. A flat rate of motor car tax of £10 per car was introduced. Petrol cost 2/1d a gallon of which 36 per cent was tax. Blackburn's new Bombardier engine broke ground in two ways. The first Cirrus derivative engine to have fuel injection, it was also the first engine by this company to 'go Metric' in its dimensioning. The Kemsley Flying Trust was formed to help groups buy aircraft. Petrol rationing restricted all motoring and flying and shortages forced tighter control on leisure activities.

M1/3/1F	--/Feb	Chrislea CH.3 Super Ace Series 2	Wing and tailplane of metal construction fabric covered
M1/0/1F	--/Jun	Slingsby Motor Tutor	Powered version of Tutor two seat glider as single seat ULA
R1/1/1F	--/Oct	Cierva W.14 Skeeter 1	Two seat experimental helicopter, Jameson engine
R1/4/1F	5/10	Westland S.51 Mk.1A	First Yeovil-built American-designed helicopter

Engines:
- 110 h.p. Jameson FF-1
- 180 h.p. Blackburn Cirrus Bombardier
- 145 h.p. de Havilland Gipsy Major 7
- 145 h.p. de Havilland Gipsy Major 8
- 145 h.p. de Havilland Gipsy Major 10 Mk.1/Mk.2
- 160 h.p. de Havilland Gipsy Major 30

CHRONOLOGY OF LIGHT AIRCRAFT AND ENGINES

1949

Auster J/5B Autocar.

Austerity now officially much worse than during the war years. Public, hitherto with stoic resolve to situation, became restless as the Cold War generated new fears of yet a fresh war and more restrictions. North Atlantic Treaty Organisation (NATO) formed in April. The cost to member countries would be huge and the campaigners wondered, rightly, if we could afford it all. The real threat to the world, we were entreated, was Communism and the Chinese Red Army. By the end of the year all mainland China was under the control of Mao Tse Tung. American president Truman sided with South Korea against North Korea and the Republic of China creating a destabilising conflict that all alert Britons deeply feared. The Cirrus Bombardier engine was first flown in a Miles Messenger in February 1949. The engine developed 180 hp at a dry weight of 350 lb.

M1/0/1F	9/Jan	Heath Parasol	First British-built example (Blackburne Tomtit engine) first flight
M1/3/1F	--/Aug	Auster J-5B Autocar	Four seater tourer and club machine
M1/3/1F	--/Aug	Auster J-1B Aiglet	Originally for crop-spray duty. First public demo 1950 SBAC Show
R1/4/1F	15/Sep	Westland S.51 Mk.1B	First Yeovil-development of American-designed helicopter
M1/3/1F	21/Nov	Chrislea CH.3 Srs 4 Skyjeep	Four seater or air ambulance/light freighter

Engines:
- 180 h.p. Blackburn Cirrus Bombardier
- 197 h.p. de Havilland Gipsy Major 50 (formerly Gipsy Major 3S Supercharged)

1950

Red China sent 'volunteer' armies into Korea to contest what was officially a US and UN force, but was really mostly Americans under General MacArthur. The horror a fresh World War, the third in 46 years, loomed large. Worries rose as Moscow and Communist China signed a 30-year 'treaty of friendship, alliance and mutual assistance'. Back home, the General Election returned the Socialists to power but with a reduced majority. An international radio conference in Copenhagen acceded to Denmark's demand for a new frequency allocation for a high-powered station. The only frequency suitable was 1,224-metre wavelength which happened to be that used by Airmet. Amidst tremendous uproar from all quarters of aviation, not the least private and club flyers, Airmet went off the air on March 15th. Despite hopes for frequency allocation, it never resumed. Private flying

Scottish Aviation Prestwick Pioneer (Alvis).

had been subjected to fuel rationing which had imposed severe restrictions on all aspects of operation, not the least flying training and club operations. In April the Chancellor slapped a massive 9d increase on fuel tax. All aircraft owners had petrol coupons and a complicated paperwork system became tougher as the huge rise in the cost of fuel from last year's 2/1¾d per gallon to 3/0½d per gallon revealed the

153

government's tax leaping from 34.95 per cent to 49.65 per cent. Then a welcome, if uncharacteristic surprise as, on Saturday May 27th, the Minister of Fuel and Power announced the immediate ending of rationing. Tens of thousands of coupons printed and distributed to aircraft owners were binned. There was a significant change in the licensing of pilots: the long-established 'A' and 'B' Licence system (private and commercial) was replaced by a new Private Pilot's Licence while professional flyers had to have a Commercial Pilot's Licence. Novice, trainee flyers had to have a Student Pilot's Licence for which a medical examination needed to be passed. The requirements for the PPL called for basic training of 40 hours of which a certain proportion had to be undertaken solo. Certain flying schools could operate an 'approved' training programme whereby the student completed his whole flying training within a short and concentrated period of time which could be a total of 30 hours. Complaints that the hours of flying to qualify would cost so much more instead of an average of ten hours for the old licence. The Helicopter Association of Great Britain held its first rally at Hanworth Aerodrome, West London. In the world of engines, the ARB increased the overhaul life of the 90 hp Cirrus Minor Series 1 to 800 hours between complete overhauls. This brought it into line with the Cirrus Minor 2, already with an 800-hour 'life'. Meanwhile special sanction had been granted to run several Mk.1 engines to 1,000 hours with a view to a further extension. Some Mk.2 engines were already on dispensation for the magic 1,000 hours to the delight of Taylorcraft and Auster-operators.

| M1/3/1F | 5/May | Scottish Aviation Pioneer 2 | Former Prestwick Pioneer now with Alvis Leonides |
| M1/0/1F | 4/Aug | Britten-Norman BN-1F | First version with JAP engine; subsequently rebuilt after crash (1951) |

Engines:
- 520 h.p. Alvis Leonides 503 Series 5, 6, 7
- 560 h.p. Alvis Leonides 514 Series

1951

War in Korea took a turn for the worse as North Koreans and Chinese pushed invaders south of the 38th parallel. Government disarray over health service charges and increases in defence spending forced a fresh General Election which, as expected, was won by the Conservatives. They put the now-controversial Winston Churchill back at the head of the country with Anthony Eden as foreign secretary. Petrol had embarked on a steady rise in cost with the average cost per gallon standing at 3/3¾. The population of Britain hit 50m with 8.3m in London alone. An MP, speaking during a debate on civil aviation in the House of Commons, told Members that club pilots and private owners were being slowly squeezed out of the air. The pattern was there for all to see, he proclaimed. The prototype of a new Auster variant, carrying the B Conditions marks G-25-1, was demonstrated at Rearsby after which was registered G-AMKF for display at the SBAC Show. This utility four-wheeled box-car looked set for a good market amongst farmers and all who needed to transport light goods.

Miles M.75 Aries.

M1/3/2R	--/Feb	Miles M.75 Aries	More powerful, faster version of Gemini
M1/3/1F	--/June	Auster J-5F Aiglet Trainer	First demo at Auster Rally on June 2nd 1951
M1/3/1F	7/Sep	Auster B.4	Auster's four-wheeled freighter; one only
M1/0/1F	26/May	Britten-Norman BN-1F	Revised model with Lycoming engine
M1/0/1F	--/May	Dart Kitten Mk.III	Post-war revival of 1938 design

Engines:
- None

1952

On February 6th the sad news of the death of King George VI. Many considered it the passing of the last vestiges of the Georgian era at best remembered for all the wrong reasons. It was not a good omen for a year that brought no new aircraft to the fold but the Americans invented the first birth-control pill. Shock as America exploded the world's first hydrogen bomb on November 6th. A sharp reminder of how poor was our atmosphere (which often rendered the horizon invisible and gave pilots barely a few miles of visibility even on a sunny day) came in December with the arrival of the infamous 'smog' which brought the country to a standstill and killed many with frail lungs. The late King's elder daughter Elizabeth and her new husband were preparing to take over as head of the Empire. Petrol cost 4/3d a gallon with tax at 62.74 per cent.

| | | No new aircraft designs | |

Engines:
- None

Chronology of Light Aircraft and Engines

1953

Miles M.77 Sparrowjet.

Russia's feared leader, Joseph Vissarionovich Stalin, died on March 5th. The nation was elated as, on June 2nd, Elizabeth was crowned Queen at Westminster Abbey. The new age of television brought continuous live images of the entire event to every house in the land that had television and was served by one of the growing number of transmitters. On the same day it was announced that the summit of Mount Everest had been reached for the first time – by Edmund Hillary with the Sherpa, Tenzing Norgay. For the first time since the war ended there was a general feeling that things might be getting better. Petrol rose again but the government softened some of the blow by cutting its tax – but only slightly. At 4/5½d a gallon, tax was dropped to 56.13 per cent.

| M1/0/1F | --/-- | Hants & Sussex HS.1 Herald | Single seat JAP-powered tubular steel low-wing monoplane |
| M1/0/1F | 14/Dec | Miles M.77 Sparrowjet | Single seat twin turbojet built from 1935 Kings Cup winner |

Engines: None

1954

Misguided but influential Wisconsin Republican senator Joseph McCarthy expanded his hitherto more localised activities and created huge nationwide anti-Communism uprising in America which continued until 1958 and denounced many leading personalities. First experiments in Britain with vertical lift engines in the 'flying bedstead' memorably described by the BBC as 'a flying test-bed'. The Vickers Viscount enters service and the first Comet crashes.

| | | No new aircraft designs | |

Engines: • None

1955

The year started badly with the Sutton Coldfield rail crash that claimed seventeen lives and injured many more. The year would end with another train tragedy at Barnes taking thirteen more lives. Before that, though, was a further bad winter with long-term ice and snow which disrupted transport and hit industry extensively. On April 5th Winston Churchill resigned as Prime Minister, age and ill health being given as the reasons. He was succeeded by Anthony Eden who reformed the Conservative ministry with Harold Macmillan as foreign secretary. Commercial television was introduced on September 22nd by the Independent Television Authority. May saw the end of the occupation regime in West Germany which was admitted as a member of NATO. Christopher Cockerell made the first experiments which led to the invention of the hovercraft. Auster Aircraft introduced its latest Auster Autocrat variant – the J-1N Alpha which had a Gipsy Major engine. ML's curious inflatable aircraft aroused thoughts of the truly portable camping-bag aeroplane. De Havilland's pioneering Comet jet airliner embarked on a round the world sales tour and waved a bold Union Jack in far places. West London's Heston Airport closed ahead of the M4 motorway which would cross it.

M1/1/1F	--/--	ML Utility Mk.I	Inflatable non-rigid experimental aircraft
M1/3/1F	1/Jul	Auster J-1N Alpha	Four seat Autocrat with bigger engine
R1/4/1F	23/Aug	Westland S.51 Srs 2 Widgeon	First UK-designed variant of American helicopter
M1/1/1R	8/Oct	Somers-Kendall SK-1	Two seat all-wood jet-powered racer
M1/(1)/1F	8/Dec	Auster B.8 Agricola	First low-wing Auster for spray/dusting duty
M1/1/1F	21/Dec	Edgar Percival EP.9	Designed for agricultural and freight use

Engines: • None

1956

The Suez crisis in October and November posed a serious threat to petrol supplies as the year advanced until, on December 1st, rationing was once more introduced in an attempt to curb use. The essential liquid now cost on average 5/4d a gallon with 56.25 per cent going into the Exchequer's pocket. Britain's conflict in the Canal Zone drew international condemnation and bankrupt Britain was denied the American cash loans it sought. Prime Minister Anthony Eden was virtually oblivious to the state of the country and rapidly lost public support. The Helicopter Association of Great Britain held its second rally at private grounds at Ripley, Surrey, five years after its first 'annual' event.

| M1/3/1F | --/-- | Auster J-1N Alpha | Autocrat upgrade with Gipsy Major I |

Engines: • None

1957

A growing interest in basic human flight led to the formation of the Man-Powered Aircraft Committee in January at RAF Cranfield. On January 9th Anthony Eden resigned as prime minister; Harold Macmillan took over the following day with R A Butler as Home Secretary and Selwyn Lloyd as Foreign Secretary. Meanwhile as Britain lagged behind the rest of Europe in aircraft ownership and the number of licensed pilots, current figures reinforced oft-stated claims that apathy was forcing us out of our own sky. In March petrol rationing ended. The expected euphoria was somehow lost as people, accustomed to constraint, took a long while to accept freedom. The same happened in the air. Auster made a curious attempt at building an American lookalike with white plastic upholstery and trim calling it the Atlantic. It was shown at Farnborough in the autumn without its wings. Meanwhile down at Thruxton somebody had engineered a super-wide fuselage to get four people into a Tiger Moth. While no more than the Fox Moth managed (with pilot that could take five), the Jackaroo was a reminder of how forgiving a Tiger could be, even with its looks. A significant event of this year was the formation by Norman Jones of Rollason at Redhill of the Tiger Club to enable a small but select group of enthusiasts the opportunity to create a 'team' for racing, sporting and aerobatic light flying. With the prime aim of encouraging sporting flying, the club had four standard Tiger Moth aircraft converted to single seat aerobatic 'specials'. Each was fitted with a high-compression engine and metal propellers and was covered in lightweight fabric. The removal of anti-spin strakes and the repositioning of the fuel-tank in the former front cockpit created sleek and fast machines. Increased elevator chord and a strengthened stern-post combined with modified fuel and oil systems to enable inverted flying made these special aircraft indeed. The Rollason-built Turbulents were to fly under the auspices of the Tiger Club whose familiar logo adorned each machine. At the beginning of August the government announced plans to support light aviation. With immediate effect, the Ministry of Aviation would pay for up to 25 per cent of the cost of training sponsored flying instructors up to CPL and IR standard. The MoA would also pay £500 per annum to all flying clubs that maintained commercially-licensed instructors. During recent hard economic times, the number of approved clubs had fallen by 20 per cent as instructors shifted to higher-paid airline employment.

Miles M.100 Student.

M1/3/1F	--/--	Auster C.6 Atlantic	Four seat executive tourer prototype G-APHT
B1/3/1F	--/Mar	Thruxton Jackaroo	Four seat conversion of DH.82 Tiger Moth
M1/1/1F	14/May	Miles M.100 Student	Two seat single jet trainer built as private venture
M1/1/1F	12/Dec	Druine D.53 Turbi	First British-built example

Engines: • None

1958

Figures of the world's licensed pilots made miserable reading. In terms of numbers, America came first, France second and we were third before Germany, Italy and Australia. However, in terms of numbers of pilots per million population it was a very different picture. America still led with 2,880 but we were in seventh place at a mere 125 per million. It's those nations that beat us which was the humiliating bit. Switzerland was in second place followed by Australia, France, Sweden and, would you believe, Chile in sixth place. A debate on why our aircraft industry was so moribund drew a well-informed, impeccable-reasoned reply from Edgar Percival who, commenting on the success of the US industry, said that over there 'practically every manufacturer of light aircraft has received at some time a sizeable order from either the US Air

Garland-Bianchi Linnet.

Force, the Army, or the Navy. These orders sometimes amounted to as many as 150 aircraft or more at a time, and it was needless to point out what beneficial effect this had upon amortization of tooling and development costs. [Here] the building of small aircraft should receive some form of government recognition or support, until the business became mainly self-supporting. It was supported in a most practical manner in other countries. In France, the Army bought 425 Max Holste Broussards, and the German Government had placed an order for over 400 Dornier Do 27s. Both of these aircraft were in the small 'executive' class and had proved to be of great value to their owners. In the national interest, the SBAC would have to play its part and take a wider view than they had in the past'. A brilliant address but with predictable outcome – nothing.

M1/3/1F	22/Feb	Auster J-1U Workmaster	Agricultural variant of Alpha design
M1/3/1F	25/Jul	Auster C.6 Atlantic	Attempt to copy US lightplane; damaged before first flight; scrapped
M1/1.1F	1/Sep	Garland-Bianchi Linnet	First flight of first British-built example
B1/0/1F	11/Sep	Currie Wot Series	Post-war revival of 1938 design
M1/0/1F	12/Dec	Druine D.31 Turbulent	First British-built example

Engines: • None

Taylor JT.1 Monoplane.

1959

In October the nation went to the polling booths and Harold Macmillan's Conservative government was re-elected for another term. Ten million homes in Britain had a television receiver: the 'consumer boom' had started but still didn't reflect growth in private aviation. The British Gyrocopter Association was founded (later to become British Gyroplane Association after the death of its founder and his wife in an airliner mishap). In June the English Channel (or France's La Manche) was crossed for the very first time by hovercraft, the Cowes-built SR-N1 making the historic traverse in a cloud of spray. The hot topic was man-powered flight and added impetus was garnered when, in November, Henry Kremer put up two huge cash prizes – one for a 'simple' land flight and the other for the impossible – a Channel crossing! The size of the prizes fostered the challenge and designers started thinking about the impossible…

| M1/1/1F | 28/Feb | Marshal MA.4 | Experimental high-lift Auster derivative |
| M1/0/1F | 4/Jul | Taylor JT.1 Monoplane | Single seat homebuilt |

Engines: • None

1960

May 3rd saw the coming to fruition of the European Free Trade Association (EFTA) offering 20 per cent tariff cuts between members starting July. There were 6.5m cars registered in Britain. Petrol cost on average just under 4/8d a gallon. On October 7th it was announced that a new company had been formed, called (ultimately) Beagle Aircraft, created out of Miles Aircraft, Auster Aircraft and Pressed Steel Corporation. The plan was to mass-produce light aircraft rather like motor cars and to put Britain back into the world of production light-planes. The news was received with cautious optimism for it was by then an old and familiar tune, the difference being that it was being sung by Auster and Miles.

But *Pressed Steel*? As the year drew to its close came astonishing news of the world's tiniest turboprop aircraft and, what's more, a home-built one at that! Vivian Bellamy of Eastleigh had successfully fitted a 60 hp TP.60 Rover gas turbine into a Currie Wot biplane. It was, he suggested, only a bit of fun. But the aviation world and the popular press lapped it up. Imagine a jet-propelled biplane, they all said!

M1/0/1F	--/--	Fairey-Tipsy Nipper	Belgian-designed, later taken over by Slingsby
M1/3/1F	--/Aug	Auster 6A Tugmaster	Glider-towing Gipsy Major powered
M1/3/1F	10/Jan	Beagle D.5/180 Husky	Upgrade of the Auster J-1N Alpha
M1/1/1F	12/Feb	Beagle D.4/108	Upgrade of Auster J-2 Arrow
M1/1/1F	22/Apr	Tawney Owl	All-metal twin boom pusher crashed first flight
M1/3/1F	9/May	Beagle D.6 Husky	Upgrade of Auster J-5B Autocar

Engines: • None

1961

On August 10th, Britain applied for membership of the European Economic Community: three days later East Germany sealed off the border between East and West Berlin and within a week, the infamous Berlin Wall was under construction. The year drew towards its end with some very positive news for amateur flyers when, on November 30th, the Ministry of Aviation said that the Permit to Fly system was to be extended to aircraft of up to 1,750 lb (from 1,200 lb) and engine power of 115 hp (increased from 75 hp). It was also permissible to have a stalling speed of 50 mph or 60 mph where an 'approved' engine was fitted. Hitherto, stalling speed with flaps down had to be no more than 45 mph. This proclamation marked the successful end to protracted representations by the PFA and consultation with the ARB and resulted in the decision to broaden the scope of the scheme under which ultra-light aircraft could be built to simplified airworthiness requirements and qualify for a Permit to Fly instead of a C of A. Amateurs could now consider building two or even three seaters without the enormous expense of a C of A. 'The changes', said the Wallahs of Whitehall, 'are designed primarily to encourage the design and construction of two seater ultra-light aircraft.'

Auster/Beagle A.61 Terrier.

R/1/0/1F	--/--	McCandless M-4 Gyroplane	Single seat gyroplane
M1/3/1F	13/Apr	Auster/Beagle A.61 Terrier	Conversion of the Auster 6B
M1/3/1F	16/Apr	Beagle A.109 Airedale	Four seat Americanised Auster derivative
R1/0/1F	--/Jul	Napier Agricopter	Experimental crop-sprayer derived from Bensen
M1/1/1F	--/Aug	Druine D.62 Condor	First flight of first Rollason-built prototype
R1/0/1F	2/Aug	Wallis WA-116 Agile	Wallis-designed single seat rotorcraft
M1/4/2R	15/Aug	Beagle 206/206S9	Five seat all-metal executive light transport
M1/2/1F	18/Aug	Beagle E.3/A.115	Three seat STOL dev. of Auster Mk.8, sole example G-ASCC

Engines: • None

CHRONOLOGY OF LIGHT AIRCRAFT AND ENGINES

1962

Beagle 206Y (enlarged version of 206).

This year marked the final curtain for two great names in light aircraft manufacturing when, on May 10th, Miles, as Beagle-Miles Aircraft at Shoreham, and Auster, as Beagle-Auster Aircraft at Rearsby, disappeared in the amalgamation under the one heading of Beagle Aircraft Limited. The business was under the chairmanship of M A H Bellhouse, a Pressed Steel Company man. Two deputy chairmen were J R Edwards, another Pressed Steel fellow, and Peter Masefield – the only one of the top echelon to know anything about aircraft. With Masefield at the helm (more or less), the whole thing couldn't (well, shouldn't) go wrong! Could it?

M1/3/2R	17/Feb	Bellamy Hilborne BH.1/Hampshire Halcyon	Damaged in early taxi trials. Unflown
M/1/6/2R	12/Aug	Beagle B.206Y	Enlarged BV.206 G-35-5/G-ARXM
M1/3/2R	19/Aug	Beagle 218X	4 seat executive tourer with retractable u/c
R1/0/1F	30/Aug	Brookland Mosquito Mk.1	Single seat gyrocopter

Engines: • None

1963

France blocked Britain's application to join the EEC and, on January 29th, Britain was officially turned away. On October 18th, Harold Macmillan resigned as PM to be succeeded by Sir Alec Douglas-Home. In commercial and military aviation things were suddenly hotting up! The Ministry of Defence ordered a 100-strong production of our new and outstanding TSR.2 fighter while America's two biggest airlines – Pan Am and TWA – took an option on half a dozen of the world-beating Concorde supersonic airlines – a lead that would shortly be followed by Air India which put its name down for a brace. Everything was starting to go right at last, although the light aircraft scene was still a bit daunting for Beagle who seemed to be spending a lot of money with none of the promised flood of light planes emerging from within the workshop. Up at Rearsby, as the Airedale and Terrier 2 conversion programme came to an end most of the old Auster production lines were swept away and the space allocated to the manufacture of the Beagle 206.

Clutton FRED (Flying Runabout Experimental Design).

M1/0/1F	4/May	Luton LA.4A Minor	First flight of updated pre-war design for amateur building
B1/0/1F	30/Aug	Isaacs Fury Mk. 1/2	Home-built biplane derived from the Curry Wot
M1/0/1F	3/Nov	Clutton FRED	First flight of design for amateur building, choice of engine

Engines: • None

1964

A year after taking office, Alec Douglas-Home resigned as PM and Labour minister Harold Wilson formed a new government with Patrick Gordon Walker as foreign secretary and George Brown as secretary of state for economic affairs. Wilson is remembered for one particular innovation – the creation of a Ministry of Technology under former TGWU leader Frank Cousins: it wasn't much of a ministry with not much of a minister running it. Petrol cost 5/0½ of which almost 60 per cent was tax. The last conversions of Auster 6 to Terrier I and Tugmaster ended in September and the last new Auster-type aircraft to be built was a Beagle Husky, G-ASNC, gaining its C of A on April 23rd. Rather a sad day for the old lags at Rearsby who had been in there at the start of the Taylorcraft high-wingers. Production of the Auster at Rearsby had lasted just over 25 years and in this time a grand total of 3,573 aircraft were turned out. Meanwhile the lightweight autogiro (with its American contraction 'gyrocopter') had arrived here in a big way. Flight using rotating wings gained rapid popularity and resulted in a supporting body The British Rotorcraft Association (BRA for short) being formed to cater for enthusiasts' interest. Quickly designers worked to improve the Bensen concept.

Campbell-Benson Gyrocopter.

| R1/1/1F | --/-- | Campbell-Benson Gyrocopter | Single seat version of US design |
| M1/3/2R | 27/Aug | Beagle B.242X | Scaled-down Beagle B.206 as 4 seat tourer |

Engines: • None

1965

This year was dominated by a mounting balance of payment deficit, the biggest since the war. The devaluation of sterling was unlikely to help this time. It began in October with the introduction of an imports surcharge of 15 per cent as heralding an examination of ways to cut public expenditure. This was reflected in Chancellor Callaghan's crisis Budget of November 11th. This raised National Insurance contributions, the duty on petrol and the promise that Income Tax would rise 'next spring'. It was followed, on November 23rd, by an increase in the Bank Rate to a record seven per cent. On June 13th, Auster Autocrat G-AGVI undertook its first flight as a turboprop aircraft with an experimental installation of a TP.90 Rover Gas Turbine carried out by Vivian Bellamy of the Hampshire Aeroplane Co at Blackbushe. The 118 hp engine gave the already-old Auster a level speed of 115 mph at 2,000 ft at an engine shaft speed of 46,000 rpm and a jetpipe temperature of 625 deg.C. The engine cost around £1,800 and the total cost of converting an existing aircraft was estimated at about £2,500. Fuel consumption was 12 gallons an hour! Meanwhile down at Shoreham things were not so happy and the year got off to a bad start as no real production runs of aircraft materialised. Lots of designs, ideas, plans, projections, but nothing to earn income with. Beagle's rate of expenditure soon outstriped its funds and on Friday February 12th Parliamentary Secretary to the Ministry John Stonehouse announced that the government had stepped in with a grant of £600,000 to assist in the development of the Beagle 206 and 242.

Beagle B.206S

| M1/1/1F | --/Feb | Luton LA.5A Major | First flight of updated pre-war design for amateur building |
| M1/6/2R | 23/Jun | Beagle B.206S | 340 hp R-R Continental-powered light transport |

Engines: • None

1966

This year marked the boom in new-age universities, not just the up-grading of technical colleges (Loughborough) but the formation of green-field establishments (Guildford, Birmingham and Uxbridge) and the creation of 30 new polytechnics. Petrol cost on average 5/5d a gallon. In February the government announced it was to give that £600,000 cash grant to Beagle towards the cost of development and marketing. This same month came the first doubts about the Beagle firm as the *Daily Telegraph* air correspondent suggested a government take-over of the firm was likely following news that the British Motor Corporation had taken over Beagle's owner, Pressed Steel. BMC was said to have told the newspaper it was not interested in producing light aircraft. Beagle MD Peter Masefield said that Beagle had been discussing with the government ways of increasing the company's export potential but it was 'ill-conceived' to see this as a harbinger of a take-over. Masefield also hotly denied *Telegraph* suggestions that Pressed Steel was about to reduce its support for Beagle. On December 12th it was announced by the Minister of Aviation, Frederick Mulley, that the government was to acquire the assets of Beagle for £1m. He told Parliament that: 'Pressed Steel Fisher Ltd, on account of their other commitments, do not wish to retain their interest in the light-aircraft field'. The new development, Parliament was told, should enable Beagle to command an increasing share of the world market. Ah! Those rose-tinted spectacles were out again!

Gowland Jenny Wren

| M1/1/1F | --/-- | Hants & Sussex Rover Chipmunk | One-off gas turbine shown SBAC Show in Sept |
| M1/½/1F | 2/Sep | Gowland GWG.2 Jenny Wren | Homebuilt Luton Minor derivative; extra child seat |

Engines: • None

Beagle B.121 Pup.

1967

On November 18th, sterling was devalued from £=$2.80 to £=$2.40. American goods leapt in price here as a result including imported light aircraft. Petrol prices remained unchanged at 5/5d a gallon but the tax share jumped to more than 66 per cent. The rosy prospects for the Shoreham company soon evaporated (as did the taxpayers' million). Things were not going right for Beagle when, at the end of the year, its attempts to sell fleets of B.206-S aircraft were scuppered. Initially, it seemed certain that substantial contracts had been secured but this was not to be. The first was from the South African Government which had ordered eighteen aircraft for air-sea rescue duty as well as fishery protection duties. This contract was blocked by the American State Department because the Beagles, powered by US-built Continental engines, would be flown by quasi-military pilots and might then be used for internal security operations to enforce apartheid regulations. Britain appealed against this on the grounds that the South African security forces already used fleets of Cessna 182 aircraft. The second hiatus concerned an order for fourteen aircraft for the Argentine Air Force. Here the problem was 'tit for tat' in that we had placed a ban on beef imports because of an outbreak of foot and mouth disease. We couldn't have one without the other. Not for the first time would we find to our cost that orders for one thing would be blocked in strange ways that involved some totally different matter. This was the age of some pretty abstruse political shenanigans. The world of business became ever more convoluted even from within, and obstructions to the rudiments of marketing did not always emanate from overseas: remember that Beagle, a true British company if ever there was one, was regularly excluded from exhibiting at the SBAC's annual Farnborough air show because it used American engines! Some said this was taking 'British-made' a bit too far.

M1/0/1F	4/Jan	Taylor JT-2 Titch	Single seat high-performance homebuilt
R1/1/1F	--/Apr	Gadfly HDW.1	Two seat metal autogyro with spin-up device
M1/0/1F	21/Apr	Rollason-Luton Group Beta	Winner of the Midget Racer Design competition
M1/3/1F	8/Apr	Beagle B.121/150 Pup (B,121)	Low-wing all-metal trainer/tourer; full dual control
M1/0/1F	23/May	Mitchell-Proctor Kittiwake I	Single seat sport & glider-tug home-built
M1/0/1F	20/Jun	Slingsby SE.5A Replica	Replica aircraft for film work
M1/0/1F	4/Aug	Ward Gnome	Non-approved single seat homebuilt

Engines: • None

1968

At the start of January work began on a new factory at Shoreham for the production of Pups. The 60,000 sq.ft extension was to be completed by the summer. Questions asked in Parliament as to how much actual money the government had advanced to Beagle and whether such sums were in the form of grants or loans and if the latter whether interest was payable. The Minister of Technology Mr Wedgwood Benn gave a written Parliamentary answer on February 2nd to questions from Mr Nicholas Ridley who had asked whether the £2.4 million advanced to Beagle as part of the company's capital was a grant or a loan. He stated that the sums were grants, not loans and therefore no interest was payable. Meanwhile Peter Masefield spoke at the British Light Aircraft Centre dinner held in London on February 9th. In a speech responding for the guests, he let it be known that the Pup was attracting great interest and that the first 115 examples would be delivered by the end of the year and that the first production Pup-100 was 'being painted at the weekend'. The Shoreham School of Flying, we learned, was taking delivery of this example so that the makers could check its use in service. Harbingers of a clean sweep of what remained of the old and our heritage, the first decimal-currency coins were issued. But in economic terms we were still in a state of deep distress. In a bold attempt to curb what was seen as an out-of-control increase of consumer spending, on November 1st, the government announced increased restrictions on hire purchase. The minimum deposit on all goods was increased from 33⅓ per cent to 40 per cent and the maximum period for repayment was reduced from 27 months to 24 months. This same month, petrol went up by 5d per gallon eventually hitting an average of 6/2d a gallon. Beagle sold off its last-remaining interests in the former Auster company (meaning after-sales, support and spares) to Hants & Sussex Aviation Ltd at Portsmouth.

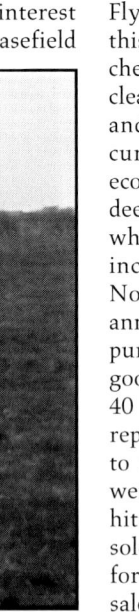

Storey TSR.3.

M1/2/1F	15/Feb	Slingsby Type 49C Powered Capstan	Capstan two seat sailplane with pusher engine
M1/1/1F	--/May	Ord-Hume/Gardan GY-201 Minicab	First British-built example to revised drawings
R1/0/1F	--/Jun	Brookland Mosquito Mk.11	Single seat gyrocopter
M1/0/1F	27/Jul	Storey TSR.3	Racing homebuilt

Engines: • None

1969

The government of Prime Minister Harold Wilson was in disarray as once more the country was on the verge of bankruptcy. A hard line on wage increases angered the coal-miners: other unions united workers in all sectors as strikes spread. The economy, analysts told us, is in 'melt-down'. On October 10th a part of British tradition was tossed away as a 50 new pence coin replaced the 10s note. Beagle entered a crucial phase as the government refused to advance more money and the carrot of a 'full order book' did not generate a rush of investors. In response to ever more concerned meetings and arguments, Beagle remained a chronic spender of what were now public funds with no certainty of a date when the flow of cash might be reversed. Any thought of profit was so far into the future that it became an end-of-the-rainbow type of forecast. The company issued an urgent plea to be granted an additional £6m of taxpayer's money for continued development. The Minister of Technology said 'no' several times and on December 2nd put the firm into the hands of an official receiver.

Campbell Cricket.

M1/3/1F	17/May	Britten-Norman BN-3 Nymph	US-style tourer for low-cost production. Only one made
M1/2/1F	19/May	Beagle B.125 Bulldog	Military version of Pup suitable upgraded
M1/0/1F	14/Jun	Jodel D.9 Bébé	First British-built example first flight
R1/0/1F	July	Campbell Cricket	Single seat gyrocopter
R/1/3/2F	18/Aug	Cierva CR. LTH-1 Grasshopper 3	Four seat helicopter, twin engines, contra-rotating rotors
M1/0/2F	20/Sep	Slingsby/Osbourn Twin Cadet	Twin-engined single seat conversion of Cadet glider

Engines: • 130 h.p. Rolls-Royce/Continental O-240-A (British developed)

1970

The British public voted a weak Labour government out of power and on June 19th a shattered and demoralised Harold Wilson was replaced by a Conservative administration led by amateur yachtsman Edward Heath with Sir Alex Douglas-Home as Foreign Secretary and Reginald Maudling as Home Secretary. Britain was promised 'better times ahead' as Scottish Aviation took over production of the Bulldog as Beagle was wound up. Our last light plane industry hopes faded. The discovery of oil in the North Sea by British Petroleum was heralded as a major discovery and an economic boost, for it was proclaimed we might be independent from Middle East oil and price cartels and become self-sufficient. Petrol remained the 'cash cow' for the government with the average price per gallon now 6/6½ of which government took a whopping 67.5

Jodel D.11.

per cent in tax. We were promised low-cost fuel now that we were on the road to becoming independent of Arab-dominated cartels as regards oil and petrol. There were said to be 293 television receivers per thousand population in Britain as well as 15 million cars on our roads. We were admitted to the European Union and joined the Common Market. No cash or incentive, though, for industry of any sort.

M1/1/1F	--/--	Pilot Sprite	All-metal side-by-side two seater (not flown until 16/6/76)
R1/1/1F	5/Apr	Penn-Smith Gyroplane	Derived from Bensen design
M1/1/1F	27/Nov	Jodel D.11	First flight of first British-built example

Engines: • None

1971

The year started with a national postal strike, Ford ceased car production in Britain and we said goodbye to pounds, shillings and pence as we 'went decimal'. Heath's promised 'better times' would ultimately result in more strikes, more wage freezes and culminate, later, in the so-called 'three-day week' with massive restraints in the use of electricity. Britain returned to the wax candle as a means of domestic (and some office) lighting. With the passing of the familiar we conceded defeat to other light plane-building nations. Slingsby Sailplanes began production of its first powered aircraft.

M1/1/1F	8/Feb	Slingsby Motor Falke	First flight of Slingsby-built prototype
M1/0/1F	24/Aug	Lockspeiser Land Development Aircraft	Scale model of larger machine
M1/1/1F	10/Oct	Shield Xyla	Home-built two seater

Engines: • None

The first production Autocrat was a more familiar shape and amongst the earliest customers was the Elstree-based United Services Flying Club which had several examples right from the beginning including this one, G-AGXJ. The aircraft passed seamlessly into the ownership of Elstree Flying Club when the USFC was disbanded and reformed under the new name.

CHAPTER NINE
The Makers of Post War Light Aircraft

At the time when private aviation was allowed to re-start in 1946, the number of significant manufacturers of light aircraft was exactly three – Auster Aircraft Ltd, Miles Aircraft Ltd, and Percival Aircraft Ltd. Others with wartime engagement in sub-contracting, doubled this number. In the few years that followed, a couple more were added to the clique. It was hardly a giant industry. It has already been explained how the possibility of a return to the pre-war style of activities was hobbled by the super-abundant austerity that affected every aspect of life.

There remained the chronic shortage of parts, materials, even basic tools. Manufacturing itself had changed. The old labour-intensive days of skilled woodwork no longer equated with the high-speed production methods that wartime production had forced industry to adopt and adapt to. The aircraft industry had changed almost out of all recognition. As much as anything else, it was a faster place and speed of manufacture – the one characteristic that had underpinned the immense growth of the light aircraft industry in America during the 1930s – was seen as the cornerstone of any revival of manufacture.

Most raw materials were either not available or were rationed by suppliers. Permits from the government's Board of Trade were still required before the purchase of wood, steel and many finished goods. The old wartime adage that supplies were curtailed 'for the duration' were replaced with the wryly humorous response 'don't you know there's a peace on?' Foreign engines could not be bought on the open market because of the currency restrictions and British-made engines were in short supply and very expensive.

The austerity that affected every aspect of life thus hit hardest at those industries where specialist materials and supplies were most in use and among these the most sensitive was light aircraft. The shortages were selective, though. Some materials, such as dope and, to a certain extent, fabric, were readily available because the firms that produced them had been engaged full-time in war-production of the same material. Turnbuckles, stranded flexible control cable and AGS (Aircraft General Spares) parts like nuts and bolts, were freely available, mostly through yacht chandlers who had bought up very large quantities: people taking up sailing used these parts extensively on small boats.

Such availability did not apply, though, to small-sized wheels and tyres, low-reading light plane-suitable instruments and associated equipment, virtually none of which could be made available for the civil market simply because suitable products were not in production. Military aircraft wheels and tyres, for example, were not suitable for small aircraft while cockpit instruments were similarly unsuitable for aircraft which operated at the lower end of airspeed and altitude. Fortunately, a restricted number of suitable instruments had been produced for gliders and enthusiasts trawled the market for the limited surplus items.

Of course, there were some exceptions: airspeed indicators and altimeters for Tiger Moths, for instance, could be acquired as 'surplus' goods, but they were not what one might call elegant dials for civil use. The instrument-makers were keen to develop marketing opportunities but this was achieved at a price. It was for this reason that Taylorcraft Austers were produced with plastic throttle control knobs: they were cheap and easy to make 'on site' using contemporary saucepan-lid-knob technology. It was truly a period of 'make-do-and-mend' when it came to putting an aircraft together.

These conditions had an affect on those who may have been moved to start or re-start aircraft building. Those that tried suffered an uphill battle of paperwork none of which was straightforward and all of which seemed to be in triplicate (the use of carbon-paper for copying not being allowed, of course).

One subtle change from the 1930s was the much wider use of welding. Once an almost elitist and expensive technique, gas welding was now considered a common replacement for the skills of aircraft carpentry. Where woodwork remained the order of the day, the increasing use of synthetic resin glues, quite unheard of in the 'thirties, ousted the ever-popular (but non-gap-filling) caseins while an increasing application of glass fibre and epoxy-resin use offered manufacturing advantages that were both new and exciting.

Some noted manufacturers of the pre-war years did not survive the outbreak of peace. Among these many makers that disappeared for one reason or another were Redwing Aircraft (who became jig, tool and component manufacturers or contract builders to firms like Planet, while abandoning their own complete light plane construction), General Aircraft and, to a major extent, de Havilland.

There was no shortage of ideas, though, and an increasing number of companies established themselves as aircraft manufacturers. These extended from enterprises such as Elliotts of Newbury and Chrislea, both long-term businesses in the aviation world, through overtly enthusiastic business concerns like Rollasons, down to small and even one-man concerns. It was this latter sector that began to dominate the British light aircraft scene as the decades advanced.

Along the way there were several monumental disappointments such as the Planet Satellite and the Tawney Owl. Of these the former was a high-profile failure since so many personalities were involved and much investors' money was lost. The latter represented the opposite end of the scale but because it was quietly built and actually did fly (which the Satellite barely did), its failure was more a disappointment than a huge disaster. These individual type histories are recorded in Chapter Eleven. Because the failures were as important historically as the successful machines, those that built them are accorded a space in history.

With the disappearance of Auster, then Miles and finally Beagle, our light plane heritage gradually ebbed away. It transferred from the world of business and finance to return to one where enthusiasts once more reigned. It was left almost entirely in the hands of the private or amateur sector. As time would tell, this was not a bad thing for in the hands of the small operator light aircraft flourished and was soon of such strength and magnitude that it was able to self-sustain. Foreign aircraft were imported at one end of the scale, and enthusiasts built their own light planes at the other end.

These, then, are the names of the people who designed and built the last 'commercial' light aeroplanes through the quarter-century that is covered by this present volume. Be advised that some enterprises, as with the designs and projects covered elsewhere, tend to straddle the arbitrary cut-off date of 1970. Do not be surprised, therefore, to find references to enterprises that reached fruition (or failure) a few years outside that date. The criterion is that they were conceived generally no later than 1970.

Aerogypt High Speed Development Company Ltd,

Caxton Street, London, SW1.

Founded in 1945 by Eqyptian-born Saleh Helmy to develop his pre-war light aircraft design, now known as the Aerogypt IV. Helmy's operation was based at White Waltham Aerodrome near Maidenhead, Berkshire. On June 6th 1947 a new company, Helco (England) Ltd, was registered as a private company with £500 start-up capital to operate as importers, exporters and manufacturers &c of aircraft. Directors were Saleh Helmy, Dorothy F Helmy, Anne M L Arkell, Gordon B Cockell and Ethel May Cockell. The registered office was Helmy's home, Barn House, Cherry Gardens Lane, Maidenhead. On November 26th 1947 Helmy and his wife Dorothy (who was also a pilot) embarked on a flight from White Waltham to Egypt with a first stop at nearby Northolt to clear Customs. On the approach the aircraft snagged a wire of the perimeter fence and was badly damaged in the ground impact that followed. A Coles aircraft lifting crane was summoned to raise the damaged machine but at a height of ten feet, the cable broke, dropping the aircraft hard and resulting in damage that rendered it beyond repair. Helmy went on to become UK representative of Misr Egyptian Airlines and remained at his UK home at Maidenhead Thickett where the remains of his aircraft were stored in the open.

Airmark Ltd,

Water Lane, Storrington, Pulborough, Sussex,
also Redhill, Surrey.

With a London address at 1, Stewart's Grove, SW3, Airmark Ltd was created as a private company early in 1969 with directors D A Hood and K Platt and Thomas M Storey as managing. Initially the business was concerned with certification of the Wallis WA-117 autogyro but by 1970 had acquired all rights in Tom Storey's TSR.3 racing monoplane which it manufactured. With the hope of introducing American-style Formula I air-racing into the UK, the business acquired the European agency for plans and kits for the Cassutt single seat racing monoplane. Designed by a Trans World Airlines' captain, Tom Kenneth Cassutt (1917-2015) of Huntington Station, New York, in 1954 and improved over subsequent years, three slightly modified examples called the Cassutt 3M were produced by the company between 1969 and 1972. These were powered by a 90 hp Continental C-90-8F engine and the first made its debut at the Goodyear Trophy Race held at Halfpenny Green on September 1st 1969. The company seems to have disappeared after 1972.

Airmaster Helicopters Ltd,

c/o Bering Ltd, Doman Road, Camberley, Surrey.

During 1970, D J Fry designed and built what was described as the smallest, smallest, simplest lowest-cost two seat helicopter possible. Designated the Airmaster H2-B1, it was registered G-AYNS on December 21st 1970 and subsequently made its first flight thirteen months later in January 1972. In 1971 a company called Airmaster Helicopters Ltd was established to develop the machine but nothing further materialised and the business faded.

Auster Aircraft Ltd,

Britannia Works, Thurmaston, Leicester, *[then]* Rearsby Aerodrome, Leicester *also with* works at Syston and Thurmaston, Leicestershire.

Developed from the original British company, Taylorcraft Aeroplanes (England) Ltd, which was formed on November 21st 1938 at Thurmaston, Leicester for the licence-manufacture of the American-designed Taylorcraft Model B light aircraft. Production began at Thurmaston in February of 1939 and the first British Taylorcraft Plus Model C, flew for the first time at Ratcliffe (the one-time privately-owned Leicester

Airmark began operations in 1969 with certifying the Wallis WA-117 autogyro seen here.

aerodrome) on May 3rd 1939. With the outbreak of war, a modified version of this design was selected as the AOP aircraft for the RAF who gave the Taylorcraft monoplane the name 'Auster'. This machine and its subsequent developments were used throughout the war on every front in Europe and the Far East. The pre-war activities of the Taylorcraft business are related in Ord-Hume [37]. It was towards the end of the war that, on April 14th 1944, company founder Alexander Lance Wykes and company chief test pilot Geoff Edwards were killed during an Army demonstration of an AOP Auster at Abbey Park, Leicester. After the war, military Austers were also used operationally in Palestine, Korea, Malaya, Kenya, Cyprus and Aden. Taylorcraft returned to the production of civil aircraft in 1945 and changed the name of the business from Taylorcraft Aeroplanes Ltd to Auster Aircraft Ltd on March 7th 1946 at the same time shifting its principal factory to Rearsby Aerodrome. The registered capital was £15,000 and in February 1947 this was increased by £45,000. Directors were: Frank Bates (managing), Percival Wykes (chairman), Ken Sharp (works director), A J Pickering and F A Pratley. Sales manager was J Lester Pendleton, chief designer R F Davis, test pilot (until 1946) Geoffrey Edwards who was succeeded in that June by George Norman Snarey. Previously he had been pre-war assistant test pilot to Westland Aircraft. Born on April 4th 1907, Snarey had served as second test pilot to Westlands between 1938 and 1940 and had been a production test pilot for Vickers Supermarine on, among others, the Spitfire. He left in 1948 and was replaced by Ranald Porteous. From 1947 onwards, chief designer was Ronald Edward Bird who was appointed a director in 1957. The company set up an eight-strong team of nationwide distributors, a move which probably marked a first for any British light aircraft company (see advert in Flight, March 7th 1946, pp.ii). In October 1960, Auster Aircraft Ltd was absorbed by Beagle Aircraft Ltd and Auster's current designs dual-masted for a time as 'Beagle-Auster' aircraft. The Beagle-Auster tie remained until 1962 when the Auster name was suppressed. Beagle's production at Rearsby continued but Beagle's losses associated with its factory at Shoreham and its production and development of Pup and Bulldog aircraft eventually caused the receivership and closure of the whole enterprise in 1970.

Aviation Traders Ltd,

21, Wigmore Street, London W1.

Private company registered October 17th 1947 with £100 initial share capital for the purpose of acting as merchants and distributors and agents for aircraft. Directors: Frederick Alfred Laker (1922-2006) and Alfred L Hughes. This business gave rise to Aviation Traders (Engineering) Ltd of Southend Airport, Essex. This latter business was a private company registered on March 15th 1949 with a £5,000 initial capital. Its purpose was the design, manufacture and production of aircraft. Directors were F A Laker, Mrs Joan M Laker, Myles Dermot Norris Wyatt (chairman and MD of Airwork Ltd), and R L Cumming. Other executives were John Robert Batt (sales director), Eric Church and John Loader. In 1956 this company acquired a huge quantity of Percival P.40 Prentice trainers from the Royal Air Force and placed them on the civil register – the largest block of aircraft types ever to appear on the register. The plans to convert these machines for civil use occupied the company for several years. Among the duties planned were club trainer, private owner, light freight and agricultural dusting/spraying: for one reason or another it was unsuited to any of these. Of the total of 253 aircraft, only 28 were found a buyer and the rest were broken up either at Stansted or Southend: an expensive end to a largely futile plan.

Beagle-Auster Aircraft Limited,

see under Auster Aircraft Ltd,
also Beagle

Beagle (British Executive and General Aviation Ltd).

Sceptre House, 1269 Regent Street, London WI,
also Rearsby Aerodrome, nr, Leicester,
also Shoreham Airport, Shoreham-by-Sea, Sussex.

The formation of what was first described as BEAGLE was announced on Friday, October 7th 1960 in a form that was guaranteed to stimulate something. The new firm was solidly guaranteed by the Pressed Steel Co Ltd, makers of motor car bodies, railway rolling stock and refrigerators. Earlier that year the business had taken over the lease of Oxford Airport at Kidlington. The entire share capital of Auster Aircraft had been acquired by the new BEAGLE and with it that maker's experience of over 20 years of light aircraft manufacture. In recent times, and despite being a full member of the SBAC, that company's dependence on American-made engines rather than British motors had debarred them from giving their usual Farnborough demonstrations. The technical and manufacturing liaison arranged with F G Miles Ltd offered a virtual guarantee to the forward-thinking of the design team. And, as managing director, Peter Gordon Masefield, former MD of Bristol Aircraft Ltd, was an obvious choice. While no designs were immediately revealed, there was no doubt that the new firm would be challenging markets presently dominated

Auster J/5B Autocar first registered March 28th 1952.

by makers based in Wichita, Lock Haven and Bethany. Masefield foresaw 'a good opportunity of being able to sell into the States'. Described as a subsidiary of the Pressed Steel Co Ltd, it was created to design and manufacture a new range of executive and light aircraft for the home and export markets. Discussions were in hand with Rolls-Royce with a view to the production of a series of power-plants. Chairman of BEAGLE was Michael Alexander Hamilton Bellhouse, deputy chairman of Pressed Steel. Born in 1906 he was an ex-RAF man with education at Oundle and Magdalen, Oxford. Also from the Pressed Steel board was Joseph Robert Edwards, P S's managing director. Auster's managing director Frank Bates was also on the board initially along with Peter Wright Brooks. George H Miles was to be technical director of a co-ordinating board formed under the chairmanship of Peter Masefield. It was announced that development of the Auster line of aircraft would continue but with the greater financial backing of Pressed Steel and therefore at a greater rate. Pressed Steel was not new to aviation and besides owning Kidlington Aerodrome operated several business aircraft in order to liaise between the company's five factories in the British Isles. In the past the company had also made aircraft components including complete Hunter rear fuselages. From the moment of foundation, Auster Aircraft Ltd became Beagle-Auster Ltd, and F G Miles Ltd became Beagle-Miles Ltd. On May 10th 1962 British Executive and General Aviation Ltd formed a subsidiary company called simply Beagle Aircraft Ltd which absorbed the two subsidiary companies, Beagle-Auster and Beagle-Miles. The duties of deputy chairman were now divided between Masefield and Edwards. Two other executives, commercial director Sir Mark Norman and sales director Wg-Cmdr Tim Vigors, resigned at this point. Back in mid-October 1960, the chairman of Pressed Steel Co Ltd, Alexander Abel-Smith, had claimed that the BEAGLE Group intended to produce a 4/5 seater executive aircraft to sell at 'around £25,000'. Later that month George Miles stated that, following his appointment to the Beagle board, planning was now going forward on the basis of technical partnership between the company and the group and future activities are being worked out, 'any project that involves the design or construction of aircraft is essentially a continuing process – especially when it also involves the development of new business partnerships within a group with such objectives as this. The technical relationship between ourselves and BEAGLE, for instance, must necessarily be different from that between BEAGLE and Auster, the whole of whose share capital was acquired by the group. Obviously the close working relationships which are envisaged in future will be to the benefit both of F G Miles as a company, and of its employees.' Clearly Miles was taking steps to emphasise the difference between his own company's involvement and that of Auster. The announcement at the beginning of November 1960 that Rolls-Royce Ltd had acquired a licence for the manufacture of Continental piston engines in the UK from Continental Motors Corp of Muskegon, Michigan was very much tied in to the Beagle deal. R-R's chief executive and deputy chairman, Sir James Denning Pearson said that the production of Continental engines would take place in the company's Crewe factory where a newly-formed Light Aircraft Engine Department was being set up under John P Herriot who had been chief development engineer on the early Whittle turbojets. Rolls-Royce-built Continental engines would be installed in Beagle Executive and Auster/Beagle aircraft. As the year wore on there were conflicting reports of what might be emerging from the new company and stories of a five seater costing £25,000 were adjusted to a 4-5 seater at about £20,000. The company asserted its activities were not confined to one type or specification of aircraft and that neither prices nor seating capacity had been finalised. The design team, said Beagle, was still being formed and the company was not in a position to say more. Meanwhile the rumours and counter rumours continued and the company began leaking its own rumours. The Pressed Steel plant at Linwood in Renfrewshire, it was hinted, might be making components for Beagle aircraft while Peter Masefield stated early in November 1960 that: 'We have not yet got to the extent of deciding production arrangements but I think it is possible that components might be produced at Linwood. The prospect of building and assembling in Scotland is not likely'. Linwood at that time was producing parts for Rover cars. Matters took a fresh turn soon afterwards. At the end of November 1960 arrangements were concluded for the acquisition of F G Miles Ltd of Shoreham Airport, Sussex. At the same time it was announced that 44-year-old Ronald James Brabant Woodhams had been appointed chief designer. He had been with Bristol Aeroplane Co for five years and prior to that he was with Air Service Training Ltd. However, he didn't last long: by 1965 Thomas D R Carroll was chief designer and chief engineer. In 1966, Beagle managing director was Keith Nicholas Myer, a man with a fine background in general engineering and sewing-machines within which industry he had previously run the Singer company. Other directors were Peter G

Beagle A.109, formerly G-25-11. This was the prototype Airedale, first registered, in February 1961. It was withdrawn from use in April 1963.

Beagle B.206C Series 1. It was subsequently sold to Spain as EC-BJF.

Masefield (chairman); Peter Wright Brooks (deputy managing), T N Ritchie, Col F T Davies, E P Hewson, Eric Stanley Greenwood, G C John Larroucau (chief engineer and chief designer), Ian Chinchen (deputy chief designer) and Margaret V Lawrence (company secretary). Chief demonstration pilot was Charles Masefield. By this time its London office was 2 Buckingham Gate, SW1, and it listed its 'works' as being at Shoreham Airport and Rearsby Aerodrome. Company demonstration pilot and salesman was Benn Gunn. It was announced on December 12th 1966 that the British government intended to acquire Beagle Aircraft Ltd to ensure the continuation of a British light aircraft manufacturing industry. An associate company was formed called Beagle Aviation Finance Ltd. At the end of 1969 things began to happen. In 1968, the government bought Beagle lock, stock and barrel from Pressed Steel. At the end of 1968, Beagle Aircraft Ltd sold off its entire interest in Auster aircraft to **Hants & Sussex Aviation Ltd** [qv]. General manager of Beagle's factory at Rearsby, Ambrose V Hitchman, was appointed manager of Hants & Sussex's Auster section. A new marketing director was appointed in the shape of D W Gray who had been European vice-president of Singer Corporation of New York – Keith Myer's old outfit. Beagle now made an urgent plea to receive an additional £6m of taxpayer's money considered necessary for expansion and continued development. The Ministry of Technology declined. The cries for salvation became louder but, following the Ministry of Technology's final decision on December 2nd 1969 not to grant the firm the extra money that it considered necessary for continued development and expansion, the government put the firm into the hands of an official receiver. At that time, Beagle had orders for 397 Pups and 116 Bulldogs of which 276 still had to be delivered. By the start of 1970, things were at tether's end and mid-January there was a flurry of talks with the German company Messerschmitt-Bölkow-Blohm and amid rumours that there was talk of a takeover, the confirmation from Germany that talks were definitely not on plunged the once-great company into the depths of despair. Talks with the Delaney Group, which had earlier expressed some interest, fell through after the company accountants had looked into the figures and concluded that it was very doubtful whether there could be any return on the large investment necessary. In the middle of all this, the company's test pilot, popular J W C 'Pee Wee' Judge, was killed at the Farnborough Air Show demonstrating a Wallis autogyro. Earlier the American group Ling-Temco-Vought, which had expressed some interest in acquiring the firm before a receiver was appointed, had withdrawn when the British government announced its decision not to put any more funds into the business. The increasing reluctance of the government to spend more money on keeping Beagle afloat while possible takeover talks continued meant that the last sands in the hour-glass were about to flow. A certain irony may have been missed by most that fateful January, for one of the reasons why Britain's light aircraft industry was in such a parlous state was the rich and rewarding activity of one American maker – Piper Aircraft Corporation. On January 15th 1970, William Thomas Piper Snr died at Lock Haven, Pennsylvania aged 89. His tenuous connection with Auster (via Taylor) should not go unnoticed. Beagle was subsequently wound up and the Bulldog production project was sold to **Scottish Aviation Ltd** [qv].

Beagle-Miles Aircraft Ltd,

see under Miles Aircraft Ltd,
also Beagle

Botley Aircraft,

7, Winchester Street, Botley,
Nr Southampton, Hampshire.

A small private business founded in 1968 by Dr John Hewlett Brabazon Urmston (b. 1924; d. 2016) who purchased the rights to the Currie Wot ultra-light biplane from Vivian Hampson Bellamy (b. 1919; d. 1998) of the **Hampshire Aeroplane Club Co Ltd** [qv] who himself acquired the design after the war from the original designer, J 'Joe' R Currie. Urmston produced revised and updated drawings for the aircraft and through his work the

1937 design found a fruitful post-war life with a variety of models one of which was the world's smallest turboprop aircraft. Eventually the design rights were passed on to Phoenix Aircraft Ltd before reverting to the Popular Flying Association on the closure of Phoenix.

British Executive & General Aircraft Ltd,

see under Auster Aircraft Ltd, *also* Beagle

Britten-Norman Ltd,

Bembridge Airport, Bembridge, Isle of Wight.

A small company that can trace its origins to 1948, Britten-Norman ultimately became a major manufacturer producing one of Britain's most successful post-war small airliners, the twin-engined BN-2 Islander and, later, the triple-engined Trislander. The company is also remembered for the single seat BN-1F and BN-3 Nymph light aircraft. The business was begun as a partnership between Forester Richard John Britten (1929-1977), eldest son of Col F C R Britten and one-time Isle of Wight Magistrate, and one-time RAF pilot, Nigel Desmond Norman (1929-2002), son of Henry Nigel St Valery Norman, aeronautical consultant and one-time owner and operator, with Alan Muntz, of Airwork Ltd and Heston Airport. Both men had met as students at the de Havilland Aeronautical Technical College, Hatfield. The two began their activities with the design and construction of a single seat ultra-light that was styled the BN-1F. Under the attentive eye of the newly-formed Ultra Light Aircraft Association which hoped it would make a new-generation amateur kit-plane or at least a set of construction plans. The sole example was built for them in the hangar at Bembridge Airport by a local carpenter, Peter Gattrell. The first airframe was badly damaged in early trials and a second fuselage built with a different engine. Through many trials and tribulations this aircraft was not a success. The firm progressed from the garage in the garden of Britten's home, St Denis, Bembridge, to the former Unity Hall, Star Street, Ryde which adjoined the Commodore Cinema, part of a small cinema chain owned by Col Britten and managed by John's brother Robin Colville Britten (1932-1988). Initially the business was involved with the design and manufacture of crop-dusting and spraying apparatus for DH Tiger Moths. Assistant chief designer and production manager was Arthur W J G Ord-Hume. The company designed a then-unique rotary atomiser called the Micronair which came to be made in a number of sizes. In 1955 the firm became a limited-liability company and formed a subsidiary contracting business called Crop Culture (Aerial) Ltd. Encouraged to undertake work in the Sudan, the new business identified a need for a small twin-engined airliner that would cost under £25,000 for short-field, tropical operation. Loosely planned as a Dragon Rapide replacement, a space-saving feature was to be 'char-a-banc'-style seating – full-width bench seats with each seat having its own door at one side, this alternating from side to side with alternate seat rows. Britten-Norman decided to design and build their own and, in January 1964, they decided to go ahead with the construction of a prototype: it was rolled out on June 10th 1965 and was shown at that year's Paris Air Show. By 1968, the directors of the business were Alan Frank Bartlett, F R J Britten, Frank Herbert Mann, James Matthew McMahon, Nigel Desmond Norman, and Walter Oppenheimer. Chief designer was John Allen, replaced two years later by Denis A Berryman. In 1969 the company had a final flirtation with light aircraft, this time the BN-3 Nymph. Built in just 53 days, this all-metal Cessna/Beagle look-alike was a head-to-head design with too many other four seaters and consequently found no market. It was to serve as something of a catalyst in the company's affairs. In the early part of 1970 the company began to experience the inevitable problems of fast growth and a highly successful product but insufficient capital: in 1971 Britten-Norman Ltd went into receivership. On November 23rd 1971 a new company was formed called Britten-Norman (Bembridge) Ltd with directors that included John Britten, Desmond Norman and Maurice 'Monty' Eckman of Price Waterhouse, the Receiver. In August 1972, The Fairey Co Ltd acquired the whole of the share capital of the business for approximately £4.1 million. The business, without its founders, was now absorbed by the Fairey Group becoming affiliated to Fairey SA at Gosselies in Belgium. After Fairey itself went into receivership in 1977, the Britten-Norman assets were transferred by January 1979 to the Swiss company, Pilatus Flugzeugwerke. Shortly before his death from leukaemia aged just 49 in 1977, John Britten (who was appointed High Sheriff of the Isle of Wight in 1976) designed another light aircraft, aptly called the Sheriff and designed as a cheap twin-engined trainer. Co-founding director Desmond Norman went on to undertake a number of projects in aviation none of which proved totally successful. Popular publicity manager for the company in its hey-days of the late 1960s-early 1970s was R M J (Mike) Straw, killed in a road accident near Guildford November 1st 1974.

Brookland Rotorcraft Ltd.

Run by Brian R Luesley and R E Luesley, this business succeeded that of **E Brooks** (*see next entry*) and produced the Brookland Hornet in 1969. Later the same year the business changed its name to Gyroflight Ltd with C Golightly as managing director and Brian Luesley as test pilot and project manager. The premises were at Dean and Chapter, Ferryhill, Co Durham, and the company produced a machine called the Gnat, a rotorcraft glider in which basic training could be provided. Following the death of Brian Luesley in June 1970, the business became dormant.

E Brooks,

Brookland Garage, Coulson Street, Spennymoor, Co. Durham.

Ernest Brooks began by converting a Volkswagen engine to power his Druine Turbulent (G-APOL) and then, in 1960, he began the development of an ultra-light gyroplane fitted with the VW motor. This was the Brookland Mosquito. On March 9th 1969 while flight-testing an example of this aircraft (G-AVYW) at Tees-side Airport, Darlington, the machine crashed killing its 30-year-old designer. He had just begun limited production of the Mosquito at his Spennymoor premises. Following this set-back, production was continued and a new company set up called **Brookland Rotorcraft Ltd.** One example of the Mk.3 Mosquito was known as the Gyroflight Hornet.

Campbell Aircraft Ltd,

Everland Road, Hungerford,
also Membury Airfield, Lambourn, Newbury, Berkshire.

Founded in 1959 by Donald Campbell (known then as 'the Glider Doctor'), S J Bartram and N Campbell for the purpose of acquiring the UK rights to American-designed Bensen autogyros. Besides building complete Gyrocopters and Gyrogliders (Bensen terminology), the firm also sold sets of drawings and kits of parts. Its own version was called the Campbell-Bensen B-88 Gyrocopter, the prototype (G-ASPX) being delivered early in 1964. On November 4th 1967, Don Campbell lost his life in the crash of an Iberia Caravelle airliner, EC-BDD, which flew into Black Down Hill, Fernhurst, Surrey, in fog killing all on board. As a result, the business was re-structured by Don's brother John Campbell and Jeremy Metcalfe. During 1968, Campbell Aircraft produced 'a slightly more refined version' of the Bensen which it called the CB.8S. The first machine, registered on February 26th 1968 as G-AWDW, claimed to be 'the cheapest rotating wing machine in the world' with a fly-away price of £1,250, a kit of parts for £880, or as a glider for £232. By 1969 the company had undergone a change of ownership in partnership with Montague Curzon-Herrick who injected 85 per cent of the capital. The board now comprised A M W Curzon-Herrick (chairman), Jeremy P Metcalfe (managing and sales director) and Geoffrey Whatley with C G Harwood as secretary. The company product had moved sufficiently far from Bensen's original to warrant a different name: the product was now the Campbell Cricket single seat autogyro designed by Peter Lovegrove and the construction of the prototype (G-AXNU) started in June 1969, the first flight being made that November. At the same time a two seat cabin machine called the Curlew was designed and a mock-up of the prototype (G-AXFJ) was shown at the Paris Air Show in May, 1969: the actual aircraft was never completed. Other projects were postulated including a version of the Cricket for crop-spraying, but these failed to materialise. Later the company built a two seater called the Cougar (G-BAPS). Later the business closed but a subsequent firm called Campbell Gyroplanes Ltd appeared as did Leyzell Gyroplanes Ltd briefly.

Chilton Aircraft Ltd,

Hungerford, Berkshire.

The business was formed in 1936, by Alexander Reginald Ward (1915-1987) and the The Hon William Henry Andrew Dalrymple (1914-1945), for the design and construction of light aircraft and gliders: the pre-war activities are described in an earlier book *[37]*. The firm re-started after the war and it was projected to revive two 1939 designs that war had caused to be postponed, one being the two seat cabin monoplane (which was almost complete when work had to be stopped) and a light five seat twin-engined cabin monoplane. The company's prospects changed dramatically when Dalrymple lost his life in a curious accident that occurred on Christmas Day, 1945, on the family estate (and aerodrome) at Hungerford. With Chilton's test pilot Dennis Phillips, he was flying a Fieseler Storch that had been brought over from Germany. Structural failure occurred; watchers saw the starboard wing break away soon after take-off. Both men lost their lives in the subsequent crash. It was said afterwards that, knowing defeat was imminent, some German aircraft engineers had anticipated that a number of aircraft would be captured by their enemies and with this in mind had sabotaged certain aircraft so that eventually in-flight failure would take place. On June 5th 1946 the company was re-structured as **Chilton Aircraft Co Ltd**, capital £5,000 and directors listed as A R Ward and P F F Bush. By 1948, Ward described himself as owner and managing director. Although the company was involved for a time in glider manufacture (which it contracted to Elliotts of Newbury Ltd *[qv]*, it never regained a position in the post-war light aircraft scene and eventually moved into domestic electrical goods under the name Chilton Electronics Ltd.

Chrislea Aircraft Co Ltd,

Heston Airport, Hounslow, Middlesex.

This company was originally formed as The Chrislea Aircraft Co Ltd on October 2nd 1936 for the design and manufacture of light aircraft. The directors were Richard Constantine Christoforides of 12 Warrington Crescent, London W9, Bernard Victor Leak and E H Jacobs. Co-founder Leak was born on May 27th 1907, was apprenticed to Boulton & Paul,

worked for Handley Page, then went to America and joined Taylor Aircraft of Bradford, later to become Piper Aircraft. Returning to England he was successively with Westland Aircraft, Vickers and de Havilland before becoming director and chief engineer for Chrislea. On the outbreak of war, Leak served in America on the British Air Commission after which he joined Folland Aircraft as chief designer but died in his fortieth year on October 18th 1947. Richard Christoforides was of Turkish origin and was born on April 14th 1915. Educated at Bradfield College, his home was in Devon but he had a London address at 37, Crooked Usage, the unusually-named road in Finchley. The Chrislea premises were a small shared workshop off Mornington Crescent, Camden Town, North London. It was here that the little Mikron-engined Chrislea Airguard was built. With the outbreak of war the company made small components for aircraft, predominantly the Fairey Swordfish. In 1940 the firm took over part of the Acme Furniture Company's premises at 77 Fortess Road, Kentish Town, NW5, where it remained for the rest of the war years. Here a 60-hour 6-day working week was established producing parts for, among others, the Bristol Beaufighter. Early in 1944, Richard Christoforides began design work on a light aircraft. Believing that the war must end soon and, anticipating an immediate demand for a light plane, he opened a small additional workshop where a wooden mock-up of the cabin of what would be the CH.3 Chrislea Ace was made. A lathe was modified for the purpose of accurately cutting the angles of steel tubing for the fuselage. Remarkably, advertisements for the Ace first appeared in December 1944 from

Fortess Road advertising the machine as 'a full four seater' with an 'approximate' selling price of £475. Immediately the war ended six months later, the company moved into one of the Airwork hangars at Heston Airport where, in February 1946, construction of the Ace began in earnest with the assistance of a former Miles Aircraft man Ralph Marshall as designer. Directors at this time included J W Hick and E E Christoforides. On May 17th 1947 a new private company was registered as Chrislea Aircraft Co Ltd (no preceding definite article) with a £1,000 capital. While first director was still Christoforides, the other directors were named as Joseph Green and Aubrey A Green. Test pilot for Chrislea (1946-1948) was Rex F Stedman previously test pilot to Blackburn Aircraft throughout the war years and who had, while a member of the Bradford & County Gliding Club in 1933, designed and built a novel and elegant two seat sailplane which he called *City of Leeds* (first flown Baildon, July 21st 1934; BGA 213). The Ace was a curiously attractive light aircraft fitted with a tricycle undercarriage. Subsequent versions known as Super Ace and Skyjeep never matched the simple and pleasing lines of the prototype. A novel and unconventional control system created sales resistance and eventually forced a change to a more normal type. Needing more space for production and aware of the imminent closure of Heston Aerodrome, by the end of 1947 the company transferred its operations to Exeter Airport, Clyst Honiton. On May 10th 1947 the company changed its name to Beam Aircraft Co Ltd, but continued to be known as Chrislea Aircraft Co By the summer of 1948 the firm was experiencing difficulties, announcing, in July, that 'shortage of raw materials and components' was the reason why the factory was closing down for two months and adding, darkly, 'home and export orders will be affected'. The possible reasons for those 'material shortages' came a little clearer when, on July 21st, the business held a meeting with its creditors to submit details of a scheme centred on a six-month moratorium on its debts to enable it to complete the aircraft work that was presently on hand. It took the opportunity to state that 'the various Ministries concerned had sponsored the manufacture of the Chrislea Ace and loaned an American engine for the prototype. A request for an import licence for more than 12 engines was however refused. As a result

Chrislea CH.3 Super Ace 2 first registered March 8th 1948.

of this, the production programme was set back by a substantial period'. It went on to cite as a further factor an order received from Spain for six aircraft that May only for their clients to be denied the necessary import licence and sterling'. Presumably to boost their plea for their creditors to hold back, three weeks later photographs were released showing a line-up of nine Super Ace aircraft 'ready for delivery' with the advice that 'as soon as the material supply position improves it is hope to put the next batch in hand'. Apparently overseas interest, particularly from Commonwealth and South American countries, had been encouraging. Staff were now dispensed with, one of the first to go being test pilot Rex Stedman. In September 1949, Christoforides, managing director and chief designer, left the company following drastic but necessary economies due to slack sales. A new board of directors took over in 1950 comprising Eric A Doran (managing), A A Green and J Green with senior executives named as R F Marshall (chief designer) and Donald Lowry (sales, publicity manager and test pilot), and C A L Morton (chief inspector). In January 1951 it registered a capital increase of £9,000 over its registered capital of £1,000. Unfortunately the company did not survive for much longer and later that year the assets of the Chrislea company were acquired by C E Harper and the company name was changed to C E Harper Aircraft Company Ltd on October 18th – and a receiver was appointed. Lowry resigned on August 1st 1951. All partly-constructed aircraft, comprising seven Super Ace and two Skyjeep machines, were then scrapped. Christoforides subsequently returned to the West London area where, in 1955, he was operating a business at 292, Worton Road, Isleworth, called Jarc Motors Ltd trying to develop a lightweight utility vehicle using a vertically-mounted 250 cc Excelsior Talisman engine in the centre: he called it the 'Little Horse' and it was priced at £347.16s. He died in 1967.

Cierva Autogiro Co Ltd,

Southampton Airport, Southampton, Hampshire.

The Cierva Autogiro Company was formed on March 24th 1926 and the firm's pre-war activities have already been related *[37]*. After the Second World War, the directors were Air Commodore James George Weir (chairman), the Hon Hugh Kenyon Molesworth Kindersley (who was also managing director of bankers Lazard Brothers as well as a director of Whitehall Trust), Colonel John Josselyn as managing director, succeeded later by Cyril George Pullin (managing and chief designer). Chief mechanical engineer was Ken Watson (formerly with J G Weir), senior technical officer Jacob S Shapiro and head of design and stress Harold Bolas (who coined the saying 'all problems are soluble in beer'). Cierva's post-war activities centred on two helicopters, one being among the largest in the world (the W.11 Air Horse) and the other being one of the smallest. This was the two seat Skeeter intended as a low-cost vehicle for the club and private flyer. Planned to sell at around £3,000, it was powered by the 106 hp Jameson engine but early tests proved that it was underpowered. A second example was built fitted with a 145 hp Gipsy Major 10 engine. Very different from the prototype, this was a satisfactory flyer but it suffered from ground-resonance problems that ultimately resulted to its destruction on the ground. By now it was also clear that the hoped-for civil market for the Skeeter would not materialise and, following the fatal accident to the Air Horse (in which company test pilot Henry Alan Marsh was killed), the Cierva company wound down. In January 1951 the firm ceased operations as an independent company. The business was bought by Saunders-Roe (Saro) as a diversification from its waterborne projects and on the understanding with the Ministry of Supply that it would take on and complete the Skeeter programme. Saro duly continued with the Skeeter programme but now it was directed at Service use with trials for the Royal Navy. Ground resonance plagued the design and test pilot Ken Reed was severely injured in another instance of on-ground disintegration. Saunders-Roe funded research and development to remedy this short-coming, eventually succeeding. The later models of the Skeeter were highly successful, serving as trainers with the Army Helicopter Training Flight. The Skeeter's success was, unfortunately, long after Cierva had ceased to be involved and that was far from the original plan that it should be a private aircraft. *See also:*

Cierva W.14 Skeeter 1 prototype powered by a Jameson engine.

Cierva Rotorcraft Ltd,

South Block, Redhill Aerodrome, Surrey.

On August 15th 1965 it was announced that 'The Cierva Autogyro [sic] Co Ltd' had changed its name to Cierva Rotorcraft Ltd having purchased the share capital of **Rotorcraft Ltd** [qv]. Claiming lineal descent from the original Cierva Autogiro Co, the curious spelling may actually have been no more than a careless piece of PR by Informat, the Piccadilly-based agency that handled the announcement. Certainly those behind the new firm comprised several members of the original Cierva Autogiro Co Ltd. This brought together the resources of Rotorcraft and the management and brains of Cierva. The directors were Air Cmdr James George Weir (chairman), A G Douglas, Jacob S 'Yasha' Shapiro (technical director & former chief technical officer of Cierva Autogiro Co), G R L Weir (commercial director and company secretary). Shapiro (b. Poland, November 3rd 1911; d. London, May 1983 aged 71), then described as a consulting engineer, was also MD of ServoTec Ltd as well as having been a director of Rotorcraft. The new company designed a machine called the CR.LTH-1, a 5 seat twin-engined helicopter and this, registered G-AWRP on October 14th 1968, first flew in August 1969. Shown at the SBAC Show, Farnborough, 1970, first production aircraft were planned to appear during 1972. The project was abandoned.

Eric Clutton, 92, Newlands Street,

Shelton, Stoke-upon-Trent, Staffordshire

Originally a high school teacher in Stoke-on-Trent, Eric Clutton designed and built, with the aid of Ernest Sherry, a single seat ultra-light aircraft that he called FRED (Flying Runabout Experimental Design). The six-year project culminated with a first flight at Meir Airfield in November 1963. Over the following years numerous engine installations were tried and the aircraft progressively evolved, removable wings replaced by foldable. In mid-1967 Mr Sherry left the partnership, his place in the team being taken by Albert Tabenor. At various times the names **Clutton-Sherry** and **Clutton-Tabenor** were associated with the FRED and sets of plans were issued for amateur construction under the various forms of Clutton. In recent years, Mr Clutton has retired and emigrated to the United States where he lives in Tennessee. The original FRED followed him and is still flying regularly around his home, 913, Cedar Lane, Tullahoma, TN 37388.

Clutton FRED with wings folded and attached to a motocycle combination.

James R Coates,

The Spinney, Breachwood Green, Hitchin, Hertfordshire, SG4 8PL.

Flt-Lt James R Coates was a holder of the DFC and one-time Queen's Flight pilot. His first attempt at amateur aircraft construction was in 1950 during his Royal Air Force service when at RAF Waterbeach in Cambridgeshire he built a LA.4 Luton Minor, G-AMAW (which he named Swalesong SA.I) and which was constructed from pre-war *Practical Mechanics* magazine plans. During the early 1960s he designed and built a two seat low-wing monoplane that he named SA.II Swalesong: it was registered G-AYDV on May 18th 1970. In response to requests from other amateur constructors, Coates redesigned the machine in 1972 as the Swalesong SA.III to make it simpler for home constructors: the prototype was registered G-BAAH on July 31st 1972. Coates died aged 70 on May 15th 1987.

De Havilland Chipmunk Mk.22 operated by Elstree Flying Club (The London School of Flying) in 1956.

Dart Aircraft Ltd,

Market Place, Chalfont St Peter, Buckinghamshire.

Dart Aircraft Ltd owes its origins back to 1935. The pre-war history of this company is related in *Ord-Hume [37]*. With the revival of amateur flying, designer and founder Alfred Richard Oscar Weyl decided to revive the design that had proved so successful in the immediate pre-war years – the single seat Kitten ultra light. Weyl served on the executive committee of the Ultra Light Aircraft Association and in 1950 he decided to try to reintroduce the machine and obtain for it a Type Certificate of Airworthiness. Above all the plan was to reintroduce it as a set of plans for amateur construction. Weyl was essentially a one-man business and in the final analysis only one new Kitten was produced – G-AMJP – in January of 1952. In that year, Dart established itself in Chalfont St Peter and at the same time Air Vice-Marshal Donald C T Bennett acquired a controlling interest in the organisation. Dart did not pursue its potential, though, and the Kitten never enjoyed the hoped-for revival through lack of finance and, above all, no suitable engine. Weyl (*b.* Berlin; *d.* 23rd February 1959 aged 61 years) left the firm the following year.

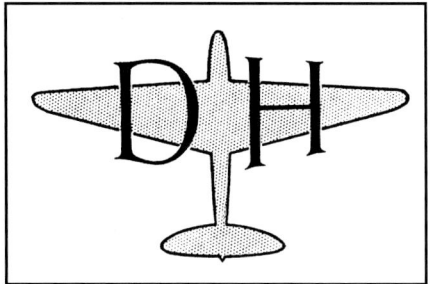

De Havilland Aircraft Co, Ltd,

Hatfield, Hertfordshire.

The DH business was far reaching and extensive. Founded in 1920, the business played a key role in private, club and commercial aviation up to the outbreak of war after which it concentrated on military machines. An exception was the Chipmunk originally designed and built by the de Havilland Aircraft of Canada Ltd at Toronto as a Tiger Moth replacement. The project was transferred to England and the subsequent versions of the Chipmunk were built initially at Hatfield and latterly at Chester. The company was absorbed by Hawker Siddeley in 1960 its famous logo, pictured left, would enter the realm of history and its art deco headquarters demolished..

Edgar Percival Aircraft Ltd,

Stapleford Aerodrome, Romford, Essex.

Edgar Wikner Percival had founded Percival Aircraft Ltd in the pre-war era. When his company was absorbed by Hunting and eventually his name removed from the business, he resigned and founded a new business at Stapleford Tawney, Essex, in 1954 to build a utility aircraft that he called the EP.9. Directors of this company were E W Percival (chairman and MD) and D Ross. Ultimately he sold out to Samlesbury Engineering Ltd, retaining a directorship of the operating company until the end of 1959. Percival died on January 21st 1984: he was 86 years old. *See under* **Lancashire Aircraft Co Ltd.**

Dart Kitten Mk.3 registered May 25th 1951. Owner Geoffrey Bramhill survived a crash at Hillington, King's Lynn, on June 5th 1966: the Kitten didn't.

W H Ekin (Engineering) Co Ltd,

158, King's Gate, Aberdeen, AB2 6BR, Scotland.

This business, which had a proliferation of addresses (its headquarters were in Northern Ireland at 59, Mill Road, Crumlin, Co. Antrim, its registered office at 4 Malone Hill Park, Belfast BT9 6RL, and its alternative address was 'An Stac', Durris, Banchory, Kincardineshire) was formed in March 1969 for the purpose of producing the McCandless Mk.IV Gyroplane under the new name WHE Airbuggy. The directors were Dr William H Ekin and Mrs M J H Ekin. The prototype Airbuggy first flew in February 1973 and is thus outside the scope of this present work. Dr Ekin lived at The Park, 12, Nutts Corner Road, Crumlin, Co. Antrim. Ekin undertook extensive redesign of the original machine resulting in the production of a new prototype, G-AXXN, that flew for the first time on February 1st 1973. In 1970 Ekin opened a gyroplane training school at Nutts Corner, Belfast, with Sqdn Ldr Desmond Mock as CFI and an hourly flying charge of between £2 and £3. *See also* under **McCandless Aviation Ltd**.

Elliotts of Newbury Ltd,

Albert Works, Newbury, Berkshire.

Elliotts was an old-established woodworking company with a strong position in the furniture trade. It began in business in 1895 and in 1939 turned its attention to aircraft production. Around the time of the First World War, it had been joined by the brothers Buckingham – Horace C G and Cecil de Vere. Horace Buckingham had been a director of the business since 1921 and, in 1938, became chairman of the firm. During the war years, Elliotts became sub-contractors for, among others, Airspeed and, in the first

year of operating this contract delivered 100 complete Airspeed Oxford fuselages. Other wartime work included components for both the Horsa and the Hamilcar military transport gliders as well as parts for the Spitfire, Mosquito and Tiger Moth. At the end of the war the directors comprised Horace C G Buckingham, Cecil de Vere Buckingham (joint managing), and William Goodyear. Company pilot was James Norman Ampthill. With the return to peace, Buckingham decided to capitalise on the aircraft experience that his company had established and so entered into an arrangement with Chilton Aircraft to build a modified version of the Meise sailplane. Production began in 1947 at Newbury and more than 150 examples were built, an event that provided the British gliding movement with its first and most satisfactory post-war sailplane. The company exhibited at Farnborough in 1947 showing the Olympia, Primary and Baby gliders. The following year, besides the same three gliders, they displayed the Newbury EoN light four seat monoplane. First flown on August 8th 1947 by Philip J Stanbury, chief test pilot for Gloster Aircraft Ltd. Development of this aircraft was planned but although it offered attractive features and specification, sales were not forthcoming. It was widely demonstrated usually towing one of the company's EoN Baby gliders. Despite an extensive and prolonged sales and demonstration tour, orders for the aircraft failed to materialise, the market being dominated by cheap ex-Service machines. Plans for an improved model were put forward. Finally the loss of the sole prototype aircraft in a mishap that resulted in a Court sequel, the project was abandoned. Early in the 1950s the company produced the outstanding Olympia 4 series of sailplanes, a later development of which won events at the 1963 British National Championships. In the spring of 1966 Elliotts, second only to Slingsby in glider manufacture, gave up manufacture and concluded an agreement that saw all servicing, spares and any future manufacturing rights of the EON Olympia 463 sailplane handed over to Kirkbymoorside. Horace Buckingham died in 1965 in his 65th year.

Essex Aero Ltd,

Albion Works, Canal Side, Gravesend, (*also* Gravesend Aerodrome) Kent.

With registered offices in Gravesend's Queen Street, this firm of aeronautical engineers was an associate member of the SBAC and specialized in magnesium construction, door frames and fuel tanks. The founder, managing director and chief designer was Reginald Jack Cross (*b.* Bristol, November 26th 1902) who had begun an engineering career with engine-makers Brazil Straker of Bristol before transferring to Douglas Motors Ltd and then Bristol Aeroplane Co. He then worked with Imperial Airways in the Middle East before transferring as chief engineer to Hillman's Airways where he served between 1932 and 1934. In that year, he formed a separate aircraft servicing company with Edward Hillman called Hillman & Cross Ltd, aeronautical engineers, with the registered address given as Maylands Aerodrome, Romford. With the unexpected sudden death of 45-year-old Hillman on December 31st that same year, Hillman & Cross Ltd was re-named Essex Aero Limited on May 8th 1936 and the two directors were then shown as Reginald Jack Cross (then living at The Homestead, Camer Corner, Meopham, Kent) and Miss Ivy Teesdale with the registered address as Queen Street, Gravesend. On March 5th 1937, Essex Aero took out a debenture to raise £550 for property and tools in the name of Miss Ivy Teesdale who was by now Jack Cross's fiancé. The business specialised in the overhaul of aircraft and made a name for itself in the preparation of record-breaking aircraft, notably Clouston's DH Comet G-ACSS which, in 1938, he flew with Ricketts to Sydney and back, and then Alex Henshaw's Mew Gull G-AEXF. Henshaw writes (*The Flight of the Mew Gull*, John Murray, London. 1980) that Cross was a brilliant engineer and adds that at various times Henshaw and his father put money into the business. Cross went on to specialise in the development of wrought magnesium for aircraft and wrote two seminal books on magnesium fabrication including one on welding this inflammable metal. During the war the business concentrated on the design and manufacture of light and ultra-light alloy fuel and oil tanks of which it built vast numbers. It was also responsible (in 1955) for the design and production of many tanks for special requirements to meet urgent tactical needs, the largest being the 5,000-gallon overload fuel tank for the Royal Air Force's Vulcan bomber. After the war Cross revised the business, now describing himself as managing director and chief designer with A C Crockford (assistant chief designer) and Sqdn-Ldr Alan Francis Eckford as technical sales manager and test pilot. Other directors were G E Weber and E Louis (secretary). General manager was Dennis Bliss Winter, AFRAeS. Chief chemist and metallurgist was E F Maillard with V V M Ernst as chief technical assistant. Cross announced in 1947 the design and construction of a two seat light aircraft to be known as the Sprite. It was to incorporate a number of novel if not radical design features based on the firm's considerable experience in the application of magnesium-alloys for aircraft components. Unfortunately this forward-looking design was abandoned shortly after the cessation of the Nuffield engine project by Morris Motors in 1948, and nothing further was heard of it. The fate of the 'almost completed airframe' is unknown. It is alleged that early in 1956 Martins Bank Ltd appointed a Receiver and the company was wound up.

Fairey Aviation Co Ltd,

Hayes, Middlesex.

The founder of this pioneering aircraft company was Sir Richard Fairey (b. Hendon, May 5th 1887; d. September 30th 1956). Fortunately he did not live to see the nationalisation of his company which took place in May of 1960 with the enforced acquisition of the whole business by Westland Aircraft, so marking the end of this long-established independent aircraft name. In 1947, Fairey designed and built a prototype machine called the Gyrodyne, part helicopter, part autogiro. Unfortunately this revolutionary four/five seater was not proceeded with. The company's only involvement with fixed-wing light aircraft was through its Belgian subsidiary. In 1931, Fairey opened a factory at Gosselies near Charleroi in Belgium as Avions Fairey SA which was known as The Fairey Company Ltd. Operated by the outstanding light aircraft

designer Ernest Oscar Tips, a long-standing offshoot of the Fairey concern was **Tipsy Aircraft Ltd** [qv]. On April 1st 1959, The Fairey Aviation Company Ltd was re-named The Fairey Company Ltd as a holding company for Fairey Engineering Co Ltd (formerly the Stockport Aviation Co Ltd) and Fairey Aviation Company Ltd. After the financial restructuring of the Britten-Norman company [qv] in 1971, Avion Fairey acquired the whole of the share capital of the business from the Receiver Maurice Eckman for approximately £4.1 million and began production of the Britten-Norman Islander. Avions Fairey went into liquidation in 1977 and was restructured the following year as Sonaca SA.

Fairtravel Ltd,

Boyn Hill Road, Maidenhead, Berkshire,
also Blackbushe Airport, Camberley, Surrey.

Private company registered on June 28th 1950 with £100 initial capital. Directors Mrs Elsa Bennett and Donald Clifford Tyndall Bennett. Travel bureau, tourist agent and contractors, the registered office was Deepwood House, Farnham Royal, Buckinghamshire. Air Vice Marshal Don 'Pathfinder' Bennett had a number of irons in the fire at this time including an airline subsidiary called Fairflight (this owned an Avro Tudor II, was formed in August 1949, and was sold to Surrey Flying Services in November 1951; Fairtravel was shown as owning one Avro Lincoln transport) and there was some interaction between the similarly-named businesses. Fairflight had succeeded another Bennett enterprise called Airflight Ltd. Fairtravel was revived in 1962 when Bennett decided to take over the manufacture of the British version of the Piel Emeraude, a project previously handled by Garland Aircraft Ltd and Garland-Bianchi Aircraft [qv]. The aircraft, known as the Fairtravel Linnet, was powered by a 105 hp Continental O-200. Three aircraft were built between 1963 and 1965, the last two of which were constructed at Blackbushe. By 1968 the address of the business was still given as Deepwood House but it seems to have ceased business shortly after that date. 'Fair' seems to have been a popular Bennett company-name prefix: he and his wife also ran a business called Fairthorpe Ltd named after the house in Toowoomba, Queensland, Australia where he was born on September 14th 1910. He died on September 15th 1986.

Farm Aviation Ltd,

Rush Green, Langley, Hitchin, Hertfordshire.

Founded by G C Beckwith, William S Bowker and Michael A Pruden to take on the development of the agricultural version of the de Havilland Chipmunk after the collapse of Agricultural Aviation Co Ltd with which Bowker worked as chief engineer. It took over the prototype G-APOS and subsequently modified three more examples, G-AOTF, G-ASPW and G-ATVF. The firm also operated as an agricultural aviation contractor. Between 1970-71 the company built a single seat American-designed racing aircraft called the Owl Racer. Designed by a Californian named George Owl, Farm Aviation's example, G-AYMS, first flew on April 13th 1971 but six weeks later was involved in a fatal accident. Later Farm Aviation's activities were continued under the name Bowker Air Services.

Firth Helicopters Ltd,

32, Clarges Street, London W.1
and Thame, Oxfordshire.

Private company registered on June 16th 1947 for the purpose of developing helicopters and to enter into an agreement with the American firm Landgraf Helicopter Company. Initial registered capital £72,500 increased by £4,000 six months later. The aim of the company was stated to be to enter into an agreement with Landgraf Helicopter Co (of Los Angeles) to build the firm's designs in Britain. Directors were Lord Bruntisfield of Boroughmuir, Frederick Anson Firth (managing), W E Hole, John Nelson Dundas Heenan, R L Hutchins. Heenan, whose position was described as 'consultant', was also the designer of the Planet Satellite which, at the time this company was formed, had yet to be completed. Frederick Anson Firth had been chief technical officer of the British Air Commission's Western Area. The Landgraf was a non-starter for it did not have a production engine: the American prototype had flown with a pre-war Pobjoy engine. In the late 1940s the Firth company designed and built a helicopter (G-ALXP) using the second and unfinished fuselage of the Planet Satellite, but it was not completed so did not fly. On January 30th 1950 a receiver was appointed to wind up the company by which time its address was shown as being 24, Old Broad Street, EC2. *See also* **Planet Aircraft Ltd**.

Folland Aircraft Ltd,

Sydney Lodge, Hamble, Southampton, Hampshire.

Directors: Charles L Hill, R J Norton, Henry Phillip Folland (managing), Edward Norman Egan (assistant MD and secretary), Thomas Gilbertson (general manager). Although its potential in the post-war light aircraft business is quite forgotten today, Folland's name should not be excluded from this list. The business was originally formed in February 1936 as British Marine Aircraft Ltd for the purpose of building American Sikorsky flying boats under licence but that project fell through. In June 1937 it was completely restructured and Folland became managing director: that December the company name was changed to Folland Aircraft Ltd. Much of its important work on defence projects was lost through changes in government policy but it contributed to the Brabazon airliner, and Vickers' aircraft such as the Viking and Valetta and de Havilland's Dove and Vampire. Henry Folland (1889-1954) began as chief designer of the Royal Aircraft Factory at Farnborough replacing Geoffrey de Havilland who resigned to set up his own business as Airco. The aircraft for which he is best remembered is the SE.5 and SE.5A. He left the Royal Aircraft Factory and joined the British Nieuport Company where he was responsible for the design of the Nighthawk, later joining Gloster where he produced the designs for a number of famed aircraft including the racers, the Grebe, the Gauntlet and Gladiator as well as the legendary Bamel. Wartime contract work was extensive and included the conversion of four Spitfire seaplanes. Shortly after the end of the war, Folland announced the design of several light aircraft projects, foremost among these being the Fiona. None was proceeded with. At this time, chief designer (under Folland's guidance) was Bernard V Leak (1907-1947) who had been with Chrislea [qv] before the war and later with Cunliffe-Owen after which he worked in America until 1945. In 1948, Arthur Beavan took over. Formerly with Vickers, Beavan had been with Cunliffe-Owen on the Burnelli project and, latterly, bomber modification work, until April 1946 in which month he joined Folland as assistant chief designer. Ill-health forced Folland's retirement in 1951, his position as managing director having been taken by William Edward Willoughby Petter the previous year. It was under Petter's leadership that the company started work (in 1951) on a private-venture jet fighter, the two models of which became the Midge and the Gnat. In charge of design after Folland's departure was ex-Bristol Aeroplane man Frederick Henry Pollicutt, but he only stayed two and a half years before transferring to Hunting Percival early in 1954. Lack of Royal Air Force interest in volume ordering of the Gnat trainer forced the Folland company to merge with the Hawker Siddeley Group in September 1959. Henry Folland died on September 5th 1954. *See major entry* in Chapter Twelve.

Gadfly Aircraft Co Ltd,

Andover, Hampshire.

Private company set up around 1966 by S/Ldr M Ogilvie-Forbes (chairman), D Hyman (managing) R J H Goodfellow. S/Ldr James Edward Doran-Webb and M Boston. Subsidiary of **Thruxton Aviation & Engineering Co Ltd** [qv]. Built a two seat cabin autogyro initially called the Thruxton Gadfly ES.101 but later reworked as the Gadfly HDW.1. This was designed by Eric Smith of the Patent Lighting & Engineering Co of Hayes, Middlesex. One example only, G-AVKE, evaluated at Thruxton in 1967. The project was not proceeded with and the machine was dismantled for long-term storage.

Garland-Bianchi Aircraft Co,

Boyne Hill Works, Maidenhead, Berkshire,
also White Waltham Aerodrome.

A private company formed in 1955 by P A T Garland and Douglas Edward Bianchi to produce an English version of the Piel Emeraude and known as the Garland-Bianchi Linnet the prototype of which (G-APNS) flew in September 1958. The selling price was a little over £2,000. The following year a new business was set up as Garland Aircraft Ltd, also operating at White Waltham (but with its base as Dale House, Clewer Green, Windsor, Berkshire), which built two examples before closing in 1960 to be succeeded by **Fairtravel Ltd** [qv].

Garland Bianchi Linnet prototype of June 1958.

Glos-Air Ltd,

Staverton Airport, Cheltenham, Gloucestershire.

Aeronautical engineers having as chairman Sir Derrick Thomas Louis Bailey (also of Aurigny Air Services Ltd), Charles Poole (managing director), A H Luscombe as chief engineer and N E Wright as chief inspector. By 1971, Wright had been elevated to managing director. Company formed for the construction assembly and sales of the Australian-designed Victa Airtourer aircraft as manufactured in New Zealand by AESL and which it re-named the Glos-Airtourer. Between 1965 and 1966 the firm erected twelve examples. *See also* **Trojan**.

Hampshire Aeroplane Co, Ltd,

Southampton (Eastleigh) Airport, Southampton, Hampshire.

Directors of the firm were Vivian Hampson Bellamy (1919-1998), Mrs L Bellamy and R W Cross (secretary). In 1958, members of the Hampshire Aeroplane Club built an example of the Currie Wot designed in 1937 by John R Currie who was the club's maintenance engineer. The Currie Wot was subsequently taken over by **Botley Aircraft** *[qv]*. During 1959-60, a twin-engined four seat light aircraft was designed by Ray J Hilborne (1930-2008) and designated the BH.1. Of advanced design and construction, the all-wood aircraft was registered G-ARIO and was built during 1961 partly by John Owen Isaacs. However, during early taxi trials late in the spring of 1962 the rear spar fractured due to overloading caused by a basic design stressing error, and the aircraft was scrapped. The two-Mikron-powered Hampshire Halcyon was thus built but never flown. In 1962, disappointed by the Halcyon failure, Bellamy sold the business.

Hants & Sussex Aviation,

Portsmouth Aerodrome, Portsmouth, Hampshire.

Albert Holmes 'Jimmy' Hawes (1893-1971) joined Portsmouth, Southsea & Isle of Wight Aviation Ltd as chief engineer in 1933. He had previously been with Robert Blackburn and later F G Miles. During the war, Hawes and Frederick George Lewis were heavily involved in the planning and operation of the aircraft maintenance and repair contracts (*see under* **Portsmouth Aviation Ltd** for details of this involvement) as well as the building of the Portsmouth Aerocar. When in 1946 Portsmouth Aviation's projected production plans for the Aerocar appeared realistically to be some way ahead (they eventually foundered), Hawes and Lewis left the company and began in business in part of Bailey's of Bognor Ltd's builders yard at Felpham, a property that had belonged to Portsmouth Aviation. Two private companies were formed. The first was Hants & Sussex Aviation Ltd registered October 23rd 1946, £4,000 capital, purpose to acquire business carried on by A H Hawes and F G Lewis at 448 London Road, Portsmouth. The second was A H Hawes & Sons Ltd. Soon afterwards Hants & Sussex Aviation Ltd moved to the Rampart site on the north side of Portsmouth Airport close to the railway line. Here the business of aircraft repairs and engineering began in earnest. Albert Edward 'Ted' Hawes, son of Jimmy, became general manager in 1947 and managing director in 1968. After the war, Hants & Sussex Aviation designed and built the Herald, originally planned as a two seater but which only every flew as a single seater. Registered G-ALYA on February 3rd 1950, this did not meet expectations and was eventually broken up. In 1966, in conjunction with Vivian Bellamy and the Rover Gas Turbine Company, the company built the sole Rover Turbine Chipmunk powered by a Rover Wolston engine. Hopes were that the Rover Chipmunk would be marketed but this was not to be. At the end of 1968, **Beagle Aircraft Ltd** *[qv]* sold off its entire interest in Auster aircraft to Hants & Sussex Aviation for £35,000. General manager of Beagle's factory at Rearsby, Ambrose V Hitchman, was appointed manager of Hants & Sussex's Auster section.

Helco (England) Ltd,

Barn House, Cherry Gardens Lane, Maidenhead, Berkshire.

A business registered June 6th 1947 with £500 capital for the purpose, among others, of manufacturing aircraft &c. Directors were Saleh Helmy and Dorothy F Helmy (both directors of Aerogypt High Speed Development Co Ltd), Anne M L Arkell, Gordon B Cockell and Ethel May Cockell. The Helmy Aerogypt aircraft, originally a three-engined machine with a cabin-top high-lift section and later rebuilt as a twin-engined tricycle-undercarriage machine, is related in *Ord-Hume* [37]. While the prototype of this unusual and attractive machine was constructed in Britain in the pre-war years, post-war development was intended to be transferred to Egypt and it was to that country that the unlucky Helmy and his wife were flying when their hopes and aircraft were dashed to the ground at Northolt on November 26th 1946. The remains of G-AFFG were to be seen in the back garden of Barn House for many years afterwards.

A fine air-to-air picture of the Currie Wot, a diminutive Moth lookalike

Heston Aircraft Co Ltd,

Heston Airport, Hounslow, Middlesex.

The Heston Aircraft Company was founded in June 1934 by the acquisition of the assets including premises, but not the staff, of the former Comper Aircraft Ltd. The pre-war activities of this firm have been described elsewhere [37]. After the war years, during which the business undertook considerable defence work including aircraft production, modification and repair, the management comprised Sir Norman James Watson (chairman), B R S Jones (managing director), George Alexander Lingham, Lt-Col G C Golding, Grp-Capt G H Bowman with George Cornwall (*b.* May 30th 1896) as chief designer. In 1948 the company undertook the building of the sole example of the Youngman-Baynes experimental high-lift aircraft. This was designed by R T Youngman in conjunction with Leslie Everett Baynes and incorporated some Percival Proctor components. Following the eventual closure of Heston Airport in the early 1950s due to Heathrow proximity plus the urge to drive the M4 Motorway across its fine turf, Heston Aircraft Co remained in business at the airfield site for some years, changing its name first to Heston Aircraft & Associated Engineers Ltd and then, in 1963, to Hestair Ltd. With the redevelopment of the site, the company premises took a new postal address in 1967 as Southall Lane, Hounslow and in that year became Hestair Sherpa Ltd, described as manufacturers of aircraft lifting tables, wheel-changing equipment and Sherpa Stackers. *See also* **Alan Muntz & Co Ltd**.

John O Isaacs,

42, Landguard Road, Southampton, Hampshire.

In January 1961, John Owen Isaacs (1920-2001) began work on a 7/10 scale wooden version of the Hawker Fury based loosely on the Currie Wot airframe, the proportions of which were used as a design stressing model. Called the Isaacs Fury, it proved extremely successful and the designer marketed sets of construction drawings for the aircraft from his home address. He went on to design and develop a three-fifths scale Spitfire, again for which he marketed plans.

Jackaroo Aircraft Ltd,

Thruxton Aerodrome, Andover, Hampshire.

This business was established in 1956 for the purpose of modifying de Havilland DH.82a Tiger Moth aircraft to carry four people, or as agricultural conversions. It began as a subsidiary of two principal organisations based on the airfield - **Thruxton Aviation & Engineering Co Ltd** and **The Wiltshire School of Flying Ltd.** Directors of the firm were Sqdn-Ldr J E Doran-Webb (managing), Air Vice-Marshal N C Ogilvie-Forbes, Sqdn-Ldr M F Ogilvie-Forbes, R Giddings, E J Heaton, Capt D M Spencer-Smith, Eric H Smith (chief designer). In 1961 it was announced that The Wiltshire School of Flying had developed a four seat Tiger Moth conversion that was to be called the Thruxton Jackaroo. The prototype was said to have flown for the first time on March 2nd 1957. The activities of Jackaroo Aircraft Ltd were taken over in 1961 by **Paragon Aircraft** at the same address. The directors were Doran-Webb, Capt R Aird, Eric Smith and E Ellis. In the 1962-63 edition of *Janes' All The Worlds Aircraft*, the company announced that it was building three new light aircraft but nothing further materialised and the assets of the business were ultimately acquired by the Hampshire School of Flying.

Jones, Norman –

see under Rollason Aircraft & Engines Ltd

Lancashire Aircraft Co Ltd,

Samlesbury Airfield, Nr Blackburn, Lancashire,
then Squires Gate, Blackpool.

A wholly-owned subsidiary of Samlesbury Engineering Ltd, this business was formed at the beginning of 1960 to undertake the production of the Lancashire Aircraft Prospector. The Samlesbury company had acquired the design and manufacturing rights to the EP.9 general purpose monoplane from **Edgar Percival Aircraft Ltd** [*qv*] in October 1958. It acquired two complete aircraft, seven incomplete airframes, all the jigs and tools and the goodwill of the business. The chairman and managing director was J Eric Rylands and other directors were Lord Wakefield of Kendal (Sir Wavell Wakefield) and David Gaunt. The Earl of Bective was appointed sales manager and in 1960 G F Sharples became chief designer. Edgar Percival, who was for a short while after the sale, a director of Samlesbury Engineering, severed all contact with the business and the aircraft at the end of 1959. With the EP.9 renamed the Prospector, the new business acquired premises at Squires Gate Airport, Lytham St Annes in Lancashire although the main production facility remained at Samlesbury. The machine remained in production until 1962 in which year the company, an associate of Skyways Engineering Ltd of Stansted Airport, Essex, moved its operations to Lympne Airport in Kent. The business closed the following year.

Lancashire Prospector EP.9 prototype first flown at Squires Gate October 9th 1959.

Lockspeiser Aircraft,

14 Manette Street, London W1.

David Lockspeiser (1927-2014), a Hawker Siddeley test pilot (and son of Sir Ben Lockspeiser, a leading figure in the wartime Ministry of Aircraft Production and later Ministry of Supply's chief scientist), formed this business to produce a utility aircraft with multi-rôle capability. With the registered address given as his then home address, 4 Princes Buildings, Clifton, Bristol, Lockspeiser was MD with Christopher E Bean as company accountant and secretary. Other directors were George Smith and Richard Lucraft who provided the Manette Street, London address and was in charge of publicity. Lockspeiser designed what he called a 'Land Development Aircraft' in 1965-71. A 70 per cent scale prototype of this tandem-winged aircraft first flew in August 1971 registered initially G-AVOR and much later as G-UTIL. By 1974 a new limited liability company had been formed called Lockspeiser Aircraft Ltd with its registered address at 652 Grand Buildings, Trafalgar Square, London, WC2. While the project was progressing its development, it was destroyed in an arson attack on its hangar-workshop at Old Sarum on January 16th 1987. This brought all development to an untimely end.

Lockspeiser Land Development Aircraft in first form with four-wheeled undercarriage.

Lockspeiser LDA with revised tricycle undercarriage.

Lockspeiser LDA in dismantled form showing kit of parts, all of which could be carried inside a LDA aircraft.

Marshalls' Flying School Ltd,

Airport Works, Cambridge, Cambridgeshire.

Founded as Marshalls (Cambridge) Ltd on December 29th 1934 as a private company with £9,000 capital. First directors were David Gregory Marshall (1873-1942) and Arthur Gregory George Marshall. In the post-war years, Sir Arthur Marshall was chairman with R D Horsbrough (commercial director), R O Gates (chief engineer) and Norman Sellars as sales manager. Until 1962, this business was known as Marshalls Flying School Ltd at which time its name changed to Marshall of Cambridge (Engineering) Ltd. Its speciality was the modification, repair and overhaul of military and commercial aircraft but it also conducted experiments in high-lift research. One of these was the experimental high-lift Auster variant, the Marshall MA.4, a research vehicle to study boundary layer control.

McCandless Aviation Ltd,

Newtownards Aerodrome, County Down, Northern Ireland.

Private company formed by Rex McCandless and W A C McCandless and operating as an ARB-approved aircraft maintenance, repair and design organisation at Newtownards. In 1961, he bought a Bensen-type gyrocopter with which to gain experience before embarking on his own design. Aided technically by Frank Robertson, then chief of preliminary design for Short Brothers & Harland Ltd, McCandless developed his M4 Gyroplane, the first flight being in 1961 (G-ATXW). Several later (1974-1976) examples were built by **W H Ekin (Engineering) Co Ltd** [qv] of Crumlin, some of which (G-AXYX-G-AXZB inclusive) were subsequently redesignated as the WHE Airbuggy powered by the 1600cc VW engine. William H Ekin lived at The Park, 12, Nutts Corner Road, Crumlin, Co. Antrim.

F G Miles Limited,

Redhill Aerodrome,
then Shoreham Airport, Shoreham-by-Sea, Sussex.

The new private company which succeeded the former **Miles Aircraft Ltd** [*qv*] was registered on December 4th 1948 as F G Miles Ltd with a capital of £100. The directors were Frederick George Miles (chairman and managing director), Mrs Maxine Francis Mary Miles, Dennis Daybell (who was also a director of the Miles-Martin Pen Company Ltd), J W P Angell and Mrs O M Wadlow (secretary). The last two names joined the board on the reformation of the company in 1951 shortly before it moved to Shoreham. Purpose described as the repair and service of aircraft as well as research, development and design of aircraft. Work at Redhill involved pioneering research into the use of moulded phenolic-impregnated asbestos (this was called Durestos) in connection with a two seat high-performance sailplane to be called the M.76. In collaboration with Hugh Kendall, a glass-fibre sailplane was built in 1950. The company also set about the conversion of earlier Miles designs, predominantly the improved larger, faster and more powerful version of the Gemini known as the Aries, and carried out the conversion of the pre-war Sparrowhawk G-ADNL into the King's Cup-winning Sparrowjet. After the move to Shoreham in 1952 it formed a plastics division which built an experimental wing of Durestos. Miles conducted much experimental work with the Hurel-Dubois ultra-high aspect-ratio wing using an Aerovan in March 1957. This experience went towards the development of Short's twin-engined feeder-liner, the Skyvan. Miles' last major activity was the design and manufacture, in the summer of 1957, of a private-venture jet trainer called the Student. In October 1960, F G Miles Ltd was absorbed into the Beagle complex first as Beagle-Miles Aircraft Ltd, and then after 1962 as simple Beagle Aircraft Ltd whereupon it ceased to exist as an entity.

Miles Aircraft Ltd,

Woodley (Reading) Aerodrome, Berkshire.

Originally as Phillips & Powis Aircraft Ltd. In June 1947 the company increased its share capital beyond its issued £300,000 by £700,000. Chief sales executive was Leonard Arthur Hackett who had started out in the days of Phillips & Powis in 1935. Frederick George Miles' personal assistant was R L Robinson under whose guidance the company produced the Miles Actuator (an aircraft control-operating device), the Miles Co-Pilot (a cockpit flight-assistance system), the Philidas (a variety of stiff [self-locking] nut to rival the similar products of Simmonds and Oddie) and the Biro divisions operated by a separate business called the Miles-Martin Pen Co Ltd. Chief technical officer was Donald L Brown. In 1946 the company was expanding with a Messenger production line operation in Northern Ireland and what F G Miles described at the 10th AGM at the end of 1946 as 'widening aspects' of the firm's activities. On April 30th 1946 a new private company, Miles Aircraft (Northern Ireland) Ltd, was registered in Belfast with a £50,000 capital. The registered office was Banbridge, and the factory was at Ards Airport, Newtownards, Co. Down, under the management of Charles Owen Powis, formerly the partner in the original Phillips & Powis of Reading. That summer also saw the formation of a subsidiary company, **Fletcher Airscrew Division** (*see Chapter 10*). Miles Aircraft Ltd entered financial difficulties in 1947, problems that were exacerbated by the severe winter and fuel crisis that heralded the year and prevented much of industry from operating during February and March. That September the company was restructured with S R Hogg appointed receiver manager and other directors being appointed by creditors as A F Jopling, J C Murley and J R Valentine. Principle creditors were Blackburn Aircraft (for Cirrus engines), De La Rue Extrusions, Smiths Aircraft Instruments and Sperry Gyroscopes. By this time, Miles Aircraft had already diversified into the manufacture of the Biro ball-point pen and Copycat office duplicators, divisions of the business that, like Messrs Philidas Ltd, were profitable but insufficient to cover the losses of the aircraft department which was now well involved with the development of the Marathon commercial aircraft. Hopes that a liquidation could be avoided came to an end on November 14th when cellulose dope makers Titanine Ltd petitioned for the winding-up of the company. Titanine, not one of the original petitioners, now forced the issue and a creditors' meeting was held on November 19th. While the original petitioners were owed in total £62,000, Titanine's debt was only £5,837. The sum total of other creditors' indebtedness was £234,000 and these now opposed the petition. It was, though, to no avail and Miles Aircraft Ltd was in due course formally wound up, its assets (including the development of the Miles Marathon) being taken over along with its Woodley premises by Handley Page which formed a new company, Handley Page (Reading) Ltd, in June 1948. Six months later, on December 2nd, the name of Miles Aircraft Ltd was changed to Western Manufacturing Estate Ltd: this name being altered to Western Manufacturing (Reading) Ltd on May 1st 1952. Meanwhile, a new company, **F G Miles Ltd** [*qv*] sprang from the Woodley ruins.

Miles Sparrowjet single seat twin-engined wooden jetplane converted from a pre-war two seater.

M L Aviation Co Ltd,

White Waltham Aerodrome, Maidenhead, Berkshire.

This company was originally founded in 1935 as R Malcolm Ltd, designers and manufacturers of radio-controlled pilotless targets, high-speed target-towing apparatus, as well as various other kinds of aircraft equipment. Directors Sir Eric Noel Mobbs (managing), Marcel Jules Odilon Lobelle (1893-1967; chief designer), R O Mobbs, J P and A J Wilson. The name of the new company came from the initials of Mobbs and Lobelle (who had been chief designer at Fairey Aviation Co Ltd from 1925 to 1940). Developed an inflatable and portable light aircraft a prototype of which (the ML Utility) appeared in 1954 and an improved version, the ML Light Aircraft Mk.1, was built to a Ministry of Supply prototype contract in 1955. It was hoped that the machine might have a light civilian application but this did not come to pass. The parent company, M L (Holdings) Ltd acquired an interest in **Slingsby Sailplanes Ltd** [qv] in the 1980s.

C G B Mitchell,

'Clouds', 17, Tavistock Road, Fleet, Hampshire.

Originally in business with Roy G Proctor as **Mitchell-Proctor Aircraft Ltd** [qv], C G B Mitchell formed his own company in 1968 to concentrate on developing a two seat version of the original Kittiwake II aircraft. The prototype Kittiwake II (G-AWGM) was built for Mitchell by Robinson Aircraft Ltd of Blackbushe, Hampshire.

Mitchell-Proctor Aircraft Ltd,

Chorley, Lancashire

Private company formed around 1965 by C G B Mitchell and Roy G Proctor to build and develop an all-metal single seater for amateur construction called the Kittiwake I. Business partnership dissolved around October 1968 after which both partners formed new businesses around their own names. Proctor retained rights to the Kittiwake I and announced the development of the two seat Proctor Petrel, construction of which began 1972-73 at West Byfleet in the hands of Southborough Engineering Ltd. See also **Robinson Aircraft Ltd**.

ML Light Aircraft Mk.1 of 1955 was built around an inflatable wing.

Alan Muntz & Co Ltd,

Heston Airport, Hounslow, Middlesex.

This company was formed in 1937 to develop and produce the Pescara gas generator and turbine for industrial use. An aircraft section was set up soon afterwards with Leslie Everett Baynes as chief designer, initially to modify the Pescara engine to aircraft use. Work was well advanced when war interrupted. The company also carried out work on the Maclaren drift or castoring landing gear and during the war was engaged in defence production work. In 1946 the business had as directors F A I Muntz, J E D Shaw (of Slingsby Sailplanes Ltd), Jan Horodyski and G W Duncan. Owners of Heston Airport and the Heston Aircraft Co, the company was responsible for the building of the Youngman-Baynes experimental high-lift aircraft in 1948.

D Napier & Son, Ltd,

211, The Vale, Acton, London, W.3

This ancient and respected company was established in 1808 and incorporated in 1913. During the First World War it established a reputation for the design and manufacture of aircraft engines, a business in which it shared a world dominance until the years following the end of Second World War. At that time the directors were Sir George Henry Nelson (chairman), G A Riddell (deputy chairman), Peter John Daglish (managing director), P Horsfall, H E C de Chassiron and The Viscount Caldecote. In 1961 the business decided to move into agricultural aviation and with this in mind purchased three basic kits of parts for building the Bensen Gyrocopter from the designer. In conjunction with the chemical company Pan Britannica Industries Ltd, Napier modified the aircraft and produced a spray version called the Agri-Copter. This flew under B Conditions as G-29-3. After demonstration at Napier's Luton Airport test ground on July 20th 1961, it was handed to PBI for evaluation at G-ATWT. All aircraft work was abandoned soon afterwards when the company was absorbed by Rolls-Royce Ltd.

Navarro Aircraft Construction Company,

Hanworth Aerodrome, Feltham, Middlesex.

Joseph George Navarro's obituary in *The Aeroplane* described him as having 'spent his life trying to build aeroplanes'. Indeed, the overwhelming evidence is that while his name regularly appeared in the aviation scene, the sum total of his work inescapably erred on the side of failure. Born around 1881, his first aircraft design was completed in 1909 and was for a triplane. His next machine, the Navarro Biplane, formed the subject of a patent in 1910 and heralded a lifetime desire for devising patentable features. During the First World War he formed an eponymous aircraft manufacturing company at Burton-on-Trent from which he subsequently and very publicly disassociated himself from. Next he devised the Navarro Bullet with a 200 hp Hispano engine which was claimed to be the fastest fighter of its time. Rather like F G Miles, Navarro married an aircraft designer and spent the 1920s trying to popularise flying at seaside resorts. In 1925 he announced a transatlantic air service using flying boats with a string of station ships stretching across the Atlantic. His flying boat was to have a total of 5,000 hp. In 1929 he built the three-engined Navarro Chief at Hanworth which was rich in eccentric innovations (a split rudder to act as an airbrake, differential elevators to help turning and an unstallable wing of unusual shape). The aircraft didn't fly and the designer ran out of money. He suffered the loss of his wife and went on to run a training school, and then to manage Fairey's aerodrome at what is now Heathrow. During the war years he worked in design and immediately after the war announced three new designs, one (the amphibian Naiad) with sponsons which housed the retracted land undercarriage and which he was able to patent. A chance meeting in 1947 with The Hon Simon Warrender proved potentially fortuitous and Warrender was so taken with the Naiad design that he at once secured finance through one Douglas Johnston Reoch. Joseph Navarro's luck appeared to turn with the creation, that summer, of the Navarro Aircraft Construction Company and premises at Hanworth Aerodrome. He was wrong again, for he died at Market Harborough on September 9th 1947 aged 66. His backers, unwilling to abandon everything, went on to form **Sponson Developments Ltd** *[qv]* to redesign the Naiad into the Tribian. The Navarro hubris, however, was eventually to win in the end.

Nipper Aircraft Ltd,

East Midlands Airport, Castle Donington, Derby.

Founded by David Patrick Leith Antill and Mrs D Patricia L Antill in 1966, in that year the company bought the world rights for the Tipsy Nipper aircraft from Belgium. The aircraft was manufactured for Nipper Aircraft by **Slingsby Aircraft Co Ltd** at Kirkbymoorside in Yorkshire, production in 1968 being at the rate of about four machines per month. By 1970 the business had expanded with Sir Montague Cholmeley heading the board and with the addition of J G Faber. The business handled the Nipper Radio, acted as agents for Siai Marchetti, operated the Nipper Flying School and undertook maintenance and hangarage. The company went into receivership in May 1971 but on October 20th 1971 a new company was formed called **Nipper Kits & Components Ltd** of 1 Ridgeway Drive, Bromley, Kent, BR1 5DG. The directors comprised D P L Antill (chairman), A F Ayles, R Marshall and A S Pearcey, and the business continued to supply Nipper plans for amateur constructors.

Norman Jones

see under Rollason Aircraft & Engines Ltd.

Arthur W J G Ord-Hume,

Sandown, Isle of Wight, *later* Chiswick, London, W4.

A founder of the Ultra Light Aircraft Association (later the Popular Flying Association), he rebuilt a pre-war Luton Minor in 1949 and received the first Permit to Fly to be granted for a totally-rebuilt old aircraft with a 'new' (non-type attributed) engine. He then redesigned the aircraft and secured its approval for amateur aircraft construction. This was the first post-war design to gain such status, the French-designed Druine Turbulent being the second. After building and restoring several other Luton Minors and further improving the type, he approached the original 1930s designer, Cecil Hugh Latimer-Needham and suggested they create a business to promote the aircraft. **Phoenix Aircraft Ltd** *[qv]* was formed in April 1958 for the purpose of marketing drawings for the new Luton LA.4A Minor along with kits of parts and complete aircraft. Unfortunately, although many sets of plans were sold, there proved to be no market for kits or complete machines. Also at this time Ord-Hume undertook the complete redesign of the pre-war Luton Major for which no drawings existed. He also negotiated with de Havilland Aircraft Ltd at Hatfield concerning a projected Phoenix-designed collaborative venture light aircraft. Ord-Hume resigned from Phoenix Aircraft in 1965 retaining the design rights to the Luton Minor and Major aircraft. Meanwhile he had acquired the full rights to the French-designed GY-201 BabyClub/Minicab two seat low-wing monoplane and devoted two years to the redesign and re-stressing of the aircraft followed by the drafting of an up-dated English-language set of drawings. The two seat Luton LA.8 Minor-Two (which used mostly standard Minor parts) came next. Other designs followed of which the cabin and the folding-wing variants of the Luton Minor were built and flown, and the O-H4-B Minor built. During the 1950s he was chief designer for the Middlesex Aviation Syndicate (*see* Chapter Eleven). In 1988 he retired to Surrey.

E Wayne Osbourne,

17, Everard Road, Bedford, Bedfordshire.

In 1969 Mr Osbourne converted a Slingsby Cadet glider into a twin-engined light aircraft using two motorcycle engines on the lift struts. At a later date he replaced these with a single Triumph motorcycle engine in the nose. Both versions of the same aircraft shared the registration G-AXMB. No further aircraft were produced.

Paragon Aircraft Ltd,

Thruxton Aerodrome.

This business was formed in 1961 to take over the activities of **Jackaroo Aircraft Ltd** *[qv]* and continued to convert Tiger Moth aircraft into the four seat Jackaroo, but ultimately abandoned plans to build certain designs that Jackaroo had proposed including the Plover and the Paladin. It ceased operations during 1964 at which time its assets were transferred to the Hampshire School of Flying. *See under* **Jackaroo Aircraft Ltd**, *also* **Thruxton Aviation & Engineering Co Ltd.**

Patent Lighting & Engineering

Company of Hayes, Middlesex.

This company was sub-contracted by **Thruxton Aviation & Engineering Company Limited** to build the original Gadfly HDW-1 autogyro.

Percival Aircraft Ltd,

The Airport, Luton, Bedfordshire.

Edgar Wikner Percival (cousin of Geoffrey Neville Wikner of pre-war aircraft-makers Foster, Wikner) was born on February 23rd 1897. The pre-war establishment of his company and its activities are described in [37] and need not be repeated here. Shortly before the outbreak of war the business was restructured with the Marquess of Londonderry as chairman and Hubert Edward Peter Dyke Ackland, who had been with Vickers Ltd, became managing director. Percival himself resigned in 1940 and Arthur Andrew Bage, who had joined the company in 1934 and was responsible for all Percival designs, became chief designer. Former Vickers man P D Ackland was appointed managing director. Percival lost its independence in September 1944 when the company was acquired by the shipping and oil company Hunting & Son Ltd of Newcastle-on-Tyne. Ackland retired at the end of that year. The new management board now comprised Percy Llewellyn Hunting (chairman), William Arthur Summers (managing), Gerald Lindsay Hunting, Charles Patrick Maule Hunting, Borras Noel Hamilton Whiteside, M R Cooke, K D Morgan with James Alexander Mackenzie as general manager. The name of the business was not altered and Percival Aircraft Co Ltd remained. In April 1948, Wing Cmdr Harry Proctor Powell (*b*. December 2nd 1911) was appointed chief test pilot to the company. Later that same year, in November, Bage retired and Leslie George Frise joined the company as chief engineer. Born July 2nd 1997, Frise had been responsible for the design of the aileron form that bore his name (1921) and in the same year the ducted radial engine cowling while at Bristol Aeroplane Co. In charge of public relations and, later, sales, was the popular White Russian aristocrat, Prince Yurka Galitzine. In 1954 the company name was changed to Hunting Percival Aircraft Ltd which name was retained until 1957 when the Percival name was dropped. The 1939-vintage Percival Vega Gull became the Proctor series of military aircraft, a number of which entered the Civil Register at the end of the war. The Percival Prentice RAF trainer also entered the civil market although by no means as successfully or in such numbers. By this time, Edgar Percival had re-entered the aircraft manufacturing business under his own name as **Edgar Percival Aircraft Ltd** [*qv*]. Hunting Aircraft Ltd ceased to be independent in September 1960 when it became part of the British Aircraft Corporation. Here Hunting's design for a short-haul jet-powered airliner, designated the P.107, was developed and produced at Weybridge as the BAC One-Eleven. The old Percival Aircraft Ltd factory at Luton Airport became BAC Luton until closed in July 1966 with the loss of 1,850 jobs: the Jet Provost trainer was in production that was now transferred to Preston, Lancashire. The premises were taken over briefly by Vauxhall Motors Ltd but shortly afterwards all buildings were razed for re-development of the site as a trading estate. Percival remained in business from his London address, 72 Chesterfield House, Curzon Street, where he was involved in other projects. He died aged 86 on January 21st 1984.

Phoenix Aircraft Limited,

St James Place, Cranleigh, Surrey, *then* Shoreham Airport, Sussex.

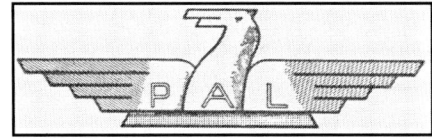

The pre-war Luton Aircraft Company ceased aviation activity on the outbreak of the war, its premises near Gerrards Cross becoming a war-effort production facility. While machining magnesium an accident with water caused a fierce fire that gutted the building and destroyed an adjacent store that housed the aircraft drawing office, the prototype Luton Major and six part-built production models among other items. After the war, Arthur W J G Ord-Hume acquired a crashed pre-war-built Minor and, after rebuilding, eventually succeeded in being allowed legally to fly it. He subsequently redesigned the aircraft and restressed it to accommodate larger engines. Using photographs and a few fragments of burned drawings, he then fully redesigned the Luton Major two seater. After completing this work and with the original designer, Cecil Hugh Latimer-Needham, then in retirement, he founded Phoenix Aircraft Ltd in April 1958 for the purpose of marketing drawings, kits of parts and complete aircraft. Unfortunately, although many sets of plans were sold, there proved to be no market for kits or complete machines. The undercapitalised company then created a design for a crop-spraying aircraft and was in talks with de Havilland Aircraft Co Ltd at Hatfield with a view to co-designing and manufacturing a new post-war light plane but this did not materialise. Ord-Hume resigned in 1965 and Latimer-Needham continued but only as a retailer of plans for the Minor and Major as well as the French Jodel D.9 and D.11, the American EAA Biplane and later, following an agreement with **Proctor Aircraft Associates Ltd** [*qv*], the Mitchell-Proctor Kittiwake I. Darrol Stinton became chief designer soon afterwards and designed several aircraft one of which, the Stinton-Warren ST.32-2, based on the Warren-Hall designs, was the subject of a full-scale mock-up at Cranleigh but projected prototype construction was abandoned when wind tunnel tests proved the design unairworthy. Shortly afterwards Stinton left the firm (early in

Phoenix Aircraft Luton LA.4A Minor built to plans sold to Australia. This, a classic example with JAP engine, was one of many to be constructed 'down-under'.

1969) to join the Air Registration Board, and Latimer-Needham resigned, moving to Canada where he died in 1975 aged 75. The business was revived and moved to Shoreham Airport where it continued selling plans. At this time the managing director was David Rendel. Then the firm was again restructured and the board was now headed by James Gray (managing) with directors Derek Page MP, John Owen Urmston and James L Bainbridge. It formed an association with Proctor Aircraft Associates Ltd to market plans/kits for the Mitchell-Proctor Kittiwake I but this seems to have fallen by the wayside. Through John Urmston, the business added the Currie Wot to its coterie of plans for sale. In March 1969 the directors approached Warden Aviation & Engineering Co at Old Warden (home of the Shuttleworth Collection) with a view towards collaboration but this came to nothing. In 1971, a new company was formed, Phoenix Aircraft (Development and Holdings) Ltd to take over the assets of Phoenix Aircraft Ltd. The old company held a 51 per cent stake in the new firm but on January 15th 1972 Phoenix Aircraft Ltd went into voluntary liquidation. With the final disappearance of the original Phoenix Aircraft Ltd, the design rights to the post-war Luton Minor and Major reverted by covenant to its designer, Arthur W J G Ord-Hume.

Phoenix Aircraft Luton LA.6 Major G-AVXG with 100 hp Continental engine. This particular example has a non-standard fin.

Pilot Magazine,

Lernhurst Publications Ltd,
189, Victoria Street, London SW1.

This magazine, edited by Brian Healey, decided to sponsor the design of a two seat light aircraft to be of all-metal construction. The outcome was the Pilot Sprite designed by two Loughborough University lecturers, Peter Sharman and Lloyd Jenkinson. *See under* **Practavia Ltd.**

Planet Aircraft Limited,

29, Clarges Street, London W.1,
also Croydon Airport *then* Redhill, Surrey.

Planet Aircraft Ltd was formed on September 11th 1946 as a subsidiary of Magnesium Elektron Ltd, makers of magnesium metal, electron alloys and associated products. Magnesium Elektron was anxious to promote the use of this metal in aircraft construction and planned to build an aircraft entirely out of it. With an initial capital of £21,000. Planet's board of directors was chaired by Maj Charles James Prior Ball (1893-1973) who was also chairman of Magnesium, The Distillers Co Ltd, Sterling Metals Ltd, F A Hughes Ltd, British Petroleum Chemicals Ltd and a number of other businesses involved in plastics, metals and chemicals. Ball was one of the 'big-name' industrialists of his era and his involvement with Planet highlights both its City expectations and the industrial 'clout' behind it. The Planet board had as managing director Grp Capt Francis Henry Louis Searl who, like Ball, had a background in the petrol, oils and chemical industries. Other executives included Maj John Nelson Dundas Heenan (chief designer and senior partner in Heenan, Winn and Steel), Rt Hon Lord Waleran, Maj W H P Burnyeat, and Grp Capt Hugh J Wilson. The registered capital was quickly increased to £30,450 and in July 1948 this was further increased by £22,050. In that same year, the Blackburn Aircraft Co took an interest in the venture and its sales and marketing director, Sqdn-Ldr James Leonard Neville Bennett-Baggs, joined the Planet board. The industrial backing for the project thus included ICI, Distillers and Blackburn. The complete aircraft was made by Redwing Ltd at its factory in Thornton Heath, but in the end major design and aerodynamic problems resulted in the Air Registration Board refusing permission to fly. In November 1948 it was announced that the Satellite fuselage was to be used as the fuselage of a new helicopter, the Firth, two prototypes of which were already under construction at the Thame Airport works of maintenance firm Airtech Ltd. Firth Helicopters Ltd was another company in which Heenan held a directorship and its registered offices were also at the Clarges Street address. It was said to be designing and constructing commercial helicopters based on the designs of the Landgraf Company of Los Angeles which was the brainchild of Fred Landgraf. On March 9th 1949 Searl resigned as Planet's MD and left the board of directors: Planet chose not to announce his departure until May by which time things were starting to fall apart for the firm. The demise of the much-vaunted Satellite marked a tremendously expensive failure and Planet Aircraft Ltd faded virtually overnight from the scene, shareholders having rejected the opportunity to pour more money into the venture.

Portsmouth Aviation Ltd,

The Airport, Portsmouth, Hampshire.

Founders and joint managing directors were Lionel Maxwell Joachim Balfour (1905-1973) and Francis Logan Luxmoore (1897-1985). The early days of this company and its activities are described in [37] and need not be repeated here. During the war years the former airline operating company survived on Ministry of Aircraft Production service and repair contracts operating as part of the Nuffield repair organisation. It undertook extensive work on Airspeed Oxford, Miles Master and Avro Anson aircraft as well as Horsa gliders. Portsmouth Aviation's association with the Airspeed company had begun in the mid-1930s when both firms had their bases at Portsmouth Airport. As early as March 1943 designer

Luxmoore had submitted plans to the Army for a general purpose aircraft capable of meeting military requirements. Although Whitehall ignored the submission, the design was evolved into the novel Portsmouth Aerocar, construction of which was undertaken at the beginning of 1946. At this time the directors included, besides Balfour and Luxmoore, Walter H Jenks (company secretary), Geoffrey W Foster, and Dudley Escott (works director). Escott was one of the oldest employees having joined the firm in 1932. On March 30th 1946 the board was joined by Edgar Louis Granville, Liberal MP for Eye (Suffolk) who had, before the war, been a director of British Airways: much later he would become Lord Granville. By 1948 he was chairman and managing director, Balfour and Luxmoore becoming vice-chairman and assistant managing director respectively. Granville resigned in 1951 to be replaced by Dudley Escott. The test pilot for the company was Denys Alan Evan Jones (*b*. June 2nd 1918). In December 1946 the Board of Trade allocated the company 80,000 sq.ft of factory floor area comprising the former erection bays at the East end of the Short Brothers (Rochester & Bedford) Ltd airport factory at Rochester and the intention was to employ in excess of 400 staff, the majority sheet-metal workers, building the Aerocar. On October 9th 1948 an associated business, Portsmouth Aviation Developments Ltd, was created with Edgar L Granville and Sydney P Escott as directors. An associate company was formed, Portsmouth Aviation (Nawanagar) Ltd, Jamnagar, Kathiawa, India, to handle construction of the aircraft in India. The trials and tribulations of the Aerocar design are related elsewhere; suffice it to say here that the failure to be able to produce the aircraft through circumstances beyond the control of the company, and the failure through political unrest of advanced plans for production in the Far East, resulted in the near-collapse of the firm at the end of 1949. Astute work by Dudley Escott and a new board of directors ultimately pulled the business round and it survives today, but not in aircraft manufacture. The connection between Portsmouth Aviation and **Hants & Sussex Aviation Ltd** is related under that heading.

Practavia Ltd,

Wycombe Air Park, Buckinghamshire.

A company formed in 1970 to take over the development of the Pilot Sprite all-metal light aircraft from Pilot [*qv*]. Directors were Brian Healey (editor of *Pilot* magazine and described as project executive), Lloyd Jenkinson and Peter Sharman, both lecturers at Loughborough University and the designers of the aircraft. *See under* **Pilot Magazine**.

Proctor Aircraft Associates Ltd,

Greenball, Crawley Ridge, Camberley, Surrey.

Formerly as **Mitchell-Proctor Aircraft Ltd** [*qv*] until October 1968 when Roy G Proctor and C G B Mitchell severed their business partnership. Proctor then advertised plans for sale to build the Kittiwake I and also announced the impending construction of a derivative two seater to be called the Proctor Petrel. The new business began in November 1968 with directors R G Proctor, Roger H White-Smith, Lionel and Barbara Alexander, and Paul Minton. Ann Proctor was described as company secretary. Much later, in 1978, Alan R B Nash acquired a controlling interest in the business and changed its name to Nash Aircraft Ltd moving it to the Trading Estate, Farnham, Surrey. Roy Proctor remained on the board, a third director being R C Nash. The aircraft now became the Nash Petrel, a two seater based upon the Proctor Kittiwake Mk.I and first flown in 1980.

Redwing Ltd,

Bensham Works, 340, Bensham Lane, Thornton Heath, Surrey.

Formed before the war as Redwing Aircraft Co Ltd, this company was contracted to build the Planet Satellite by project designers, Magnesium Elekton Ltd. One complete machine was erected by **Planet Aircraft Limited** at Redhill Aerodrome but despite protracted tests it failed to fly. A second incomplete fuselage was used in the Firth helicopter project.

Reid & Sigrist Ltd,

Shannon Corner, Kingston By-Pass, New Malden, Surrey.

This major manufacturer of aircraft instruments was created around 1930 by Sqdn-Ldr George Hancock Reid and Frederick Sigrist (1884-1956). The firm produced the first practical turn indicator which was fitted first to Hawker Tomtit G-AFTA. In 1937 it created an aircraft division and designed and built a twin-engined trainer called the Snargasher. Only the prototype was made. During the war the company built 700 Boulton Paul Defiants and carried out a large

Portsmouth Aerocar showing fuselage emergency skids for use in the event of hydraulic failure.

programme of repair and modification to American-built Mitchell bombers for the Royal Air Force. The company also operated five Elementary Flying Training Schools (EFTS) on behalf of the Air Ministry. In 1945 it introduced its second own-design aircraft which was called the Desford and named after the town in Leicestershire near which it was built. The post-war directors were George Hancock Reid (chairman and managing), E A M Reid with H P Maskell (general manager), with Charles Bower as chief designer. Test pilot was C F French. By 1948 the business had moved to Walton Lodge, Kirby Muxloe, near Leicester, with works at nearby Braunstone. Frederick Sigrist, formerly T O M Sopwith's partner and chief engineer, retired from the business during the war and passed away at Nassau, Bahamas, aged 72 on December 10th 1956. A shrewd and successful businessman, he died a millionaire.

Robinson Aircraft Ltd,

Blackbushe, Hampshire.

A business associated with C G B Mitchell. Constructed the two seat Mitchell Kittiwake II all-metal side-by-side two seater in 1972. *See also* **Mitchell-Proctor Aircraft Ltd.**

Rollason Aircraft & Engines, Ltd,

Croydon Airport, Surrey,
then Shoreham-by-Sea, Sussex

This aircraft and engine servicing business was founded by William Arthur Rollason (1899-1955) as W A Rollason Aircraft Services Ltd in 1929. In 1930 he moved from Brooklands to Croydon and created Rollason Aviation Ltd. He toured the country flying a Desoutter for British Hospitals Air Pageants Ltd. By 1933 was trading as Rollason Aircraft Services and, on February 28th 1935, he registered Rollason Aircraft Services Ltd as a private company with £10,000 capital. By 1936 it employed some 700 workers and operated as a sub-contractor to Vickers reconditioning Harts and modifying Wellesleys. That year the business was sold to British Continental Airways and in 1939 sold it on to the Hunting Group. After the war was over, Rollason returned to Croydon and set up three new companies – W A Rollason Ltd, then Rollason Aero Engines Ltd and thirdly Rollason Aeroaccessories Ltd. Upon his death at his Epsom home in November 1955, he left the businesses in the hands of his other directors, Messrs Bennett and Millard. In 1956 the undertaking was acquired by Norman Herbert Jones (*b.* July 17th 1905) who was to become one of the most significant people in post-war light aviation. The new Rollason Aircraft & Engines Ltd was re-organised headed by Norman Jones, Alan Sproxton and Mrs W M Rollason with W V Fitzmaurice as secretary. While the aircraft maintenance business was continued, Jones embarked on a new business that earned him the respect of a connoisseur of vintage aircraft. He undertook the formation of the renowned Tiger Club and in 1957 put into limited production the French Druine Turbulent and Condor light aircraft. Additionally the business acted as the UK agent for several foreign machines, among them the French Jodel Mousquetaire for which the firm secured C of A validation in the Public Transport category. Norman Herbert Jones was born on July 17th 1905 and educated at Marlborough. His father was director of Samuel Jones Ltd, makers of paper adhesives. This business, which had premises at Ware to the north of Hertford, had been founded in 1880 by his uncle. As a young man he developed an interest in aviation that was fostered by his parents. He became a member of the London Aeroplane Club at Stag Lane where, together with Mrs Eliott-Lynn, he owned a DH 60 Moth. In 1925 he joined No 601 (County of London) Squadron, Royal Auxiliary Air Force, as a 'weekend flyer' and survived two major landing mishaps while piloting DH.9A aircraft. In the 1930s he became interested in offshore racing and shared a boat named *Maid of Malham* with the yachtsman John lllingworth. This experience stood him in good stead when the Second World War began for the Royal Naval Volunteer Reserve at once enrolled him. His war service was distinguished and he was twice Mentioned in Dispatches. After the war Norman Jones threw himself into developing the family business into one of the leading stationery suppliers marketed under the Butterfly brand-name, chosen after the Camberwell Beauty species. Specialising in envelopes, the business grew rapidly. Floated on the London Stock

Rollason built a number of Druine Turbulents with full C of A like this Tiger Club example.

Norman Jones' company also put the cabin two seat Condor into production.

Exchange in 1963, he sold it in 1964 to paper merchants The Wiggins Teape Group. His interest in aviation, meanwhile, remained undiminished and back in 1957 in a conscious attempt to revive the golden age of light aeroplane flying between the wars, he founded the Tiger Club. In 1969, at the age of 63, he won the 100-mile Manx Air Race, accompanied in the cockpit by his Jack Russell terrier, Dickie, also dressed in flying-jacket and goggles. The next year he took part less successfully in the London-Australia Air Race relating that he did it merely for fun and had to make 20 stops for petrol. At his Croydon Airport hangars Jones specialised in producing special variants of the Tiger Moth. His highly innovative versions included the Super Tiger, which boasted a much enhanced performance, the Sea Tiger, and a Ski Tiger. Rollasons provided refurbished Tiger Moth aircraft and a comprehensive airframe and engine spares service for many years, and the majority of current owners have availed themselves of Rollason's support at some time so much so that had it not been for Norman Jones' enthusiasm at a critical period in that particular aircraft's post-Service history, fewer Tiger Moth machines would have survived. Special Rollason/Norman Jones Tiger Moths included G-ANZZ, the single seater called *The Archbishop*; and G-AIVW, *The Sea Tiger*. This was fitted with floats taken from an Aeronca Sedan. He also manufactured an excellent conversion of the VW engine to fit in the Turbulent light aircraft. Rollasons ceased production of aircraft and engines in 1975. Norman Jones died in 1990 aged 85 years.

Rotorcraft Ltd,

Feltham Trading Estate, Middlesex.

A company formed in 1959 to develop a two seat helicopter called the Grasshopper designed by former Cierva technical officer Jacob S Shapiro and with a head office address at 3, Bedford Square, London WC1. Founded in conjunction with the Mitchell Engineering Group, the parent company was ServoTec Ltd who had an office at 265, Finchley Road, London NW3. Shapiro was managing director of this business which was described as, among other things, a consultant in helicopter engineering. Chairman of the firm was E B N Mitchell and other directors were E F E Battle and J F R Mitchell with R C Sparrow as company

Rollason sponsored a Midget Racer design contest (see Appendix Two) and the winner was this, the Luton-designed Beta.

secretary. The Grasshopper was built and registered but after initial trials in March 1962 proved unsatisfactory, a second version was built which flew in November 1962. Despite attractive lines, the project faded. Jacob Shapiro had several attempts to make inroads into the rotary-wing market after he left Cierva in 1951 and was at one time working on what would become the Grasshopper at Denham Aerodrome. In 1965 a new company called Cierva Rotorcraft Ltd was set up by several members of the original **Cierva Autogiro Co Ltd** [qv] including Shapiro to develop the Cierva Rotorcraft CR.LTH-1. This also was a short-lived enterprise.

Samlesbury Engineering Ltd,

Samlesbury, Blackburn, Lancashire.

A private company registered on May 16th 1947 with a capital of £50,000 for the purpose of carrying on a business of motor body and coach-builders as well as aircraft. Directors were Joseph Eric Rylands, Robert Hardman and Joseph M Twiss, all described as directors of Lancashire Aircraft Corporation Ltd. The registered offices were at Market Place, Market Rasen, Lincolnshire. In 1958, Edgar Percival sold his company Edgar Percival Aircraft Ltd of Stapleford Tawney Aerodrome, Essex, to this firm which then reorganised production. Percival was initially a director of the newly-formed **Lancashire Aircraft Co Ltd** [qv] (which renamed the aircraft as the Prospector) but what was described as differences of opinion led to his severing all connections with the business and the design at the end of 1959.

Saunders-Roe Ltd,

Cowes, Isle of Wight.

The formation and pre-war activities of this company, also known by the contraction Saro, are related in *Ord-Hume* [37]. After the war, the company comprised Sir Alliott Verdon-Roe (president), Alfred Eustace Chambers (chairman), Arthur Gouge (vice-chairman), Edward Denman Clarke (managing director), the Rt Hon Viscount Cowdray, the Hon Harry N Morgan-Grenville, L Lister Walsh, and Robert Verdon Perfect. Director and chief designer was Henry Knowler. This company's traditional background was in flying boats and amphibious aircraft. In January 1951, after the Cierva Autogiro Company ceased operations as an independent company, Saunders-Roe bought the business as a diversification from its waterborne projects. There was also an understanding with the Ministry of Supply that it would take on and complete the Skeeter helicopter programme. Besides setting up a helicopter division, Saro continued with the Skeeter programme but now it was directed at Service use with trials for the Royal Navy. The Skeeter's success came long after Cierva had ceased to be involved and that was far from the original Cierva intention that it should be a private aircraft.

Scottish Aviation Ltd,

Prestwick Airport, Ayrshire, Scotland.

This business was established in 1935 for the purpose of developing and operating the then-new Prestwick Airport and flying school. After the war, the management comprised The Duke of Hamilton (chairman), Bernard Boxall (deputy chairman), Edmund Digby Maxwell Robertson (managing director), David Fowler McIntyre, and The Earl of Selkirk, Sir Ernest H Lemon. Chief designer was Robert McIntyre. Test pilots Ronald C W Ellison and Noel John Capper. During the late 1940s the company designed a five seat single-engined aircraft called the Prestwick Pioneer which first flew in 1950. This gave rise to a twin-engined aircraft that, although called the Twin Pioneer, was non-derivative but a wholly-new design. After the collapse of Beagle, the company took over the production of the Bulldog and, following the dissolution of Handley Page Ltd, assumed the development and production of the twin-engined Handley Page Jetstream. The former project was controlled by a subsidiary known as Scottish Aviation (Bulldog) Ltd. The company suffered a period of bad luck. Twin Pioneer G-AOEN was being demonstrated at Tripoli in Libya in December 1957 when fatigue failure collapsed the port wing, killing managing director David McIntyre along with the pilot and engineer officer. On March 10th 1960, D A Templeton was killed in an accident to a Twin Pioneer (G-ANTP) he was demonstrating at Johat, Assam, and the following month Ian C Reid, sales manager, fell ill and died in a New Delhi hospital while on a sales promotion tour. Ranald Porteous, former Auster chief test pilot, then Beagle sales manager, joined Scottish Aviation Ltd at the start of 1969 as marketing manager.

Shapley Aircraft Ltd,

The Foundry, Swan Street, Torquay, Devon.

Founded by Errol Spencer Shapley (*b.* April 16th 1906, Torquay), an accountant by profession, who lived at High Street, Totnes, Devon. The founding of this business and its pre-war activities are related in *Ord-Hume* [37]. In 1946 Shapley had plans to produce the Kittiwake Mk.II and was pursuing arrangements for its certification when, in December that year, the Ministry of Civil Aviation's nominated test pilot, who was known to be prejudiced against the aircraft, allegedly got it into an inverted flat spin from which he could not recover despite being at considerable altitude. He jumped out, the aircraft crashed on Dartmoor and was destroyed – and Errol Shapley's plans brought to a sudden and quite unnecessary end. Shapley's business ceased and he emigrated. His two pre-war designs are described in Ord-Hume [*op.cit*].

Shield, G W,

Grammar School, Maple Road, Mexborough, Yorkshire.

George W Shield, BSc, was headmaster of the Mexborough Grammar School and having built and flown a Luton LA.4A Minor (G-ATFW), designed and built his own single seater aircraft which he called the Xyla. Construction began in 1968 and the machine (G-AWPN) flew successfully in 1971.

Slingsby Sailplanes Ltd (later Slingsby Aviation Ltd),

Ings Lane, Kirkbymoorside, North Yorkshire

Directors: Frederick Nicholas Slingsby (managing director and chief designer), Major John Edward Durrant Shaw (who was also chairman of The Tipsy Aircraft Co Ltd), Lt-Col G R D Shaw, J R Archer, Mrs A J Shaw. Chief engineer was John Watson Leach (who also doubled as company test pilot), works manager F E Deeley and test pilot (for Martin Hearn Ltd) Capt Rimmer. The connection with Martin Hearn Ltd was a long-standing business friendship. Martin Nieto Hearn (*b.* June 1906) had been with the Lancashire School of Aviation and had also served with Berkshire Aviation Tours Ltd and Alan Cobham Aviation Ltd. He became Slingsby's agent and distributor for a short while in the immediate post-war years. Major Shaw lived at Welburn Hall, Kirbymoorside, and in the 1930s was president of Scarborough Aero Club Ltd. Slingsby was born on November 6th 1894 and subsequently served in both the Royal Flying Corps and the Royal Air Force. Upon leaving the Service in 1920 he bought a partnership in a woodworking and furniture business with premises in Queen Street, Scarborough. Slingsby was an early enthusiast for the revival of the British gliding movement in 1930 and in February that year formed the Scarborough Gliding Club using a Dagling glider. This was frequently broken and Slingsby was continually engaged in restoring it at his woodworking factory. Quickly he built up a team of skilled woodworkers and was soon considering diversifying into the new work on a full-time basis. The venture began in a small way with the importing of several dismantled German-designed Falke gliders. He built these first machines at his furniture works in Scarborough but, with the rapid growth in demand for gliders, he moved first into disused tram sheds belonging to the Town Corporation (where he advertised as 'Slingsby

Slingsby Motor Tutor of October 1947 was intended to be flown solo with just glider experience.

Sailplanes, Scarborough') and then, in the second half of 1934, ordinary woodwork and furniture-making was finally abandoned and the nascent business moved to the village of Kirbymoorside (as it was then spelled) on the northern edge of the Vale of Pickering. It was here that he founded Slingsby Sailplanes Ltd early in 1935. In 1939 a new factory was built at Ings Lane south of the village. At the end of the 1939-45 war the company comprised F N Slingsby, Maj J E D 'Jack' Shaw, Lt-Col G R D Shaw, G E Shaw and J R Archer, all shown as directors. Philip Aubrey Wills, gliding champion and record-holder, became chairman in 1957-58 and a holding company called the Shaw-Slingsby Trust Ltd set up which owned the entire share capital of the business with the purpose of distributing all company profits to the British gliding movement. F N Slingsby remained as managing director and works manager was A Brayshaw. Unfortunately, the intended function of the Trust met with opposition from the Inland Revenue and so the business was acquired by the Bradley Group of York which itself went bankrupt soon after. In November 1968 the factory was almost entirely destroyed by fire and the following summer the company (by then the sole remaining British sailplane designer and manufacturer) entered receivership following a financial crisis. A year later, in November 1969, the shipbuilding and engineering business of Vickers Ltd (which also held a 40 per cent interest in British Aircraft Corporation) acquired the assets of Slingsby Aircraft Co Ltd for £179,150 and changed its name back to Slingsby Sailplanes Ltd. The purpose was declared to be twofold: first to return to glider production (which it successfully did shortly afterwards), and second to engage in research into glass- and carbon-fibre structures for application in both aviation and shipbuilding. The new managing director was George Burton, a well-known British gliding competition pilot. The company built the Tipsy Nipper light aircraft for Nipper Aircraft Ltd [qv] and also powered gliders. After 1982, however, the company was reformed as Slingsby Aircraft Ltd and became exclusively concerned with powered aircraft manufacture, becoming part of M L Holdings Ltd. The name of Kirbymoorside itself underwent a subtle change in the 1960s when local historians discovered that the correct name of the village should have been Kirkbymoorside: thereafter the second letter 'k' entered the name. Fred Slingsby died aged 78 on May 21st 1973. Today the company is known as Slingsby Aviation Ltd.

Somers-Kendal Aircraft Ltd,

Panshanger Aerodrome, Hertfordshire.

Private company formed around 1953 to design and build the SK-1 light jet trainer and sporting aircraft. Directors were racing pilot John Nathaniel Somers (b. June 26th 1909), and Hugh McLennan Kendall (b. November 26th 1914) who was test pilot for Miles Aircraft (1957) and a post-war racing pilot. Secretary of the company was W J Miles. The registered office was Eagle House, 109 Jermyn Street, London SW1, and the workshop was at Woodley Aerodrome, nr Reading, Berkshire. A projected assembly line workshop/hangar was erected at Panshanger but remained empty. Successful though the single-engined pure jet aircraft was, the Royal Air Force found it unsuitable for Service training and the racing career of the sole example was troubled with technical difficulties. The project was abandoned and the company disappeared shortly afterwards (1957).

Sponson Developments Ltd,

3, Albermarle Street, London W1.

A private company registered on December 29th 1947 with a share capital of £500. Purpose described as 'to carry on the business of aeronautical consultants and designers, manufacturers and repairers of and dealers of aeroplanes, seaplanes, etc'. Permanent directors were given as the Hon Simon George Warrender (in charge of sales), Douglas Johnston Reoch, Wing Cmdr Reginald Herbert Stocken (technical), W J W Brodie and C R Hutchinson. The company was formed to acquire the designs and patents of the newly-deceased Joseph George Navarro and the still-born Navarro Aircraft Construction Co [qv]. The outcome was the redesign of Navarro's Naiad amphibian which now became the Sponson Tribian amphibious aircraft, the prototype of which was to be constructed at Redhill by Tiltman-Langley Laboratories Ltd. T-LL was the independent research and development consultancy set up in the autumn of 1944 by Alfred Hessell Tiltman, Marcus Langley (the original partners), Jacobus Johannes Gerritsen, H W Roberts and others (registered September 19th 1947) and which possessed fully-equipped workshop facilities. Sponson Developments undertook exhaustive fact-finding trips using a Percival Proctor Mk.III flown by Ian Brown to Greece, Siam, Malaya and New Zealand to determine the market for its five/six seater. A mock-up was built but the project was abandoned.

Storey, T M,

1, Stewarts Grove, London, SW3. – see Airmark Ltd.

Tawney Aircraft Ltd,

Stapleford Tawney Aerodrome, nr Romford, Essex.

A business set up as a subsidiary of Thurston Engineering Ltd, aircraft, engine and automobile maintenance specialists. Directors were Eric F Thurston of Theydon Bois and Anthony M Creedon of Harlow, Essex. The purpose was to develop and build a two seat pusher light aeroplane called the Tawney Owl designed by Creedon. On April 22nd 1960, the aircraft attempted its first flight but crashed. The company and the project faded.

John F Taylor,

25, Chesterfield Crescent, Leigh-on-Sea, Essex.

John Franklin Taylor developed a small single seat monoplane (G-APRT) first flown in July 1959. Taylor adopted the pre-war words of Mignet that amateur aircraft ought to be built in the home – in his case an upstairs living room. Over the following years he sold sets of plans for this machine for amateur construction. He designed a second aircraft, the Titch, which flew in January 1967. This attractive and highly successful design was also aimed at the amateur but regrettably Taylor lost his life in the prototype, G-ATYO, at Southend on May 16th 1967. For some years afterwards, the sale of plans for his aircraft designs was continued by his widow, Mrs Taylor, and these are today handled by his son, Terry Taylor.

Taylorcraft Aeroplanes (England) Ltd,

Britannia Works, Thurmaston, Leicester.

The pre-war history of this business, which was registered on November 21st 1938, is related in *Ord-Hume* [37]. During the war, the Taylorcraft aeroplanes used by the military were named Austers and on March 7th 1946 the company name was changed to Auster Aircraft Ltd. The American Taylorcraft company was declared bankrupt in 1946: several attempts at reviving the US business resulted in repeated failure. *See under* **Auster Aircraft Ltd**.

Tipsy Aircraft Co Ltd [Nipper]

20, Elmwood Avenue, Feltham, Middlesex.

Formed in February 1937 as a sales outlet for the Tipsy S single seat ultra-light aircraft and then the Tipsy B two seaters. The founder of the original Belgian company was Ernest Oscar Tips. This company became a subsidiary of the Fairey Aviation Co Ltd as Avion Fairey (Gosselies). The British business was wholly-owned by British interests (it was a subsidiary of Fairey Aviation Company at Heston) and undertook the construction of Tipsy aircraft in Britain. It also had facilities at London Air Park, Hanworth. Re-formed on September 1st 1946, directors were Major J E D Shaw (chairman) William White MacArthur (managing and also director of Fairey; general works manager for Blackburn Aircraft Ltd in 1937), Flt-Lt George Birkett, J G Crammond, Walter Gaskin, E O Tips and Cecil Clifford Vinson (who was a chartered accountant). Factory and workshop premises were secured at 183-7, Liverpool Road and 798, Weston Road, Slough Trading Estate, Buckinghamshire. Here the company assembled Belfair two seaters starting in the autumn of 1946. It soldiered on until the 1960s when, with the arrival of the Tipsy Nipper, construction was taken on (initially) by Slingsby Sailplanes, a company of which Major Shaw also happened to be chairman. The company closed after the Fairey Co Ltd was forced to allow itself to be bought by Westland in May 1960.

Thruxton Aviation & Engineering Co Ltd, *and* The Wiltshire School of Flying Ltd,

Thruxton, Hampshire.

The Wiltshire School of Flying announced in 1961 that it had developed a four seat Tiger Moth conversion that was to be called the Jackaroo. Thruxton Aviation & Engineering Co Ltd was set up in 1962 as a subsidiary of the Wiltshire School of Flying. The chairman was J Connolly with Eric H Smith (managing director), R J H Goodfellow and Sqdn-Ldr James Edward Doran-Webb. Under this name the company converted a number of Tiger Moths to four seat Jackaroos. Later that year a fresh company was formed called Jackaroo Aircraft Ltd *[qv]* while the original company set about designing and building a light two seat autogyro called the Thruxton ES.102 Gadfly, the work of Eric Smith. At one point in 1965 the firm was known as Gadfly International but within a year the business had been restructured as **Gadfly Aircraft Ltd** *[qv]*. Doran-Webb appears to have formed a number of related businesses to cater for his many projects, among them another called **Paragon Aircraft Ltd** *[qv]*. While a mock-up was made of his low-winged Paragon project, no further aircraft were made after the Jackaroo and the company faded.

Trojan Ltd,

Purley Way, Croydon, Surrey

A notice appeared in *Air Pictorial*, September, 1970, advising that: 'Airtourer. Trojan Ltd, a member of the Lambretta-Trojan Group, are to build the AESL Airtourer under licence at their Croydon factory. The type is at present being imported from Aero Engine Services Ltd, New Zealand, and assembled by Glos-Air at Staverton. Trojan-built machines will be powered by 130 hp Rolls-Royce Continental O-240-A engines and will be taken to Biggin Hill for final assembly and test-flying. The company hopes to reach a production rate of 150 aircraft a year'. Nothing further is known of this venture by this car manufacturer. *See under* **Glos-Air Ltd**.

Twyford Moors (Helicopters) Ltd,

Twyford House, Chestnut Avenue, Eastleigh, SO5 3HJ.

Private company founded in 1967 by E H Doe, O Hill, F E A Mitchell and K M Reed to acquire the UK licence for the manufacture and marketing of the American-designed Enstrom F-28 designed by the R J Enstrom Corporation of Menominee, Michigan. One aircraft was assembled by the firm in October 1967, the parts air-freighted to London (Heathrow) on September 22nd 1967. This was G-AVUK. A second aircraft was imported (G-BAAU) with the intention of producing a version to be called the Twyford-Enstrom F-28A Solent, but nothing further transpired.

Thruxton Jackaroo four seater Tiger Moth was a short-term success.

Wallis Autogyros Ltd,

121, Chesterton Road, Cambridge *also* Reymerston Hall, Norfolk.

Private company founded in the autumn of 1964 by Wing Cmdr Kenneth Horatio Wallis (1916-2013), G V Wallis and P M Wallis in Cambridge and moving to the Norfolk address in 1969. The popularity of the small Bensen-type autogyro encouraged Wallis to embark on the design and development of a series of improved autogyros the prototype of which (G-ARRT) first flew in August 1961. Since that time Wng Cmdr Wallis has produced a large number of designs. The business became associated with **Beagle Aircraft Ltd** *[qv]* as Beagle-Wallis which carried out a £50,000 design survey, structural proving and flight programme on the WA-116 in the hope of interesting the British Army. Delays in obtaining type approval slowed the project until Beagle embarked on its long period of retrenchment: upon its final closure, the WA-116 programme reverted to the Wallis family. To Wallis goes credit for popularising the autogyro through the part played by a WA-116 in the 'James Bond' film *You Only Live Twice* where it was immortalised as *Little Nellie*. Wallis became Sean Connery's 'stunt pilot' in the film. The name was a family nickname based on word-play and derived from the pejorative term that referred to someone doing outrageous things as 'a bit of a Nellie', that expression being itself derived from the name of the Glasgow-born music hall performer, Nellie Wallace, who took London by storm in 1924 and remained a popular entertainer up until her death in 1948. Wing Cmdr Kenneth Horatio Wallis was found dead in his workshop hangar in September, 2013.

M Ward,

4, Eagle Road, North Scarle, Lincolnshire.

A joiner by trade and a keen aeromodeller, Michael Ward designed and built an exceptionally small single seat monoplane that he called the Gnome. It was powered by a 1925 motorcycle engine and the first flight took place on August 4th 1967. No plans were announced regarding any future development of this interesting project. In 1980 he built a diminutive biplane that he called the Elf.

Wren Aircraft Co Ltd,

Kirklinton, near Carlisle, Cumbria.

Extant in 1946. Described as designers and constructors of light personal aircraft. Owner/designer R G Carr of Milltown, Carlisle, built a low-wing single seat monoplane he called the Wren Goldcrest. It seems the goal was production but the designer was consistently unsuccessful in his negotiations with the Ministry of Civil Aviation which refused to let his aircraft fly. Ultimately and thoroughly exasperated, he allegedly burned the prototype and abandoned the project.

Wallis WA.116 Srs.1 gyroplane of 1961 being demonstrated hands and feet off.

CHAPTER TEN
Light Aircraft Engines and Propellers

Throughout the course of this work we have repeatedly seen evidence that the immediate post-war engine scene in Britain was distinguished by a general lack of incentive. Those pre-war engine designers upon whose experiments great hope was invested, were, in general, all gone. Inventors such as Cyril Francis Caunter (1899-1988), Frank Metcalf Aspin (1913-1976) and Charles Benjamin Redrup (1878-1961) were spent forces. We were left with a few bright and new promises in motors such as the Jameson, Monaco, Nuffield, Fedden and Coventry Victor. It would emerge that none would succeed.

Our aircraft designers desperately wanted these new engines and despite the government surplus Gipsy Majors and the preponderance of Cirrus Minors, everybody felt that there had to be something better just around the corner. What was wanted was another genius in the engine world – a new Frank Halford or a Douglas Pobjoy. Both these great bastions of past engine-development were getting on in years but were far from old when they died. Pobjoy was the first to go, meeting his premature end in July 1948 in a historic mid-air airliner collision in poor weather. Halford died less dramatically seven years later in 1955 aged just 61 years. Curiously both these great men ended their days within a half-mile of each other – Halford quietly at his home in Northwood, Middlesex, and Pobjoy cruelly in an inferno set in a damp, lonely wood also in Northwood.

If engine technology advanced rapidly during the war years then it was largely to engines well beyond the power output of the light aircraft motor. There was, in fact, no great improvement in this area during the years of conflict. For this reason, the great name of Bristol was never to appear again in the realm of light aircraft as the company's impressive large engines, not all of which were sleeve-valved remember, moved them further and further into the realms of military and commercial aircraft.

The Paris Air Show in November 1946 coincided with the announcement of two new British aero engines for light aircraft. First a flat four, the 100 hp – 70 hp cruise Nuffield engine. Fuel injection, we were told, may be developed later but to begin with the engines were to have downdraught carburettors. The second engine was the Fedden flat-six sleeve valve giving 160 hp for takeoff and about 120 hp for cruise. The Fedden engine was to be amazingly shallow – marginally over 12 inches (12.25 inches) – which would enable it to be buried in a wing just 14 inches thick.

The inspiration was the buried-engine concept first seen in the pre-war de Havilland Albatross and projected during the war years by designers as a way ahead for post-war civil aircraft. Designers of aircraft to meet the Brabazon Committee requirements suggested buried engines as did George Miles in many of his futuristic designs. Unfortunately, the impending arrival of the pure jet and then the turboprop curtailed this potential while powerful and compact American horizontally-opposed motors had showed that the format was not just possible but was actually in production meaning that it was fully developed in the form of both flat-four and flat-six motors.

Naturally, as far as British designers were concerned, experimenting with a new engine, even if from the drawing-board of a man of Fedden's reputation, was not really a viable alternative. Curiously America's Lycoming company picked up on Fedden's design and produced its own version – the ultra-slim eight-cylinder 320 hp GSO-580 – which, despite achieving a similar 1.9 lbs/hp for 20-inches in height, was equally unsuccessful and, for the same reasons as that of Fedden, failed.

Work on the Nuffield project, the work of youthful engine genius Tom Brown, had occupied the latter part of 1945 and most of 1946 and became a talking point within the industry. The thought of a light aircraft power plant that not only weighed less than two pounds per horsepower but could be mass-produced in large quantities was attractive: the difficulty lay in the way of building light aeroplanes at a suitable price had always been the high cost of the power plant. This, of course, was directly connected to the quantity of engines produced. It is for these reasons that tremendous interest was aroused immediately the intention of the Nuffield Organisation became known especially in view of its long experience in volume production.

Many remembered the period between the two wars during which a very great deal of work had been done by Wolseley Aero Engines Ltd (part of the Nuffield Organisation) to the benefit of the private and civil market, which had resulted in the production of a series of radial engines of medium power and for which a great future was foreseen. Unfortunately, as related earlier, as a result of a clash with the Air Ministry, Lord Nuffield decided to drop the whole thing. Nuffield was effectively snubbed, being disparagingly referred to in high (Air Ministry) places as a mere car-maker when his aircraft engine contribution was of the highest order. Nuffield never even made into the 'establishment' trade directories whose editors lacked the courage to do their jobs properly in the face of pressure from others in the industry they served. It was a shameful dereliction of historical accuracy and therefore quite despicable.

Somewhat prematurely, observers were quick to note, news of the projected motor was leaked to the technical press and others. It seemed somewhat early days in view of the fact that the engine (described as an air-cooled flat four of 100 hp) had still to conclude its various type tests. In fact, it hadn't even run yet. Even so, in May of 1946 details and installation drawings were circulated to what the Engineering branch of the Nuffield Organisation coyly called 'various aircraft constructional interests'. One of these was Auster Aircraft where Auster historian Ian W O'Neill has found a schematic of the Arrow with this motor. It is significant that the hide-bound rules of the SBAC had prevented Auster from demonstrating the Arrow at its 1946 beanfeast because of its American-made engine, hence the firm's interest in a British-made alternative. The unique document is dated '5-46' and shows the approximate weight of the engine to have been a fairly precise 192.5 lbs.

Auster, however, was committed to Blackburn for its Cirrus engines.

193

Blackburn only really had two customers – Miles and Auster – and so it was imperative that the engine-maker preserve his outlets. While it cannot be proved, I have been told on reliable authority that pressure was applied to Auster to drop the Nuffield proposal otherwise, said Blackburn, it 'could not guarantee' to supply any of Auster's bread-and-butter Cirrus motors. Here one should remember that Auster Aircraft Ltd was never financially strong enough to take risks or gamble with its smooth running, that it was dependent on Blackburn for the fulfilling of its military contracts and that anything that might jeopardise these contracts would produce a huge question-mark over the firm's future. The bluff worked, Auster was forced to back off, abandoned risking a potential boat-rocking exercise and nervously dropped the Nuffield like a hot coal.

For Nuffield, things were grim. There was no way the project could be moved ahead unless there was some genuine interest from the aircraft industry. It is believed that Miles Aircraft at Woodley (the management of which had a thoroughly open and friendly relationship with its opposite numbers at Auster) received the same offer from Nuffield, the same response from Blackburn – and, like Auster, was forced to take the easy way out. Clearly, lack of competition in supplies allowed the manufacturers to get away with what you and I would call blackmail.

One particular aircraft, however, had been expressly designed with the Nuffield in mind. This was the butterfly-tailed Essex Aero Sprite. The prototype was described as being in an advanced stage of construction in May 1947. By the end of that year it was fairly obvious which way things were going for Nuffield and the short answer was 'not very far'. Had Auster and/or Miles been allowed to sign up, production could have begun but without any prospect of an order, the hard-nosed car-industry background of the Nuffield dictated a resounding 'No!' The project was dropped and, although Essex Aero said it would proceed using another engine, the Sprite died as well.

Meanwhile the Jameson, although further down the line, had also got off to a bad start and was in any case underfunded for serious production. Some in the industry, those that feared boat-rocking risks, quietly rejoiced.

As the year opened, Monaco (appreciably heavier in lbs/hp than the Nuffield) was getting some very satisfactory and encouraging results from its new engine running at its Elstree Aerodrome-based test facility, but further capital was needed to build up a programme of prototype engines and finance for development of jigs and tools for production. It needed investment. There wasn't any.

In March, the company put out a fresh statement. It claimed that the delay in developing the Monaco engine was in part due to the difficulty in producing Mr Cross's complexly-valved cylinder head and although the company had reached a stage where they could confidently produce a four-cylinder aero engine ready for type test, they decided to abandon further development 'for the time being'. Monaco said it was willing to dispose of its rights to the aero engine for a figure less than a quarter of the amount spent on it already. Monaco then entered more pressing financial difficulties, was re-structured – and then dissolved. What happened to its test engines (which were extensively trialled on that test-rig at Elstree Aerodrome) is unknown.

There was only one significant new engine produced throughout the time and that was the 180 hp Cirrus Bombardier that was first flown in a Miles Messenger (G-ALAC) during February 1949. This motor had a dry weight of 350 lb giving a weight per horsepower of 1.94 lbs/hp. It had run for the first time on June 19th 1946. That exercise was to receive a set-back when the aeroplane, making its maiden public appearance in the South Coast Air Race, force-landed and was written off.

If this was a very light engine in terms of power-weight ratio, Coventry-Victor's claimed 55 hp Flying Neptune was a massive heavyweight. A sweet runner when it wanted to be, it probably gave no more than around 45 hp for a dry weight of 130 lbs or a massive 3.75 lbs/hp. It really was too heavy for its power.

Without the Nuffield or the Monaco, we were left with the 110 hp Jameson. All these three motors (plus the Coventry-Victor), significantly, were of the new horizontally-opposed four-cylinder type, long popular in America but only just being seen in Britain in the form of Lycomings in Austers. But while it was the only one of the three to enter limited production and to fly, the Jameson faded, too.

It was not that we were starved of this size of engine for there were the Cirrus Minor Series I of 90 hp; Cirrus Minor Series 2 of 100 hp, and the Cirrus Minor D 503 together with DH and its Gipsy series offering from 130 to 145 hp.

Reverting for a moment to that Paris Air Show of 1946, it set a precedent that was hardly appreciated at the time. A party of two VIPs attended Paris travelling in the Nene-powered Avro Lancastrian. It was the first jet transport and the first 'service' carrying passengers between two countries. From London to Paris took 50 minutes with Rolls-Royce's chief pilot Capt Ron T Shepherd in command. It was a portent of things to come.

Meanwhile in America by 1946 the flat engine ruled supreme so the news of an inverted inline four-cylinder came as a bit of a surprise. One Everett S Cameron of The Cameron Aero Engine Corporation based at Reading, Pennsylvania, announced three engines – a 125 hp weighing under 200 lbs, a 185 hp and a 370 hp one. Unusual feature of this long-stroke series was the positioning of the valves on the sides of the cylinders. The valves were push-rod operated horizontally opposed and positioned transversely across the engine. One purpose was to ensure that cool induction charges flowed onto the exhaust valves so helping to cool them while at the same time vaporising the charge. But the American market was in no mood for an inverted inline when it had a good generation of trained flat-four-experience engineers under its belt.[1]

To complete its range of engines, and to avoid the huge cost of trying to design and develop its own light motors, Rolls-Royce took the decision to find a suitable American engine and secure the licence production. It looked at the only two major makers that had anything to offer – Lycoming and Continental – and settled for the latter, taking a useful power-bracket of products. R-R did, however, go one better than the Americans by taking over the design of one engine that Continental had decided not to proceed with. Rolls-Royce managed to make a good motor out of it. This was the O-240-A.

The arrival of the gas turbine for small aircraft, an event underwritten by Rover Gas Turbines Ltd, posed a range of exciting possibilities for the light

---

1. This was not America's first air-cooled inverted inline motor. The pioneering work, in that country, of Albert S Menasco (1897-1988) should not be overlooked. A self-taught engineer he produced a range of first-class inverted inline engines in the 1930s, most famed of which were probably the Menasco Pirate and Buccaneer motors. Probably remembered today more for his associations with the American film actor Clark Gable, Menasco resigned from his Los Angeles, California, company in 1938 and that marked the end of his eponymous motors. He died aged 91 years on November 14th 1988.

aeroplane, none of which would be taken up. Admittedly the spiralling cost of fuel has acted against the widespread adoption of this style of power unit, but the immense structural benefits and design opportunities in terms of lightness and simplicity have been translated from a technological breakthrough into a lost cause. Nobody took up the challenge and, without the enterprise of Vivian Bellamy, we would never have had the creation of a turboprop-powered Currie Wot, Auster or Chipmunk.

So what of the pure jet for light aeroplanes? Here the possibilities were equally attractive yet many more times less practical. Small jet engines had appeared, but to employ them as small jet engines for aircraft use highlighted the supreme shortcoming of the genre. While in terms of thrust the small jet such as the French-made Turboméca Palas produced ample thrust to keep a light aeroplane going fast through the air (the engine was rated at 330 lb static thrust), it provided barely sufficient power to get the aircraft moving by itself in long grass. The engines also required an external power source for starting and even then proved to be a temperamental starter. 'Scrambling' a home-made jet-plane could demand more calendar than stop-watch...

Both of the pure jet light aircraft built in the 1950s had proven engines, yet the take-off acceleration, particularly on grass, was pretty poor. Racing pilot J N 'Nat' Somers, regarding test-flying the Somers-Kendall SK-1, told the author on one occasion at Panshanger Aerodrome: 'Unless they cut the grass, we'll never get off and we'll end up in the hedge!' He was exaggerating a little, but the fact remained that while there was enough thrust for fast flight, there was insufficient to counteract long-grass rolling resistance, let alone provide the acceleration needed to give a quick take-off. One understood why jet-powered fighters relied on boosting systems for take-off!

This proves, rather sadly, that jet aircraft need immense quantities of excess power (meaning thrust) to get airborne, even though they can cruise comfortably on around just 38 per cent of that thrust. It also shows that, however attractive the pure jet may seem as a light plane power unit, it can probably never be an economic proposition. It must always have a superabundance of power which means a bigger engine and more fuel which means more weight which means higher operating costs. Expressed simply, to have a reasonable range, even allowing for an enhanced cruising speed, any benefits in weight-saving would be annulled by the need to carry possibly five times the fuel for the same range with a piston-engined plane.

The small pure jets, then, must exist as a novelty and, like the motor enthusiast's 'hot-rod', have little application in the real world. The situation boils down to a perplexing reversal of what happens in the realm of larger aircraft. Here the pure jet has virtually captured the whole market, long-since ousting turboprops. In the light plane world, though, the pure jet is impractical compared to the turboprop which has a strong advantage that even as this book is written remains unexploited to the full.

Of course, in recent times these arguments have been coloured by the problems of fuel costs and, with a sigh, we have to accept that small jets (and, come to that, rocket motors) are never going to influence the world of the small aeroplane even if only because they would be too expensive to run. This suggests that we shall continue to be dependent on the technology heralded by Belgian engineer Jean-Joseph-Étienne Lenoir's invention back in 1860 when he thought up the internal combustion engine. Until, that is, we have a suitable electric motor which, in the year 2022, seems now just around the corner.

The sections that follow are divided into products by manufacturers. Generally speaking, all the engines shown are post-war designs but, in some cases (such as the Gipsy Major), the design may have originated in the pre-war era.

In terms of rated power output, engine specifications are frequently conflicting. Even contemporary reports and descriptions are notoriously unreliable. This lack of continuity means that quite often the same engine would be shown as capable of more than one horsepower output. While the goal has been absolute accuracy and the information shown here has been checked from as many sources as possible, in some instances it may not be reliable in every respect.

Manufacturers themselves were not consistent in their power-rating basis for their motors. Some listed their engines at maximum take-off power, others at maximum continuous cruise – two very different portions of the performance curve. It was probably thought in the best interests of the company to quote the higher figure, although this could only make for confusion. And occasionally manufacturers quoted both power outputs separated by a stroke or slash. To avoid confusion over published horsepower output, the tables that follow adhere to the manufacturers' published claims where available.

The provision of the engine compression ratio as part of an engine specification did not become standard practice until approaching the mid-1930s. Even in post-war times this information was not always available. In all cases, however, compression ratios are shown as relative to the numeral one, $i.e.$ 5.6 means 5.6:1. Where across the life of an engine type its compression ratio has been increased (upgraded), this will be shown as, for example, 5.1/5.45.

By far the largest user of light aircraft engines after 1945 was Auster Aircraft Ltd which used both of the popular British-made light engines – the Blackburn Cirrus range and the de Havilland Gipsy Major series.

Few original illustrations grace this section since little contemporary expenditure was undertaken by makers for whom main markets lay way beyond small engines and wooden propellers.

Throughout this section the standard abbreviations are used for the original specifications as follows: rpm = revolutions per minute; hp = horsepower; bhp = brake horsepower; hp/rpm = given or stated horsepower at a given engine speed measured in revolutions per minute; lb/hp = pounds weight per horsepower; cc = cubic centimetres [or lit = litre] (as a standard of capacity); shp = shaft horsepower.

The calculation for pounds weight per horsepower (lbs/hp) is in general based on the continuous rated output rather than the maximum-available or short-term power output. For instance, an engine developing 185 hp at take-off rpm, producing 155 hp at maximum continuous cruising rpm and weighing 355 lbs will be shown as having a lbs/hp ratio of 2.29 rather than 1.92.

Once again, original styles of presenting or calibrating weight, power, volume and dimensions are retained. The anomaly of metric capacity and imperial units for everything else is a curiosity of great antiquity which I am happy to sustain. For those of today's readers to whom horsepower and inches are anathema, consult other references under the heading 'measurements' in the General Index.

As far as propellers (airscrews) are concerned, if the science and technology of the aircraft engine underwent a fairly dramatic development during the war, then so did that of the humble propeller. Although it can be argued that a propeller is a simpler device and, in basic terms (and in its common form), it has no moving parts *per se*, much effort went into improving the performance of airscrews under a variety of conditions.

The outcome of all this was that in 1946 Britain had a highly-refined airscrew industry that could design and make a propeller to suit a specific and detailed application. The 'downside' was that as engines became larger and moved further away from the light aircraft scene, so did propellers. It took courage and not a small portion of faith to revert to a single piece of whirling wood.

Fortunately, small wooden propellers had not exactly fallen by the wayside, for enormous numbers were produced for light aircraft. After all, the Royal Air Force's principal training fleet – Tiger Moths and Magisters – all had wooden airscrews, while the Army's Auster aircraft also had small propellers.

There were, however, some differences between the pre-war and post-war propeller industry. While Fairey, as Fairey-Reed, had been offering metal propellers for a small number of aircraft since the 1920s, metal propellers became acceptable for more aircraft as engine crankshafts were provided with suitable hubs.

There were other changes. While adjustable-pitch propellers were rare amongst light aircraft in the 1930s, they gradually became more commonplace in the post-war light aircraft. Again engine hub design offered splined shafts and designers were more inclined to avail themselves of the adjustable propeller.

At the same time, variable-pitch airscrews, virtually never found on anything smaller than a large aircraft engine, were adapted for smaller engines. Although this was an American influence it was both inevitable and beneficial to the British light aeroplanes above a certain size. The touring aeroplane was, in Britain, no mere post-war novelty but virtually the norm for four seaters and upwards. For them, the optimum engine management scheme was an increasing dependence on the variable-pitch propeller.

Specialist propeller-makers began to emerge in the 1960s. These were in general skilled amateurs who had a flair for propeller design and fabrication. These tiny firms are not listed here but their work played a far from insignificant part in the home-built aircraft scene. Blade forms that were impossible or difficult to manufacture on economic grounds by the established makers were often exploited by these people. The almost unique self-adjusting one-piece propeller of scimitar shape was adopted to produce both visually attractive and practically impressive propellers.

This cottage industry was a welcome aspect of propeller-making for it de-mystified airscrew manufacture and established a broad and practical middle ground between the rather crude (but nevertheless perfectly satisfactory) instructions on building and carving a home-made propeller produced by Henri Mignet, and the scientific approach taken by the experts.

It was easily overlooked that the professionals were often as much in the dark regarding design matters as the amateurs: one eminent propeller-maker confessed that when instructed by a client to design and make a new airscrew, he always supplied three – one conforming precisely to the theoretical and mathematical ideal, one that was slightly on the lower side of the calculations, and a third that was slightly above them! That way he could be 'reasonably certain' that one would work!

One final trend appeared as the 1970s approached and this was the introduction of the plastic propeller blade. This was to be a move of tremendous importance later in the 20th century for the trend in engines was towards higher and higher crankshaft speeds. While conventional propellers give of their best at comparatively low rotational speeds (between 1,500 and 2,500 rpm is calculated to be the ideal), shaft speeds in excess of 3,000 rpm were becoming commonplace.

This had two major effects. One was to increase propeller noise because of the blade form and diameter, and the other was to put greater loads on the blades themselves. It had been known for many years that by increasing the number of blades on an airscrew, not only did you keep the diameter down to a reasonable size (important on a small aircraft) but you absorbed the power at lower engine revolutions. A useful corollary to this was that the greater the number of blades (within reason) the less obtrusive the propeller noise.

The reason was simple. Expressed in rather basic terms, the more blades employed, the narrower the chord required for each blade and the less overall diameter needed. This reduced the propeller-blade tip-speed (the prime cause of noise) and the result was less sound.

Ultimately, the plastic propeller blade has developed into the ground-adjustable three and four-bladed light aircraft propeller resulting in a marked improvement in engine/propeller efficiency at higher rotational speeds, an improved margin of ground clearance and a reduction in the induced noise of light aircraft. This last-mentioned feature is probably one of the most important as an increasing per centage of people find it easy to complain about noisy light aircraft, somehow completely unaware that the more egregiously antisocial flying machine of all time, in terms of noise to those on the ground, is the business executive's helicopter.

LIGHT AIRCRAFT ENGINES AND PROPELLERS

The Engines

Alvis Ltd

Coventry Civil Airport, Coventry, Warwickshire.

Directors: A E Nicholson (chairman), John Joseph Parkes (managing), George Thomas Smith-Clarke (chief engineer and general manager), S W Horsfield, R W Rutledge, Lt-Col J C Chaytor, Capt H S Harrison-Wallace. Makers of aircraft engines. The company had started in 1919 with the formation of T G John Ltd later to become Alvis Limited. Between 1937 and the outbreak of war this firm designed a series of large radial engines that were named after star groups in the Heavens. These included Alcides, Maeonides and Pelides. At the end of 1947 the company celebrated its 25th anniversary. Its core business was the manufacture of quality motor cars and an auto-platen printing machine. In July 1949, Parkes became chairman to succeed Nicholson who, while retaining his membership of the board, stepped down from the office of chairman. At the same time, Rutledge, a director since 1939, became deputy chairman and financial director. Its aviation engine division was primarily associated with the development of the Leonides series of radial engines developed from a 1937 design known as the 9ARS. These engines all featured a Farman-type epicyclic reduction gear either 0.625 or 0.5 depending on the particular model. Power ratings by this maker tended not to relate so much to rpm as to altitudes, maximum given at sea level and continuous cruise at 2,780 ft. The so-called 515 hp Leonides (with an international rating of 425 hp) completed its 50-hour air test in an Airspeed Oxford (LX119) in the late summer of 1946. There were many variants and precise cataloguing of these is today almost impossible. Leonides engines were noted for their light weight in terms of horsepower ratio. Those of the fairly large Leonides series that found use in light aircraft (Scottish Aviation Pioneer, Fairey Gyrodyne, &c) are itemised below: these are all single-row radials; the Leonides Major (fitted to the prototype Handley Page Herald) was a two-row 14-cylinder motor. By the early 1960s, production of Alvis aircraft engines had dwindled to nothing and the business concentrated on its core work of making armoured vehicles for the military. Through its Rover Gas Turbine subsidiary, a series of small turboprop engines were tried out in light aircraft. *See under* **Rover Gas Turbines Ltd**.

SPECIFICATIONS

Name of model	Cyls [No]	Layout of cylinders	Cooling system	Comp. ratio	Cubic capacity	Super-charged	Gear ratio	HP Rating	Max Take-off [hp/rpm]	Continuous [hp/rpm]	Weight [lbs]	Lbs/hp
Leonides	9	Radial	Air	6.8	11,780 cc	Medium	0.625	505	505/3,000	400/2,800	760	1.5
Leonides 530	- do -	- do -	- do -	6.5	12,800 cc	- do -	- do -	615	615/3,000	590/2,800	860	1.4
Leonides 501	- do -	- do -	- do -	- do -	11,780 cc	- do -	0.5	600	600/3,000	590/2,800	790	1.3
Leonides 522	- do -	- do -	- do -	- do -	- do -	- do -	- do -	540	540/3,000	515/2,800	820	1.52

Armstrong Siddeley Motors Ltd,

Parkside, Coventry.

Originally part of the Siddeley-Deasy Motor Car Company, Armstrong Siddeley Motors Ltd was founded in October 1919. In 1937 it produced the Cheetah radial which was developed throughout the war and manufactured into the late 1940s. Directors: Sir Frank Spencer Spriggs (chairman), Thomas Octave Murdoch Sopwith, Harold Thomas Chapman (general manager), Col C D Siddeley, W T Johnson (secretary). Designers and manufacturers of aero-engines specialising in gas turbines and medium-sized piston engines. Those post-war engines with light aircraft connections (Edgar Percival EP.9, Lancashire Aircraft Prospector) are listed below.

SPECIFICATIONS

Name of model	Cyls [No]	Layout of cylinders	Cooling system	Comp. ratio	Cubic capacity	Super-charged	Gear ratio	HP rating	Max Take-off [hp/rpm]	Continuous [hp/rpm]	Weight [lbs]	Lbs/hp
Cheetah X	7	Radial	Air	6.35	13,660 cc	Medium	Direct	360	367/2,425	304/2,100	720	2.37

Blackburn Aircraft Ltd manufactured the Cirrus range of engines at Brough in East Yorkshire. Immediately after the war the company embarked on a brief but impressive advertising campaign for its products which ran head-to-head with de Havilland's Gipsy motors. As DH phased out its lower-powered models it left Blackburn in a sole position for inline engines. Here the early generations of 90 hp Minor and 150 hp Major inlines get eye-catching promotional artwork.

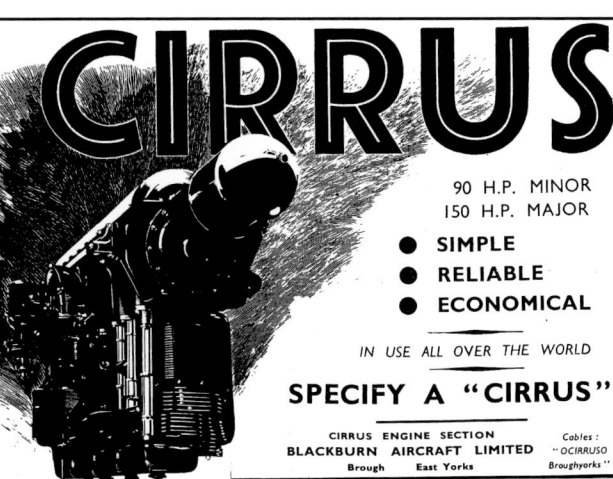

Blackburn Aircraft Ltd (Cirrus Engine Division),

Brough, East Yorkshire.

Directors: Robert Blackburn (managing), Maj Frank Arnold Bumpus, Sir Maurice Denny, Capt Norman William George Blackburn, Sqdn-Ldr James Leonard Neville Bennett-Baggs, A F Jopling. Manufacture and development of the Cirrus inverted inline engines. The Cirrus engine dates back to the work of Frank Bernard Halford at the Aircraft Disposal Company Ltd, Croydon, in 1925. The early history and development of the Cirrus engine is related in [37] and [39]. In 1934, the manufacture and further development of these engines was taken over by Blackburn Aircraft Ltd and a new series of engines produced starting with the Cirrus Minor and Major ranges. In 1948 the company announced a trio of new piston engines to be called Bombardier (4-cylinder, normally aspirated, 180 hp); Musketeer (6-cylinder, normally aspirated, 265 hp); and Grenadier (6-cylinder supercharged, 320 hp). All were to be direct fuel-injection engines resulting in increased power output and eliminating carburettors and their associated complications. Of the three engines announced, only the Bombardier was built, the first appearing in 1948 and, generally, being categorised as an 'improved' Cirrus Major Series III. Cirrus engines went through a rather difficult period in the late 1940s and early 1950s when they earned a reputation, not totally justified, for 'throwing con-rods', a problem traced to the oscillating piston-type oil pump used on the Cirrus Minor. This was already obsolete and there was a changeover to a gear-type pump which gradually supplanted the earlier type on all engines. In 1948 Blackburn introduced a new

Perhaps more commonly known to most, especially engineers and pilots for whom servicing and operating manuals were available, was the Cirrus logo the origins of which can be traced back to the 1930s.

By the time the more powerful Cirrus Major Series II and Series III engines came along, Blackburn advertisements followed a familiar theme updated accordingly. For Blackburn, however, it was a diminishing market and the range of aircraft powered by these engines steadily decreased.

version of the Minor called the D503 which could be fitted with a de Havilland manually-operated variable-pitch propeller. The larger Blackburn Cirrus Bombardier 203 also had provision for a variable-pitch propeller. Essentially a military engine, it was fitted to the Auster AOP.9 and the Auster B.4. The Bombardier 702 was a civil version of the earlier motor and was used in the Auster B.4, Cierva W.14 Skeeter IIIB prototype and the Miles M.38 Messenger Mk.5. Most significant was that it had fuel injection. An amusing aside is that when Major Halford originally designed the first Cirrus engine at Croydon, it created something of a precedent as being 'all-Metric' in its dimensioning. From that day forward, all Cirrus engines were drawn and measured in millimetres. With the Bombardier, Blackburn made a point of announcing, among its improvements, it was taking the opportunity to change over to English measurements, hence the 120-mm bore of the old Cirrus Major became a nice modern 4.8-inches (actually 122-mm!). Nevertheless, the Bombardier was the first British engine to have passed the ARB's approval tests. First flight was in a Miles Messenger.

SPECIFICATIONS

Name of model	Cyls [No]	Layout of cylinders	Cooling system	Comp. ratio	Cubic capacity	Super-charged	Gear ratio	HP rating	Max Take-off [hp/rpm]	Continuous [hp/rpm]	Weight [lbs]	Lbs/hp
Cirrus Major II	4	Inv. In-line	Air	5.8	6,300 cc	No	Direct	145	150/2,450	138/2,200	338	2.33
Cirrus Major III	- do -	- do -	- do -	6.5	- do -	- do -	- do -	146	146/2,450	138/2,200	345	2.36
Cirrus Minor I	- do -	- do -	- do -	5.8	4,000 cc	- do -	- do -	82	90/2,600	78/2,300	238	2.9
Cirrus Minor II	- do -	- do -	- do -	6.25	- do -	- do -	- do -	100	100/2,600	82/2,300	247	2.47
Cirrus Minor D503	- do -	- do -	- do -	- do -	- do -	- do -	- do -		98/2,500	80/2,300	-	-
Bombardier 702	- do -	- do -	- do -	7.1	6,524 cc	- do -	- do -	180	180/2,600	165/2,300	379	2.1

David Budworth Ltd.,

Harwich, Essex.

This company was formed in 1952 for the purpose of developing and manufacturing a very small gas-turbine initially for driving emergency electrical generating and water-pumping equipment. So successful were early trials that it was decide to develop the engine for aircraft use either as a turbojet or, with a reduction gear, as a turboprop and for use in light helicopters and/or fixed-wing aircraft. Directors of the company were David D Budworth, Mrs J M Budworth and J Blewitt. The first engine, called the Puffin, was a described as a centrifugal free-turbine turboshaft or turboprop dependent on the manner in which the basic engine was finished. It featured a two-stage axial unit with separated coupling. The rotor blades were carried on an overhung disc cast in Nimonic PE10 high-temperature alloy. This form contributed to the small size and physical length of the engine: 15 inches in diameter and 30 inches in overall length. It was rated at 180 lb static thrust. As a turboprop, the continuous output was 200 hp. Starting was by electric DC motor at the intake end. By 1970, progress with the Puffin was well advanced and its ground-testing programme on the waterfront at Harwich was going according to plan

Light Aircraft Engines and Propellers

when David Budworth was killed in a newly-bought American light aircraft following control failure: it was found that wing flap brackets were were severely corroded and had not been detected during maintenance. One broke and he crashed. The assets of the Budworth business were subsequently acquired by a company called Noel Penny Turbines Ltd of Coventry. Founded in 1972 it was planned to take over the development of Budworth's design. While in the fullness of time the Budworth Puffin was abandoned, a curiously similar engine was produced by an American company (with whom Budworth had been in negotiation) shortly afterwards. This was an engine that, although low-powered, offered tremendous potential, especially as a turboprop. But it was American...

SPECIFICATIONS
180 lb s.t. Puffin Turbojet
200 h.p. Puffin turboprop

Name of model	Cyls [No]	Layout of Cylinders	Cooling system	Comp. ratio	Cubic capacity	Super-charged	Static Thrust	HP rating	Max Take-off [hp/rpm]	Continuous [hp/rpm]	Weight [lbs]	Lbs/hp
Puffin Turbojet		Single-stage	Gas Turbine				180 lb	-	-	-	110	-
Puffin Turbo-prop		Single-stage	Gas Turbine				-	200	-	-	125	-

- *Designer's estimates based on initial test-rig results.*

Coventry Climax Engines, Ltd,

The Grange, Newbold-on-Stour, Stratford-on-Avon
later Mill Lane, Coventry, Warwickshire.

Directors: H Pulham Lee and Leonard P Lee. Founded by a former Daimler engineer, this company had specialised in internal combustion engines since 1903. Made special racing engines for cars during the 1920s and 1930s but, following the Depression during which many car-makers folded, the business shifted into stationary engines for electric generators. The management was strengthened by the addition of Pulham Lee's son, Leonard Pulham, who identified a potential market for aircraft engines. Shortly before the outbreak of the Second World War, Coventry Climax Engines acquired the manufacturing licence for the American Continental four-cylinder horizontally-opposed air-cooled aero-engines from the Continental Motors Corporation of Detroit, Michigan. The firm advertised a five-strong range of Continental engines – 40 hp, 50 hp, 65 hp, 75 hp and 85 hp – well into the war years (as late as June 1942) but with the return of peace did not renew its options on the deal leaving it to Rolls-Royce to negotiate a fresh UK manufacturing deal fifteen years later. Coventry Climax produced vast numbers of light stationary engines for airfield and other use during the war and reverted to industrial motors, never again looking towards aviation. Reformed as Coventry Climax Ltd, the business was acquired by Jaguar Cars in 1963, that business becoming part of British Leyland in 1968.

Coventry Victor Motor Co Ltd,

137-139 Cox Street, Coventry.

Directors: W A Weaver and T E Morton, secretary: S J Cordery. Major William Arthur Weaver had been associated with flying since the early days and had entered an aeroplane in the first Blackpool Flying meeting in 1909. The Weaver Ornithoplane No.2 made a free flight of about 400 yards at Hampton-in-Arden about 1907 [*see* Goodall, Michael H, and Tagg, Albert E: *British Aircraft before the Great War*, Schiffer, Atglen, Pennsylvania, 2001]. He went on to set up Coventry Victor Motor Co Ltd, a firm which had a long history of light three-wheeled cars and motorcycles as well as horizontally-opposed piston engines for industrial purposes since 1911. In the years immediately before the Second World War produced an aircraft engine based on its Neptune four-cylinder industrial motor. After the war, under the direction of managing director Maj W A Weaver, his son Alfred N Weaver and chief engineer E W Wright, a new and updated version was produced called the Flying Neptune. A motor with a relatively flat power-curve, the overhead valve Flying Neptune had a cylinder bore of 85 mm and a stroke of 80 mm. It underwent its first aircraft installation in 1955 when it was put through a series of tests in an American-designed Piper Cub light aircraft, G-AIYX, by BKS Engineering Ltd (the business operated by J W Barnby, T D Keegan and C J Stevens) at Southend Airport where test-flights were completed by Peter G Masefield. The engine was subsequently handed over to Arthur W J G Ord-Hume who modified it for installation in the British prototype Druine Turbi, G-APFA, where certification tests were completed by Ord-Hume at Bembridge Airport. This marked the conclusion of the development and unfortunately no further work was undertaken, the project being abandoned.

SPECIFICATIONS

Name of model	Cyls [No]	Layout of cylinders	Cooling system	Comp. ratio	Cubic capacity	Super-charged	Gear ratio	HP rating	Max Take-off [hp/rpm]	Continuous [hp/rpm]	Weight [lbs]	Lbs/hp
Flying Neptune	4	Hor. Opp.	Air	7.2	1,825 cc	No	Direct	55 hp	57/3,340	53/3,000	225	4.33

De Havilland Aircraft Co, Ltd,

Stonegrove, Edgware, Middlesex, *then* Leavesden, Watford, Hertfordshire.

Directors: Maj Frank Bernard Halford (chairman), Alan Samuel Butler, Sir Geoffrey de Havilland, Wilfrid Ernest Nixon, Francis Edward Noel St Barbe, John L P Brodie, Hugh Buckingham, Aubrey Francis Burke (general manager). Designers and manufacturers of light piston engines particularly the four-cylinder inverted inline Gipsy Major series through to the six-cylinder Gipsy Queen. The Gipsy Major I Srs I owes its origins to 1934 yet flew in a number of Austers (including Taylorcraft) as well as the Miles Messenger and Saunders-Roe (Cierva) Skeeter. The Gipsy Major I Srs II dated from later the same year yet a dozen years later was to be found powering Messenger and Gemini aircraft from Miles. The larger Gipsy Major IC powered Tiger Moths, Autocrats, Geminis and the Thruxton Jackaroo. The first post-war Gipsy Major variant was the 145 hp Model 7 of 1946 used in some Auster. Its derivative, the Mk 8, was virtually the same but made to run on leaded fuel with sodium-cooled exhaust valves. This was used in the Chipmunk and featured a self-indexing gas cartridge-starter. The Gipsy Major 10 Mk.1 had aluminium heads, used 80-octane leaded fuel and was available with a splined propeller-shaft. An electric starter was available. This engine saw service in many aircraft from Chrislea Super Ace through the Austers and the Miles aircraft. The Gipsy Major 10 Mk.2 of 1948 was really a civil version of the Mk.8 and was available with a manually-operated variable-pitch propeller. Again it was used in Austers, particularly the Aiglet Trainer, and the Miles Gemini 3C. The 160 hp Gipsy Major 30 and the 197 hp 50 were both bigger-bored models intended for the Chipmunk while the 200 hp Mk.200 was just about the most powerful of the original four-cylinder Gipsy Major. Using 100/130 grade fuel it was intended for the Cierva Skeeter as was the Mk. 215 which, by using exhaust-driven supercharging, pushed the output up to an incredible 220 hp. The six-cylinder Gipsy Queen series were used in the de Havilland Rapide, the range of Percival Proctors, the Scottish Aviation Pioneer and the Percival Prentice. The Queen 3 and its derivatives could accommodate the manually-adjustable variable-pitch propellers developed by the de Havilland company. The significant engines are listed below.

The de Havilland Gipsy Major was perhaps the most widely known of all the inlines and, in various models, powered aircraft from the RAF's Miles Magisters and Tiger Moths through to post-war Miles aircraft and many others. Here is a neat and revealing installation of a Gipsy Major 10 as installed in the Fairey Primer. Stub exhausts were sometimes replaced with a manifold which could be connected to a silencer. Here the engine is fitted with a Fairey-Reed metal propeller which was essentially a twisted strip of shaped aluminium alloy.

SPECIFICATIONS

Name of model	Cyls [No]	Layout of cylinders	Cooling system	Comp. ratio	Cubic capacity	Super-charged	Gear ratio	HP rating	Max Take-off [hp/rpm]	Continuous [hp/rpm]	Weight [lbs]	Lbs/hp
Gipsy Major I Srs I	4	Inv. In-line	Air	5.25	6,124 cc	No	Direct	130	130/2,350	120/2,100	305	2.35
- do - Srs II	- do -	- do -	- do -	6.0	- do -	- do -	- do -	138	140/2,400	125/2,100	310	2.21
Gipsy Major IC	- do -	- do -	- do -	- do -	- do -	- do -	- do -	130	142/2,350	- do -	- do -	2.38
Gipsy Major ID	- do -	- do -	- do -	- do -	- do -	- do -	- do -	- do -	- do -	- do -	312	2.4
Gipsy Major IF	- do -	- do -	- do -	5.25	- do -	- do -	- do -	- do -	- do -	- do -	310	2.38
Gipsy Major 7	- do -	- do -	- do -	6.0	- do -	- do -	- do -	145	145/2,550	138/2,300	- do -	2.14
Gipsy Major 8	- do -	- do -	- do -	- do -	- do -	- do -	- do -	- do -	- do -	- do -	313	2.16
Gipsy Major 10 Mk.I	- do -	- do -	- do -	- do -	- do -	- do -	- do -	- do -	- do -	- do -	318	2.19
Gipsy Major 10 Mk.2	- do -	- do -	- do -	- do -	- do -	- do -	- do -	- do -	- do -	- do -	325	2.24
Gipsy Major 30*	- do -	- do -	- do -	6.5	- do -	- do -	- do -	160	160/2,500	136/2,200	340	2.12
Gipsy Major 50	- do -	- do -	- do -	- do -	- do -	Full	- do -	202	202/2,500	166/2,300	345	1.71
Gipsy Major 200	- do -	- do -	- do -	6.0	- do -	No	- do -	200	200/2,500	194/2,600	400	2.0
Gipsy Queen II	6	- do -	- do -	- do -	10,178 cc	- do -	- do -	210	210/2,400	195/2,150	508	2.42
Gipsy Queen 30-2	- do -	- do -	- do -	6.5	- do -	- do -	- do -	240	240/2,500	206/2,250	525	2.19
Gipsy Queen 32	- do -	- do -	- do -	- do -	- do -	- do -	- do -	- do -	245/2,400	235/2,200	510	2.12
Gipsy Queen 34	- do -	- do -	- do -	6.3	- do -	- do -	- do -	250	250/2,500	235/2,100	566	2.23
Gipsy Queen 70-1	- do -	- do -	- do -	6.5	- do -	Medium	0.711	340	340/2,800	330/2,400	685	2.01

Formerly known as the Gipsy Major 3.

Roy Fedden Ltd,

Stoke Orchard, Nr Cheltenham, Gloucestershire.

Designers and manufacturers of light piston aero-engines. This company was formed in 1945 to specialise in the development of low-drag power-units for small and medium-sized aircraft. Directors: Sir Alfred Hubert Roy Fedden, C H Young, R G R Goldby (secretary). Chief engineer was Donald Raymond Price Amor who, like Roy Fedden, was one of the most experienced inter-war engine designers. In overall charge of piston engine design was Alexander Senkowski. The company also produced medium-sized gas turbines. The Fedden Flat-Six high-compression piston engine was exhibited at the Paris Air Show in 1946 although it was unclear whether at that time it had run. It was still described as under development in 1947 and incorporated a number of unusual features for its type. Besides being designed for a 'fully-submerged' mounting within a wing, it was a sleeve-valve engine of remarkably shallow dimensions. While measuring 31.7 inches across the cylinder heads, it was only 14.75 inches high. Fuel-injection was standard and the weight per horsepower comfortably broke the 2 lb/hp barrier. The engine was to be available in two forms, one direct and one geared to give greater power further up the power curve. This was an advanced-concept engine that was designed in the belief that buried engines in wings were the likely trend in medium-to-large aircraft design. In fact the first generation of jet engines effectively stole this market and the Fedden Flat-Six was still-born. All figures given here are manufacturer's estimates.

SPECIFICATIONS

Name of model	Cyls [No]	Layout of cylinders	Cooling system	Comp. ratio	Cubic capacity	Super-charged	Gear ratio	HP rating	Max Take-off [hp/rpm]	Continuous [hp/rpm]	Weight [lbs]	Lbs/hp
Fedden Flat-Six	6	Hor. opp.	Air	8.0	5,300 cc	No	Direct	160	160/2,750	145/2,550	310	1.94
- do -	- do -	- do -	- do -	- do -	- do -	- do -	Geared	185	185/3,400	175/3,100	340	1.84

Jameson Aero Engines Ltd,

Spring Works, West Street, Ewell, Surrey.

Director: Joseph Lambert Jameson. Described as 'machine tool makers', this company was involved in the long-term development of light engines that unfortunately were not accorded the success they deserved. The chief engineer was A E Moser who had designed a four-cylinder four-stroke light aircraft engine in 1943. Featuring magnesium alloy crankcase and a balanced double-throw crankshaft, the engine had no cylinder offset and was thus symmetrical. After the end of the war, the engine was built and underwent extensive proving culminating in the completion of an Air Ministry Development Test in 1946. Two years later it was subjected to a Type Test for final certification but unfortunately following a valve-spring failure, it was only granted a 100-hour clearance for civil flight. The motor was developed further by the fitting of a gearbox and in this condition it was used to power the Cierva W.14 Skeeter prototype. It was also flown experimentally in the Miles M.18 Mk.1 G-AFRO (U-2; U-0222). The company only produced one model, the FF-1. The propeller shaft was provided with a spur reduction gear and it was a relatively high-compression motor at 7.4.

SPECIFICATIONS

Name of model	Cyls [No]	Layout of cylinders	Cooling system	Comp. ratio	Cubic capacity	Super-charged	Gear ratio	HP rating	Max Take-off [hp/rpm]	Continuous [hp/rpm]	Weight [lbs]	Lbs/hp
FF-1	4	Hor. opp	Air	7.4	3,280 cc	No	.691/1	110	110/3,200	106/3,060	290	2.64

Monaco Engines Ltd,

King's Langley, Hertfordshire.

This little company originated in 1935 as the Monaco Motor & Engineering Co Ltd of High Street, Watford, Hertfordshire. At that time the directors were P R Monkhouse and I F Connell. Prior to the outbreak of war it was only concerned with automobile engineering but during the war it undertook sub-contract work for aircraft and aero-engine manufacturers under the auspices of the Ministry of Aircraft Production. The firm was an Associate Member of the SBAC. At the end of the war, the company at once announced its intention to build and develop two light aircraft engines. These were to be of the then-unusual horizontally-opposed format that was already well-established in America. The engines would develop 75 hp and 100 hp and there were to be three basic types of each: Sport, De Luxe and Wing, the last-mentioned being provided with an extension airscrew shaft for mounting within a wing. All models would be adaptable for pusher installation or for use in helicopters. This ambitious programme seemed perfectly attainable and the first engine was running and undergoing tests by 1947. In September that year it announced that air tests were expected to begin shortly using an Auster. During that year, the business was reformed as Monaco Engines Ltd and moved to Kings Langley. The new board of directors comprised C W Reeve (chairman), P R Monkhouse (managing); H R Mayes (chief designer), I F Connell (sales manager); P Emmet-Love (works manager), G E Still, R G Eagle. The engine contained some advanced thinking, not the least of which was the use of silent hydraulic tappets that were completely self-adjusting. The inlet manifold was cast integrally with the sump and submerged in oil to give improved fuel vaporisation as well as additional cooling of the lubricating oil. A very neat and compact engine, the Monaco could be fitted with a variable-pitch propeller. Test facilities were rented at Elstree Aerodrome where an engine was put through extensive and prolonged testing without problem. However, it gradually became clear that the company did not have the funding to put its engine into production and attempts to raise investment failed. Monaco Engines Ltd disappeared quietly in the late 1940s. The details that follow are taken from specifications published by the company in 1946. They apply to the Sport variants: in the De Luxe type, shrouded ignition cables, air-cleaner, air intake thermometer, ice-guard, silencer, cabin heater, mechanical variable-pitch propeller, generator, starter (hand or electric) vacuum pump, air-compressor, fuel-injection, Kigass primer, reduction gear, and so on were optional extras.

SPECIFICATIONS

Name of model	Cyls [No]	Layout of cylinders	Cooling system	Comp. ratio	Cubic capacity	Super-charged	Gear ratio	HP rating	Max Take-off [hp/rpm]	Continuous [hp/rpm]	Weight [lbs]	Lbs/hp
Monaco	4	Hor. opp.	Air	6	3,600 cc	No	Direct	75	75/2,200	65/1,900	230	3.1
- do -	- do -	- do -	- do -	- do -	- do -	- do -	- do -	100	100/2,800	80/2,350	245	2.45

The Nuffield Organisation, Engine Branch,

Cowley, Oxford.

This was part of Morris Motors, Ltd of Courthouse Green, Coventry, Warwickshire and was an associated company of the Nuffield Organisation, Cowley. Wolseley Aero Engines Ltd had been founded in 1935 to acquire the aircraft engine manufacturing business of Wolseley Motors (1927) Ltd of Drews Lane, Ward End, Birmingham. In 1937 this new company purchased Nuffield Mechanizations Ltd as a going concern and subsequently changed its name to Nuffield Mechanizations Aero Ltd. This was altered to Mechanizations Aero Ltd. in 1939 and again to Nuffield Mechanizations Ltd. in 1942. In the post-war period the firm was concerned with agricultural machinery, rather than military equipment. The whole enterprise was lead, in the post-war period, by Sir William Miles Webster Thomas who, in 1949, would become better known as the chairman of British Overseas Airways Corporation. The company announced in 1946 that it was undertaking the design and construction of a four-cylinder horizontally-opposed engine suitable for private aircraft. Its principal features included overhead valves, large cooling area of cylinders, heads and crankcase sump and provision for either pusher or tractor use. An updraught carburettor was fitted with a 12-volt electrical system having a gear-driven dynamo and an integral pre-engagement-type starter motor. Initially manually-operated altitude control would be used although automatic operation would be available as an option. An automatic means of controlling warm and cold air to the carburettor was under development and the development of fuel-injection was foreseen at a later stage. Fuel consumption was estimated at six gallons per hour. The man behind the engine was designer Tom Brown who, as one of the youngest designers in the motor industry, was a man with great vision and, as a private pilot, he had first-hand interest in light aircraft engines. With a bore of 111mm and a stroke of 98.4 mm the engine was, for its time, high-revving, yet would have been a responsive motor. It was rumoured that a likely selling price would be in the order of £100 but that was dependent on high-volume production. Less impulsive pundits put the price nearer to £200 – still an expensive motor but one that, on paper, offered a very great deal. The goal of between 25/- and 30/- per horsepower nevertheless seemed attainable given volume production. Approaches to aircraft manufacturers such as Miles and Auster initially showed interest as did newcomers Chrislea, but vested interests in the form of Blackburn Cirrus intervened suggesting to Auster and Miles that if they associated with the Nuffield engine, then their supplies of Blackburn Cirrus motors might be compromised. It was a bluff that produced the desired result and both aircraft builders declined the Morris offer. Unfortunately the late 1940s marked a period of great fluidity not just in the light aircraft business but also in the motor car industry and when Morris Motors became part of British Leyland, work on the aircraft engine was abandoned – curiously with no attempt at seeking a transfer of the technology. The Nuffield, like its contemporary the Monaco, was a worthwhile and practical proposition. While the Monaco was built and ground-tested, the Nuffield remained but a paper motor. Tom Brown left Nuffield in June 1948, never to get the chance to see his fine engine built. And Sir Miles Thomas turned his back on Lord Nuffield's once great empire for Heathrow Airport.

SPECIFICATIONS

Name of model	Cyls [No]	Layout of cylinders	Cooling system	Comp. ratio	Cubic capacity	Super-charged	Gear ratio	HP rating	Max Take-off [hp/rpm]	Continuous [hp/rpm]	Weight [lbs]	Lbs/hp
Nuffield	4	Hor. opp.	Air	6.3	3,820 cc	No	Direct	100	100/2,600	70/2,300	192.2	19.2

Rollason Aircraft & Engines, Ltd,

Croydon Airport, Surrey,
then Shoreham-by-Sea, Sussex

For details of the founding of this business see Chapter Nine. In 1946, Grp-Capt William Arthur Rollason set up three new businesses – W A Rollason Ltd, Rollason Aero Engines Ltd and Rollason Aero Accessories Ltd. Rollason Engines Ltd was the trading name for the second of these businesses. In October 1949 Rollason Engines was joined by L M McPherson from the position of general manager of W A Rollason Ltd. After the death of W A Rollason at his Epsom home on November 16th 1955, the businesses were acquired in 1956 by Norman Jones who was to become one of the most significant people in post-war light aviation. The new Rollason Aircraft & Engines Ltd was re-organised headed by Jones, Alan Sproxton and Mrs W M Rollason with W V Fitzmaurice as secretary. The company acquired a manufacturing licence from Roger Druine in France who had developed an excellent conversion of the VW car engine which he developed for the Turbulent. This was the 30 hp Ardem 4CO2. Rollason put this motor into production at Croydon and it flew in a number of ultra-light aircraft including the American-designed Evans VP-1 Volksplane, the Luton LA.4A Minor, the Rollason-built Druine Turbulent and the Tipsy Nipper variants. This was a very reliable and important motor. Norman Jones died in 1990 aged 85 years.

SPECIFICATIONS

Name of model	Cyls [No]	Layout of cylinders	Cooling system	Comp. ratio	Cubic capacity	Super-charged	Gear ratio	HP rating	Max Take-off [hp/rpm]	Continuous [hp/rpm]	Weight [lbs]	Lbs/hp
Ardem 4CO2	4	Hor. opp.	Air	6.6	1,192 cc	No	Direct	30	30/3,000	28/2,700	133	4.43

Rolls-Royce, Ltd,

Nightingale Road, Derby, Derbyshire.

Designers and manufacturers of gas turbine and large piston aero-engines. The immediate post-war directors were Capt E C Eric Smith (chairman), Ernest Walter Hives (later as Lord Hives, managing director), Harald Peake, Albert George Elliott (chief engineer), William Tait Gill, The Hon Maurice Fox Pitt Lubbock, F Llewellyn Smith. Frank Nixon was chief quality engineer. This famous company made its first aero-engine in December 1915 and since that time has been in the forefront of aircraft engine design and manufacture. In the immediate post-war years, the business underwent numerous management changes, an event that often created great problems in the matter of continuity. A number of these 'management restructurings' were of considerable magnitude. At the end of the war, Rolls-Royce had a strong inventory of high-power and high-performance engines. With no lightweight, low-power piston engines in its portfolio, the company accepted there was a market for engines in the 85 hp to 145 hp bracket and therefore took steps to source suitable designs. In 1960, and following on Coventry Climax Engines Ltd's failure to revive the licence deal concluded in 1939, it signed a licence agreement with a well-known American maker, Continental Motors Corporation, giving Rolls-Royce exclusive rights for the sale of all Continental horizontally-opposed piston aero-engines and spare parts throughout the world with the exception of the continent of America. Selected models from the maker's range, namely light aircraft engines of 95, 100, 130 and 145 hp, were consequently manufactured by Rolls-Royce Motor Car Division at Crewe and the company formed a Light Aircraft Engine Department to handle the licence manufacture of Continental engines. One of these engines was developed by Rolls-Royce in Britain and that was the O-240-A which, while designed by Continental, was shelved in favour of a new range. Rolls-Royce took over the programme in 1968 and undertook the final development to production of this motor: production deliveries began in mid-1970 and the engine was also successfully exported to America for sale there through Continental. This motor was being heralded, in 1969, as 'the Gipsy Major of the 1970s' as market assessments all pointed to the market potential as excellent. In essence this engine combined four cylinders from the existing 1O-360 engine with the crankshaft design of the O-200 but Rolls-Royce raised the original compression ratio from 7 to 8.5 with concomitant strengthening of the crankshaft and improvements to the crankcase. Indeed this engine was far more 'Rolls-Royce' than any of the other British-built Continentals. One tiny but significant change was to extend the propeller shaft by 1¼-inches compared with that of the O-200. The main reason for this was to improve the cowling lines of light aircraft installations. Hydraulic tappets were fitted with dual valve springs. A spectacularly low weight per horsepower was achieved. By making these engines in Britain, Rolls-Royce was able to market them at competitive prices in spite of somewhat smaller volumes than those built in America. This was because UK manufacture sidetracked the 25 per cent freight duty and Customs charges otherwise levied on American imports. Details of the Rolls-Royce-built Continental engines are found below. Note that these engines are generally rated to produce maximum power on a 'continuous' basis: in the instance of the Rolls-Royce-developed O-240, however, the continuous power is rated at an economical setting.

SPECIFICATIONS

Name of model	Cyls [No]	Layout of cylinders	Cooling system	Comp. ratio	Cubic capacity	Super-charged	Gear ratio	HP rating	Max Take-off [hp/rpm]	Continuous [hp/rpm]	Weight [lbs]	Lbs/hp
C90	4	Hor. opp.	Air	7	3,280 cc	No	Direct	95	95/2,625	90/2,475	188	1.98
O-200-A	- do -	- do -	- do -	- do -	- do -	- do -	- do -	100	100/2,750	100/2,750	190	1.9
O-240-A	- do -	- do -	- do -	8.5	3,933 cc	- do -	- do -	130	130/2,800	97.5/2,540	219	1.68
O-300	6	- do -	- do -	7	4,900 cc	- do -	- do -	145	145/2,700	145/2,700	277	1.91

Rover Gas Turbines Ltd,

Holyhead Road, Coventry, Warwickshire.

The Rover Company was responsible for initial production of the original Whittle-type turbojet engines in 1941-42. Later the company developed a series of small gas-turbine engines for industrial uses. Early in 1968, the aviation activities of the company were transferred to Alvis Ltd of Holyhead Road, Coventry, where further development work was undertaken. Both Rover and Alvis were then member companies of British Leyland Motor Corporation. The directors were virtually all the Alvis board, comprising A B Smith, W F F Martin-Hurst, John Joseph Parkes (who was also chairman and managing director of parent company Alvis Mechanisation Ltd) George Russell Howell (the Alvis director and chief accountant), R N Penny and R E Nicholl (sales manager). Chief engineer was Arthur Francis Varney, another Alvis man. Early in 1960, Rover Gas Turbines produced a pair of small gas-turbine engines that could drive a propeller through a reduction gear. While the larger model was mainly used as an auxiliary power unit in aircraft such as the Avro Vulcan and the Armstrong Whitworth Argosy, it was the smaller of the two that first saw service as an aircraft prime-mover. This was flown in a Currie Wot biplane at Eastleigh. Four years later a slightly larger engine, the TP.90, was installed in an Auster Autocrat by the same man – engineer Vivian Bellamy following a successful installation in a Chipmunk by Hants & Sussex Aviation. Despite the success of these installations, the high cost of the engines contributed to the demise of the venture. Both engines were described as centrifugal-flow turboprops and both engines weighed the same inclusive of reduction gear but excluding the starter. The smaller model had a compressor pressure ratio of 2.95 and an air mass flow of 1.45 lb/sec. The larger had a compressor pressure ratio of 2.80 and an air mass flow of 1.88 lb/sec. The specific fuel consumption of the smaller engine was 1.5 lb/shp/hr; that of the larger slightly less at 1.22 lb/shp/hr. Average jet pipe temperature was 625 deg.C and an automatic fuel trimmer prevented the temperature exceeding 675 deg C.

SPECIFICATIONS
70 h.p. TP.60
120 h.p. TP.90

Name of model	Cyls [No]	Layout of Cylinders	Cooling system	Comp. ratio	Cubic capacity	Super-charged	Static Thrust	HP rating	Max Take-off [hp/rpm]	Continuous [hp/rpm]	Weight [lbs]	Lbs/hp
TP.60		Single-stage Gas Turbine					-	60	65/47,000	60/44,000	140	-
TP.90		Single-stage Gas Turbine					-	116	118/46,000	115/44,000	140	-

* *Designer's estimates based on initial test-rig results.*

The Propellers

The Airscrew Company,

Weybridge, Surrey

This company was formed in 1923 and its inter-war history is related elsewhere (*see* Ord-Hume [37]). After the war, it returned to the making of propellers for civil aircraft. In October 1946 the directors were John D Titler (chairman and managing), A H Sherry, B G Haycock, R J Blackadder, F C Lynam (chief designer and technical manager), and E C F Pash, sales director. The chief engineer was G Deal Haye. During the war, much work had been done on improving wood for airscrews, one major development being the creation of compressed, resin-bonded laminated timber for which the company registered the name Jicwood. Not only could this be used for making propellers but also it was ideally suited to the making of small-run press tools and rubber-presses. At an extraordinary general meeting held on January 3rd 1950 it was decided to change the name of the business to The Airscrew Company & Jicwood Ltd. This company made propellers for almost all light aircraft and could design and produce experimental propellers for test work. It also made detachable blades for the de Havilland manually-adjustable variable-pitch airscrew.

Constant Speed Airscrews Ltd,

Wharfe Street, Warwick.

Shortly before the war this company acquired the licence to build the German VDM airscrew in this country but in the event no manufacture of this interesting propeller was carried out by the firm. Its efforts were concentrated on the design and production of spinners for use with airscrews from other manufacturers and consequently had very little involvement in the light aircraft scene.

De Havilland Propellers Ltd,

Hatfield, Hertfordshire.

The activities of this old-established company have already been related (*see* Ord-Hume [37]). Suffice it to repeat that it was the 1935 acquisition of a manufacturing licence for the designs of the American company Hamilton Standard Propeller Co that put DH on the road to becoming one of the two largest – if not the largest – propeller-manufacturing company in the country. Much of the development in the 10 year period to 1946 was encouraged by the war effort but it placed the company in an ideal position to play a commanding role in the post-war propeller scene. Among the most important airscrews it built was the two-bladed constant-speed counterweight type which was the smallest CS airscrew in the DH range. It used Duralumin blades with steel counterweights to assist in pitch-changing and was suitable for engines between 100 and 300 hp in diameters up to 7 ft 6 ins. Complete with spinner this weighed between 83½ and 88½ lbs complete with control unit. There was also a two-bladed manually-adjustable variable-pitch propeller suited to the very light aeroplane. This had two wooden blades which could be set to any angle within a 15-degree range by turning a handle mounted in the pilot's cockpit so as to allow the optimum pitch to be set for any flight conditions. With spinner and cockpit control this weighed from 50 to 55 lb and was available in diameters from 6 ft 6 in to 7 ft 6 in. In 1947 the company introduced a manually variable-pitch airscrew which was approved on a Miles Aerovan and was then evaluated on a Rapide with Gipsy Queen III engines. The weight penalty was only 20 lbs per airscrew. Additionally, the company made a large range of Hydromatic three- and four-bladed propellers including constant-speed and feathering type as well as one with reversing pitch (called, at that time, braking). These were not for light plane application, though.

Fairey Aviation Co Ltd (Propeller Division),

Hayes, Middlesex.

Fairey entered the propeller-manufacturing business in 1936 producing the Fairey-Reed all-metal fixed-pitch airscrew for engines in the 60 to 200 hp power bracket. Designed and patented by an American named Sylvanus Albert Reed who was a pioneer in the development of metal airscrews, it attracted the attention of Charles Richard Fairey who secured a UK manufacturing licence as early as 1925. This airscrew, which re-entered production for the civil market after the war, used a blade that was machined from a flat billet of Duralumin and subsequently twisted to the required aerodynamic form after which it received

There were two main producers of wooden airscrews – Hordern-Richmond in Haddenham, Buckinghamshire and The Airscrew Company of Weybridge, Surrey. The former hardly ever advertised while the latter rarely took promotional space in the aviation press. This is an advertisement from *Flight* of April 11th 1946 at a time when the industry retained high hopes.

appropriate heat-treatment. A two-bladed controllable-pitch model was introduced in 1947 having blade-angle regulation operated from the cockpit using a three-position lever. This was available in three sizes for engines from 60 to 120 hp, 120 to 220 hp and 220 to 400 hp. The smallest of these fitted the Cirrus Major and Minor engines with mechanical control, while the largest had electrical control. Total pitch variation of these airscrews was five degrees, considered adequate for all normal operations, but a maximum of eight was available. Weights were 37½ lb for the smaller and 45 lb for the larger model. Fairey also produced larger airscrews up to and including a six-bladed electrically-operated contra-rotating airscrew but that was hardly suited to light aircraft.

Jablo was less concerned with making light aircraft propellers but had patented a form of compressed wood called Jabroc which behaved like metal and thus had attractive properties for lamination into the roots of separate airscrew blades used in variable-pitch wooden propellers. Compressed wood was also made by The Airscrew Company (known by the trade names of Weyroc and Jicwood) and Hordern-Richmond (Hydulignum).

Fletcher Airscrews,

The Aerodrome, Reading, Berkshire.

Wartime propeller-maker Anthony A 'Tony' Fletcher resumed airscrew design in the summer of 1946 forming a company called Fletcher Airscrews of which he was chief designer. This became a subsidiary of Miles Aircraft Ltd through its Philidas Ltd division. The head office of Philidas, makers of stiff nuts, was at Maclise Road, London W.14 while the business also had offices and factory at Reading Aerodrome. During the war Fletcher had produced propellers for Tiger Moth, Magister and Messenger aircraft, as well as the Auster Mks.IV and VI, and the Airspeed Oxford. The new company announced it would design and manufacture wooden airscrews specialising particularly on light aircraft types. It was also associated in providing Miles Aircraft Ltd with its propeller needs. With the problems faced by Miles Aircraft Ltd that resulted in its dissolution (*see Chapter 9*) the Fletcher enterprise disappeared.

Hordern-Richmond, Ltd,

Hydulignum Works, Haddenham, Buckinghamshire,

Private company registered August 6th 1947 for the purpose of acquiring company of exactly the same name, in voluntary liquidation, at Haddenham, Buckinghamshire, to manufacture propellers &c. Directors: David S Jackling, John G H Barton, Lewis W le Gros, and Ronald S A Simmons. Manufacturers of the Aeromatic compressed-wood variable-pitch airscrew blades (under licence from the Everell Propeller Corporation of America), fixed-pitch airscrews, helicopter rotor blades and so forth. Original founder Edmund Hordern died in 1992.

Jablo Propellers Ltd,

Jablo Works, Mill Lane, Waddon, Croydon, Surrey.

Bruno Jablonsky had founded his company in 1936 (*see Ord-Hume [37]*) to capitalise on his patents for the manufacture of airscrew blades made from reinforced wood and the application of a surface finish that ensured their maximum durability. Jablo had little direct involvement in the light aircraft scene other than through Rotol Ltd [*qv*] for whom they made the majority of all their wooden blades. Jablo also specialised in the manufacture of helicopter rotor blades. The firm became Jablo Plastics Industries Ltd in the 1960s.

Rotol Ltd was mainly concerned with larger airscrews, in particular those for light gas-turbines – it made the airscrews for the turbo Auster, Currie Wot and Chipmunk – and in 1946 launched a small and light weight two-bladed mechanically operated constant-speed airscrews for light aircraft. After the war, Rotol was one of two major airscrew-makers in Britain, the other being de Havilland.

Rotol Ltd,

Cheltenham Road, Gloucester

Directors: Sir G Stanley White, Lord Hives, A E Russell, A G Elliott, W R Verdon Smith, W T Gill, Lt-Gen Sir John Evetts. This business was established in May of 1937 as a joint enterprise between Rolls-Royce and the engine division of Bristol Aeroplane Co to combine the propeller sections of both companies. The name Rotol was an amalgamation of the two company names. During the Second World War the business provided airscrews for many military aircraft and after the war became one of the two largest airscrew manufacturers in the land, the other being de Havilland. Rotol's pioneering work in propeller design for gas-turbines made possible light aircraft such as the Currie Wot and DH Chipmunk turboprop variants but it was the introduction in 1946 of the firm's two-bladed mechanically operated constant-speed airscrews for light aircraft that brought the firm firmly into the large light aircraft scene. Suitable for engines between 100 and 170 hp, this had blades of reinforced wood (made by Jablo – *qv*) and a metal hub, changes in pitch were attained by axial translation of a transfer bearing connected by links to the blade roots. In simple terms, it owed something of its design to the principle of the engine sleeve valve and was both light in weight and simple to operate with little to go wrong. The average weight of this propeller and its spinner was 49 lb 11 oz, the hand controls weighed 5 lb 5 oz and the electrical controls 11 lb 5 oz making it an extremely light unit.

The original Gardan GY-20 Minicab design was acquired in 1955 by Arthur W J G Ord-Hume and re-engineered as the GY-201 to meet British requirements. He produced a new set of engineering drawings which were marketed extensively across Britain, Australia, New Zealand and North America. One of the earliest builders in Britain was F Stanley Jackson of BAE at Preston. Here in 1965 is the fuselage of his finely-constructed aircraft posed on his lawn. Ultimately G-AWEP, this was test-flown by 'Roly' Beamont on June 21st 1969 powered by a Continental C90-8F.

Stan Jackson's completed Minicab displays its neat lines and superb finish.

Hotelier J B Evans of Niton, Isle of Wight, built GY-201 Minicab G-AZJE which was first flown at Bembridge in September 1974 after a six-year build time.

Continued in Volume Two